Counting the Cost of Freedom

CIVIL WAR AMERICA

Caroline E. Janney and Aaron Sheehan-Dean, *editors*

This landmark series interprets broadly the history and culture of the Civil War era through the long nineteenth century and beyond. Drawing on diverse approaches and methods, the series publishes historical works that explore all aspects of the war, biographies of leading commanders, and tactical and campaign studies, along with select editions of primary sources. Together, these books shed new light on an era that remains central to our understanding of American and world history.

A complete list of books published in Civil War America is available at https://uncpress.org/series/civil-war-america.

AMANDA LAURY KLEINTOP

Counting the Cost of Freedom

The Fight over Compensated Emancipation
after the Civil War

The University of North Carolina Press *Chapel Hill*

This book was published with the assistance of the Fred W. Morrison Fund of the University of North Carolina Press.

© 2025 The University of North Carolina Press
All rights reserved
Set in Arno Pro by Westchester Publishing Services
Manufactured in the United States of America

Library of Congress Cataloging-in-Publication Data
Names: Kleintop, Amanda, author
Title: Counting the costs of freedom : the fight over compensated emancipation after the Civil War / Amanda Laury Kleintop.
Other titles: Civil War America (Series)
Description: Chapel Hill : The University of North Carolina Press, [2025] | Series: Civil War America | Includes bibliographical references and index.
Identifiers: LCCN 2025013269 | ISBN 9781469688640 cloth | ISBN 9781469688657 paperback | ISBN 9781469688664 epub | ISBN 9781469688671 pdf
Subjects: LCSH: Slaveholders—Southern States—History—19th century | Enslaved persons—Emancipation—Southern States | Compensation (Law)—Southern States—History—19th century | United States—History—Civil War, 1861–1865—Reparations | Southern States—Economic conditions—19th century | BISAC: HISTORY / United States / Civil War Period (1850–1877) | SOCIAL SCIENCE / Slavery
Classification: LCC E453 .K58 2025 | DDC 306.3/62097309034—dc23/eng/20250408
LC record available at https://lccn.loc.gov/2025013269

Cover design by Lauren Smith. Cover art courtesy of the Rubenstein Library, Duke University.

This book is derived in part from the article "Life, Liberty, and Property in Slaves: White Mississippians Seek 'Just Compensation' for Their Freed Slaves in 1865," published in *Slavery and Abolition* 39, no. 2 (2018): 383–404. Copyright Taylor & Francis, available online: www.tandfonline.com/10.1080/0144039X.2017.1397334.

For product safety concerns under the European Union's General Product Safety Regulation (EU GPSR), please contact gpsr@mare-nostrum.co.uk or write to the University of North Carolina Press and Mare Nostrum Group B.V., Mauritskade 21D, 1091 GC Amsterdam, The Netherlands.

Contents

List of Illustrations vii

Introduction 1

CHAPTER ONE
The National and International Origins of Compensated Emancipation Schemes 11

CHAPTER TWO
Wartime Emancipation Policies: Compensation and the Contested Status of Property in Persons 36

CHAPTER THREE
Emancipation and Reunification: The Persistence of Arguments for Compensation after Confederate Surrender 63

CHAPTER FOUR
Writing Compensation Out of the Constitution: The Making of Section 4 of the Fourteenth Amendment 88

CHAPTER FIVE
Debt Relief and Repudiation: The Legal and Economic Consequences of Uncompensated Emancipation 110

CHAPTER SIX
Writing Uncompensated Emancipation into the Lost Cause 137

Conclusion 165

Acknowledgments 173
Notes 177
Bibliography 225
Index 255

Illustrations

FIGURES

Elihu Burritt 31

Hon. Garrett Davis of Kentucky 43

"The Restoration of the Union—Inauguration of Hon. Michael Hahn" 54

"No Accommodations!" 87

Slavery and treason "buried in the same grave" 92

Jonathan J. Wright 121

Horace Greeley eats his words and deeds 143

Hon. John H. Williamson 153

TABLE

Emancipation in former Confederate states 71

Counting the Cost of Freedom

Introduction

When the United States ended slavery in the South amidst civil war without paying enslavers or the formerly enslaved, it destroyed almost 50 percent of the South's wealth in an unprecedented move.[1] Americans today tend to take for granted that enslavers in the South would not have been compensated for their lost property in people, but some historians have noted that emancipation as it happened—immediately, and without compensation to former enslavers—was exceptional. In contrast, many countries in the Atlantic world and Northern states ended slavery gradually before 1865 to alleviate the financial burden of emancipation on enslavers, paying them or compensating them indirectly with access to the coerced labor of ostensibly free apprentices. In 1833, Great Britain passed the Slavery Abolition Act, which abolished slavery while requiring freed people to work as apprentices for four to six years, and allowed for former enslavers to be paid direct monetary reimbursements. In the early 1800s, Latin American nations like Gran Colombia abolished slavery gradually, with payments made to enslavers, in their efforts to shove off Spanish rule. In 1791, enslaved people in the French colony Saint-Domingue rebelled against enslavers, sparking a revolution that created an independent Haiti, the first Black republic. Decades later, France strong-armed the country into paying an indemnity for property lost in the Haitian Revolution, including enslaved people, in exchange for recognizing the Haitian government.[2] In the aftermath of the American Revolution, Northern states ended slavery so gradually that a few people remained "apprentices for life" until the Civil War.[3]

Unlike emancipation in these times and places, where slavery ended in colonial struggles, slavery ended in the US South after four years of bloody civil war and the defeat of the Confederacy. Still, enslavers in the South expected that they would receive compensation, too. *Counting the Cost of Freedom* reveals that even in defeat, enslavers and their allies in the former Confederacy petitioned federal reimbursements for the value of freed people because enslaved people were seen as a species of property under the law. They believed they had a right to own people—and to profit from that right. They argued that the Constitution and international precedent were on their side.

From 1864 well into the 1870s, they cited prior moments of emancipation in the Atlantic world and the Fifth Amendment's takings clause, insisting that the United States could not take private property "for public use without just compensation."[4] They continued to seek compensation after the war and the passage of the Thirteenth Amendment in 1865 because they believed that the federal government had invalidly confiscated their property in people.

If we consider emancipation in the South alongside other regions and nations, we see that immediate, uncompensated emancipation was not an inevitable outcome of US victory. *Counting the Cost of Freedom* recovers the histories of enslavers' resistance to immediate, uncompensated emancipation in the Civil War era and how that resistance relates to subsequent debates about the legacies of US slavery. I argue that immediate, uncompensated emancipation was the outcome of a series of disjointed policy decisions and legal debates at the state and federal levels. Neither US military victories, nor a growing sense of slavery's moral repugnance, nor the Thirteenth Amendment's abolition of slavery ensured that emancipation in the South would be immediate and uncompensated. Instead, it resulted from a postwar contest in which Americans leveraged their understandings of wartime loyalty and slavery's role in the law and the economy to direct Reconstruction.

White Southerners' ultimately fruitless claims for compensation changed US law and Americans' views of emancipation. This book joins a growing literature that understands emancipation not as the work of one proclamation or amendment but as a contingent reimagining of American legal, political, and economic institutions by many actors, all of whom faced the chaotic conditions of war and its aftermath. Historians including Eric Foner, James Oakes, and Michael Vorenberg have described the political and legal processes by which American politicians like President Abraham Lincoln reimagined the status of enslaved people under the law, and how the Thirteenth Amendment changed Americans' understandings of freedom and constitutional law.[5] Other scholars, and especially those associated with the Freedmen and Southern Society Project, have revealed the complexities of emancipation on the ground. Freedom seekers, enslavers, US army officers and soldiers, and politicians in the United States and the Confederacy sought to define freedom for their own goals until, as historians Ira Berlin and his fellow authors wrote, freedom seekers' actions "gradually rendered untenable every Union policy short of universal emancipation."[6]

Looking to the broader political culture of the era, I seek to explain how Americans mobilized their understandings of US law, politics, and finance to decide who would bear the financial burden of emancipation. I hope to illuminate major legal and political developments concerning emancipation and reunion that prior scholarship has underexamined.[7] In the pages that follow, I will show that white Southerners demanded compensation long after the Civil War and that their practical arguments were only put to rest by adoption of the Fourteenth Amendment, whose fourth section prohibited any state or the United States as a whole from paying "any claim for the loss or emancipation of any slave" when it was ratified in 1868.[8]

I will also show that debates over former enslavers' compensation lingered in American politics through the end of the nineteenth century. Historians have not addressed the unsettled nature of this argument until now. But as I will demonstrate, this history is not well known, because when white Southerners lost this battle, they sought to obscure it. By the 1890s, white Southern elites and Confederate veterans erased postwar debates over compensated emancipation as part of their larger "Lost Cause" narrative that the Civil War had been a war about state sovereignty rather than slavery.

As we will see, former Confederates made widespread claims for compensation. Published and unpublished government documents, presidential papers, congressional records, and postwar state constitutional conventions reveal the breadth of white Southerners' claims for compensation and appeals for relief from debts for the value of slaves at the state and federal levels. So, too, do a range of state archival sources, including governors' papers in Texas, Mississippi, Georgia, North Carolina, and South Carolina. Different states preserved different kinds of records, so evidence of claims for compensation vary state by state. Federal sources help fill the gaps, however, and reveal how US policy demarcated Southerners' state-level debates and was affected by them in turn.[9] Black and white newspapers from across the country, memoirs, and veterans' groups' records enabled me to document the legacies of uncompensated emancipation in broader American political culture.[10]

While I focus on the former Confederate South, conversations about compensated emancipation were national and occurred at every level and branch of government, including the border states—slave states that never seceded—and Indian Territory. The people and places in this book reflect where these debates were most prominent or, in some cases, where they expressed a unique idea about reimbursing Southern enslavers. Most claims came directly from state and federal politicians, particularly in areas where white Southern Unionists—largely former Whigs residing in Confederate states who had opposed secession—exercised some political control, and places where many had invested in human property. Some border state politicians were also vocal supporters of paying at least enslavers loyal to the US. Though some of these politicians play active roles in this book, I do not detail the process of emancipation in the border states. Because they did not secede, enslavers there could and did make different claims to the federal government regarding the legality of uncompensated emancipation.[11]

DEBATES ABOUT COMPENSATING ENSLAVERS shaped postbellum politics, economics, law, and American memory in underappreciated ways. To contemporary readers aware of Confederate defeat, the atrocities of slavery, and renewed conversations about reparations for the enslaved, enslavers' claims may sound ridiculous or ill-conceived. Yet such claims were based on longstanding legal and political disputes that shaped the outcomes of emancipation and reunion in the former Confederate South. By documenting the history and legacies of these claims, this book makes three major interventions in the history of the Civil War and Reconstruction.

First, I argue that Americans finally decided that uncompensated wartime emancipation could remain permanent, if not legal, only by changing the Constitution in response to resistance from former enslavers and their allies—twice. During and immediately after the war, white Southerners persistently and powerfully insisted that they were entitled to be compensated for the loss of human property they claimed. They based their claims on antebellum state laws and financial practices that recognized enslaved people as chattel property as well as people under the law. Slave states established legal doctrine to protect and regulate property rights in people, and many argued that the Constitution's protections for property rights generally applied to property in people as well. They mobilized constitutional arguments because Americans regarded the Constitution as sacrosanct. However, their legal theories about eminent domain and emancipation were never tested in court and therefore had virtually no doctrinal grounding.[12]

Without clear doctrine, no one was certain how these arguments applied to emancipation as it unfolded during the war. Congressional action involved cautious steps, but only the Constitution could make clear where government could intervene on the question of compensation. While many accepted that the United States could emancipate enslaved people claimed by enslavers in rebelling states under war powers without reimbursing them, even President Lincoln and other Republicans worried whether the United States could abolish slavery without paying enslavers in the border states. Enslavers there, many argued, remained loyal, retained their property rights in people, and were therefore owed compensation as citizens of the United

States. The precedent to pay loyal enslavers was so strong that Congress used its constitutional powers over Washington, DC, in 1862 to abolish slavery there by paying enslavers up to $300 for each person freed. Policymakers also questioned the longevity of wartime emancipation. Would these federal policies and confiscations be enforceable after the war ended, even in seceded states? Republicans designed the Thirteenth Amendment in part to make those confiscations permanent under constitutional law.

When Confederate armies surrendered before the amendment was ratified, new avenues for opposition to immediate, uncompensated emancipation opened up. Enslavers in both the border states and Confederate states pushed for compensation in earnest when emancipation was all but guaranteed by military defeat and the Thirteenth Amendment. They fought for federal payments to enslavers for overlapping economic, political, and legal reasons. They continued to cite precedents for compensated emancipation in the Atlantic world and the Fifth Amendment's takings clause, and they also mobilized other arguments specific to the circumstances of emancipation during the Civil War. They invoked natural rights, arguing that neither governments nor military might could revoke enslavers' rights to property in people or, at least, the value of enslaved people. Unionist politicians from Louisiana and the border states asked that the United States compensate loyal enslavers as a reward for their loyalty. Some described compensation as necessary for regional economic stability and financial protection for dependent white widows and orphans. One did not need to claim ownership over people to support this right; indeed, some of the most vocal proponents of compensation did not. For example, two of the most vocal supporters of compensation for enslavers in Mississippi had not claimed ownership over anyone in 1860, while the most vocal opponent of the policy did.[13]

White Southerners' insistence that immediate, uncompensated emancipation violated the Constitution was strong enough that Republicans responded with another constitutional amendment. Thanks in part to enslavers' persistent resistance to emancipation after the war, Republicans in Congress who viewed the Thirteenth Amendment as an abolitionist victory insisted that the United States could end slavery without reimbursing enslavers because Americans had already paid in bloodshed. And rather than rehash legal debates about property rights in people, emancipation, and the Fifth Amendment, Republicans mobilized Americans' outrage after four years of war to ensure that former Confederates would not regain political power until they relinquished their claims for compensation. To these ends, Radical Republicans successfully included language in the Fourteenth Amendment, passed in 1866 and ratified in 1868, that voided "any claim for the loss or emancipation of any slave."[14]

The second major argument this book makes is that section 4 of the Fourteenth Amendment, which historians and legal scholars have long neglected or dismissed as unwarranted punishment against the white South, represented a significant and necessary constitutional change in its time. Republicans did not take it for granted that Union victory in the Civil War guaranteed immediate, uncompensated emancipation because their political opponents continuously challenged it. By countermanding enslavers' claims for compensation, section 4 recognized in retrospect the complicated ways in which pro-slavery politicians had used the Constitution to protect property rights in people. Given white Southerners' resistance to immediate, uncompensated emancipation in 1864 and 1865, Republicans' goals were as politically motivated as they were legally necessary to prevent enslavers from receiving compensation. As legal scholar Mark Graber has argued, Republicans used the Fourteenth Amendment to reform the Constitution for political ends: to punish enslavers and the disloyal, prevent their return to political power, and favor Republican political movements.[15]

This book adds to the histories of constitutional reform that the framers of section 4 attempted to alter the relationship between the US economy and slave law. By refusing to compensate enslavers, Republicans and other federal policymakers intended to prevent enslavers' and former Confederates' return to economic power. Enslaved people had represented vast wealth, and compensation for slavery—whether paid to former enslavers or freed people—would have put money back into the Southern economy and helped reconstruct it in an economic sense. Instead, congressional Republicans forced enslavers to shoulder the cost of their rebellion. The federal government's choice to abolish property rights in people without paying enslavers for their lost property or the enslaved for their stolen labor contributed to impoverishing the formerly rich region, making it one of the poorest parts of the country for decades.[16]

Section 4 discredited enslavers' claims that the Constitution protected their right to profit from property in people, but constitutional change was insufficient to unravel slavery's legal and financial architecture. Legal scholars and historians of Reconstruction such as Michael Vorenberg have long concluded that Republicans' constitutional reforms built on the country's original structures without tearing them down. Republicans wanted to abolish property rights in people, not all property rights. Instead of instigating lasting economic reform, congressional Republicans stopped short at immediate, uncompensated emancipation in the Thirteenth and Fourteenth Amendments. Former enslavers could continue to mobilize other aspects of slavery's legal and financial practices to seek compensation or other forms of relief after the adoption of the Fourteenth Amendment.[17]

For example, many slave buyers owed debts for purchasing enslaved people on credit or mortgaging them before emancipation. After the war ended, slave sellers sought full payment from buyers—many of whom were cash poor and unable to pay their debts. Some debtors or their allies suggested that they should not have to pay their debts for the value of a person who was no longer property because they never received compensation from the state for their emancipation. Some even suggested that section 4 invalidated *all* claims for slaves, including outstanding debts for the value of enslaved people. Congress and other politicians refused to intervene, and such cases made their way through state and federal courts over time. When these cases reached the Supreme Court in 1871, the court dictated that outstanding contracts for the value of enslaved people remained valid because slavery was still legal when those contracts were created.

This book helps explain why federal policymakers did not intervene in these postwar legal conflicts despite many debtors' and state lawmakers' belief that section 4 sanctioned it. Significantly, lawmakers, most judges, and the Supreme Court affirmed wartime, uncompensated emancipation as it happened despite Southern resistance. However, in a process that mirrored how they grappled with the question of secession's legality after the war, Americans sought a return to legal and economic stability and predictability. Lawmakers and judges sought to stabilize legal doctrine regarding emancipation and the Southern economy. As historian Giuliana Perrone has shown, the court left the complicated process of unraveling how emancipation affected existing laws and financial practices to states and localities, where judges limited the meaning of the Thirteenth Amendment to nothing but freedom. Former enslavers, their descendants, judges, and regional policymakers, could still use property rights, contract law, and other legal mechanisms to recoup their economic power and preserve the political and legal hierarchies that had governed the slave South, hierarchies made possible by the antebellum category of property in people.[18]

The third major argument I make is that American politicians mobilized promises to compensate enslavers for political ends. Regionally and nationally, both during and long after the war, those in power used the compensation issue to build political coalitions, win elections, and direct Reconstruction toward their desired ends. Over the course of the war, compensated emancipation, particularly for enslavers loyal to the United States, evolved from a moderate compromise position to an unpopular conservative policy. By the war's end, the compensation debates were litmus tests by which Americans judged enslavers' loyalty to the United States. As recent historians have shown, Civil War–era Americans used conceptions of loyalty as a political act, a language, and a set of state policies to define who was entitled to the rights of citizenship in both the United States and the Confederacy.[19] By 1866, I argue, Congress had determined that the loyal enslaver whom Unionists defended was a fiction. All enslavers were disloyal, and all should pay the price of their rebellion by shouldering the financial burden of emancipation—whether they lived in former Confederate states or the border states. Republican policymakers expected former enslavers to disown slavery by disavowing any right to compensation. Only then could former Confederates regain their citizenship status and could their states re-enter the Union.

Even after the ratification of the Fourteenth Amendment, the political value of talking about compensation for enslavers remained, sometimes in tandem with talk of compensation for the formerly enslaved. Republicans won national elections by threatening well into the 1880s that Democrats would arrange to pay enslavers from federal coffers if they returned to power. In the 1890s, some third-party congressional candidates in Alabama and North Carolina, hoping to gain a foothold against established Democrats, suggested paying former enslavers—alongside the formerly enslaved—to build interracial coalitions and challenge incumbents.

These 1890s politicians were not the first to suggest paying enslavers and the formerly enslaved. Before the Civil War, radical abolitionists often asked proponents of compensating enslavers why the enslaved should not be paid as well—or instead. After emancipation in the United States, many freed people expected and fought for what we would today call reparations: for the United States to divide and redistribute land from large plantations to the formerly enslaved and for full citizenship rights. However, many others did not take proposals for payments or land redistribution seriously. The precedent to pay enslavers was much stronger.[20]

By the 1890s, however, promises to compensate enslavers had lost credibility. A few third-party candidates suggested that paying former enslavers and the formerly enslaved *alike* could support the South's faltering regional economy, including by providing funds to impoverished African Americans who might spend them in white-owned businesses. They made these suggestions around the same time that congressmen like Walter Vaughan and the mutual aid group the National Ex-Slave Mutual Relief, Bounty and Pension Association proposed federal pensions for the formerly enslaved. However counterintuitive, the positions of white enslavers who sought compensation and Black Americans who sought payment shared some of the same logic; most notably, they both saw slavery and the Civil War as being fundamentally about profits, money, property, and labor, as organized and sanctioned by law. These discourses were not tightly linked, but journalists often discussed—and dismissed—them in the same columns. Sometimes advocates of paying the formerly enslaved justified their claims by citing past precedent to pay enslavers. Conversely, opponents pointed out that enslavers never had been and never should be compensated, so neither should the formerly enslaved.

These campaigns failed, but they drew attention from the national press. At a time when Democrats consolidated political power regionally and nationally by emphasizing white solidarity, white Southern elites, Democrats, and Confederate veterans realized that claims for compensation hurt their chances of recouping political power. They damaged their credibility with white Northerners and drew attention to class divisions among white Southerners by offering relief to those who had been the richest. Confederate veterans ceased tolerating attention to the legal and profit-making side of enslavement and downplayed past claims for compensation.

In keeping with the Lost Cause narrative, elite white Southerners obscured the history of white Southerners' claims for compensation from their larger narrative of Civil War history. They insisted that the Civil War had been a war about state sovereignty rather than the preservation of slavery, and they minimized the economic significance of slavery to the South by suggesting it was unprofitable. They erased the fact that abolition annihilated an entire category of valuable property—and that many white Southerners had fought hard for compensation during and immediately after the war. Their efforts undermined third parties, upstart candidates, and emerging claims to compensate the formerly enslaved, sometimes alongside former enslavers. One long-term result of this purposeful forgetting was that future historical accounts offered the false idea that white Southerners had accepted the immediate, uncompensated abolition of slavery, an idea that fed into the larger myth that slavery had been unprofitable and discredited reparations claims.[21]

THE CHAPTERS THAT FOLLOW detail chronologically how Americans debated and obscured the history of claims for compensation for enslavers in the nineteenth century. Chapter 1 surveys the antebellum arguments and precedents for compensated emancipation in US law and the larger Atlantic world. Chapter 2 explores wartime conversations about compensated emancipation through the lenses of four different groups of Americans who contested the legality of immediate, uncompensated emancipation throughout the war: Frederick Douglass, Senator Garrett Davis of Kentucky, President Abraham Lincoln, and Unionists in occupied Louisiana. Chapter 3 focuses on white Southerners' continued opposition to immediate, uncompensated abolition even after Confederate armies surrendered in 1865, defending their property rights in people based on the Fifth Amendment's takings clause and the need for economic relief. Chapter 4 centers on Congress's response, and particularly the Republican political drive to pass section 4 of the Fourteenth Amendment.

Chapters 5 and 6 focus on white Southerners' continued arguments for compensation after 1868, chapter 5 discussing how their efforts to seek relief forced courts to grapple with the practical legal implications of the Fourteenth Amendment and section 4. Chapter 6 argues that even though section 4 and the courts restricted white Southerners' claims, they did not stop until their efforts proved politically inexpedient, at which point Confederate veterans and pro-Confederate historians sought to cement the myth that white Southerners neither wanted nor needed compensation, perpetuating this tale from the 1890s through the early 1900s.

The conclusion returns to the comparative perspective and explores how this historical erasure obscured white Southerners' claims for compensation in US history books and memory. These deeply contingent but nevertheless unsuccessful debates over whether enslavers needed to be or should be compensated for the value of slaves reflected and exacerbated the entangled legal, economic, and political conflicts that led to the Civil War. They shaped the course of emancipation in the United States and continue to shape how Americans wrestle with the costs of slavery. Today, when discussions of reparations to people of African descent for the wrongs of slavery and other forms of racial subordination are on the agenda, it is helpful to understand that slavery was so embedded in US legal and financial systems that enslavers sought compensation for the value of freed people even after Confederate defeat. They lost, but their resistance succeeded in focusing postwar historical and political debates on what the nation owed enslavers, not what it owed the enslaved.

CHAPTER ONE

The National and International Origins of Compensated Emancipation Schemes

Nor shall private property be taken for public use, without just compensation.
—US Constitution, Fifth Amendment

In April 1864, after three years of civil war, a group of Louisiana Unionists assembled in New Orleans for a state constitutional convention intended to usher their state out of the Confederacy and back into the Union. The delegates arrived knowing that they had to abolish slavery, but some believed they could shift the policy that President Abraham Lincoln mandated—immediate emancipation—in former enslavers' favor. At the end of the convention, the delegates petitioned Congress to compensate loyal enslavers in some measure "for the great sacrifice they have made for the general welfare." The "loyal people of Louisiana" were "impoverished" by emancipation and the "destruction and devastation" of war, and the "whole burden" of losing $150,000,000 of human property "ought not to fall on" them, the delegates beseeched. The convention had ended slavery in their state, and Louisiana would "expend large sums of money in the education and moral culture of these emancipated slaves" in the future. In return, the federal government should reimburse loyal enslavers for the value of freed slaves.[1]

Delegates' memories of moments of compensated emancipation in the Atlantic world influenced the petition. During the convention, one delegate reminded his colleagues that no state that abolished slavery after the American Revolution had "freed a single slave" when they "rid themselves of slavery." When Pennsylvania abolished slavery in 1780, it had freed "all children born of slaves, after the passage of the Act," at the age of twenty-eight. The delegate explained to the convention, "The legislators of old Pennsylvania saw and appreciated the difficulties and the injustice of tearing away from legitimate owners hundreds of millions of property, and it did not deem it right or politic to adopt such a measure as I fear will be adopted by this Convention." The same delegate also cited state and federal jurisprudence. Up to "four or five thousand" court cases, he quoted from the infamous 1857 *Dred Scott* decision, "all tending in the same direction," recognized "slaves as property." Similarly, the petition itself pointed out that Great Britain abolished slavery while directly reimbursing former enslavers, "with signal success in . . . her West India colonies."[2]

The Louisiana delegates were some of the first politicians from a former Confederate state to claim federal compensation for the value of slaves freed during the Civil War, but they were not the last. From 1864 through 1866, white Southerners from every former Confederate state petitioned their states and the federal government to reimburse former enslavers for the value of enslaved people freed during the Civil War. Despite the different plans proposed, two fundamental justifications usually supported their claims. First, they pointed out that the overwhelming majority of states and nations in the early United States, Latin America, and Great Britain abolished slavery gradually, with direct or indirect reimbursements to former enslavers. Second, they argued that state and federal law protected property in people from immediate, uncompensated emancipation. In particular, they cited or alluded to the US Constitution's takings clause and eminent domain, the principle that no government could take any form of property for public use without compensating owners. If the federal government was going to abolish slavery and destroy enslavers' property rights in people, it had to reimburse them.

Though precedents for emancipation in the Atlantic world represent roads untaken in the US South, they help us understand why compensated emancipation did not happen before or during the Civil War except in Washington, DC. Southern historians usually write about emancipation as a domestic question but debates about emancipation in the United States occurred in the broader setting of the Atlantic world. From the nation's founding, Americans mobilized compensated emancipation as an important discursive tool in US slavery debates just as politicians had throughout the Atlantic world. This chapter explores how compensation schemes could reinforce or destabilize slavery; at different times, the various factions argued that paying enslavers—directly or indirectly—was a compromise measure to further the cause of abolition; was national absolution for the sin of slavery; was a way to prevent further violence and discord; or was a method to stymie abolition altogether.[3]

Reacting to emancipation movements throughout the Atlantic world and fearing insurrection, enslavers and pro-slavery advocates in the United States sought legal means to protect the institution where it existed and expand it where it did not. They worked to ensure that their state laws protected property rights in people and obstructed state-sponsored emancipation schemes. They mobilized legal theories of property, particularly eminent domain and the Fifth Amendment's takings clause, to defend slavery against state-sponsored emancipation. The staunchest defenders of slavery insisted that the federal government could not interfere with the institution of slavery where it existed. On the other hand, the staunchest antislavery politicians and abolitionists insisted that no natural right to property in people existed and so the government could abolish it. Other, more moderate pro-slavery advocates who hoped to maintain a tenuous alliance with free state politicians conceded that government-sponsored emancipation was possible but warned that the Fifth Amendment's takings clause required the United States to reimburse enslavers. These politicians and supportive legal scholars emphasized the impossibility of paying millions of dollars to indemnify enslavers to discourage abolition, even if they admitted the federal government had the power to end slavery. Abolitionists and antislavery politicians contested that the takings clause applied to property in people, arguing that no property right overrode people's natural right to own and control themselves. Nevertheless, abolitionists were sometimes willing to compromise on this point to end slavery by offering enslavers direct or indirect reimbursements. In so doing, they acknowledged enslavers' right to profit from property in people.

Pro-slavery advocates' arguments about the Fifth Amendment as it applied to emancipation were never tried in courts, and no compensation scheme came to fruition before the Civil War because enslavers doubled down. Though no federal legal doctrine affirmed enslavers' right to be compensated for freed slaves in the event of emancipation, pro-slavery politicians succeeded in pushing the terms of the slavery debates ever more conservative. By the time national debates over the expansion of slavery peaked in the 1850s, they had ensured that state and local law would protect their investments in human property, and they pushed the federal government to do so as well. They regarded compensation schemes apprehensively, seeking not to end slavery but to expand their investments in human property. Rather than concede to end slavery by paying enslavers, they wanted guarantees that the federal government could never abolish it.

The Problem of Compensated Emancipation

Compensated emancipation schemes emerged as compromise measures that helped mitigate the tensions between abolitionist ideals about self-ownership and enslavers' property rights in the revolutionary era. Throughout the late 1700s and early 1800s, European colonies in Latin America, the Caribbean, and North America defied colonial rule to gain national independence while espousing the ideals of American liberty and freedom. Compensated emancipation schemes attempted to address the dilemmas that some of these new nations faced as they fought against colonial rule yet sought to preserve existing social and political hierarchies and economic systems. The architects of these schemes established legal ideologies that shaped debates about emancipation through the Civil War.

From the beginning, proponents of compensation schemes sought to balance political pragmatism with their moral principles and the law. On the one hand, revolutionaries understood slavery as a product of colonial rule. Some, alongside abolitionists and the enslaved, saw independence and abolition as inseparable goals.[4] They saw that if freed, enslaved men could be important allies and soldiers in the fight for independence. They began to relate revolutionary calls for liberty to freedom for the enslaved. Black abolitionists developed new arguments condemning slavery by connecting their mission to revolutionary rhetoric surrounding natural rights, rights so basic that they were beyond the reach of government.[5] They argued that slavery violated the natural rights of the enslaved to life, liberty, and property. Writers of the Declaration of Independence and future US state constitutions echoed this argument—based in Christian belief as well as Aristotelian and Enlightenment principles—and upheld the notion that "the purpose of government was to preserve natural rights to 'life, liberty, and property.'" For proponents of abolitionists' natural rights discourse, the new governments of the Americas needed to abolish slavery in order to realize these goals.[6]

On the other hand, enslavers and their allies pointed out that property rights, too, were core revolutionary ideals and natural rights. While the most radical abolitionists would have countered that the right to own property in people was a theft of the enslaved's natural rights to life and liberty, many other contemporaries would have seen the desires to protect individual freedoms and preserve property rights as one and the same. In the United States, legal scholars understood that enslavers' human property was protected by vested rights, an English common-law doctrine that protected property owners from any confiscation of property without their consent. Enslavers also likened their legal relationship to the enslaved as a contractual relationship. They argued that the enslaved owed them their future labor in perpetuity. To force enslavers to free those they claimed ownership over, they suggested, was akin to making creditors release their debtors from their obligations.[7]

Seeking compromise, many state policymakers of the revolutionary era understood the emancipation of future generations of Black people and respect for enslavers' property rights in people to be reconcilable policy goals.

After the American Revolution, many Northern states moved to abolish slavey on the condition that legislation respect enslavers' property rights. One New Jersey newspaper doubted that emancipation legislation would pass unless abolitionists "devise[d] a scheme that would guarantee that *'no one has his slave forced from him or* [is] *put to necessary trouble and expense in bringing them up without an equivalent.'*" Abolitionists in New England acknowledged that enslavers claimed enslaved people by government sanction and implied that the state could end the practice only if it offered compensation to them.[8]

Although no northern state abolished slavery by direct monetary payment, historians suggest that there was strong agreement that enslavers should be compensated for the value of their slaves. The insistence that governments could not abolish slavery and deprive someone of their property in people without purchasing the enslaved to free them raised a number of logistical questions—namely, Who would pay? Around 1775, Connecticut clergyman and abolitionist Levi Hart wrote a letter to Samuel Hopkins, a fellow clergyman and abolitionist in Rhode Island, to address the question. He told Hopkins that "the public faith is, in effect, plighted to protect & support [enslavers] in the possession of their Slaves, or indemnify them if they are taken away." Hart suggested that the cost of slavery was the responsibility of the entire public.[9]

However, state policymakers did not relish the idea of paying for emancipation. Policymakers concerned about who would pay also considered whether they were legally obligated to compensate enslavers. Emancipation could be considered a compensable taking for public use under the principle of eminent domain, which defined the right of a government to confiscate private property for public use with just compensation and was enshrined in the US Constitution's takings clause. Eminent domain required transferring the title of the confiscated property from the owner to the government for public use. But it was unclear whether emancipation, which destroyed the title to an enslaved person (or transferred it to them under some legal thought), was eminent domain. Emancipation might instead be a noncompensable taking. Throughout the antebellum era, states regulated and sometimes extinguished individual property rights—as opposed to transferring titles—for the public good. Governments did not always compensate property owners for such regulatory actions executed under a state's police power. Jurists and lawmakers understood that property owners' claims were validated by public law and governance in the first place, and they viewed these regulatory acts as the price of a well-run society. In any case, confiscation made property owners nervous. They could imagine a slippery slope where governments could use eminent domain or their regulatory powers to take, destroy, or modify the value of any property. They suggested instead that vested rights protected their property in people, making them untouchable to government.[10]

Convinced that paying enslavers would be prohibitively expensive but unwilling to dispossess enslavers of their property rights in people, policymakers in New England and the Mid-Atlantic avoided the question of whether emancipation was a compensable taking. According to historian George William Van Cleve, contemporaries rarely discussed abolition legislation as an exercise of police powers. Historian Arthur Zilversmit suggests instead that gradual emancipation enabled states to exercise their regulatory powers without requiring direct compensation to enslavers because no living enslaved person was freed, only their future children. Many northern states abolished slavery gradually with "free womb laws," which dictated that children born to enslaved mothers after a certain day would be free but must work for their mother's enslaver as unpaid apprentices until a certain age. Pennsylvania passed a free womb law in 1780. Rhode Island and Connecticut followed in 1783 and 1784, respectively. Over twenty years later, New York and New Jersey passed them in 1799 and 1804, respectively.[11]

Legislators, enslavers, and non-enslavers accepted free womb laws because they shifted the cost of emancipation from enslavers and taxpayers almost entirely onto the enslaved and free people of African descent. St. George Tucker, an enslaver and professor of law and policy at the College of William and Mary by 1788, wrote that decades of apprenticeship satisfied the need for "just compensation" in the event of emancipation, enabled enslavers to plan financially, and prevented unrest and rebellion by keeping enslaved people under the control of their enslavers. More recently, historian Sarah L. H. Gronningsater has argued that Northern politicians supported free womb laws because they knew enslavers would more readily relinquish their ownership over children than adults, and because apprenticeship programs were familiar legal practices. Existing structures of poor relief could regulate freed people, and children's labor would reimburse enslavers for their upkeep and education.[12]

Although the value of enslaved people tended to decline quickly after a state passed free womb laws, these laws cost relatively little—except for enslaved people and their kin. In states that passed free womb laws and in Massachusetts, where the state supreme court effectively abolished slavery in *Commonwealth v. Jennison* (1783), enslavers could continue to exploit enslaved people's labor and that of their ostensibly free children. They could also protect their financial investments in people in other ways. In Massachusetts, enslavers sold people to places were slavery was still legal, posted notices for runaways in newspapers, and kidnapped and sold enslaved people out of state. Enough enslavers sold people out of New Jersey that its legislature enacted a statute that discouraged such sales without agreement from the still-enslaved person. However, such laws that protected imminently and already free people were difficult to enforce.[13]

No Northern state directly reimbursed enslavers, but these state-level conversations reached the national scale as the United States expanded in the early 1800s. For example, many colonization schemes that arose in this time would also have compensated former enslavers. Colonization, an idea popularized by white abolitionists and entertained in some states and Congress, proposed to free and remove African Americans from their states for a number of reasons: to ease the process of gradual emancipation or individual manumission for white people by removing the formerly enslaved, to preserve slavery, to spread Christianity and republicanism abroad, to secure US sovereignty over recently captured native lands, and to limit Black citizenship in the new nation. As historian Samantha Seeley notes, "depending on who controlled the venture," colonization "could symbolize exclusion or political autonomy." After the Revolution, some African American abolitionists hoped to leave the United States and emigrate to accelerate abolition and grant Black communities economic independence and more political rights. Proponents joined together to form the American Colonization Society in 1816, but members differed over the degree to which they embraced emancipation.[14] Offering to pay for freed people incentivized enslavers' participation in colonization schemes and reinforced their property rights.

Both colonization and compensation were moderate solutions to the problem of emancipation because they would preserve the existing logic of white supremacy and property rights. By advocating for gradual emancipation and removal of freed people from the body politic, abolitionists attempted to appeal to enslavers, who tended to reject both colonization and compensation in the interest of preserving enslavement.[15] Moderate enslavers and abolitionists met in the middle. By 1819, as the Missouri Crisis divided the nation over whether to admit Missouri as a free or slave state, enslavers like James Madison and Thomas Jefferson viewed colonization and compensated emancipation as favorable alternatives to extending slavery in the West. Like others before him, Madison suggested that the sale of Western public lands would pay for reimbursements to enslavers without burying the nation in debt. Madison believed that property in people was recognized by the

Constitution and, as such, "could not be constitutionally taken away without just compensation." Madison's suggestion was different from the logic of Northern states' free womb laws. Distinct from legal conceptions of vested rights or police powers, he used the takings clause to argue that no government had the power to deprive enslavers of their property in people without their permission and reimbursement.[16]

Congress also mobilized compensation schemes to reinforce the principle of property in people. Congress repeatedly tried to secure reimbursements for enslaved people from foreign powers. During the War of 1812, British forces promised to welcome any Americans who defected and emigrated from the United States to British possessions in North America and the Caribbean. Although the proclamation never specified the enslaved, an estimated 3,000–5,000 enslaved people from Virginia and Maryland took advantage of the offer. The British had enacted a similar policy during the American Revolution. In 1775, the royal governor of Virginia, Lord Dunmore, issued a proclamation granting freedom to enslaved people claimed by rebelling colonists who could fight in the British army. Though the United States had pursued compensation for those freed by Dunmore's proclamation, commissioners failed to secure it. In peace negotiations after the War of 1812, US commissioners, including abolitionist John Quincy Adams, attempted to force the British to return all previously enslaved Americans. The British refused, but after twelve years of international arbitration, they did agree to pay American enslavers over $1.2 million for the freedom seekers. Because so many US enslavers claimed compensation from the fund, it was depleted within two years, before all claims were paid.[17]

Paying for the National Sin

Madison and other Americans mobilized formalist legal distinctions to justify their positions on compensation, but their arguments were untested under US law. Gradual emancipation schemes had set a precedent to compensate enslavers, if indirectly. Elsewhere in the Atlantic world, it was common for nations to pay for manumission, as the British did in 1812, which buttressed enslavers' property rights in people. Indeed, historian Maya Jasanoff has argued that the British willingness to pay American enslavers after 1812 underscored the "novelty" of their refusal to do so during the Revolution.[18] Shortly after, Latin American nations and, later, the British ended slavery by direct or indirect compensation to enslavers for a variety of reasons, including the need for soldiers in wartime and in recognition of the nation's culpability in perpetuating slavery. Not only would these examples influence US policies during the Civil War, but they also changed the shape of the slavery debates in the United States. After the British example, abolitionists in the United States began to emphasize the immorality of paying enslavers to end slavery.

Many nations believed they had to pay enslavers for freed slaves not necessarily out of legal obligation but to recognize their sacrifice and shoulder the national burden of emancipation. In their independence movements against colonial powers, Latin American revolutionaries were pulled between enslavers' interests and their need for soldiers. They adopted antislavery policies, and enslaved men joined revolutionary armies in pursuit of their freedom. Latin American antislavery activists and revolutionaries argued that enslavers' right to own people could not overrule enslaved people's right to self-ownership. At the same time, revolutionary governments needed planter support to establish their legitimacy and defend against colonial powers. New Latin American nations amassed that support from the enslaved and enslavers alike by freeing enslaved people gradually, with some direct reimbursement to former enslavers for the value of the enslaved.[19]

The British would adhere to this norm in 1833, when Britain abolished slavery throughout its empire. According to historian Nicholas Draper, direct compensation to enslavers for the value of freed people was a precondition to passage of the Slavery Abolition Act of 1833 in Parliament. The act abolished slavery gradually and paid 20 million pounds to enslavers as compensation. The enslaved received no recompense for their own and their ancestors' labor; instead, the act required them to labor for their former enslavers during four to six years of apprenticeship, beginning on August 1, 1834.[20]

Although they provided it, enslavers and abolitionists in Great Britain did not believe that compensation to enslavers was legally required. Draper writes that the legal framework governing slavery in Great Britain was "underdeveloped," and thus debates about emancipation were primarily moral, rather than legal. Instead of claiming a definitive legal right to own people, British enslavers emphasized that lawmakers in London, as well as British colonization practices, had compelled them to purchase people. As Levi Hart similarly suggested in Connecticut, because Parliament sanctioned slavery, it could not abolish it without reimbursing enslavers.[21]

Instead, British enslavers successfully appealed for compensation by arguing that the ill-gotten profits of slavery suffused the nation. Enslavers and abolitionists alike accepted national culpability for slavery and the slave trade. The institution of slavery contributed to the nation's wealth, and therefore no one group should be punished for their investments in people. As their counterparts across the South would later do, British enslavers opined that widows and orphans would be destitute without compensation. They insisted that former enslavers who did not claim ownership over anyone at the time of emancipation were just as guilty as those who did because they had profited from selling people over whom they claimed ownership before abolition. Notably, James Madison, Levi Hart, and Americans in the Civil War era echoed the idea that slavery was a national sin. In Madison's words, abolition was only "just" if accomplished "at the national expense."[22]

By reimbursing enslavers, British abolitionists found a pragmatic policy for emancipation that nonetheless capitulated to enslavers' political and economic arguments. Both groups claimed that they wanted to prevent the collapse of the nation's credit system because the entire nation would be economically vulnerable if enslavers lost the value of enslaved people. But abolitionists had long argued that slave labor was inherently inefficient and sapped the nation's wealth. This premise highlighted differences between enslavers' and abolitionists' economic arguments. Enslavers convinced the nation that slavery was so efficient and productive that emancipation would impoverish them even as abolitionists reassured the nation that it could survive without the inefficient labor system of slavery.[23]

After the act was passed, enslavers collectively received about half the value of the enslaved directly from the British government. They filed claims in the colonies where the enslaved lived and worked, with local slave registries supplying supporting documentation. In London, the Slave Compensation Commission approved the payments and the National Debt Office paid them. The process took years. Claimants who owed money for the value of an enslaved person sometimes conflicted with creditors over who would be awarded the compensation. Lawyers, rather than the commission itself, usually resolved such conflicts, although the commission heard appeals. By 1839, the commission had arbitrated and settled over 50,000 claims and disbursed 20 million pounds in compensation. Former enslavers were happy enough: the West India Committee of absentee enslavers and West India merchants presented a silver ewer to the full-time commissioners in 1841 in appreciation of their work.[24]

The Slavery Abolition Act's apprenticeship system also compensated British enslavers for the value of enslaved people in the empire indirectly: The act freed only enslaved children under the age of six in 1834; freed people six and over became apprentices who were legally bound to work for their former enslavers for four to six years, depending on their occupation. After widespread protests from freed people and religious groups, however, Britain granted full emancipation for all enslaved people ahead of schedule in August 1838. Economic historian Stanley Engerman estimated that four years of apprenticeship yielded roughly one-half of the price of an enslaved person before emancipation, which meant that all told, former enslavers secured almost full compensation for the formerly enslaved when the value of apprenticeship was added to the direct reimbursement.[25]

Rather than inspire similar plans in the United States, international emancipation schemes dissatisfied many abolitionists. Immediately after the passage of the Slavery Abolition Act of 1833, Americans began to discuss the British example in the context of their antislavery debates. Some US abolitionists continued to see immediate emancipation with compensation to former enslavers as a compromise measure that could encourage abolition in the South, but many disagreed about whether former enslavers should be compensated. Impatient with moderate antislavery thought, Black abolitionists, who had been advocating for immediate emancipation at least since the American Revolution, radicalized many of their white allies. Throughout the Atlantic world, enslaved people had participated in and led revolutionary overthrows of colonial governments in Latin America and Saint-Domingue. In the United States, too, the enslaved rebelled against bondage and petitioned for freedom and redress for enslavement after the Revolution.[26]

For years after the act passed, US abolitionists sought to prove that payment to enslavers was immoral and economically unnecessary. In 1862, noted abolitionist, women's rights activist, and writer Lydia Maria Child published *The Right Way, the Safe Way*, a treatise for immediate emancipation in the United States that echoed arguments from one of her earlier publications, *An Appeal in Favor of That Class of Americans Called Africans* (1833). Child suggested that the enslaved, not enslavers, should have received a remedy for the national sin of slavery: "The slaves received nothing from the British government for centuries of unrequited toil. But £20,000,000 ($96,900,000) were paid to the masters, for ceasing to extort labor by the lash." Without explicit analysis of the policy, she presented indemnities to enslavers as neither a net positive nor a net negative. She quoted British planters who reflected, both before and after the Slavery Abolition Act passed in 1833, that they did not need government indemnities. Their profits increased after emancipation, she told readers. However, Jamaica, whose economy deteriorated after 1833, plagued her case. Avoiding discussion of rebellion there, she argued that the postwar economy failed despite the money enslavers received. Planters used the funds to pay off their considerable debts, but they had little money left to pay laborers. Ultimately, Child concluded that slavery and coercive labor conditions, not emancipation, led to economic precarity. The treatise ended with an example from the Dutch Empire, where, she said, many enslavers refused to take the compensation offered by the government, "while others took it and gave it to the emancipated slaves, who had worked so many years without wages." The possibility that freed people could benefit from compensation schemes intrigued Child, but she used it to emphasize the injustice of compensation to former enslavers if not the justice of reparations.[27]

As Child's work suggests, by the Civil War, most Black Americans and some white abolitionists denounced slavery as a crime and rejected any emancipation plan that would reimburse enslavers for their sins. As the slavery debates escalated in the United States, antislavery legal theorists insisted that the enslaved were people, not property, under the law. An 1827 legal treatise by George M. Stroud argued that emancipation was incompatible with compensation to former enslavers because people could not be property. Men, he wrote, "by nature, are equally free," and therefore it was impossible to "acquire a right over the person of another unless by his consent." Later, in 1853, abolitionist William Goodell also rejected the compensation argument, claiming that it identified "slaveholding with human chattlehood" even though enslaved people were human beings.[28]

However, enslaved people and abolitionists routinely purchased themselves and paid to manumit enslaved people in order to reunite with loved ones and free others from bondage. Among the more famous examples, Quaker abolitionists in Britain purchased Frederick Douglass's freedom in 1846 when he was on a speaking tour there to prevent his re-enslavement. Some US abolitionists believed that Douglass and his friends had conceded the right of property in people by purchasing him, but Douglass called the purchase a "ransom," or "money extorted by a robber." As William Lloyd Garrison, a cofounder of the American Anti-Slavery Society, said when he defended Douglass, "I see no discrepancy in saying that a certain demand is unjust, and yet being willing to submit to it, in order to save a brother man, if this is clearly made to be the only alternative left to me." Nevertheless, some abolitionists drew a line at ransoming the enslaved en masse for government-sponsored emancipation while others endorsed it, knowing that enslavers had repeatedly rejected such offers.[29]

These national and international precedents for gradual and compensated emancipation radicalized abolitionists and enslavers alike. Onlookers in the United States celebrated the republican but not necessarily antislavery principles of Latin American independence movements, which abolished slavery gradually enough that it was less threatening to US observers. Faced with uprisings and resistance, the Haitian Revolution, and abolitionists' growing commitment to immediate, uncompensated emancipation, proslavery politicians and enslavers reacted by securing the institution of slavery in state and local law and dodging any national conversation about emancipation, be it compensated or not. Historian Edward Rugemer writes that the dominant proslavery view was that abolitionists, given the opportunity, would work with British "fanatics" to violate enslavers' constitutional right to own people. Seeing how abolitionists used compensation to end slavery, pro-slavery advocates developed new legal interpretations of the takings clause to support their property rights in people. By the 1850s, most pro-slavery Americans sought to protect slavery, not compromise it by entertaining any possibility of abolition with reimbursements.[30]

Emancipation and Eminent Domain

Given that their economy, credit, and wealth relied on the complex legal and financial machinations that supported the institution of slavery, enslavers went to great lengths in their states to preserve it. In response to growing threats to slavery, pro-slavery advocates of the early 1800s mobilized evolving concepts in American law, most notably eminent domain, to reinforce rather than end slavery and protect it from political interference. This accounts for their unique stance by the 1850s—opposition to the more familiar model of compensated emancipation.

Throughout the first half of the nineteenth century, pro-slavery advocates developed theories of property rights, case law, and legally sanctioned slave-trading practices that ensured that state governments, at least, would protect their investments in human property as commodities.[31] Given the enslaved person's agency and the amount of money required to purchase a person, a buyer assumed much greater risk when purchasing an enslaved person than that associated with any other form of property. As a result, historian Jenny Wahl writes, "slave buyers tended to enjoy more legal protection than buyers of other commodities."[32] Compared with laws for the sale of other kinds of property, laws governing the sale of the enslaved assigned more responsibility to sellers because they had more information about the slave market and the enslaved's history. In courtrooms, judges recognized enslaved people's free will and knew that they could intervene between buyers and sellers by conveying information about themselves to manipulate a sale or by running away. Enslavers could also secure their investments by purchasing life insurance for enslaved people as assurances against injury or death, and these insurance policies could be transferred as credit, too, to build more profit.[33]

Enslavers' or buyers' prerogatives came second only to creditors'. When enslavers bought the enslaved on credit or mortgaged them, they jeopardized their legal protections by introducing a third party into the relationship—a creditor. By the mid-nineteenth century, nearly all states prioritized the rights of creditors over debtors, to say nothing of the enslaved. In 1837, the extent to which the law protected creditors was noted by one treatise writer, Jacob Wheeler, in a footnote. He wrote, "As slaves are considered as property upon which creditors have a right to look for the payment of their debts due by the owners of slaves, regard must be had to the rights of the creditor; and no emancipation is valid when those rights are violated." It is unclear what this practice meant for a freed person, but a separate practice regarding manumission by will might offer a hint. Wheeler observed that if an enslaver died indebted to a creditor, the creditor was entitled to the value of the enslaved, even if they were manumitted in the debtors' will. These freed people would not be re-enslaved, but they would be held liable for their enslavers' prior debts.[34]

Creditors' legal claims to an enslaved person's value structured the everyday experiences of the enslaved and white Southerners alike. Even Solomon Northup, a Black man born free in New York, quickly learned to navigate slavery's financial world after he was drugged and kidnapped in Washington, DC, and sold into slavery in the South in 1841. As many enslavers did, Northup's first enslaver, William Ford, gave him to a neighbor, John M. Tibeats, to satisfy a debt in 1842. Northup's value was greater than Ford's debt, so Tibeats owed Ford another $400, and he mortgaged Northup to Ford for that value. Tibeats therefore did not own Northup outright, even though Northup worked under his command. That mortgage, Northup later wrote, saved his life. When Tibeats threatened to whip him soon after he was sold, Northup refused to strip down and struck Tibeats in self-defense. Tibeats and his posse restrained Northup, bound his wrists and ankles, and dragged him to a tree, intending to hang him for his resistance. Ford's overseer, Mr. Chapin, intervened. He held up a gun to the vigilantes and told them, "Ford holds a mortgage on [Northup] of four hundred dollars. If you hang [Northup], he loses his debt. Until that is canceled you have no right to take his life. You have no right to take it any way. There is a law for the slave as well as for the white man." Thanks to Ford's monetary interests in Northup's value, Northup escaped further assaults and was later rescued from bondage and returned to the North as a free man.[35]

The enslaved's status as property enabled Tibeats to threaten Northup and also enabled Chapin to save him. Northup recalled the exchange between Tibeats and Chapin as a seminal moment in his time enslaved, representing for him and Northern readers both the physical violence of slavery and the dehumanization of commodification. Chapin's admonishment of Tibeats and his posse, as well as his power to stop them, stemmed from laws that prioritized a creditor's due over an enslaver's or overseer's prerogative to control the enslaved. After emancipation, creditors and enslavers would expect the same legal protections to recoup the value of people who were no longer property from debtors.[36]

Enslavers and their allies reinforced these financial protections with the principle of eminent domain. Throughout the antebellum era, pro-slavery politicians added takings clauses to their state constitutions at times when the future of the institution was unpredictable or they could not control political decision-making. In those moments, according to political scientist Stephan Stohler, slave states usually adopted takings clauses to secure reimbursements in the event of emancipation or unrest, or make abolition so expensive that voters would reject any emancipation proposals.[37] Not all policymakers agreed that state-sponsored emancipation required paying enslavers according to these clauses; however, they gave pro-slavery advocates enough legitimacy to dissuade their colleagues from abolishing slavery altogether.

We can best understand pro-slavery politicians' emerging arguments regarding eminent domain and its relationship to slavery in the 1830s, when enslavers had more reason to fear for the security of slavery. One of the best-known uprisings sparked debates in one slaveholding state about emancipation and just compensation. In August 1831, over a year after Virginia ratified a new state constitution with a takings clause very similar to the US Constitution's, an enslaved preacher named Nat Turner led six other men in rebellion against his enslaver in Southampton, Virginia. At 2:00 a.m. on August 21, they killed his enslaver and his family in their sleep and continued throughout the neighborhood, gathering more enslaved followers as they killed white people in each household. They continued until the middle of the next day, when a white militia confronted them, repulsed them, and captured some rebels. By the time the rebels dispersed, they had killed fifty-five white people. Whites in the state retaliated, capturing suspected rebels, executing fifty-five, and banishing many more. White mobs murdered hundreds of enslaved people, many of whom had nothing to do with the rebels. Turner himself was captured, tried, hanged, and skinned on November 11.[38]

What is now known as Nat Turner's Rebellion terrified white Southerners, who sought further protections and safeguards against future uprisings. The rebellion convinced many in Virginia that the best way to prevent them was the emancipation and forcible removal of enslaved people in the state for the protection of the white population. The Virginia General Assembly received about forty petitions signed by 2,000 Virginians, many calling for emancipation or removal. At least two petitions supported free womb laws and state-sponsored colonization, and others criticized any plan for emancipation without just compensation.[39]

During debates over emancipation in the Virginia House of Delegates, delegates could not agree whether state law allowed them to abolish slavery, especially without reimbursing enslavers. Delegate James Gholson, from a county near Southampton, opposed emancipation on the basis that Virginia's proposed plan was not only unwise but also illegal because it had no mechanism to pay enslavers for lost property in people. Gholson was concerned that the plan proposed taking "eighty or one-hundred millions of private property for public use, without compensation." Not only that, but he also insisted that private property was sacred, that enslaved people were property, "and that no high and overruling necessity exists for taking them from their owners." Abolishing slavery would be an abuse of Virginia's regulatory power—with or without compensating slave owners—Gholson argued.[40]

Delegates who supported gradual emancipation agreed that Virginia laws supported slavery but differed over whether enslavers required compensation. A few suggested that an emancipation policy was certainly for the public good, which justified intervention. Thomas Marshall, the son of former Supreme Court chief justice John Marshall, reminded the legislature, "Whenever the tranquility and security of society shall imperiously demand this sacrifice, the rights of property must yield to the preservation of happiness and life; but still it is a sacrifice, and one for which compensation should be made."[41] Marshall saw state reimbursements to enslavers as a recognition of their sacrifice, but others supported the state's power to regulate slavery as a form of property ownership unequivocally. William Preston, a delegate from western Virginia, suggested that the presence of Black people in Virginia endangered whites. To protect white communities, Virginia could negate enslavers' property rights in people under the state's police power and remove free Black people. Delegate Charles Faulkner argued that the House of Delegates could abolish slavery in any way it deemed fit. Enslavers "hold their slaves—not by any law of nature—not by any patent from God, ... but solely by virtue of the acquiescence and consent of the society in which they live." As soon as society ceased to tolerate that form of property, Faulkner argued, "the right by which they hold their property is gone." Enslavers held a title for human property not because they were inherently entitled to it but because Virginia law allowed it under positive law.[42]

Virginia did not abolish slavery after Nat Turner's Rebellion, but its General Assembly shared the ambivalence of northern states that had abolished slavery gradually at the turn of the century regarding compensation to enslavers. Whether the delegates believed that emancipation was an act of eminent domain or a regulatory taking, the state constitution's takings clause gave pro-slavery advocates enough ammunition to shed doubt on any emancipation scheme without compensation to former enslavers. Eminent domain also helped pro-slavery advocates evade all conversations of emancipation by emphasizing its necessary expense.[43] Though their ideas remained untested in courts, they gained traction when Thomas R. Dew, a historian and political economist at the College of William & Mary, published on the House of Delegates' debates in 1832.[44] Historians have traditionally credited Dew for popularizing the idea that slavery was not a necessary evil but good for enslavers and the enslaved. Dew also disseminated the idea that government-legislated emancipation was a taking that required compensation to enslavers. His writings became some of the leading pro-slavery works in the years before the Civil War and would be reprinted many more times into the 1850s.[45]

Ironically, Dew used eminent domain to defend enslavers' property rights in people against government-sponsored emancipation. For Dew, the right to claim property in an enslaved person was sacrosanct, and governments were bound to respect it because "the great object of government is the protection of property."[46] Consequently, Dew wrote, no enslaver was required to emancipate an enslaved person "unless his full value is paid by the state." He explained, the right to confiscate "only occurs in cases of real exigency; and secondly, ... the writers of our national law—and the Constitution of the United States expressly sanctions the principle—say, that no property can be thus taken without full and fair compensation." In the rare unconstitutional event that a government did abolish slavery, Dew held, it would have to pay enslavers.[47]

By establishing the constitutional requirement for compensation, proslavery advocates like Dew could in turn argue for the infeasibility of emancipation. Eminent domain helped Dew premise that enslaved people were like any other kind of property under the law, yet it also offered abolitionists a path to emancipation. Dew argued around that loophole. Even if a government tried to end slavery by paying enslavers, he suggested, enslaved people were so valuable that "legal," amply compensated emancipation would be impossible. After discussing the principle of eminent domain, Dew listed the value of enslaved people in Virginia and the steep costs to transport freed people from Virginia to the African coast. He asked readers, "Do not these very simple statistics speak values upon this subject? . . . the loss of $100,000,000 of property is scarcely the half of what Virginia would lose." He made emancipation less appealing to non-enslavers by asserting that government would have to pay millions of dollars in compensation to former enslavers. With that number in mind, Dew concluded that eminent domain prevented rather than enabled state-mandated emancipation in practice.[48]

Pro-slavery politicians in Congress would apply Dew's understanding of eminent domain to the Fifth Amendment's takings clause to obstruct federal interference with slavery. In 1837–38, abolitionists sent more than 130,000 petitions to Congress for the abolition of slavery in Washington, DC. On December 20, 1837, Vermont representative and Whig William Slade responded to these petitions and spoke against slavery in DC, violating the "gag rule" that Congress had implemented in May 1836 to prevent members of the House from formally debating issues surrounding slavery and emancipation. Slade rejected the idea that the enslaved were property under the Constitution and that abolition constituted a public taking. "Nobody thought," he said of the writers of the Constitution, that the takings clause was "applicable to the case of slavery: for, in the first place, the constitution no where speaks slaves under the denomination of '*private property*' but as '*persons held to service*,'" referring to the Fugitive Slave Clause. Second, he alleged, "no body had ever heard abolition spoken of as the '*taking* of private property for *public* use.'" Instead, he argued, abolition "takes from the usurpations of slavery the protection of law, and restores to men their 'private property' in themselves.'" Slade rejected arguments such as Dew's, asserting that the takings clause had no bearing on property in people because enslaved people, not the government, would own themselves after emancipation.[49]

Pro-slavery apologist and South Carolina senator John C. Calhoun denied that Congress could abolish slavery anywhere, yet he agreed with Slade: eminent domain did not apply to emancipation. In the same year as Slade's speech, Calhoun introduced a series of resolutions emphasizing the importance of slavery in Southern and Western states and discouraging any other state or the federal government from intervening in states where it existed. The fifth resolution also prevented any state, its citizens, and Congress from promoting or passing any act that would end slavery in Washington, DC, or federal territories. Calhoun's colleague, Kentucky senator and enslaver Henry Clay, tried to amend the fifth resolution to prevent abolition in DC or the territories "unless compensation were made to the proprietors of slaves." On January 10, 1838, Calhoun castigated Clay for the most "dangerous and unconstitutional" concession of appropriating public funds to purchase and emancipate the enslaved. Calhoun envisioned a slippery slope. He worried that if Congress "admitted" that it could abolish slavery with compensation to former enslavers, then "it would be very easy to complete the end the abolitionists have in view, and that wholly at our expense. If we yield that point, the work will soon be consummated." Knowing that slavery's profitability rested in the institution's capacity to grow and expand, Calhoun sought to prevent abolition at all costs.[50]

Calhoun and Clay had the same goal—to prevent abolition—but had different views on the takings clause in that shared goal. Calhoun drew a hard line, arguing that eminent domain did not apply to emancipation in order to end all debate over abolition. Clay, throughout his career, construed compensation as a necessary condition to end slavery in the District of Columbia. In 1839, he spoke in the Senate in response to another petition to end slavery in the district and sidestepped the question of whether emancipation represented a taking for public use; instead, he argued that a major impediment to immediate abolition was "to be found in the immense amount of capital which is invested in slave property." He exclaimed, "And now it is rashly proposed, by a single fiat of legislation, to annihilate this immense amount of property!—to annihilate it without indemnity and without compensation to owners! Does any considerate man believe it to be possible to effect such an object without convulsion, revolution, and bloodshed?" Where Calhoun refused to countenance compensation at all, Clay underscored its infeasible and all-encompassing enormity. Slavery was so entwined in Southern and national law and finance that it would be too expensive to abolish it.[51]

Similar to Dew, Clay evoked eminent domain to dissuade potential allies of emancipation. He used the British example of compensated emancipation to argue that "an irresistible sense of justice extorted from that Legislature the grant of twenty millions of pounds sterling to compensate the colonists for their loss of property." If abolitionists were determined to end slavery immediately in the United States, he told the Senate, they could raise "a fund of twelve hundred millions of dollars to indemnify the owners of slave property." That task would sufficiently "dissuade the abolitionists from further perseverance in their designs." Clearly, Clay did not see compensation as a compromise measure but as a safeguard against emancipation. He talked about compensation with the intention of ending talk about emancipation.[52]

An Alternative to War

Whether they thought the Fifth Amendment restricted or enabled government-sponsored emancipation, no formal legal doctrine confirmed Dew's, Slade's, Calhoun's, or Clay's arguments about eminent domain, particularly at the federal level. Nevertheless, pro-slavery advocates expected that the federal government would protect their property rights in people, and they worked to ensure it. They also counted on national ambivalence to prevent emancipation. However, that changed when tensions between pro- and antislavery forces escalated with the Kansas-Nebraska Act in 1854. The possibility of emancipation, even with payments to enslavers, began to appeal to abolitionists who believed that paying enslavers was a small price to pay to end the violent confrontations over slavery in Kansas. Hoping to prevent further bloodshed and future civil war, some abolitionists would take Clay at his word. According to historian John Stauffer, well-known abolitionist Gerrit Smith, who was in Congress for less than one term while the act was being debated, warned Congress that "slavery would 'go out in blood' unless immediate action were taken" to abolish it. Smith proposed an unpopular compensated emancipation plan in lieu of bloodshed. Realizing that Congress would not abolish slavery, he resigned after the Kansas-Nebraska Act was signed into law.[53]

Despite the evidence that enslavers did not support them, Smith continued to support compensated emancipation schemes outside Congress. In 1857 he collaborated with peace reformer Elihu Burritt to establish the National Compensated Emancipation Society. Primarily a pacifist but also an active proponent of temperance and abolition, Burritt had joined the abolitionist speaking circuit in the early 1840s. He traveled to Europe throughout the late 1840s and helped organize a series of annual peace conferences during the European revolutions of 1848. Burritt's peace work brought him into the abolitionists' orbit, yet his commitment to pacifism, willingness to work within US politics to abolish slavery, and lack of commitment to Black citizenship often alienated him from them. Hoping to end slavery without bloodshed, Burritt published a plan in 1856 to end slavery by paying former enslavers. He toured the United States from Massachusetts to Iowa and back, consulting with a number of antislavery politicians and abolitionists and speaking on his compensated emancipation scheme to what he reported to

Elihu Burritt by Henry Joseph Whitlock, albumen carte-de-visite, early 1870s. © National Portrait Gallery, London.

be enthusiastic audiences. With their support, he organized the National Compensated Emancipation Convention, held in Cleveland August 25–27, 1857, with the goal of establishing a national society to sponsor his program.[54]

The convention presented compensated emancipation as a practical policy solution to the slavery debates, as well as national redemption for the crime of slavery. Burritt and others at the convention insisted that Congress could legislate emancipation only by paying former enslavers. No one cited the takings clause as a rationale, likely because doing so would have explicitly recognized a right to property in people. Otherwise, Burritt's proposal recalled those of past politicians who suggested that revenues from public land sales would more than suffice to cover compensation to enslavers, as well as provide additional funds for Black education and "moral improvement." States had the prerogative to abolish slavery with any method and at any speed they saw fit, which, Burritt pointed out, would only make emancipation more plausible financially by staggering the timeline.[55]

Burritt and other delegates also hoped that compensated emancipation would restore "kindness and brotherly love" between the sections. Similar to British abolitionists who viewed compensating enslavers as repentance for national sin, Burritt believed that the United States could repent its own moral and economic complicity in the institution of slavery by paying enslavers. As he wrote in his 1856 treatise on the topic, "Before God and man, the North deserves to be fined heavily for its dereliction of duty to freedom. It deserves it richly, as an act of penal justice to humanity. It should be made to pay its share of the cost of extinguishing enslavement, whatever pecuniary expense it may involve." Burritt looked to the British example for guidance, and he reassured audiences that enslavers in the United States would receive more money than their British counterparts. Once again, the larger context of Atlantic world emancipation examples informed the US debate.[56]

Not all of the attendees agreed with Burritt, and a few attended specifically to argue against the idea. At the convention, as elsewhere, attendees disagreed about whether compensating enslavers implicitly recognized their legal or moral right to property in people. William Watkins, associate editor of *Frederick Douglass's Paper*, protested that enslaved people could not be held as property, and the compensation movement was more an idea for enslavers, not abolitionists. Ohio minister and abolitionist John Rankin also addressed the convention on the morality of enslavement and compensation. For him, making payments to enslavers was a small price to pay for abolition. He believed "life and freedom were more precious than money," reported a correspondent from the New York *Daily Tribune*.[57]

Convention organizers had intended only to pursue compensation for former enslavers, but attendees themselves began a conversation about advocating for remuneration for the enslaved as well. Watkins encouraged the convention to make "the slave, not the enslaver, the object of our movement." He reframed Burritt's view of compensation as national penance, telling the convention, "We should not talk of national compensation, but national retribution." The convention dismissed the idea on the first day, but the presence at the convention of other abolitionists, such as Gerrit Smith, who had long advocated to remunerate freed people with land, led the convention to reconsider. For his part, Smith supported enslavers' right to compensation as a kind of ransom. However, he critiqued the convention's conciliatory tone, encouraging the convention to acknowledge the inhumanity of slavery, even as, or if, it paid enslavers. Smith argued that without some compensation to the enslaved, other abolitionists would be unlikely to support the convention's goals. Eventually, the convention not only resolved that the federal government should provide states with the money to pay $250 for every person emancipated but also recommended that the United States should "help the emancipated also."[58]

More radical abolitionists had successfully pushed the convention to support remunerations to the enslaved, but the resulting plan was nebulous and vague. The convention concluded that "no measure of aid in this direction could exceed our wishes," and suggested that each freed person receive $25 and homes in the United States or another continent, if they desired. Unlike many prior proposals, the convention's resolutions did not unite around compensation and colonization; they left the possibility of colonization open in accordance with Black self-determination and growing emigration movements, of which attendees like Watkins were a part. However, the resulting National Compensated Emancipation Society, established during the convention to carry out its resolutions once the convention adjourned, outlined explicitly in its new constitution that its object was to compensate enslavers, not the enslaved.[59]

The National Compensated Emancipation Society operated for a couple of years after the convention with little success. Burritt began a newspaper, *North and South*, to publicize the plan, and the society met again in 1858 in New York and January 1859 in Albany. Within a year, the society had swayed a few moderates and conservatives to support a compensated emancipation scheme, but most abolitionists had abandoned any plan for emancipation that paid enslavers. Burritt had little foothold among more radical abolitionists such as William Lloyd Garrison, who had ridiculed him since the 1840s for his willingness to compromise with enslavers to preserve the Union. Further, as 1857 and 1859 convention attendees pointed out, the enslaved of the South were not for sale. Burritt received and publicized some support from enslavers, but most would not agree to the plan, even though it was designed to appeal to them. Rooted in a moral opposition to slavery, if a relatively conservative one, the movement united neither abolitionists nor enslavers, who wished to preserve slavery for the promise of future growth.[60]

IN THE ANTEBELLUM UNITED STATES, compensated emancipation was a compromise to the slavery debates that satisfied few. Northern policymakers who abolished slavery after the American Revolution believed they somehow needed to compensate enslavers for freed slaves to end slavery, but did not want to pay from the public purse. Later, abolitionists also viewed compensated emancipation ambivalently, as a capitulation to the pro-slavery ideology that denied the natural rights of the enslaved. Even when abolitionists considered paying enslavers as penance for the national sin, compensated emancipation failed because enslavers tried to have it both ways. Under threat, enslavers in the US South established legal protections for their property in people. To discourage abolition, pro-slavery politicians argued that no government could confiscate property in people, or, conversely, that emancipation was like eminent domain, and a government could abolish slavery if it guaranteed reimbursements to former enslavers.

Pro-slavery arguments may have remained mere rhetorical tools had the US Supreme Court not issued the *Dred Scott* decision. During and after the Civil War, white Southerners who supported federal compensation for freed people insisted that the decision of March 6, 1857, proved that the US Constitution protected property in people and that the federal government had to reimburse enslavers for the value of freed people in the unlikely event of emancipation. In the decision, the Supreme Court declared that Congress had no constitutional authority to ban or otherwise regulate slavery in federal territories. Historian Paul Finkelman concludes, Chief Justice Roger B. Taney argued that the Constitution "guarded" the rights of property with the Fifth Amendment. Taney insisted that Congress could not deprive a citizen of his property because he brought an enslaved person into a particular territory of the United States. Notably, Taney's argument centered on the Fifth Amendment's due process clause, not the takings clause. His decision protected enslavers' property rights in people against acts of Congress but did not necessarily guarantee enslavers compensation in the event of emancipation. Similar to Calhoun before him, Taney emphasized the sanctity of property rights to prevent future federal interference. Pro-slavery politicians used Taney's argument to defend slavery against all threats of abolition, including compensated emancipation, and defended slave ownership as a Fifth Amendment property right throughout the sectional crisis.[61]

By the outbreak of the Civil War, there was still no formal legal doctrine to explain whether federally legislated emancipation was an act of eminent domain that required just compensation to slaveholders. However, Northern backlash to the *Dred Scott* decision threatened enslavers' property rights in people. After *Dred Scott*, many Northerners joined abolitionists in rejecting the court's decision for its overreach. The Republican Party continued to advocate for the ban of slavery in new territories, and the party's most radical leaders, such as Salmon P. Chase and Charles Sumner, argued that freedom was national and slavery sectional on the basis that the Fifth Amendment's due process clause protected enslaved people's life, liberty, and property as any other person's. Echoing abolitionists' natural law arguments that insisted on the personhood of the enslaved, they admitted that slavery existed in positive law in slave states but protested that the federal government was not obligated to protect slavery or its expansion.[62]

Though this radical view of the Constitution was not accepted by a national majority, or even a majority of legal theorists, it threatened enslavers who defended their property rights in people by aligning abolitionist arguments with constitutional ones. During the 1860 presidential election, opponents of Republicans, such as Mississippi congressman and Democrat Reuben Davis, warned, "When the government gets into the hands of the Republican party, the arm of the General Government ... will not be raised for the protection of our slave property." After Republican president Abraham Lincoln was elected in November 1860, South Carolina quickly called a convention to secede from the United States in December 1860, followed by Mississippi, Alabama, Louisiana, Georgia, and Texas in January and February 1861. Many white Southerners in the Deep South believed they had lost the political battle for federal protection of their "greatest individual interest under the Government": "investments of more than forty hundred million dollars" in enslaved people and their plantation enterprises.[63]

Without a federal guarantee of their property rights in people, reactionary white southerners seceded, formed the Confederacy, and instigated the Civil War to protect these rights and their investments in human property. The Confederate Constitution, drafted in the spring of 1861, infamously reinforced the right to property in people, prohibiting any law "denying or impairing" it.[64] But in an effort to prevent emancipation—compensated or not—the Confederacy created new conditions that challenged slavery. Though unresolved, movements for compensated emancipation in the antebellum era informed Americans' conversations about the possibility of emancipation during the Civil War.

CHAPTER TWO

Wartime Emancipation Policies
Compensation and the Contested Status of Property in Persons

By the outbreak of the Civil War, enslavers and their representatives had spent decades staving off any possibility of emancipation, with or without compensation to enslavers. After Confederate states seceded, many enslaved people believed that freedom was imminent, and some took advantage of the political uncertainty by seizing it. On May 23, 1861, five weeks after Virginia seceded, Frank Baker, Shepard Mallory, and James Townsend sought shelter from their enslaver from the US Army at nearby Fort Monroe, in Hampton Roads, Virginia. The commander of the fort, General Benjamin Butler, refused to return them when their enslaver appealed. Butler called the men "contraband of war," or confiscated property.[1]

Propelled by enslaved people who had secured their own freedom and did not need constitutional sanctions or permission for their actions, Americans struggled to reconcile antebellum slave law with these new wartime realities. Beginning with the term "contraband," lawmakers reimagined what the legal category of "slave" meant in an ever-changing wartime context. The term exemplified the legal and political conundrum that confronted the Lincoln administration and the United States in the war's earliest years. "Contraband," which applied to the shipment of property by neutral parties, was not appropriate at Fort Monroe, and Butler knew it. Nevertheless, Butler used the term to controvert the Fugitive Slave Clause, which would have dictated the enslaved's return, even though it characterized enslaved people as property.[2]

When Baker, Mallory, and Townsend arrived at Fort Monroe, the federal government had not yet resolved basic questions of compensation and emancipation: Did the Constitution's takings clause guarantee enslavers a right to compensation for property in people in the event of emancipation in seceded or loyal states? Military measures such as Butler's contraband policy, the laws of war, and concerns over the loyalties of enslavers—whether in rebelling states or not—added new nuances to old questions. This chapter explores how Americans reconsidered the question of compensated emancipation in the context of civil war from the perspectives of abolitionists, border state politicians, the Lincoln administration, and Unionists in one seceded state: Louisiana.

Lawyers, activists, policymakers, and military commanders argued for or against compensated emancipation with new applications of familiar legal principles. In the early years of the war, few could be sure that the different arguments and legal actions that the United States mobilized to disrupt and, eventually, abolish slavery would be honored in peacetime. For this reason, many federal and state lawmakers continued to imagine that federal compensation for those who claimed ownership over enslaved people was a central component of Black freedom. As the United States pursued military emancipation, this chapter argues, Congress and President Lincoln offered partial compensation for the value of enslaved people as a compromise measure to achieve their ever-changing goals.

Confederate secession and war also changed the political landscape of the compensation debates. Lawmakers now considered compensated emancipation not only in terms of property law but in terms of loyalty and citizenship as well. Even the American Anti-Slavery Society acknowledged in the first year of the war the constitutional rights of faithful citizens to reimbursements for the loss of property. Many supported compensation to garner support for emancipation among enslavers in the border states—Delaware, Maryland, Missouri, and Kentucky—who still lived within the Union.[3] However, few could agree on what defined a faithful citizen. Presumably, border state enslavers remained citizens residing in the United States and privileged to constitutional guarantees. Following that logic, Kentucky congressmen, in particular, echoed antebellum enslavers who insisted that enslaved people were a kind of property, but not one subject to seizure and compensation under the Fifth Amendment's takings clause, which guaranteed that private property could not be taken for public use without "just compensation." They denied that state-sponsored emancipation was a taking for public use and insisted that the United States could not interfere with slavery in states where it existed. Their goal was to preserve slavery for as long as possible.

The rights of enslavers residing in Confederate territory and places under US military control were even more uncertain. Butler's contraband policy and ensuing laws suggested that the United States could only confiscate the property of disloyal enslavers, but did they apply to ostensibly loyal Unionists in seceded states? Some white Southerners in seceded states remained loyal to the United States, but these Unionists did not necessarily want to end slavery. They represented many different political stances and behaviors, ranging from distrust of the Confederacy to a desire to preserve slavery and the US Constitution "as it was," to actively fighting for the United States and abolition. Only when emancipation was certain and the hope of retaining property in people had faded did they earnestly pursue reimbursements from the United States. As seceded states like Louisiana and Arkansas began to re-enter the Union toward the end of the war, Southern Unionists asserted claims to federal compensation for freed slaves less as a Fifth Amendment right than as a reward for their loyalty and their state's acquiescence to US emancipation policy. But by then, the war had convinced many Americans that loyal citizens should willingly relinquish their property rights in people regardless of any right to reimbursement.[4]

Abolitionists: Frederick Douglass, War Powers, and the Natural Law Argument

As soon as the war began, renown abolitionist Frederick Douglass called for emancipation throughout the Confederacy. As he saw it, federal policy was, at best, contradictory. In a speech in Philadelphia in January 1862, Douglass condemned the Lincoln administration's careful legal language that concealed every "cause for the rebellion except the right one." When the Lincoln administration referred to enslaved people, Douglass observed, "they must be called persons held to service or labor. When in the hands of the federal government, they are called contrabands—a name that will apply better to a pistol, than to a person." Whatever words it used, the US government preserved slavery in the name of "the rights of the South under the Constitution," he explained. But property in people was precisely the principle that the Confederacy fought to perpetuate and precisely what Douglass believed the US Army should destroy.[5]

Douglass drew on the abolitionist idea that the federal government had no obligation to preserve enslavers' property rights in people because those property rights violated the enslaved's natural rights to freedom. Some early abolitionists in the US North and Great Britain had believed that emancipation should come at the expense of the public, who benefited economically from slavery. Later, abolitionists who observed British emancipation and the sectional crisis were more concerned with the morality of purchasing—or ransoming—people. Throughout the antebellum era and the early war years, as we have seen, Douglass defended enslaved people's natural rights to own themselves, and abolitionists like him crafted a theory of immediate emancipation without compensation to former enslavers based on the notion that no one could legally enslave another person. Any application of the principle of eminent domain to manumission or emancipation required accepting that enslaved people were property under the law, like any other kind of property, a notion that most radical abolitionists did not accept. At the outbreak of the Civil War, a few moderate abolitionists seemed willing to pay enslavers to rejoin the United States in the midst of the secession crisis as a peace measure.[6] But Douglass and others continued to resist the possibility of paying enslavers, determined that enslavers should shoulder the financial burden of emancipation.

Douglass urged Americans that secession and war justified federal emancipation without any regard for the property rights of enslavers in seceded states, including any constitutional justification for compensation. He insisted that US lawmakers must cease describing enslaved people as "an article of commerce" and recognize their humanity by abolishing slavery without compensation to a group of people abolitionists had long considered undeserving of such payments. However, formal legal doctrine did not corroborate Douglass's arguments about the natural rights of the enslaved, and antislavery advocates in government followed unevenly.[7]

As early as 1861, US officials argued instead that the Constitution granted Congress war power to interfere with slave laws, which had important implications for loyal and disloyal enslavers' claims for compensation under eminent domain. William Whiting, a solicitor of Lincoln's War Department, published a treatise in which he adopted Charles Sumner's "state suicide" theory of secession, arguing that seceded states forfeited their statehood and thus their residents' constitutional rights and protections. The US military could confiscate enslaved people, debts, and service or labor—it could all be confiscated for use or destruction under the takings clause. While the takings clause required the United States to pay "just compensation" to friends of the government, war powers enabled the United States to deny compensation for those whom it regarded as its enemies. The Constitution granted the president and Congress the power to decide who was a friend and who was an enemy, and any compensation Congress granted to loyal citizens residing in disloyal states was "an act of grace," not obligation.[8]

However deeply ambivalent about the possibility of compensation they might have been, many abolitionists suggested that the war gave the federal government the power to interfere with property rights in people, but not necessarily those rights of loyal enslavers living in the United States. Many shared Douglass's frustration with the United States for respecting property rights in people but nevertheless acknowledged border state enslavers' right to compensation. The United States would at least owe them compensation in the event of federally legislated emancipation there. Whiting, for example, based his arguments in favor of emancipation on the confiscation powers inherent in the takings clause. As long as border state enslavers resided in the United States and remained ostensibly loyal, they retained a right to reimbursement for emancipation. In these arguments, abolitionists relied on Revolutionary-era conceptions that considered loyalty to the state a prerequisite to legitimate property ownership. Abolitionists recognized that any argument for emancipation based on the takings clause was inescapably premised on the recognition of property rights in people; however, granting the federal government the right to interfere with slavery in loyal states represented a step toward emancipation that few Americans supported before the war.[9]

Compensating *disloyal* enslavers was unacceptable to abolitionists, who held that enslaved people were rendered forever free by the ongoing disloyalty of their enslavers. But early US policy suggested that the federal government might pay loyal enslavers in seceded states for freed slaves. After Butler's contraband decision, Congress passed the First Confiscation Act in August 1861, authorizing the US seizure of rebel property and releasing enslaved people who worked for the Confederacy from service to their enslavers. Whether the United States owed a loyal enslaver living in the Confederacy for releasing an enslaved person from service was unclear. David Lee Child—former co-editor of the *National Anti-Slavery Standard* alongside his wife, Lydia Maria Child—noted that the secretary of war, Simon Cameron, had requested that General Benjamin Butler record the names of any enslaved people who sought protection from his camp, as well as the "name and the character as loyal or disloyal" of their enslaver. Cameron predicted that with peacetime, "Congress will doubtless properly provide for all the persons thus received into the service of the Union and for just compensation to loyal masters." Though Cameron specified that only loyal enslavers would receive compensation, Child worried that the United States' commitment to the takings clause, the First Confiscation Act, and the army's recordkeeping recognized enslavers' property rights and would later leave the United States liable to compensate both loyal and disloyal enslavers.[10]

Whiting's treatise nevertheless helped antislavery policymakers avoid recognizing any Fifth Amendment claim to compensation for disloyal enslavers by reframing emancipation as a necessity for the public good in wartime. Throughout 1862, Congress maintained a commitment to remunerating enslavers residing in the United States while undermining slavery in various acts. For example, the DC Emancipation Act of April 1862 ended slavery in Washington, DC, with up to $300 (or $9,438 in 2024 dollars) payments to loyal enslavers for each person freed. Senators who first debated the bill generally agreed that the United States should compensate loyal DC enslavers in some form, whether through direct payments or through gradual emancipation without payments. While some Unionists who supported emancipation in DC argued that it was analogous to eminent domain, many Radical Republicans shared abolitionists' ambivalence about compensation.[11] Despite goading from conservative senators, radical supporters of the bill routinely submitted to its compensation measures while strategically referring to the $300 payments as anything but "just compensation" for property in people. Samuel C. Pomeroy of Kansas suggested that compensation go to freed people for their labor, as well as to enslavers for food, clothing, and other expenses they paid for enslaved people. Like other abolitionists before him, Massachusetts senator and abolitionist Charles Sumner defended Congress's power to abolish slavery in the district and called payment to enslavers a "ransom rather than compensation, so that freedom shall be acquired rather than purchased." Radical Republicans emphasized that emancipation was rubbed out in DC by the war, and compensation a "gratuity" that they bestowed generously, not by law. By their logic, Congress was not subject to the rules of eminent domain because emancipation was not a seizure of property or transfer of title. Instead, they suggested that Congress abolished a pernicious form of property that threatened the Union, which made emancipation a valid exercise of police power and therefore a noncompensable act.[12]

At the same time, Congress decided to reimburse loyal enslavers to avoid accusations that it had unconstitutionally deprived citizens of their property. Radical Republicans argued that all enslavers' rights to compensation were rubbed out by war, but they did not yet have the political support to craft emancipation policy consistent with abolitionists' arguments. As a result, the DC Emancipation Act enforced the very contradictions Douglass sought to avoid, and Congress was quite liberal in carrying out compensation measures. By the beginning of 1864, Congress had granted 930 claims to ostensibly loyal DC enslavers in full or in part and expanded qualifications for enslavers to claim compensation after the original act passed. As Congress carried out emancipation in the district, Douglass's concerns proved prescient: Historian Tamika Y. Nunley argues that the DC Emancipation Act preserved enslavers' property rights, enabling them to invalidate many freed people's claims for freedom even while their enslavers secured reimbursements.[13] Furthermore, US lawmakers set a precedent for ending slavery by paying loyal enslavers. Fearing for slavery in the border states, congressmen there continued to defend against even compensated emancipation, as pro-slavery apologists had done before the war.

Border State Enslavers: Senator Garrett Davis, Eminent Domain, and the Defense of Property Rights in People

Some of Congress's more conservative members, especially Kentucky senator Garrett Davis, were just as dissatisfied with the compensation measures in the DC Emancipation Act as Radical Republicans. An enslaver himself, Davis joined Congress at the end of 1861, condemning disunion but defending slavery. He represented a contingent of border state Unionists and Democratic congressmen who believed that property, rather than human liberty, was the most fundamental principle to the Union, and that the Constitution guaranteed property rights in people.[14]

Davis defended these ideas throughout the spring of 1862 as Congress debated the Second Confiscation Act and the DC Emancipation Act. In debates on DC, Davis, like Calhoun before him, argued that the US Constitution recognized people as property and that the Fifth Amendment's takings clause prevented abolition. Assuaging border state politicians' fears that Congress might try to abolish slavery in their states with a similar measure, Davis told congressmen, "You cannot for any purpose of overturning the institution of slavery, take a slave who belongs to a citizen" because any government appropriating property by eminent domain must use it for *public* purposes. Emancipation was not a taking, he argued. Congress would not "take the slaves" to use in service of a "governmental operation." Instead, it would free enslaved people, effectively eradicating the kind of property confiscated, and abolish the category of human property altogether. Even if Congress could take this action, he allowed, the act failed to provide "just compensation" to enslavers because the promised payments did not reflect the true value of an enslaved person in 1862.[15]

It became clear that spring and summer that many border state congressmen opposed all efforts to abolish slavery, with or without compensation, in and outside rebelling states. Davis hoped to forestall emancipation by insisting that enslavers had an inalienable right to claim property in people *and* that any government that violated that right owed them remuneration. But debates about the Second Confiscation Act regarding property confiscation in rebelling states eroded enslavers' property rights there, challenging Davis's logic. Republican senator Lyman Trumbull of Illinois proposed the Second Confiscation Act that summer to allow for the seizure of all rebel property, whether used to support the Confederacy or not. In the act, Congress sought to resolve some of the uncertainties of the First Confiscation Act of 1861, which enabled the United States to seize property used to support the rebel-

Hon. Garrett Davis of Kentucky, between 1855 and 1865. Brady-Handy Collection, Library of Congress.

lion, including enslaved people. In practice, the First Confiscation Act was difficult to enforce and appeased border state enslavers by avoiding the question of emancipation.

The Second Confiscation Act strengthened Republican's arguments about emancipation and war powers even though property confiscation divided legislators over foundational legal questions about property rights and sovereignty. Trumbull held that international law enabled the United States to confiscate rebel property and enslaved people in Confederate states without trial. Where courts were open, the United States could seize rebel property through legal process, allowing pathways for manumission in seceded and border states. During these debates, a group of conservatives emerged in opposition to Trumbull, including Davis, another Kentuckian, Congressman John J. Crittenden, and about one-third of Congress. They sought to limit the federal government's power to confiscate property. They united under their view that property confiscation was unconstitutional outside the judicial process. For example, Crittenden spoke in Congress, opposing widespread confiscation and especially the confiscation of enslaved people. He subsumed the right to own people under the "great object" of every government—the security of property—and pointed out that Congress had always defended the constitutionality of property rights in people. Even rebels retained individual rights to their property that Congress could not legitimately or constitutionally supersede, he and other border state congressmen held. Though some radicals and abolitionists wanted to dispense with due process for any disloyal person anywhere, these conservatives opposed any property confiscation except as a consequence of an individual trial for treason. They contended that judges were the only ones who could make binding decisions to deprive someone of their property. Their position was well-calculated: Treason was difficult to prosecute, and thousands of treason trials would overwhelm the courts. Conservatives thus hoped to preserve the property rights of rebels on the basis of their natural rights to property, a constitutional right to just compensation, and pragmatism.[16]

As they defended their views on property rights and the Constitution, congressmen like Davis and Crittenden often betrayed their opposition to emancipation outright, in both border states and the Confederacy. In these conversations about property rights, Davis and other conservatives held that enslaved people must be treated like any other property, but in the words of historian Silvana Siddali, they also betrayed "an uncomfortable awareness that slaves represented a type of extraordinary property." Countering Republicans' arguments that the United States could use war powers to end slavery, Davis maintained that no form of wartime confiscation could apply to property in people. Conservatives' views were consistent with Davis's arguments during the DC Emancipation debates, when he insisted that the United States could only end slavery in DC permanently if a judicial body heard each enslaver's claims for slaves and granted them full compensation.[17]

Ironically, the Second Confiscation Act undermined slavery in rebelling states by setting enslaved people apart from other property in different sections. Trumbull's initial section regarding enslaved people provided that anyone claimed by rebels was forever free, owing to the continuing disloyalty of their enslavers. In theory, the act provided for the immediate liberation of rebel-claimed freedom seekers who escaped to Union lines by transferring ownership of enslaved people's labor from those convicted of disloyalty to the United States in federal court. However, the act did not enforce that transfer in practice. It did not shift titles to enslaved people to the federal government, subject enslaved people to confiscation and sale by courts, or instruct military authorities who oversaw fugitive freedom seekers to turn them over to the courts. Nor did it acknowledge enslaved people as property; instead, it implied that it was not the enslaved person but their labor that was property. Neither eminent domain nor due process characterized the emancipation of enslaved people claimed by rebels. In practice, neither military authorities nor courts understood how to carry out the act in relation to actual enslaved people.[18]

The final version of the Second Confiscation Act represented neither Trumbull's radical view of confiscation nor Davis's commitment to a natural right to property but rather a vision of property confiscation based on loyalty. Regardless of the kind of property involved, the claimants' loyalty to the government legitimized their property ownership.[19] However, Congress could not seize property indefinitely as a punishment for *dis*loyalty. The act did not uphold abolitionists' view of property ownership as based on the will of the sovereign, contingent on the claimants' continued allegiance. Instead, the act shielded property owners from government interference. At the same time, it clarified from the First Confiscation Act that only those enslaved by "persons who shall hereafter be engaged in rebellion" against the United States would be "forever free of their servitude, and not again held as slaves." Border state enslavers were deemed loyal, and their property rights in people thereby legitimated.[20]

By preserving loyal enslavers' property rights, the Second Confiscation Act avoided any resolution of the debates over the legitimacy of property in people as a general principle or whether emancipation was eminent domain. It enabled the United States to carry out uncompensated emancipation against rebels in wartime while indemnifying enslavers within the United States. As a result, both Radical Republicans and conservatives like Davis claimed the Second Confiscation Act as a victory. Radicals and abolitionists could argue that the act gave the legislature the constitutional power to free those enslaved by rebels, while conservatives held that the act treated enslaved people like property in the event of seizure and where courts were open.[21] As long as loyalty was a litmus test for property rights, Republicans could justify interference with slavery in wartime—with or without compensation—and conservatives could argue that the federal government either could not interfere with property rights in people or at least must remunerate loyal enslavers in the event of emancipation.

Many policymakers continued to wield reimbursements to enslavers as incentives to end slavery. While Congress debated the Second Confiscation

Act, Lincoln pursued compensated emancipation schemes in the border states. On March 6, 1862, Lincoln proposed to Congress a gradual compensated emancipation plan in which the federal government would pay border states to compensate enslavers and support colonization efforts. Although Davis agreed with the principles of Lincoln's plan—it looked very much like a plan Davis himself had proposed—it lacked explicit appropriations for compensation. He sought reassurance that Congress would pay "something like the reasonable value" of enslaved people in the border states, and when that appropriation was not forthcoming, Davis and other border state representatives rejected the plan.[22]

Border state representatives continued to deny the feasibility of compensated emancipation. Davis and twenty other border state congressmen wrote to Lincoln on July 14, 1862, explaining their reluctance to accept his proposal and abolish slavery in their states, even with compensation. They insisted that if the United States were to pay the fair price of enslaved people in Kentucky, Maryland, Virginia, Delaware, Missouri, and Tennessee—which it was constitutionally obligated to do—then the cost of compensation would be prohibitive, especially, they wrote, "when the Treasury was reeling under the enormous expenditures of the war." While they accepted the constitutional principle of compensation, they rejected a proposal for compensated emancipation as not only inadequate but also cost prohibitive.[23]

In their letter, the border state congressmen resisted emancipation outright even as they required compensation for the full and fair value of enslaved people. They endorsed their states' rights under the Constitution to determine the laws and future of slavery in their state and refused to yield them. Using the principles of the Second Confiscation Act, the twenty-two congressmen defended their right not only to compensation but also to claim property in people, based on their loyalty. They blamed Congress and some of Lincoln's generals who sought to end slavery where they had military jurisdiction for subverting "the principles of the Constitution," rather than criticize Lincoln or even Confederates. In fact, the United States' efforts to chip away at slavery was the very thing that had driven otherwise loyal men to rebellion, they suggested. "We had done as much as had been required of others, in like circumstances, and we did not see why sacrifices should be expected of us, from which others, no more loyal, were exempt." They reassured Lincoln that "there was not the remotest probability that the States we represent would join in the rebellion, nor is there now." The border states remained in the United States because the only "hope for constitutional liberty" was the Union's preservation. Yet their refusal to relinquish property rights in people, even with some compensation, betrayed their rationale for remaining in the United States: Border states believed the Constitution best protected the right to profit from property in people from the uncertainties of wartime emancipation.[24] And they were right. Throughout 1862 and 1863, Congress chipped away at slavery in war-torn states, but US policymakers could not avoid the strong property claims of loyal enslavers without offering payments for freed people.

Military Emancipation and the Constitution: President Abraham Lincoln

Frustrated by his negotiations with border state congressmen, Lincoln moved toward other strategies for emancipation. In Confederate states, he pursued immediate military emancipation, as envisioned by his solicitor, William Whiting, and refined by others. In the border states, he pushed manumission and Black enlistment, as designed by his judge advocate general, Joseph Holt, who mobilized the takings clause to the administration's ends.

Lincoln and other Republicans worked to keep Kentucky and other border states loyal to the United States, but many also envisioned a future without slavery. He had warned border state congressmen that slavery would be extinguished by the "friction and abrasion" of war. Unlike Davis, who prioritized constitutional principles and rights, many Republicans viewed abolishing slavery as a foundational moral imperative that could not be decided by political principles alone. These differences led Lincoln to break with border state politicians like Davis. In July, he shared with his cabinet drafts of a military order to more aggressively confiscate the property of rebels, including enslaved people, and a draft proclamation that freed them.[25]

However, even as he took these steps toward military emancipation, Lincoln continued to imagine and implement policies that compensated enslavers in both the Confederacy and the United States. Before the war, members of the Lincoln administration, including William Seward and Salmon P. Chase, had supported compensated emancipation as a compromise with pro-slavery advocates. In the early years of the war, Lincoln pursued many avenues to abolish slavery, using constitutional and moral justifications. Similar to Davis, many of Lincoln's policies were rooted in the idea that enslaved people were legitimate forms of property under the law. In conversations about the Second Confiscation Act, he agreed with conservatives that Congress did not have the constitutional power to determine if enslaved people were a legitimate kind of property. Instead, he believed that the federal government could pay for enslaved people. Then, the United States could decide the status of the enslaved. At the same time, he embraced military emancipation to continue to dodge the question of whether enslavers had a vested right to property in people.[26]

In the fall of 1862, Lincoln combined these ideas into a few different hybrid policies. On September 22, Lincoln promised in the Preliminary Emancipation Proclamation that he would urge Congress to fund a compensation proposal for loyal enslavers in seceded states if slave states ceased their rebellion. He followed through in his annual message to Congress on December 1, recommending that Congress adopt a thirteenth constitutional amendment to abolish slavery that rewarded surrender and state-supported abolition with federal compensation to enslavers in both border and seceded states.[27]

Lincoln's proposed amendment interpreted payment to enslavers as a legal as well as a moral imperative. The proposed amendment guaranteed to states where slavery was recognized the constitutional right to compensation, to be distributed as they pleased—as long as those states in rebellion rejoined the Union. It stipulated that each state had to abolish slavery somehow before January 1, 1900, and offered federal reimbursement in the form of bonds for the total value of the state's enslaved in 1860. The federal government would deliver the bonds according to the pace of emancipation—incrementally if the state implemented gradual emancipation and in one sum if the state abolished slavery immediately. The bonds would begin to accrue interest only after every enslaved person was freed. The proposed amendment did not indicate whether or how states would distribute the income from the bonds to individuals. Lincoln did ensure, however, that if a state reintroduced or "tolerated" slavery after receiving the bonds, it had to return them. The proposed amendment also protected the enslaved, "who shall have enjoyed actual freedom by the chances of the war," and promised that they "shall be forever free."[28]

In his 1862 message, Lincoln conceded that enslaved people were property under the law, but he interpreted and rationalized compensated emancipation in many ways. One, he offered reimbursements for freed people as an incentive for slave states to cease hostilities and defended them as "both just and economical." He acknowledged arguments about property rights in people, explaining, "In a certain sense the liberation of slaves is the destruction of property—property acquired by descent or by purchase, the same as any other property," but he did not call the promised payments a "just compensation" for eminent domain. Two, and instead, Lincoln suggested that the United States should pay for peace, as abolitionists had during the secession crisis, because compensating enslavers would cost less than the war in terms of money and white lives lost. Drawing on projected population figures, he calculated that the growing population of the United States could pay off the enormous debt of reimbursing enslavers. He concluded, "A dollar will be much harder to pay for the war than will be a dollar for emancipation on the proposed plan. And then the latter will cost no blood, no precious life. It will be a saving of both."[29] Three, as British abolitionists had said of their country, Lincoln proposed that the federal government compensate enslavers because the entire nation was culpable for slavery, not because he was constitutionally bound to do so. He believed that both North and South were "responsible for the original introduction of this property," and certainly for using and profiting from the goods that enslaved labor produced, such as cotton and sugar. He asked Congress, "If . . . for a common object this property is to be sacrificed, is it not just that it be done at a common charge?" By arguing mainly in terms of fairness rather than constitutionality, Lincoln avoided engaging border state arguments that the federal government could not interfere with slavery based on their constitutional right to claim ownership over people. The tactic failed to coax border states or seceded states to end slavery, but it did align compensated emancipation with the cause of the Union.[30]

One month later, however, Lincoln appeared to abandon his strategy for compensated emancipation when he issued the Emancipation Proclamation, which declared enslaved people forever free in areas that were rebelling against the United States and that were not under US Army control. Historians have hailed the January 1, 1863, Emancipation Proclamation as the harbinger of immediate, uncompensated emancipation, but that outcome was far from certain in 1863. As historians have acknowledged, Lincoln used his powers as commander in chief to free enslaved people in territories conquered by the United States, excepting those already occupied by the military. The future of slavery was uncertain in many areas of the Confederacy, and no one knew how emancipation would be carried out where the proclamation prevailed, or if it would continue in peace.[31]

In fact, Lincoln remained committed to compensating loyal enslavers in the border states for freed people throughout the war. Contrary to historical perception, the Emancipation Proclamation created new opportunities for the Lincoln administration to manumit some enslaved men and pay enslavers based on the takings clause. The proclamation did not free enslaved people in the border states or US-occupied territories, but in it the Lincoln administration emphasized new efforts to recruit Black men into the US armed services. Before 1863, the army had already employed freedom seekers as teamsters, and after issuing the Emancipation Proclamation, Lincoln enlisted them as soldiers too.[32]

In the summer of 1863, the War Department used Black enlistment to secure freedom for Black soldiers and entice individual enslavers in the border states, as opposed to state politicians, to manumit enslaved men with compensation. In August 1863, Judge Advocate General Joseph Holt, the final arbiter of military law and a native Kentuckian, outlined a comprehensive legal argument for manumission in the border states. Holt informed the secretary of war that he could enlist and free enslaved men in these states if the United States compensated loyal enslavers, per the Fifth Amendment's takings clause. Holt explained that enslaved people were both property and persons under the law. As persons, they had the obligation to bear arms in defense of the United States. If the government asked them to imperil "their lives in defense of the Republic," they were "worthy to be free." At the same time, the United States had to compensate former enslavers for the enslaved to legally guarantee an enlisted man's permanent freedom. Up to that point, the seizure, use, or even destruction of property as part of military strategy was temporary unless civil courts declared otherwise. Now, under this plan, the title of the enslaved enlisted man was permanently transferred to the government under eminent domain.[33] To accomplish permanent freedom for some Black men, the administration continued to preserve border state enslavers' professed rights to them as property under the law by freeing them after paying "just compensation" to their enslavers.

Holt acknowledged that freeing an enslaved man claimed by a loyal enslaver to serve in the US military was an act of eminent domain, but other policies challenged border state enslavers' commitment to the Union. In April, Lincoln had issued the Lieber Code, which clarified many questions regarding military emancipation. The code acknowledged the legality of slavery in states where it existed but denied the universality of those laws. Military commanders in a conquered territory such as a seceded state no longer had to abide by state laws respecting slavery; moreover, they had no authority to extend a state's laws authorizing slavery to the US Army's policies or actions. While the code arguably applied only to rebelling and not border states, it helped the army define even residents of border states as disloyal and thus compromised their claims to property rights in people and federal compensation. This was because the code defined all enemies in war as combatants and noncombatants, or unarmed citizens of a hostile government or section, and authorized military commanders to distinguish between loyal and disloyal noncombatants. Disloyal citizens could be classified further into two categories: those known to sympathize with the rebellion without positively aiding it and those who gave aid and comfort to the rebellion without taking up arms and without being forced "bodily" to do so. The code encouraged army commanders to "throw the burden of the war, as much as lies within his power," on disloyal citizens of the rebelling section. For army commanders who dealt with enslavers in states that remained in the Union, the code noted that armed or unarmed resistance by US citizens against the lawful movement of troops amounted to treason. Thus, when border state enslavers resisted the enlistment of enslaved men, they committed treason, by at least one definition.[34] The administration's Black enlistment policies forced border state politicians to decide whether they would accept emancipation and federal payments for some freed men or resist the federal government and risk any payment at all.

The determination of a loyal enslaver, however, was more a political than a legal question and one that usually fell to Lincoln's generals and other officers to answer. Military commanders who recruited enslaved men were preoccupied with how to distinguish loyal enslavers from the disloyal. Like most generals with whom Lincoln and Stanton conferred, John M. Schofield, of the Department of the Missouri, reported to the adjutant general's office in Washington, DC, that recruitment officers "are about as likely to decide one man to be disloyal as another."[35] Despite Schofield's concerns, the War Department ordered the recruitment of Black soldiers in Tennessee, Missouri, and Maryland on October 3, 1863, without clarifying the meaning of loyalty for enslavers. The orders granted $300 to loyal enslavers for each enslaved man who enlisted, provided that they proved the man enlisted by choice and that they held the title to him and appealed to their state's slave compensation board, which would be established to hear claims for compensation to loyal enslavers. The War Department exempted Kentucky, noting that the military did not need additional troops in that area.[36]

In effect, throughout 1863, the army transformed the definition of "loyalty" from residence in the Union to allegiance to US emancipation policies through its enforcement of the administration's Black enlistment policy. Once border state enslavers could profit from Black enlistment, their noncompliance with emancipation policies cast their loyalties into doubt. Enslavers protested the policy as freedom seekers absconded to nearby recruitment camps, even though the enslaver could still claim remuneration, whether or not he consented to the enlistment. But enslavers in the border states quickly realized new financial opportunities. Missourians reportedly bought enslaved men from Confederates and Confederate sympathizers to collect the $300 compensation. About a month after the recruitment process began in Missouri, General Schofield issued new orders forbidding compensation for the services of any man enslaved to anyone who had "been in rebellion or given aid or comfort to the enemies of the Government." Schofield clearly did not consider anyone who attempted to profit by selling enslaved people to the United States to be loyal.[37]

When Congress renewed the Enrollment Act on February 24, 1864, which required states to draft men to serve in the war if they could not reach their enlistment quotas with volunteers, it expanded the administration's compensation policy by authorizing the enlistment and drafting of enslaved men in every border state, including Kentucky, in section 24. The new section promised to pay loyal enslavers up to $300 for an enslaved man who enlisted in the US Army, or $100 if the man was drafted. Border state enslavers were divided over the policy—Garrett Davis continued to disparage the low compensation rates—but the act passed handily, indicating political support for reimbursing enslavers allegiant to the United States. At the same time, as US officials carried out the policy and observed ostensible loyal enslavers' resistance to emancipation, they asked whether any enslaver deserved just compensation.[38]

Louisiana Unionists: Compensation as a Reward

Over the course of 1862 and 1863, debates surrounding congressional and military emancipation policies convinced many Americans that the United States could interfere with slavery in rebelling states.[39] However, it was still uncertain whether emancipation without just compensation to enslavers was constitutional after military conflicts ended. Early wartime policies and Lincoln's proposed amendment suggested that a loyal enslaver in a seceded state could still hope for compensation if they supported the US war effort. Unionists in Louisiana, a seceded state that the US Army occupied when it captured New Orleans on April 25, 1862, were the first politicians to test these questions. Lincoln forced Louisiana politicians to end slavery by state constitutional amendment in 1864, but so many resisted the idea that wartime policies could override staid legal doctrine that they petitioned for federal reimbursements for slaves as a reward for their loyalty.

Louisiana Unionists were in a unique position as residents of one of the earliest states to undergo Reconstruction. In late 1863, slavery still existed in the state. Lincoln exempted occupied Louisiana from the Emancipation Proclamation, and some white Louisianians continued to trade in human property. With the hopes of making Louisiana a free state, Lincoln designed the Ten Percent Plan in December 1863. The plan authorized white men in

Louisiana to elect a governor and delegates to a state constitutional convention once 10 percent of eligible voters (based on the 1860 vote count) had taken an oath of allegiance to the United States. Under the oath, men in Union-occupied areas of the Confederacy pledged their loyalty to the Constitution of the United States and their compliance with "all acts of Congress passed" and to "faithfully support all proclamations of the President" during the "rebellion with reference to slaves." In theory, the oath taker acquiesced to the end of slavery and federal confiscation legislation, but they could also claim privileges and protections from the US government—including the reclaiming of freedom seekers.[40]

Louisiana relinquished slavery only when the US military forced it. General Nathaniel P. Banks, the commander of the Army of the Gulf, helped Lincoln carry out the Ten Percent Plan as an intermediary between the president and Louisiana politicians. In December 1863, he demanded that the "numerous signs in the city relating to the sale of slaves" be removed "from the signboards of the city." Ten days later, he issued a proclamation calling for a gubernatorial election and elections for delegates to the convention and pronounced slavery "inconsistent with the present condition of public affairs." Lincoln clarified that Louisiana's new constitution should make Louisiana a free state "in the shortest possible time."[41]

In the months between Banks's proclamation and the elections for governor and convention delegates, a few Unionist political parties emerged in a fractious political field, divided by their stances on emancipation. For the most part, political candidates were loyal by Lincoln's standards and supported immediate emancipation. The moderate Free State Party supported immediate emancipation as outlined in the Ten Percent Plan, although it did not support extending suffrage to freed people. Two other parties, the Conservative Union Party and the Citizens' Free State Party, supported emancipation but not immediately. Conservative Unionists did not deny that "slavery has fallen under the footsteps of war"; nevertheless, the party held that Louisiana Unionists could write gradual emancipation laws for the state. The Citizens' Free State Party expressed similar views.[42]

Although most recognized the end of slavery by the war, many Unionists demanded that Lincoln and the United States recognize their loyalty by compensating loyal enslavers. On February 22, 1864, the Free State Party gubernatorial candidate, Michael Hahn, won the governor's race. In his inaugural address, less than a month before the elections for delegates to the convention, Hahn praised immediate emancipation and reassured listeners that "the

The Restoration of the Union—Inauguration of Hon. Michael Hahn, Governor of Louisiana, on Lafayette Square, New Orleans, March 4, 1864. Frank Leslie's Illustrated Newspaper, April 2, 1864. Historic New Orleans Collection, gift of Harold Schilke and Boyd Cruise, 1953.35.

losses, if any, incurred by this change in our labor system by the truly loyal citizens, will doubtless be properly returned to him in due season by a generous government." He suggested that compensation would be a reward for Louisiana's acquiescence to US emancipation policy.[43]

The irregularities of a wartime constitutional convention favored the Free State Party. Conservatives disputed the convention's purpose and legitimacy. Some objected that Lincoln's loyalty oath would force them to relinquish their property in people. General Banks had favored the Free State Party throughout the gubernatorial elections, casting doubt on the military's role in local politics and the extent of popular support for immediate emancipation. The elections for delegates to the convention were also unusual. The only parishes represented in the convention were those occupied by the US Army. They constituted about one-fourth of the state, and most delegates represented New Orleans. Only Louisianians who took Lincoln's amnesty oath were eligible to run for election and vote, which in one parish amounted to 20 percent of eligible antebellum voters. Furthermore, the turnout on election day was low, as few braved the cold and rainy weather in New Orleans. Unsurprisingly, the Free State Party won all but four seats at the constitutional convention in the March 28 election.[44]

Planters and conservative Louisianians were thus largely unrepresented. Reflecting the demographics of antebellum New Orleans, many delegates were born in the North but had been permanent residents of New Orleans before the war. They were largely middle class—lawyers, doctors, educators, shopkeepers, small businessmen, and civil servants who had served as US Treasury agents, sheriffs, tax collectors, postmasters, municipal employees, or clerks of court before the war or during federal occupation. This convention full of lawyers and government officials was well-equipped to debate whether the federal government could force their state to emancipate the enslaved with or without compensation to former enslavers.[45]

Most of the Louisiana delegates entered the New Orleans convention on April 6, 1864, willing to abolish slavery, but they debated how they should do so. After initial disagreement between the delegates over how to abolish slavery, the convention established the Committee on Emancipation to write the new constitution's abolition measure. Free State loyalists endorsed a measure for immediate emancipation, as Lincoln and Banks had mandated, without compensation, and prohibited the Louisiana legislature from making any law that recognized "the right of property in man." Many believed that immediate emancipation was an inevitable result of the war and that by ending slavery, the state would be adhering not only to the federal government's dictates but also to a "just" cause.[46]

Seeking compromise with the convention's more conservative members and a reward for their loyalty, delegates in favor of immediate emancipation would eventually agree to petition Congress for federal reimbursements to loyal enslavers through a process that began early in the convention, when Delegate Edmund Abell proposed an alternative to immediate emancipation: gradual, compensated emancipation that followed the traditions of gradual emancipation and apprenticeships in the British West Indies.[47] Abell represented the convention's conservative extreme. A Kentucky-born lawyer, he was elected to the convention on the Citizens' Free State ticket and ensured that his opinions were heard by arguing outlandishly and hyperbolically—he compared himself to Christ and suggested an opponent would be metaphorically eaten by cannibals. Abell initiated the monthlong debate over how to abolish slavery by suggesting that enslavers would still retain the title to their enslaved and that formerly enslaved people would have no legal right to their freedom if enslavers were not compensated.[48]

Like prior proponents of compensated emancipation, such as Garrett Davis, Abell used the Fifth Amendment, other sections of the Constitution, Supreme Court cases, and religion to challenge the constitutionality of federally mandated, uncompensated emancipation. His reasoning was consistent with antebellum slave laws and precedents. The founders and subsequent US law had supported slavery, he said, and he cited the Fugitive Slave Clause, the Three-Fifths Clause, and the *Dred Scott* decision. He did not directly cite the takings clause, but his speeches often alluded to it. Abell argued that emancipation without reimbursement to enslavers was unjust "without the consent of the master, or a fair compensation for his property." He insisted that the convention could not "divest the master of his property without doing a flagrant injustice" because enslavers "earned" the enslaved "fairly and honestly under the guarantees of" the US Constitution. Abell often referred to the "justice" of emancipation policy, concluding that even if the Constitution did not require that enslavers be compensated for freed slaves, morality did.[49]

Few Free State convention delegates argued against Abell's legal reasoning per se; instead, they argued like congressional Republicans that the Civil War had fundamentally changed Louisiana's relationship to the United States and enslavers' property rights in people despite the law's long-established tolerance of slavery. New Orleans delegate Alfred Hills reasoned that "the wisest men in the land foresaw" that "slavery was sure to bring on rebellion in this country," and that the *Dred Scott* decision was "swept away by the course of events."[50] For all intents and purposes, other delegates pointed out, slavery had already ended.

Enslavers no longer controlled enslaved people's movements—freed people were "going at large in the streets" and were "now soldiers in the ranks of the Union army"—and the military had destroyed the trade in enslaved people. The legal protections that had secured transactions for humans were unenforceable.[51] Delegates also denounced Abell's religious and moral arguments using the abolitionist defense of enslaved peoples' natural rights. Hills pointed out that enslavement was "essentially unjust in itself" because it was "a system of violence" founded in the "piracy and robbery" of controlling another person's body and labor. Morality actually demanded that delegates consider the enslaved, not the enslaver.[52]

Most delegates discredited Abell by holding up immediate emancipation as the standard of loyalty to the Union. Delegate T. B. Thorpe held that the war may not have destroyed enslavers' rights to claim ownership over people, to say nothing of compensation for their value, but that secession did. Echoing the "state suicide" theory that seceded states had forfeited their statehood, Thorpe accused Abell of being pro-slavery and betraying his amnesty oath. Louisianians, he reasoned, gave up every right they had to protections from the US Constitution when they seceded, and rather than restore those protections to them, the amnesty oath actually "separated" the delegates "forever ... from that question of slavery."[53] Although Louisiana was exempted from the Emancipation Proclamation, it was disloyal to deny that the war emancipated enslaved people there.

Delegates believed Abell's plan unrealistic and immoral, but they did not reject his idea of compensation. Though Free State delegates accused anyone who defended property rights in people of disloyalty, they were willing to entertain plans for immediate, compensated emancipation. After watching the delegates lacerate Abell's plan, Delegate George F. Brott, a merchant from New Orleans, proposed a comprehensive plan for immediate emancipation with reimbursement to former enslavers on May 5. Under his plan, Louisiana's governor would appoint and the legislature would approve commissioners to review former enslavers' claims until January 1, 1865. The commissioners would estimate the value of each enslaved person at $100, $200, or $300, and the state would reimburse enslavers in bonds after final approval of the legislature. Louisianians could only qualify for compensation if they could prove their loyalty to the Union, their past claim over the enslaved person, and the relative value of the enslaved. In a measure designed to give the state time to build up the funds, former enslavers would not be able to cash in their bonds until 1885.[54] Brott's plan placed the cost of emancipation on the Louisiana legislature and identified the State of Louisiana as the government accountable for emancipation. It satisfied some delegates, including Abell, who nevertheless protested that the level of compensation was too low.

The strongest opposition to Brott's plan came from Free State delegates who believed that the federal government, not Louisiana, owed loyal enslavers and that the cost of emancipation should fall on the United States. While protesting compensation earlier in the convention, Anthony Cazabat of Rapides Parish had railed: "I take the ground that the people of Louisiana have not a right to donate a dollar, not a single red cent from the public treasury to pay slaveholders." He supported "immediate, unconditional and permanent abolition of slavery in the State of Louisiana," but if compensation was to be granted "in the name of justice, in the name of equity, let it be made by the United States government, and then only to loyal citizens who shall prove themselves to have been such from the beginning of this unholy rebellion." Cazabat did not believe truly loyal enslavers would take the money in the end. Some feared the state could not afford it, and others protested reimbursing former enslavers at the expense of non-slaveholders, the "laboring men" of Louisiana. Those laboring men were the first to show their allegiance to the Union, a delegate suggested, and enslavers had enjoyed too many political and economic privileges, including disproportional representation in the state legislature and US Congress.[55]

These conversations about whether Louisiana or the United States should pay for compensation reflected larger issues within Southern state politics. The convention had no power to demand compensation from the federal government. They could not appear recalcitrant lest they risk their state's re-entry into the Union. But they also knew that they needed to raise support for emancipation. Promising to pay enslavers could amass that support, but it could also alienate other, non-slaveholding voters. Thus, some proposed federal compensation as a just reward for relinquishing Louisiana's property in people that would tax not only Louisianans but the entire country. They reasoned that federal reimbursement for freed people was a just prize for the discrimination and hardships that loyalists had experienced in war-torn Louisiana. Delegate Joseph H. Wilson of New Orleans asked the convention "to bear in mind that there are men—slaveholders if you will—who would sacrifice everything—aye, even life itself—to see our starry flag float again over the length and breadth of the land, and be borne in triumph over every sea."[56] Those who sacrificed for the Union, as opposed to those who actively fought against it, had earned compensation from a beholden federal government. By accepting immediate emancipation, the delegates could uphold their oaths and prove their loyalty by abolishing slavery immediately, even while securing reimbursement for loyal enslavers.

Other Free State delegates denied that the federal government owed enslavers anything, asking whether any enslaver, de facto, could be loyal to the Union. The truly loyal were "willing and ready to offer up their losses in slave labor, as a cheerful sacrifice, to secure the restoration of peace and harmony in the national and State government," Wilson established.[57] A few others agreed, suggesting that the loyalty oath that delegates pledged to regain their voting rights and other federal policies required them to relinquish slavery and any claim to compensation. These arguments did not sway the convention, but most conceded that the State of Louisiana owed enslavers nothing precisely because emancipation came with a federal mandate. The convention dropped Brott's proposal for state-based reimbursements after no delegate seconded it.[58]

Though the convention rejected all proposed plans for compensation, many delegates still sought assurance that the United States would compensate loyal enslavers for freed people.[59] On May 10, the day before the convention voted on the emancipation measure, delegates proposed a flurry of plans for immediate emancipation with compensation to loyal enslavers. Finally, when one delegate suggested that emancipation not go into effect until the year 1900, the convention floor erupted.[60] Amid the cacophony, Anthony Cazabat proposed a resolution that sought compensation for loyal enslavers. Once it passed, the convention created the Committee on the Compensation of Loyal Owners for Slaves Emancipated. The committee was composed of five members and charged with recommending "appropriate resolutions" to Congress and Lincoln that addressed "the justice and equity of ... appropriations as may be deemed proper and right for a fair compensation to loyal citizens of Louisiana for the loss of their property." The next day, the convention adopted the emancipation measure over the clamorous protests of Abell and other delegates to "enthusiastic cheers."[61]

Once the convention abolished slavery, delegates could pursue federal compensation knowing that they had fulfilled their loyalty oaths. Members of the Committee on the Compensation of Loyal Owners for Slaves Emancipated had spoken in favor of compensating loyal enslavers earlier in the convention, but they were not nearly as outspoken as Abell. Of the five members, delegates Robert W. Taliaferro and M. R. Ariail both claimed enslaved people in 1860, and delegate Thomas M. Wells's father, lieutenant governor James M. Wells, did too. Together, they symbolized Louisiana enslavers' willingness to give up their claims over enslaved people even as they requested indemnities.[62]

The committee then petitioned Congress to compensate loyal enslavers as a just reward for following the federal mandate. The report did not repeat Abell's legal arguments for compensation or contest the federal government's authority to mandate emancipation; instead, it claimed that the convention's willingness to give up slavery had earned Louisiana enslavers federal remuneration for their sacrifices. Compared to enslavers in Washington, DC, the petition maintained, Louisiana enslavers' claims to compensation were stronger because their sacrifice was "voluntary," whereas DC's was a compulsory order from Congress. Of course, the petitioners ignored Lincoln's mandate to play up the state's sacrifice. The delegates avoided framing federal compensation as a right because they knew they could do nothing to guarantee federal compensation to loyal enslavers. With that in mind, the committee did not attempt to "fix the amount of compensation or to suggest the manner in which it ought to be made." Citing British emancipation, the petition also claimed that the federal government should reimburse loyal enslavers because the entire nation had perpetrated enslavement, and the "whole burden" of emancipation "ought not to fall on the loyal people of Louisiana," who were already "impoverished" by war. By reframing compensation as a reward rather than "just compensation" guaranteed by the Constitution, the delegates hoped to demonstrate their loyalties to a sympathetic Congress.[63]

WHETHER THEY ENDED SLAVERY or resisted emancipation altogether, the policies and collective actions of the border states and the Free State Party in Louisiana revealed that many had accepted immediate emancipation but nevertheless expected the federal government to pay for it. By 1865, Kentucky and Delaware had yet to abolish slavery, and Missouri did so that January. Maryland had abolished slavery in 1864, when members of the Unconditional Union Party, riding on their party's 1863 electoral successes, convened a constitutional convention. A number of delegates there sought federal reimbursements for enslaved people and, when they failed, sought to petition Congress for payments to the state as a prerequisite for abolishing slavery in their constitution. The new constitution included a clause forbidding the state legislature from passing a law or appropriating funds to compensate enslavers, presumably overriding any additional allocation of funds from the state to carry out a February 6, 1864 act that promised one hundred dollars to the owner of an enslaved man who enlisted in the US army. However, the constitutional measure did not end claims for compensation in Maryland. There is evidence that at least some Maryland enslavers received the promised compensation from their state. After the new constitution was ratified, like Louisiana politicians, Maryland politicians petitioned the US for payments. Maryland's outgoing governor, Augustus Bradford, declared that the federal government owed the state compensation, and the state legislature sent a committee to Washington, DC, in February 1865 to confer with Lincoln and convince Congress to reimburse Maryland enslavers. The restored government of Virginia acted similarly, ending slavery while creating a committee to confer with Lincoln about securing federal compensation for former enslavers.[64]

Over the course of the war, slave states and their representatives, like Davis and Abell, had clung to slavery, rejecting even compensated emancipation, on the grounds that the Fifth Amendment protected their property rights in people and, conversely, required that the US pay for freed people. Border state politicians, in particular, used the takings clause to prevent emancipation, arguing that the federal government could not end slavery unless it could afford to reimburse enslavers. By 1864, politicians in slave states, such as the members of Louisiana's Free State Party, began to argue that loyal enslavers deserved a reward from a grateful federal government for acquiescing to abolition. This reasoning hybridized Davis's adherence to property rights with Republicans' commitment to war powers, making allegiance to the United States a condition for federal compensation.

As slave states refused to abolish slavery, federal officials answered the questions that had hounded them for decades: whether the Fifth Amendment's takings clause enabled the United States to abolish slavery, with or without compensating former enslavers. Through a series of contradictory wartime policy decisions, Republicans in power decided that emancipation was not an act of transferring the title of an enslaved person to the government or the person themselves but of eliminating slavery by war. Most Americans would not have adopted Frederick Douglass's or other abolitionists' commitment to the natural rights of enslaved people, and policymakers needed to amass enough political support to chip away at slavery. Promising to pay enslavers in the United States or the Confederacy gained support for emancipation, even if many Republicans did not believe it was constitutionally required.

At the same time, the debates about compensating enslavers called into question enslavers' loyalty to the Union. Republicans and the Lincoln administration consistently paid loyal enslavers in the United States to end slavery, but after four years of civil war and Unionists' resistance to emancipation, many came to understand enslavers as perpetrators and resented the idea that any enslaver deserved compensation. The only loyal enslaver was the one who willingly acquiesced to emancipation. For example, in January 1865,

Congress debated a new thirteenth amendment, which would abolish slavery immediately in the United States. During debates, Representative John Creswell, a Republican from Maryland, asked, "If the power of amendment extends to the abolition of slavery, and that it does is too clear to admit of a suspicion of a doubt, with what propriety can any slaveholder ask for compensation?" He criticized any hypothetical enslaver who would be "so craven as to speak of compensation for slaves when their emancipation was made necessary by the rebellion of their masters." Whatever the law said, enslavers had forfeited any right to compensation by their actions.[65] If they were truly loyal to the federal government, they would accept its authority to emancipate enslaved people without reimbursements. For the most part, those abolitionists who had not earlier agreed with Frederick Douglass had also adopted this stance and now widely condemned anyone who proposed reimbursements for their compensation schemes.[66]

Creswell articulated an important shift in policymakers' views of property rights in people. In the midst of war, loyalty to the United States—as defined by acquiescence to military emancipation policies—rather than a vested right to property in people or eminent domain would determine who, if anyone, received payments from the federal government for freed slaves. Yet keeping the possibility of federal compensation open helped federal policymakers and white Southerners alike. US officials could imply or offer outright to pay slave states or individual enslavers for freed people to incentivize cooperation with emancipation policies. Even after the passage of the Thirteenth Amendment in January 1865, reimbursing enslavers could ward off any legal challenges to emancipation. However, as Louisiana Unionists demonstrated, seceded states could—and did—seek federal payments as a reward for ending slavery. Louisiana delegates' efforts established a template for Southern politicians to do so after Confederate armies surrendered.

CHAPTER THREE

Emancipation and Reunification
The Persistence of Arguments for Compensation after Confederate Surrender

On June 24, 1865, a delegation of South Carolina politicians met with President Andrew Johnson to seek his advice on how to restore their state's place in the Union. More than two months earlier, General Robert E. Lee had surrendered his army to US forces. Only six days after that, John Wilkes Booth assassinated President Lincoln and Andrew Johnson took the presidential oath of office. Americans thereafter negotiated emancipation policy on overlapping and shifting political terrain. In his May proclamations, President Johnson began to implement his own Reconstruction policy. He appointed a provisional governor in each state who would organize elections for a constitutional convention that would redraft the state's constitution. To run for office and vote, white men had to swear to "support, protect, and defend" the US Constitution and "abide by and faithfully support all laws and proclamations which have been made during the existing rebellion, with reference to the emancipation of slaves" in a new amnesty oath. At the conventions, delegates would abolish slavery in their state's new constitution. Once their constitutions met federal approval, civil government would be reestablished in the former Confederacy.[1]

The June 24 meeting, which would be publicized in newspapers throughout the country, was one of the first public negotiations over postwar federal emancipation and Reconstruction policy. Johnson implied that former Confederate states had to abolish slavery in some fashion but gave the South Carolina delegation more leeway than the delegates recognized at the time. At the meeting, one delegate asked Johnson to clarify whether abolishing slavery in their state's constitution was "a *sine qua non*" to restoration. Johnson replied, "You must see that the friction of the rebellion has rubbed slavery out, and I assume it would be better for the people through that convention, to make it legally and constitutionally dead. The people, in coming forward, would better recognize that fact" or remain at risk of "military rule."[2]

With that, Johnson closed the door to any possibility for the conventions to write a constitution that did not end slavery. In the summer and fall of 1865, however, delegates to former Confederate states' constitutional conventions realized that they could attempt to shape emancipation policy through their own state's legal and political mechanisms. Few understood what it meant to end slavery in peacetime, and Southerners were confronting a new physical and economic landscape. Large areas of Southern cities were charred or crumbled. The US government's wartime decision to end slavery without compensation to former enslavers left many insolvent after the Civil War. Those who had purchased an enslaved person on credit or mortgaged them still owed their creditors for their value but had little means to pay off the debt. They wrote to their president and governors for aid immediately after the war, seeking financial relief. Throughout 1865, white Southerners sought alternatives to immediate, uncompensated emancipation more financially favorable to them, including different plans that would institute coerced labor systems or compensate enslavers for the value of freed people. That said, some Southern politicians who had not claimed ownership over enslaved people before the Civil War were the most vocal proponents of compensation.[3] Defeated, Southern politicians in former Confederate states defended their right to profit from property rights in people as an entitlement, a matter of fairness, welfare, and a constitutional right.

Neither former Confederate states and local governments nor the federal government had explained how to address the legal and financial questions that emancipation created. Southern politicians received different messages from President Johnson, who demanded that they abolish slavery in their state constitutions, and Congress, where Republicans advocated to abolish slavery in the US Constitution. Congress had passed the Thirteenth Amendment ending slavery in January, but by July, only twenty-three states had ratified the amendment out of the twenty-seven necessary to integrate it into the Constitution. While Republicans in Congress preferred that former Confederate states ratify the Thirteenth Amendment in their state legislatures to make it a permanent part of the Constitution, Johnson insisted that they abolish slavery in their new state constitutions. After the conventions adjourned, former Confederate state legislatures could then ratify the proposed amendment. However, former Confederate states were reluctant to ratify the amendment out of opposition to emancipation and caution. Southern politicians particularly feared that the regulatory power the amendment gave Congress to enforce emancipation in their states would expand federal power more broadly, and many would not entertain ratifying it.[4]

Many historians have concluded that former Confederates, forced to navigate Johnson and Congress, acquiesced to immediate, uncompensated emancipation as mandated by Johnson in order to quickly reenter the United States and regain control of free African Americans' labor and the postwar Southern political economy. Even if they opposed abolishing slavery in their constitutional conventions, historians have maintained, white Southerners exhibited some repentance, yielded to Confederate defeat and emancipation, and waited for conservatives to return to power in Congress.[5] These histories have portrayed attempts to secure more favorable terms, such as compensation for the value of slaves, as inevitably fruitless resistance to federal authority or as otherwise irrelevant endeavors that would obstruct future attempts to control Black labor.

But emancipation was a much more complicated process after the war than historians have described. White Southerners and politicians did not yield to Johnson or Congress easily. The question of whether enslavers would ever be reimbursed for their financial losses remained contested well after the war was over. Even in defeat, white Southerners fought vigorously to retain the financial value of enslaved people by demanding federal compensation for emancipation. As this chapter shows, they resisted the terms the US government had set for emancipation, and many Southern politicians, including the delegates to the state constitutional conventions, searched for ways to use the discrepancy between Johnson's and Congress's position on the Thirteenth Amendment to their advantage.

Delegates in Mississippi, South Carolina, Alabama, and Georgia pursued federal compensation in the name of widows and orphans and by the path and rationale of the Fifth Amendment. However, the conventions set them aside, since politicians were unwilling to jeopardize their state's readmission to the United States. Nevertheless, Southern politicians chose to end slavery in their new state constitutions in hopes of securing compensation for former enslavers once their representatives were readmitted to Congress. Far from abandoning the idea of compensation and accepting defeat on it and other matters, they hastened their representatives' return to Congress so that they could later pursue emancipation policies favorable to the white South. Their strategy yielded results: By the end of the summer, many politicians, from Unionists to conservatives, saw emancipation with federal compensation to former enslavers as a viable alternative to immediate, uncompensated emancipation.

Seeking Alternatives to Immediate, Uncompensated Emancipation

The surrender of Confederate armies throughout the spring and summer marked the end of the Confederacy, but no one was certain how to end the practices of slavery in former Confederate states' laws and financial institutions, or whether wartime measures would apply in peacetime. Taking nothing for granted, white Southerners across the former Confederacy resisted emancipation as the federal military enforced it and as Black Southerners practiced it.[6] In 1864 and 1865, some proposed vague state-level gradual emancipation policies that preserved some of their investments and property rights in humans. Christopher G. Memminger, the primary architect of the Confederate constitution who had served as Confederate secretary of the treasury, suggested apprenticeships to President Johnson in September 1865. Memminger argued that apprenticeships would "enable the emancipation experiment to be made under the most favorable circumstances" and "devise the best possible solution of the problems and afford the largest amount of good to the African race." Enslavers had alleged as early as the 1830s that freed people needed to be taught how to work in a free-market economy, which required cultural education through schooling, religion, and ethics, before they could become free, productive laborers.[7] Former enslavers carried this assumption into the postwar era, often accusing freed people of being lazy and unwilling to work unless coerced violently.[8] Such suggestions for gradual emancipation and apprenticeship programs often lacked specific plans of action, likely because many of these suggestions were serious machinations to re-enslave Black Southerners or at least indications that some white Southerners still clung to the premises of pro-slavery ideology.[9]

Proponents of gradual emancipation or apprenticeship programs believed these plans were realistic because they reflected the ideology behind even Republican emancipation policies. Before the Civil War, governments throughout the Atlantic world had abolished slavery gradually based on this Republican free labor ideology, adopting apprenticeship systems in the guise of supporting newly freed workers who had no property, money, or skills to recommend them for stable employment. Instead of burdening the state with their care, policymakers reasoned, former enslavers could continue to provide for their newly freed workers' upkeep as apprentices, tasked with working for their former enslaver for a period of six to eight years in the case of the British Slavery Abolition Act of 1833. In many states in the US North where slavery ended gradually by free womb laws, enslavers financially supported the freed children born to enslaved women while the children continued to work for them until they reached adulthood.[10]

Apprenticeship plans may have seemed feasible because the Republican Party renewed its commitment to free labor and property rights as the Civil War ended by restoring abandoned land to prior owners. In the last years of the war, formerly enslaved refugees had transformed many plantations—they had built new homes, stores, and lives on the land former enslavers had abandoned or left uncultivated during the war. In March 1865, Lincoln halted the sale of confiscated land in the South, which impeded freed peoples' efforts to purchase land privately, and Congress established the Bureau of Refugees, Freedmen, and Abandoned Lands, otherwise known as the Freedmen's Bureau. The bureau, an agency of the US Department of War, led efforts to evict freed people from plantations and to provide them with such necessities as food, shelter, and clothing as well as legal aid and education. These policies proscribed freed men from becoming independent farmers and encouraged or forced them to become contract laborers instead, reflecting the logic if not the structure of apprenticeship and free labor ideology.[11]

Despite these precedents, others suggested a more direct form of relief than gradual emancipation: federal reimbursements to former enslavers or slave states. Prewar policies and even the wartime actions of the US government gave white Southerners reason to believe they could pursue federal reimbursements for enslaved people. The 1864 Enrollment Act promised to pay border state enslavers up to $300 for formerly enslaved men who enlisted in the US Army. In February 1865, after meeting with Confederate commissioners at Hampton Roads to discuss surrender terms, President Lincoln proposed a congressional resolution to his cabinet that would appropriate $400 million (about $6 billion in 2022) to compensate Confederate states for the value of the 1860 enslaved population if they surrendered. His cabinet unanimously rejected the proposal, as did the Confederacy, which refused to surrender that month.[12]

By the summer of 1865, few appeared to have suggested state-level compensation plans. They may have realized that war-torn former Confederate states had no money to pay enslavers except in defunct Confederate currency, but more likely many landed on federal reimbursements because, as was determined at the Louisiana convention in 1864, they understood the United States to be the arbiter of emancipation and thus the party responsible for their losses.[13] Quite a few white Southerners argued that Johnson's mandate that states abolish slavery in their constitutions *required* that such payments be made. One Louisiana congressional candidate contested the federal government's policy of ending slavery without compensating enslavers. Another invoked the Fifth Amendment's takings clause. In July 1865, Mississippian B. F. Moore Jr. wrote to provisional governor Sharkey, conceding "that slavery is dead, dead, dead." Yet, he insisted, "that is not the question." The rhetorical question was, "Can the U[nited] States take away a loyal citizen's property without compensation, as the Constitution provides 'that no man shall be deprived of life, liberty, or property' without due process of law[?]" Of course not, Moore answered.[14]

Others avoided demanding compensation based on the Fifth Amendment, instead suggesting that their loyalty and willingness to end slavery entitled them to make claims on the federal government. In August 1865, newly elected US senator and former convention delegate R. King Cutler promised Louisianians that Congress "will eventually compensate all loyal persons in every Southern State for their losses in slave property." He explained that emancipation "was a national pride ... and it will be a national pride as well as a pleasant national duty to compensate all loyal persons for their loss in slave property."[15] Louisiana had obeyed Lincoln's demand to immediately abolish slavery, and politicians held out hope that at least loyal enslavers would receive reimbursement.

Along the lines of Cutler, others recommended that state conventions pursue compensation as a reward, not a demand. As Mississippi's constitutional convention convened in August, Kenneth Rayner, a former congressman, national leader of the Whig Party, and planter from North Carolina, advised Governor Sharkey to appeal to the federal government's and Northerners' "sense of justice, of generosity, of magnanimity, of humanity on the part of a victorious conqueror." Once former Confederate states abolished slavery, they could appeal to the federal government "[i]n accord and harmony" and ask for "the slight compensation of say $400,000,000 to the losses of slave property." Or, "if thought best, no special sum need be mentioned." Rayner predicted that Congress could carry out such a plan "in a shorter period than three or four years."[16]

Whether they presented their calls for compensation as a legal entitlement or a dividend for loyalty, claimants' prewar politics often betrayed their belief that former enslavers had a constitutional right to federal reimbursements for freed people. For example, before and after the Civil War, Rayner had consistently defended white men's ability to profit from human property in state and national political circles. In the three decades before the war, he served in the North Carolina General Assembly, leaving for a six-year stint in the US Congress as a member of the Whig Party, which he believed would best preserve property rights in people. After the Whig Party dissolved in the early 1850s, he campaigned for Republican candidate John C. Frémont during the 1856 presidential election to reassure enslavers that Frémont would preserve slavery. He stressed, "The position of the slave-holding States is strong enough. It rests upon the Constitution." When North Carolina considered secession, Rayner supported it, as many white Southerners did, for fear that emancipation would lead to racial equality, race war, and racial amalgamation, and that freed people would, in the words of his biographer, "drag down American civilization." He then supported peace movements late in the war to get the best possible terms, including compensated emancipation, that might prevent these outcomes.[17]

Others in favor of federal reimbursements to enslavers had identified as pro-slavery Whigs before the war but opposed secession or defended the Union amid hostile secessionists. Across the slaveholding South, former Whigs had endorsed conservative approaches to avoid the sectional conflict over slavery. For example, James Govan Taliaferro—a Louisiana judge, enslaver, and delegate to the state's secession convention—told his colleagues that secession would "impair instead of strengthen the security of southern institutions" such as slavery. Former Whigs, even enslavers, had reason to fear this. Many were businessmen, enslavers and non-enslavers alike, who appreciated the role of the US government in the region's economic growth. Secession, they concluded, would be bad for business. Given their political and financial interests in slavery, these former Whigs often stopped short of strong advocacy for the United States during the war, especially after the passage of the Thirteenth Amendment in January 1865.[18] Nevertheless, they believed that they had earned these payments because of their wartime sacrifices and allegiance to the United States. Adhering to the slogan popularized by Northern Democrats, "The Constitution as it is, the Union as it was," these petitioners argued that they had legally owned Black people, that the Constitution protected their property rights, and that the federal government should reimburse them for their former value. These Whiggish Unionists and Democrats could create a coalition in the state conventions, coordinating enough votes for more favorable terms of emancipation.[19]

Keeping "the Union as it was" had important ramifications for emancipation, especially before the Thirteenth Amendment was ratified. Johnson had also required that former Confederate states declare their ordinances of secession null and void from the date they were ratified in 1861, which would reinforce proponents of compensation's reasoning. Throughout the war, US politicians had debated the status of seceded states under the Constitution. According to the state suicide theory and the conquered province theory, military defeat transformed former Confederate states into conquered territories. Under both theories, the administration of former Confederate states would fall to Congress, which regulated territories according to the Constitution. Other theories, often professed by those who opposed the Republican-controlled

Congress, suggested that states forfeited their rights when they attempted to leave the United States, but secession was illegitimate because they could not leave without permission. The Southern theory, on which presidential Reconstruction rested, maintained that former Confederate states had remained in the United States but needed to rebuild legitimate republican governments, as required by the Constitution's guarantee clause. Many former Confederate states would readily agree to Johnson's demand and void their ordinances of secession simply to prevent Congress from controlling Reconstruction. Johnson's policies enabled them to return to the Union relatively quickly, recoup their congressional representation, and have their voting rights restored. Then, a national coalition of former Unionists and Democrats could bid for control of Congress.[20]

These theories of secession also determined white Southerners' standing to claim compensation from the United States. By nullifying their state's ordinance of secession, former Confederate states suggested not only that secession was illegitimate but that it had never happened. Therefore, the states that formed the Confederacy had never technically left the United States and their residents had not relinquished their protections under the US Constitution. If this were true, then white Southerners had legal standing to request compensation as a Fifth Amendment right. But if a former Confederate state had indeed left the Union, then enslavers had forfeited their property rights in people.[21]

Proponents of compensating enslavers hoped to unite former Confederate states around Johnson's plan so that they could pursue federal reimbursements. Rayner predicted that if Southern states acted "in concert . . . first in the conventions to be held in this Fall, and after that, press it from year to year in their legislatures," he felt "confident that in a few years it will pass triumphantly." He asked Governor Sharkey to let Mississippi, as the first state to hold a convention, "inaugurate the movement" in its upcoming constitutional convention. Rayner's letter reached Sharkey after the state convention had adjourned, and his confidence that the states would collectively agree on emancipation policy proved unwarranted.[22]

It was too difficult to unite former slaveholding states because many of them had different timelines for Reconstruction, preventing coordination. The timing of occupation and surrender often determined whether state politicians could pursue compensation. Where the United States closely oversaw states' wartime Reconstruction, such as Louisiana, few stymied the immediate abolition of slavery, but some politicians sought compensation for the value of enslaved people. In 1864, a group of Tennessee Unionists demanded reimbursements for freed slaves from their state while Andrew John-

Emancipation in former Confederate states

State	First Day of Presidential Reconstruction Convention	Date Thirteenth Amendment Ratified
Arkansas	01/04/1864	04/14/1865
Virginia	02/13/1864	02/09/1865
Louisiana*	04/06/1864	02/16/1865
Tennessee	01/09/1865	04/07/1865
Mississippi	08/14/1865	02/07/2013
Alabama	09/12/1865	12/02/1865
South Carolina	09/13/1865	11/13/1865
North Carolina	10/02/1865	12/04/1865
Florida	10/25/1865	12/28/1865
Georgia	10/25/1865	12/06/1865
Texas	02/07/1866	02/17/1870

Note: States in gray abolished slavery in their constitutions following President Lincoln's Ten Percent Plan. States in white followed under President Johnson's May proclamations. The state below the dotted line (Texas) held its convention after the ratification of the Thirteenth Amendment.

*Louisiana ratified the Thirteenth Amendment on 2/15/1865 or 2/16/1865. This and all other ratification dates are from S. Doc. No. 112-9, at 30 (2013), www.govinfo.gov/app/details/GPO-CONAN-2017.

son was governor. Johnson and his supporters opposed compensation because the state could not afford it. At an April 1864 convention of Tennessee Unionists, Governor Johnson announced that he hoped Unionists would eventually receive compensation for their enslaved people from the federal government, even if he did not pursue the policy. Yet when he was president, Johnson did not pursue federal-based compensated emancipation either, whether for Unionists or ex-Confederates. Even so, some Tennesseans continued to seek reimbursements in 1865. That summer, two white Tennesseans wrote to President Johnson opposing emancipation without "just compensation" and seeking Johnson's assistance to pay former enslavers.[23] A US Army officer also reported rumblings from white Unionists in Virginia. But by the time Rayner wrote to Sharkey to pursue compensation, some Upper South states had already abolished slavery in their states' constitutional conventions.[24] Virginia, Tennessee, and Arkansas ratified the Thirteenth Amendment before Confederate armies began to surrender in April 1865.

The timing of a state's restoration also determined whether enslavers could pursue another avenue for compensation: through the courts. While Rayner suggested political maneuvers, others believed they could challenge wartime emancipation policies through state courts or the US Court of Claims. For example, former Confederate postmaster general and acting secretary of state John H. Reagan wrote a public letter to his home state, Texas, from Fort Warren, in Boston Harbor, where he was a prisoner of war in August 1865. He told white Texans that they could not expect the US government to protect slavery. Unless they agreed to Johnson's terms, he warned, they could "neither get back into the government as citizens, nor into courts to assert your claims to slaves or any other species of property. The only wise and safe course ... to pursue is to accept promptly, unreservedly, and in good faith, the terms and policy offered, and to go forward in the work of reorganization and restoration of the union." Reagan counseled acquiescence but in part because only through reentering the Union could white Southerners go to court and challenge immediate, uncompensated wartime emancipation. Reagan did not tell his audience to abandon their claims for property in people. On the contrary, he advised white Texans to abandon enslaved labor and reenter the Union precisely because they could then possibly "assert" their claims over property in people.[25]

Given former Confederates' political status, could they have contested emancipation in court? State and federal courts were in disarray in the former Confederacy that summer. If they could even make it into court, enslavers and their allies could argue that the Emancipation Proclamation was a violation of the Fifth Amendment's takings clause, which required "just compensation" in the event of property confiscation by the federal government. One Kentucky judge did make the case. The Kentucky Court of Appeals decided a series of interrelated cases in December 1865 concerning the 1864 and 1865 Enrollment Acts, which had freed enslaved men who enlisted in the US Army and, later, their families. Chief Justice George Robertson denied the federal government's right to free enslaved men by taking the private property of loyal citizens without compensation. Of course, enslavers in former Confederate states were not loyal citizens and were not included in the Enrollment Acts, and Justice Robertson's state-level ruling had no authority over the federal government. However, that did not stop some people from making similar arguments outside the courts.[26]

Former Confederates and enslavers might also have tried to access the US Court of Claims. Congress established the court in 1855 to recommend whether a claimant was legally entitled to recover money in federal pension cases and expanded it in 1863 to hear the increasing volume of wartime confiscation and captured and abandoned property claims. However, lawmakers contested who was eligible to present claims to the court. Both the court's status and former Confederates' citizenship status remained controversial throughout the war and Reconstruction. Most people living in the former Confederacy would not have been granted access to the Court of Claims because they were assumed to be disloyal to the United States. The court required that claimants be loyal to receive compensation, and many had not been pardoned under Johnson's Reconstruction policies by the summer of 1865. Yet with every former Confederate Johnson pardoned individually and collectively through presidential proclamations, there would be more white Southerners with access to the courts, though under various restrictions, depending on the kind of property they claimed.[27]

Many cases contesting the legality of emancipation eventually made it through the state and federal court systems, but no case challenging emancipation in the summer of 1865 under the program of presidential Reconstruction has resurfaced in the historical record.[28] Many politicians could not or preferred not to invite binding judicial decisions into an already complex political arena. For example, in Texas, supporters of Reconstruction prevented their opponents from following Reagan's advice by stalling the restoration of civil government. In July and August, Texans all over the state wrote to Johnson's gubernatorial appointee, Unionist Andrew Jackson Hamilton, concerned that many white Texans resisted to disrupt occupation, the restoration of civil government, and immediate, uncompensated emancipation.[29] Four well-known Texas Unionists—James Bell, Thomas Duval, Elisha Pease, and Francis White—reported to President Johnson on August 30 that many white Texans refused to declare loyalty to the United States for fear they would forfeit their property rights in people. Their constituents believed "the Emancipation Proclamation was a violation of the Constitutional Rights of the slave states . . . and that slavery would yet be rescued." Even if slavery could not be preserved, "the Government of the United States would at least be forced to make compensation to owners."[30] Others resisted violently. As many historians have shown, white violence played an important role in shaping Reconstruction politics, including emancipation policy. Emancipation was difficult to enforce in remote counties where news of emancipation was slow to arrive and where the federal government had little influence. Some areas of Texas still lacked postal service, and the US military could not reach every remote county in the sprawling state. Furthermore, it was clear that disappointed white Texans planned to take control of the provisional government and implement more financially favorable policies to them, including emancipation with federal payments to enslavers.[31]

In light of these reports and possibilities, Hamilton enacted a political—and forceful—solution to preempt any legal claims or political movements for compensation and diminish white violence. On September 11, 1865, he issued a proclamation to the people of Texas announcing that the state's constitutional convention would be postponed indefinitely. By postponing the convention, Hamilton presented white men with a choice between their political rights or continued violence and resistance to emancipation. He assured white Texans that emancipation did not have to financially ruin the country, or even individuals—as long as they accepted that "slavery has ceased to exist in this republic. It will never, under any shape or form, be restored." He warned that if white Texans continued to exhibit "an unwillingness to recognize the truth that slavery no longer exists," the federal government might stall Texas's reinstatement into the Union, delaying white men's re-enfranchisement and the state's representation in Congress.[32]

Hamilton's tactic eventually worked to ensure that the state abolished slavery in its new constitution, but these conflicts over emancipation policy had alarming consequences for Black Texans all the same. By the time Hamilton called for Texas's convention in the spring of 1866, the Thirteenth Amendment was ratified and it was all the more difficult for white Texans to lobby for compensated emancipation. White violence continued after Hamilton's September proclamation, as white Texans were still "sore" at the "loss of property," according to multiple reports, and continued to take out their anger on Black Texans who attempted to realize freedom on their terms. On October 14, 1865, for example, Philip Holbert, an eighty-five-year-old free man from Brenham, solicited Hamilton for help "to get his rites" and reunite his family. Holbert's two daughters, Flora and Adaline, were contracted by their former enslaver, Mr. Olfred, and a man who hired Flora out, Mr. Carr. Both Olfred and Carr had beaten Flora and Adaline, and after Holbert reported those acts to the provost marshal, Carr threatened him. The provost marshal forbade Olfred and Carr from whipping them, but refused to help Holbert extricate them from their contract. Holbert wanted Hamilton to release his daughters from their contracts on the basis that their employer and former enslaver mistreated them, and that he had more claim over them as their father than their labor contracts.[33]

Holbert's efforts revealed that it took both federal military might and Hamilton's support to enforce state-sponsored emancipation. By the time the Thirteenth Amendment was ratified in December, reports of enslavers denying emancipation had diminished, presumably thanks to the combined weight of the US Army, resistance from Black Texans such as Holbert and his daughters, and Hamilton's administration. White Texans had to surrender their property rights to people if they hoped to regain their political rights. Yet during the summer of 1865, few politicians in the former Confederate South were willing to throw their political weight behind immediate, uncompensated emancipation as Hamilton had.

Seeking Compensation for Widows and Orphans

Hamilton's exceptional use of power prevented white Texans from organizing for compensation in court or otherwise, but other former Confederate states did pursue compensation in the earliest presidential Reconstruction conventions. Taking advantage of President Johnson's ambiguity, states in the Lower South used the conventions as opportunities to strategize the best route to a more favorable emancipation plan for the white South. Though the movement was somewhat similar to what Kenneth Rayner had suggested to Governor Sharkey, it was not as organized as Rayner had hoped. No one was certain about how the federal government could or should resolve questions about the lost value of enslaved people, and politicians were even less certain of what states could do. In August, Mississippi held the first convention after Johnson's May proclamation, followed by South Carolina and Alabama in the last weeks of September. Georgia and Florida held their conventions at the end of October. Delegates in the earlier conventions, particularly Mississippi, tended to contest immediate military emancipation more often than the later conventions by offering a variety of emancipation plans. The earliest conventions produced detailed journals, made available to the public in newspapers and print. Delegates were acutely aware of their historic role and the eyes of Northern audiences. They wanted to inspire other former Confederate states to pursue alternative emancipation policies but could not be too intractable lest they appear resistant to federal authority.[34]

Many of the convention delegates believed that alternative forms of emancipation were perfectly consistent with federal demands. Many Democrats and former Confederates, such as Texan John H. Reagan, were still barred from formal politics in the summer of 1865, which skewed representation toward Unionists amenable to appeals for federal compensation for freed people. Similar to Rayner and the 1864 Louisiana delegates, the majority of delegates in every convention had been either members of the Whig Party, the Constitutional Union Party, or were politicians sympathetic to those parties' views.[35] These were Southerners who probably had not supported secession, but they probably had not supported wartime emancipation either.

In Mississippi, which kept a detailed record of convention debates, conversations about compensated emancipation began almost immediately after delegates invalidated the state's ordinance of secession. Most former Confederate states quickly voted to do so to avoid further retribution from Congress and claim constitutional protections—a necessary prerequisite to federal compensation for all former enslavers, regardless of their individual loyalties.[36] The most organized group of compensation proponents emerged in Mississippi under the leadership of George Potter, a delegate from Hinds County. Potter bombastically led the convention's minority party, the eponymous "Potterites." They maintained that Mississippi had never left the Union and that Mississippians retained rights under the US Constitution, including property rights in people. Potter, a Whig and an attorney, promised in his campaign to become a convention delegate that he would vote against any proposition for the unconditional abolition of slavery. In stark contrast, most of the convention's ninety-nine delegates represented the informally named "conservative party," which maintained that Mississippi should abolish slavery unconditionally to regain admission to Congress and portrayed compensation as an obstacle to reunion.[37]

Perhaps because they faced substantial opposition, the Potterites rationalized monetary reimbursements to former enslavers using familiar arguments about the Fifth Amendment. They argued that if the federal government abolished slavery by military act, then it should pay "just compensation" for freed people. They also hoped to cast enough doubt on the legality of uncompensated emancipation that courts could intervene on behalf of former enslavers. Potter argued that the US Supreme Court would uphold former enslavers' claims for compensation if the question ever made it that far. Without "just compensation," Congress had left in question the "constitutional validity" of wartime emancipation. In light of this oversight, Potter offered an alternative plan for emancipation that reserved for Mississippians "full power to assert . . . any of their rights and claims" for compensation. He sought to buy time for state courts and the US Supreme Court to annul the acts and proclamations that abolished slavery and force the federal government to compensate enslavers before abolishing slavery in the state's constitution.[38]

At the same time, Potterites had to appear somewhat obedient to federal authority, so they mobilized other tactics. First, they used historical precedents to undermine the legality of uncompensated emancipation, citing earlier episodes of emancipation in the Atlantic world. After the "late war" with Great Britain, Potter recalled, "the British armies took Southern slaves from plantations, and after the war the authorities of the United States demanded compensation from the British Government, and that compensation was made to the owners of those slaves. They were slaves taken, in times of war, by the public enemy." Here Potter was most likely thinking of the War of 1812 and the Treaty of Ghent, in which the British agreed to return or pay for enslaved people captured in the United States. After forty-five years of negotiation by Northerners such as John Quincy Adams and mediation from the czar of Russia, the United States secured indemnities amounting to $1,204,960 for a substantial number of enslavers. Additionally, Potter cited early federal policies during the Civil War, including the DC Emancipation Act and the Preliminary Emancipation Proclamation. Potter referenced these historical precedents to remind fellow delegates that "the Federal Government has acknowledged itself, over and over again, bound in duty to make compensation to proper parties on account of their slaves emancipated by its authority."[39]

Of course, these were questionable comparisons. Enslavers in the contexts that Potter cited could negotiate the terms of emancipation as victors or citizens, not conquered parties or rebels. The United States had won the War of 1812. Enslavers in Washington, DC, had not seceded, and they had to provide proof of loyalty to receive reimbursement. Yet proponents of compensation apparently overlooked or did not notice these differences. In Mississippi, Whig delegate and judge Robert S. Hudson supported Potter's reasoning and questioned emancipation by military victory. He conjectured, "The military can rightfully do nothing not authorized by the civil authority, the President, Congress and the Supreme Court, . . . and the civil authority can rightfully do nothing, not authorized by the Constitution, and Constitutional enactments." If the convention did not meet the president's or Congress's demands for immediate abolition, he asked, would "they hold us in duress, and extort from us, by force and bayonets, an organic law, not required by the people of the State, or the Constitution of the United States?" Hudson believed that the federal government could not force Southerners to relinquish their constitutional right to profit from humans by military force or amendment. A leader of the conservatives, William Yerger, retorted that Mississippi had no "power to grasp" those "constitutional guarantees" for compensation.[40] Whatever the status of their state or the legality of military emancipation, white Southerners could not yet participate directly in government until they ratified their new state constitution and rejoined the Union.

Potterites and proponents of compensation in other states countered these arguments by qualifying and delimiting eligibility for federal remuneration.

Similar to the Louisiana delegates, who sought to unite white Southerners around compensating enslavers despite class differences by asking for federal reimbursements, Potterites argued that if no one else received it, the widows and orphans of former enslavers should. Potter's alterative emancipation plan referred to children and innocents, and delegates referenced reimbursing widows and orphans whose enslaving fathers and husbands had died during the war. In Georgia, Delegate V. M. Barnes proposed a similar measure to compensate widows and orphans and ease the financial burden of providing for these dependents of the state.[41]

Potterites in Mississippi and Barnes in Georgia argued that widows and children deserved federal funds for the value of the enslaved because they were "innocent" bystanders—but innocent of what, exactly? Few argued that widows were innocent of perpetuating slavery. In their letters to politicians, widows seeking aid more often than not emphasized their business acumen, insisting that they had run their households and invested in enslaved people reasonably. They would not be impoverished, they insisted, if not for emancipation.[42] Instead, politicians suggested that needy white women and children were not responsible for the Confederacy's war against the United States in order to dodge Yerger's objection that no citizen of a former Confederate state could secure financial protections from the government they had rebelled against.

When they proclaimed widows' innocence, delegates in Mississippi and Georgia hoped to mobilize state and federal support for dependent women and children with antebellum legal and cultural standards. Before the Civil War, dependents were sheltered under private household relations—husbands and wives, fathers and children, masters and slaves. Patriarchs—those husbands and fathers—traditionally supported members of their household financially and represented their household in public through political participation, from which dependents were precluded. A slaveholding patriarch was expected to be, according to historian Ariela Gross, the "'prudent father of a family'; he was a statesmanlike disciplinarian and a smart manager of a plantation—which meant being a shrewd businessman." Stripped of their citizenship rights, delegates after the war evoked dependency even after the war and emancipation destroyed these household economic structures. They adapted old norms with new expectations that the public should take on the responsibility of protecting dependents' previously private needs, as historian Greg Downs argues. They insisted that widows and orphans were nonpartisan, nonpolitical beings, loyal to their patriarchs and not to their governments, and therefore deserved government assistance in the form of reimbursements for emancipated slaves.[43]

Eager to claim federal money, widows and politicians alike contended that emancipation and the war had been beyond their control. Georgia's proposed measure read, "The innocent" women and children of the South "should not suffer for the acts of the guilty" because they were "incapable of engaging in arms" and therefore never aided and abetted the Confederacy. Delegates in Louisiana's 1864 convention and Potterites in Mississippi made similar statements. In other contexts and times, this strategy had worked. British politicians justified abolition with reimbursements to former enslavers in the British Slavery Abolition Act by alluding to enslaving widows' and orphans' needs, and Henry Clay defended enslavers' Fifth Amendment rights to compensation in the antebellum era by the same logic.[44]

In the context of civil war, however, opponents of compensation decried this argument. Wartime realities had discredited the cultural and legal fiction that women were innocent in war. Soldiers and citizens, men and women, had participated in the war, and elite Southern women managed the households of their husbands and fathers as men mobilized. Accordingly, US lawyers and military leaders had redefined all noncombatants living in the Confederacy as disloyal over the course of the war; only men and women who actively helped the Union could be loyal under law. Neither the ideal of women's innocence nor Unionist political sentiments secured for anyone who lived in the Confederacy their claim to the protections of the US government and Constitution. Even if widows did not themselves fight, the Confederacy had defended their interests to profit from slavery.[45]

Shifting sentiments and notions of loyalty might have undermined widows' stature and claims, but the appeal to compensate widows and orphans for the value of those enslaved by their patriarch had some basis in different aspects of nineteenth-century law, including the principle of eminent domain, personal injury law, and married women's property laws. Courts had traditionally considered the economic consequences of property confiscation to determine whether someone should receive compensation under the takings clause.[46] By claiming compensation on behalf of widows and innocents, Potter and Barnes tried to extend into the postbellum era the same legal protections that families who enslaved people had enjoyed before the war.

Furthermore, by the mid-nineteenth century, the American legal system had begun to recognize widows as a protected class. In response to changing economic developments, states created new legal mechanisms in the law of accidental injury to provide for widows and orphans in the event that their husband or father suffered an accidental injury or death. Because white male heads of households were expected to maintain women and children within their homes, states—especially in the North—enacted wrongful death statutes that made widows, dependent children, and next of kin exclusive beneficiaries of payments in death actions. Notably, many of these laws excluded husbands from receiving benefits from the death of their wives, reflecting lawmakers' belief that men should not depend on women's or children's earnings but that women and children surely depended on theirs. Courts overwhelmingly supported these laws, perpetuating the idea that upstanding families required income from a provider who was a man. Lawmakers and judges believed that without one, widows and orphans needed social support and, conversely, that the only widows and orphans who deserved social support were those whose husbands and fathers had once provided for them.[47] The discussion in Mississippi reflected this assumption.

States had also begun to shield women and children from their husbands' or father's indebtedness with new property laws before the war. After a serious financial panic, Mississippi passed the first US married women's property law in 1839, followed by a number of states in the next decades. Yet as historian Laura Edwards has argued, married women's property acts "were not designed with women's individual interests in mind." These antebellum legal practices were designed to keep the wealth from human property in the family. Before the war, savvy slaveholding families took advantage of married women's property laws to amass vast wealth in human property and expand enslavement into Western territories. As states intended, white Southerners used married women's property acts as shields to protect a family's property, especially property in people, from seizure. For example, wives might hold the title to an enslaved person on the family plantation to prevent creditors from seizing enslaved people to pay off their husband's debts.[48] Around the same time, many states began to pass homestead exemption laws, which aimed to protect small landowners' families from destitution by exempting their homes from seizure by creditors. Some of these laws gave women, children, and other dependents new rights to protect their interests in their family's landed property.[49] By adapting legal practices that enabled families to maintain their wealth in hard economic times and the idea that worthy widows and orphans deserved financial assistance, Potter and Barnes claimed direct reimbursements on behalf of widows and orphans as a mechanism to retain Southern families' wealth after a devastating civil war.

Southern politicians' appeals on behalf of widows and orphans also connected their compensation claims to wartime relief efforts. The war had disrupted the Southern economy and household hierarchy by sending patriarchs to war, inviting government intervention in widows' economic lives. Confederate states sponsored relief programs, which politicians supported as part of their masculine duty to protect those who had sacrificed for the cause, but the level of assistance families received varied over place and time. Local governments were the first to aid Confederate widows and families, but they could only help a few sporadically. So Confederates increasingly came to believe that the national government should aid the needy not only because of the war but also because so many of the poor were the suffering wives and widows of soldiers.[50]

The United States' wartime policies also gave Southern politicians reason to believe that the federal government would aid war widows. Since the 1830s, Congress had expanded relief to veterans and widows, and in 1862, Congress began what would become a century-long process of expanding pensions to Civil War soldiers' and veterans' widows and orphans. In 1864, Congress ensured that Black soldiers' widows also received pensions, opening a new avenue of relief to some Southerners.[51] The logic of these policies suggested that there was already legal and constitutional precedent, as well as an economic rationale, for compensating at least some former enslavers and expanding federal aid.

After the Civil War, such public assistance for freed people infuriated some convention delegates, who understood Black freedom to be an expense for which they were owed. During debates about emancipation and state-sponsored Black education, a couple of Louisiana and Mississippi politicians betrayed their assumptions that "innocent" widows and orphans were white. In these debates, proponents of compensation chastised their opponents for sympathizing with freed people rather than white widows. Edmund Abell, an outspoken opponent of immediate, uncompensated emancipation in Louisiana's 1864 Unionist convention, told his colleagues to "pause before you tear from the widow, the orphan, and the loyal men their slave property, and then take their money to pay for its education." Like Abell, who used "it" as a pronoun to describe freed people, Mississippi delegate Thomas G. Crawford argued that emancipation freed enslaved people at the expense of white women and children. Crawford villainized freed people and emphasized that it was the delegates' duty to protect white women and children from the consequences of war and the expansion of civil rights for Black Americans. These delegates revealed their zero-sum thinking about Black freedom: Any state money that went to support Black freedom or education was subtracted and taken from white innocents.[52]

By invoking the innocence of white widows and orphans, Potterites and other supporters of compensating enslavers compelled other delegates to address the policy. Southern politicians made claims on behalf of widows and orphans as a "tool for state expansion," according to Greg Downs. Throughout Reconstruction, state politicians "treated dependence as a strategy, a tool to mediate politics for their own benefit," and naturalized the presumed powerlessness and domesticity of women. Even as Potterites idolized worthy white women, they victimized them. Petitioners used the language of family and kinlessness to get politicians' attention, and politicians legitimized their own authority by showing constituents that they fulfilled their masculine obligations by petitioning for "weak and dependent" women and, in so doing, assumed "the mantle of the needy" for their own ends.[53]

This politics of dependency, rooted in gendered labor expectations, rationalized financial assistance from precarious Reconstruction state governments, justified the federal state's expansion, and informed American family life and welfare design into the Progressive Era.[54] Potterites and Crawford hoped to use state power to preserve white family wealth in the face of economic uncertainty and the deaths of many men and patriarchs in the war. As accidental injury law aided widows whose husbands had been financially capable of caring for them, lawmakers intended the strongest welfare programs in the country to replace the family wage for the deserving. Convention delegates practiced this politics of dependency in response to the end of slavery, hoping to stabilize the Southern economy in ways that would adapt the gendered logics of the slaveholding household to changing ideas about the roles of state and federal governments.

Rooted in American law and white supremacist assumptions, delegates' appeals for widows and orphans worked—to an extent. One of Mississippi's most vocal opponents of compensation, Amos R. Johnston, rejected any possibility of compensation based on a legal right to property in people except for the potential that Congress may "pay the orphans and helpless and innocent widows who have been reduced to beggary by this war." He named the very assumption that predicated these arguments: that women and children had no agency. Their lack of "agency," he admitted, left their "rights . . . unimpaired." Delegates' sympathy for widows and orphans did lead some to consider appealing to Congress for federal remunerations for freed people. In that way, the widows and orphans argument functioned exactly as proponents of compensation had wanted: It invited a conversation about federal compensation writ large.[55]

Potterites succeeded in making compensated emancipation a focus of the convention, but delegates still had to balance their goals with the political realities of Reconstruction. Most delegates were eager to rejoin the Union in the most favorable position possible and were therefore uninterested in risking their state's representation in Congress for the possibility of reimbursements. As one Alabama delegate put it, "Does any delegate think that we can get into the House of Representatives without admitting the destruction of slavery?" Though this delegate meant the question rhetorically, delegates throughout the former Confederate South remained uncertain. Many agreed with a Mississippi delegate that the people of the United States "who expended vast sums and hundreds of thousands of lives during the last four years" of war would never consent to compensating their "implacable enemies." Facing the uncertainty of whether their state would be represented in Congress if they did not abolish slavery immediately and without compensating enslavers, two-thirds of the Mississippi delegates voted to suspend discussion of Potter's substitute to the emancipation measure.[56] Brott's measure in Georgia was also defeated, though Georgia delegates would find another solution.

To Secure Compensation in Congress

These votes did not end calls for compensation. Unsure about the compromises required of former Confederate states, delegates tried to reconcile their desires to claim compensation and rejoin the Union by acceding to President Johnson's demand for immediate emancipation. On August 19, Mississippi's delegate Hudson introduced another revised emancipation amendment that would finalize emancipation in the Mississippi legislature only after Congress readmitted the state—and it also stipulated that nothing in the new constitution "shall be construed to prejudice any right to compensation from the United States for the loss of any slave." Delegates in South Carolina pursued similar tactics. They tried to delay by leaving abolition to the state legislature, which would only reconvene after they ratified their new constitution. Taking advantage of this postponement, Southern congressmen or state legislatures could demand federal compensation for enslaved people freed by the war after the state was restored to the Union. However, the Mississippi and South Carolina conventions defeated these measures because they feared that their states' representatives would not be seated in Congress if they passed them. The unqualified abolition of slavery in their state constitutions was the only road most politicians saw to end "military rule" and recover white Southern political power.[57]

It was not that opponents of compensation understood the US Constitution any differently than the Potterites did. They shared the same view about the legality of emancipation that many Americans at the time applied to the legality of secession. Legal historian Cynthia Nicoletti has shown that no law or policy challenged the legality of secession after the Civil War. Instead, American jurists and intellectuals turned to the metaphor "trial by battle" to resolve the discord between the "rationalism of the law" and the deaths of 620,000 men. They explained how "a violent conflict could decide a fundamental question of constitutional interpretation." Former Confederates grasped this metaphor to console themselves with the knowledge that secession had not been defeated under law; parallel to this, opponents of compensation admitted that Confederate defeat had effectively abolished slavery even if no law repudiated enslavers' property rights in people.[58] They recognized the federal government's power to abolish slavery during wartime without reimbursing enslavers, if not the constitutionality.

When they agreed to abolish slavery outright, opponents of the Potterites and others did not abandon their desire to secure federal reimbursements; they just figured they could secure them later. Many delegates across the former Confederate South agreed that no "practical good" would result from submitting any plan for emancipation other than immediate, uncompensated abolition.[59] They had to accept Johnson's terms now, and could defer the matter of compensation to a time after their states had rejoined Congress.

Key to this strategy was delegates' consensus that enslavers had an inalienable right to compensation. In Mississippi, where convention debates were most extensively recorded, even delegates who opposed seeking federal compensation during the convention insisted that abolishing slavery in their states had no effect on former enslavers' constitutional right to reimbursement for enslaved people. "If we have any right to compensation at all," Yerger said, "that fact now exists as a fixed, distinct, positive right at this time," and Mississippi's amendment to abolish slavery "in no way, shape or form, affects it." A number of delegates held that "no action of this Convention, could either abolish such a right" to compensation. If that were true, then a compensation measure in Mississippi's—or any state's—constitution was unnecessary. Though one historian wrote that members of the conservative party opposed efforts to seek compensation, these comments suggest if not similar views on the Constitution, at least an effort to appease Potterites.[60] If enslavers were entitled to remuneration, then it did not matter when white Southerners claimed their constitutional right.

The debate nevertheless convinced the majority of Mississippi delegates that they would be unwise to enshrine in the new state constitution a measure advocating former enslavers' rights to compensation. As Thomas R. Gowan, a Mississippi delegate and member of the Constitutional Union Party, laid out, addressing compensation to former enslavers in the state's constitution would "undoubtedly have a tendency to impede the progress of our speedy restoration to our Constitutional relations to the Federal Government." Gowan argued that delegates should acknowledge that the war destroyed slavery to regain control of the state and enter Congress as soon as possible. He worried that any impediment would give Radical Republicans time to implement Black male suffrage, and the only way "to avert this great calamity" would be to adopt the emancipation amendment in the state's constitution and restore civil government. Conservative leader Johnston agreed, and pleaded, "Let us do nothing that will clog our admission to the National Congress." He argued that if delegates refused to abolish enslavement in Mississippi's constitution, they would delay the state's admission to Congress and, in so doing, defeat any possibility of future compensation.[61]

Fearing the alternative, Mississippi delegates passed their emancipation amendment by an overwhelming majority, without any measure designed to delay immediate, uncompensated emancipation. Potterites balked at the convention's confidence that Congress would admit Mississippi's representatives even if the state abolished slavery. Potter warned that Radical Republicans would never admit representatives who opposed their policies. Nevertheless, the convention ended slavery in Mississippi without any means to secure former enslavers remuneration because many delegates thought that regaining representation in Congress was the best way to pursue federal compensation later.[62]

Georgia delegates, who met two months after Mississippi's convention in October 1865, found a more elegant solution to the risk that President Johnson would reject their state constitution and that Congress would reject their representatives. The Georgia convention abolished slavery in its constitution and included a section that stipulated that emancipation was "not intended to operate as a relinquishment, waiver, or estoppel of such claim for compensation of loss sustained by reason of the emancipation of his slaves, as any citizen of Georgia may hereafter make upon the justice and magnanimity of that Government."[63] Georgia maintained the possibility of federal compensation while abolishing slavery in the state without directly opposing Johnson's orders. The section passed without recorded opposition.

DESPITE THE PERSISTENCE OF a few delegates in Mississippi, Alabama, Georgia, and South Carolina, no state passed a measure endorsing federal compensation in their constitutions. By the end of 1865, no organized political efforts for compensation had succeeded because southern politicians could not organize around different timelines for Reconstruction or risk their readmission to Congress. Nevertheless, many had convinced their colleagues to accept presidential Reconstruction by promising to continue the campaign to recover former enslavers' financial losses later. As Delegate Gowan had argued in Mississippi, Johnson's plan provided their best chance to diminish Radical Republican power in Congress and gain the support of conservatives in the North to enact future policies—including compensation—that would benefit white Southerners.[64] Far from relinquishing that goal to rejoin the Union, they saw congressional representation as a plausible path to pursue it.

However, Congress would prove Potter correct. Even though President Johnson announced his intention to pressure restored state legislatures to ratify the Thirteenth Amendment on December 4, Republicans in Congress rejected Southern representatives that day.[65] In so doing, Republicans announced their intention to wrest control of Reconstruction from the president. On December 6, two more former Confederate states ratified the amendment and abolished slavery across the country—but the amendment did not invalidate claims for compensation.

Unfailing, white Southerners' claims now justified Republican Reconstruction policy. In January 1866, Texas governor Hamilton continued to receive reports that white Texans demanded "indemnity for the loss of" human "property." In March of that year, General A. L. Chetlain, a US Army general from Illinois who had been stationed in Texas and Alabama at the end of the war, told Congress that white Alabamians and Texans "talk very freely in regard to an effort being made by their members, when once in Congress, to get pay for all" the enslaved people "they have lost." In August, North Carolina governor Holden warned Johnson that white North Carolinians "intend to try" emancipation "in the Courts, at least for compensation for enslaved people, on the ground that they agreed to the amendment abolishing it, under duress."[66] Congress would now move to prevent it.

This *Harper's Weekly* illustration is captioned, "No Accommodations! Southern Congressman Elect to Clerk of the House: 'I should like very much to secure my Old Seat. Governor Perry says I'm entitled to it.' Clerk of the House: 'I am very sorry, Sir, but we can not accommodate you. All the Old Seats were broken up, and are now being thoroughly Reconstructed.'" *Harper's Weekly*, December 9, 1865. Library of Congress.

CHAPTER FOUR

Writing Compensation Out of the Constitution
The Making of Section 4 of the Fourteenth Amendment

The validity of the public debt of the United States, authorized by law, including debts incurred for payment of pensions and bounties for services in suppressing insurrection or rebellion, shall not be questioned. But neither the United States nor any State shall assume or pay any debt or obligation incurred in aid of insurrection or rebellion against the United States, or any claim for the loss or emancipation of any slave; but all such debts, obligations and claims shall be held illegal and void.

—US Constitution, Amendment XIV, Section 4

Americans realized that they needed to change the Constitution—again—as they watched white Southerners resist immediate, uncompensated emancipation in the summer and fall of 1865. When Congress reconvened in December 1865, many agreed that the process of Reconstruction that President Andrew Johnson had set in motion needed to change, but few agreed on how. After Congress rejected Southern congressmen, Pennsylvania congressman Thaddeus Stevens, leader of the Radical wing of the Republican Party, and other Republicans urged Congress to form the Joint Committee on Reconstruction to investigate conditions in the former Confederate South. Established on December 13, the committee was composed of twelve Republican and three Democratic representatives and senators.

While the joint committee collected and reviewed witness testimony from across the former Confederacy, politicians offered different ideas to address Reconstruction. In January 1866, writes historian Eric Foner, "no fewer than seventy constitutional amendments had been introduced" in Congress to grapple with the results of emancipation. Most deliberations over the amendment occurred off the public record, and scattered evidence augmented the scant records of the joint committee's work. At least four different proposals from the House and Senate influenced the resulting amendment, modified and tweaked by Republican caucuses behind closed doors. One idea that consistently emerged was an amendment to prevent any state and the United States from paying any claim for the loss of any slave.[1]

By the spring, the joint committee presented what would become the Fourteenth Amendment—five sections designed to usher former Confederate states back into the Union, protect the rights of freed people, and ensure that disloyal Confederates could not return to political power. Alongside these significant civil rights protections, section 4 combined two major economic issues: It protected the sanctity of the US public debt, accrued to fight the Civil War, and prevented states and the United States from paying any enslaver's claim for compensation for freed slaves. Though seemingly unrelated, these two provisions reflected what congressional Republicans and many Americans increasingly understood to be essential constitutional changes to prevent white Southerners' reascendancy to economic and political power as military conflicts ended.

With section 4, congressional Republicans insisted that former Confederates shoulder the cost of emancipation and war as penance for their bloody rebellion. As Pennsylvania Republican John Broomall reminded the House during congressional debates over the amendment on May 9, Confederates had refused every offer from the United States to compensate enslavers and then perpetuated a bloody four-year war to defend slavery. He insisted that Confederates, who "murdered two hundred and ninety thousand of our fellow-citizens," deserved far worse, in fact. "Let our political opponents call the dead to life," he continued, "let them restore to their homes three hundred thousand murdered American citizens, and then let them pay the debt which we contracted in putting down their rebellion, and we will renew our offer. We will then pay for their slaves."[2]

Broomall's speech brimmed with resentment for former Confederates, but his rationales were based on the familiar state suicide or conquered province theory of secession. The Republican Party united around the idea that the country remained at war. Seceded states had forfeited their status when they seceded and became conquered territories under the administration of Congress. Congress could not "punish" enslavers, he announced, because they "have now no rights" that Congress was bound to protect. To those who argued that secession was illegal and Confederate states had never left the Union, Broomall maintained, "They are the conquered, we the conquerors; and the conquered, as everybody knows, must look to the conquerors for their future political and civil position." Even if former enslavers' claims for compensation were valid, Congress now had no obligation to respect them and all the authority to intervene.[3]

Historians have seldom discussed section 4 in their otherwise expansive studies of the Fourteenth Amendment, but its inclusion in one of the most important constitutional amendments underscores how clear it was that enslaved people were considered property under the law and that former enslavers had a case for compensation. Some contemporary critics of section 4 and later historians questioned the need for a clause prohibiting compensation to former enslavers, suggesting that amending the Constitution—the United States' highest form of law—was not an appropriate strategy to resolve such a time-bound political issue.[4] Yet as Broomall argued, section 4 represented the culmination of wartime debates about secession, loyalty, and compensated emancipation. While many Americans, even abolitionists and Republicans, viewed compensated emancipation as a moderate compromise when the war began, they viewed it as an unacceptable conservative measure by 1866. With section 4, Congress rejected the long-held belief that loyal or disloyal enslavers had a right to profit from property in people, finishing what Confederate surrender and the Thirteenth Amendment had started.[5]

Section 4 also helped Republicans remain in political power and forced the slaveholding South to shoulder the financial costs of emancipation. Republicans wanted to maintain a majority in Congress and wrest control of Reconstruction from President Johnson and his political allies. They also included section 4 out of real concern for the economic welfare of the nation. They worried that payments for freed people would tax the national economy and exacerbate the unprecedented national debt accrued over the war. Republicans cast anyone who would defend enslavers' right to compensation or oppose the amendment as disloyal opponents of the war and Reconstruction.

At the same time, congressional Republicans needed to maneuver around moderate and conservative Unionists in the border states, Southern Unionists, and Northern Democrats, whom President Johnson tried to unite around his own Reconstruction policy. So they avoided the contentious legal debate over whether enslavers' rights to profit from people *had been* protected under the Constitution's takings clause.[6] Instead, Broomall and others framed the question as political, as one of loyalty. Former Confederates, they suggested, must accept the immediate, uncompensated abolition of slavery to rejoin the Union and regain their rights of US citizenship. Any border state politician or enslaver who sought compensation risked being branded disloyal. Casting all enslavers as treasonous enabled Republicans to defeat both former Confederate and border state enslavers' claims for compensation and celebrate their party and the nation as the arbiters of emancipation. Section 4 helped Republicans build coalitions against compensated emancipation, punished recalcitrant Confederates, and preserved what Republicans and many Americans now understood to be the legacies of the Civil War: national economic prosperity through immediate, uncompensated emancipation.

The Limits of the Thirteenth Amendment

When it reconvened in December 1865, Congress had last considered compensating enslavers during debates on the Thirteenth Amendment in January of that year. At that time, there was little will in Congress to add a measure reimbursing former enslavers into the Thirteenth Amendment, and it did not make any provision to pay them. But neither did Congress rescind its previous efforts to pay border state enslavers or prevent any such payments, in part because compensated emancipation for loyal enslavers remained an important compromise measure for Republicans and border state politicians in early 1865. After the passage of the amendment, Unionist and Democratic congressmen continued to suggest reimbursing loyal enslavers living in the border states and the Confederate states to end the war. Henry Grider, a Democratic representative from Kentucky who later became a member of the Joint Committee on Reconstruction, defended border state enslavers' rights to compensation based on the Fifth Amendment's takings clause even as he also asserted that the United States had no authority to abolish slavery in the first place.[7]

Given former Confederate's intransigence in the summer and fall of 1865, however, abolitionists and Republicans balked more than ever at the idea that any enslaver should be compensated. Throughout the end of 1865 and into the first months of 1866, abolitionist organs such as the *National Anti-Slavery Standard* published reports and speeches warning that, if readmitted to Congress, former Confederate states' representatives would compensate enslavers. Others warned that the president's plan for Reconstruction enabled white Southerners to quickly mobilize the Democratic Party against Republican policies and pay former enslavers.[8] More Americans echoed abolitionist arguments that enslaved people were never property under the law. In February 1866, sixty-one petitioners applauded Congress for expelling Southern congressmen and urged them to continue to do so until "adequate security has been obtained against ... any payment for ... emancipated slaves." The unknown petitioners insisted that those who "made war *for slavery*, ought now to give up *all the institutions of slavery*, ... and certainly not to be paid for what they lost by their own rebellion, *and never had any right to*."[9] Enslavers' claims to own people, the petitioners asserted in retrospect, had always been illegitimate, especially after former Confederate states started a war to defend slavery.

Republicans in and outside Congress considered a variety of ways to prevent reimbursing former enslavers, floating ideas to each other in personal

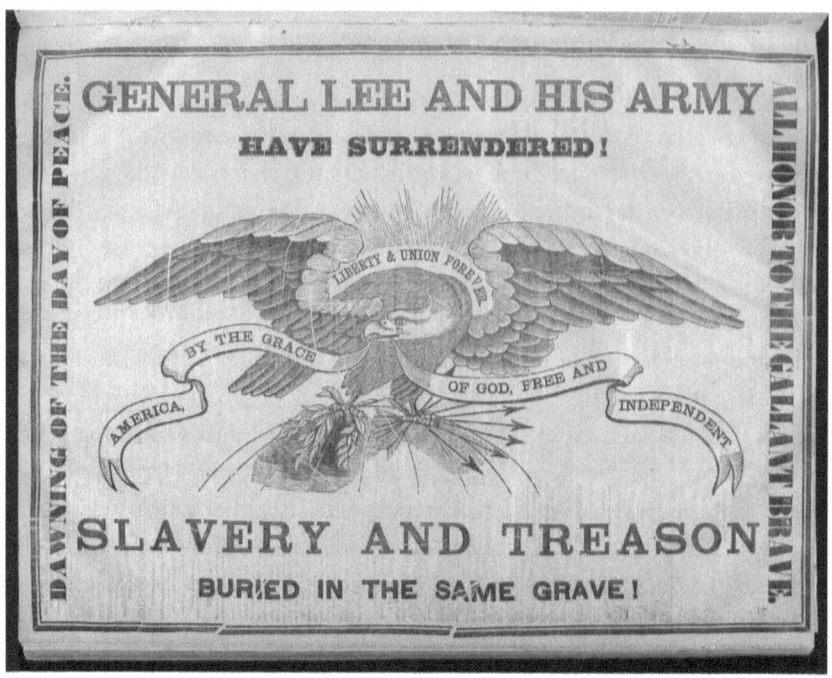

On April 10, 1865, the *Albany Evening Journal* celebrated that slavery and treason were "buried in the same grave" after the surrender of Gen. Robert E. Lee's army. The print reflects the rhetoric congressmen would use during debates over the Fourteenth Amendment. David M. Rubenstein Rare Book & Manuscript Library, Duke University.

correspondence and the press. US general Benjamin Butler supported adding an amendment to the Constitution that would prevent the United States from paying former enslavers. The New Orleans *Tribune*, which served New Orleans's Black community, proposed universal suffrage as another solution. Expand the vote to Black men, and they would balance out former Confederate, pro-slavery voters who sought payments for their property in people.[10]

As soon as Congress reconvened on December 4, 1865, Republicans moved to amass enough evidence to justify both ideas. From January through May 1866, the Joint Committee on Reconstruction heard testimony from more than 100 witnesses, including US and Confederate army officers, politicians, and loyal and disloyal citizens from the North and South. The witnesses spoke to a number of issues, including the question of whether white Southerners expected enslavers to be compensated for their freed slaves. Their observations reflected the patterns seen in the recent state constitutional conventions. Of the fifteen witnesses directly asked the question, twelve replied in the affirmative; two in the negative. The fifteenth witness, from Norfolk, Virginia, said that white Southerners did not generally expect to be paid for those they had enslaved but acknowledged that he had "heard men who have been loyal throughout express that expectation, that they were entitled to compensation for their slaves."[11] Altogether, the witnesses who answered yes had traveled in every military district of the South. Dr. James M. Turner, who had lived in different areas of the South during the war and currently resided in Louisiana, confirmed that politicians in Tennessee and Alabama planned to secure reimbursement for the value of formerly enslaved people once they reentered Congress. He informed the committee that "most of those with whom I conversed seem . . . to think that eventually they would be paid for their slaves, if they can arrange matters in Congress as they hope to do." In particular, men who were loyal to the Union throughout the war expected the federal government to reimburse them. In a June 1866 report summarizing its research, the committee observed, "There prevails, to a considerable extent, an expectation that compensation will be made for slaves emancipated and property destroyed during the war."[12]

Others found the same. President Johnson sent Carl Schurz—a German immigrant, Republican, and US general during the war—to tour the South in the summer of 1865 and report on regional conditions and the attitudes of former Confederates. That December, Schurz reported back. He had had many conversations with white Southerners who expected reimbursements. "In fact," he told Johnson and Congress, "there are abundant indications in newspaper articles, public speeches, and electioneering documents of candidates, which render it eminently probable that on the claim of compensation for their emancipated slaves the southern States, as soon as readmitted to representation in Congress, will be almost a unit."[13] Southern politicians had fulfilled President Johnson's Reconstruction policies, yet they continued to push for compensation and restricted freed people's rights in their reconvened state legislatures.

Not only was it clear that many white Southerners expected payments, but some also feared that border state politicians and conservative Unionists such as President Johnson and Henry Grider might unite with Southern Democrats, Whigs, and other conservatives around compensated emancipation. Many border state congressmen reminded their colleagues that the 1864 Enrollment Act had given many enslavers a positive claim to compensation, even if the United States had not paid most eligible enslavers. The act promised to award loyal enslavers a $300 bounty for "service" that a "colored volunteer may owe" them, and $100 for an enslaved man who was drafted.[14] In Maryland and Delaware, states that had cooperated with federal policy during the war, the War Department appointed commissioners to hear claims in 1863. In January 1865, President Lincoln had ordered the War Department to stall the payments of awarded claims and delay appointing commissioners to hear claims in Missouri, Tennessee, and Kentucky. By October 1865, Boards of Compensation in Maryland and Delaware had filed 3,981 claims for compensation, all but 114 of which came from Maryland. Only 829 had been awarded but not yet paid. Twenty-five Maryland claims amounting to $6,900 were paid before the state's commission dissolved in October 1865. Otherwise, Secretary of War Edwin Stanton explained to Congress when asked, all other payments had been suspended because money was needed to pay troops and purchase supplies.[15]

The Fifth Amendment's takings clause, which indicated that private property could not be taken for public use without just compensation, and the 1864 Enrollment Act's promise remained significant hurdles for Republicans who wished to prevent the United States from paying compensation to former enslavers. How could they legally invalidate former enslavers' claims to compensation and prevent border state politicians from allying with Northern Democrats in retaliation? The same strategy that Republicans had pursued for abolishing slavery—a constitutional amendment—might override those concerns. As historian Michael Vorenberg has written, the Thirteenth Amendment was not the first time Americans changed the Constitution, but it was the first time that a political party used the amendment process to achieve major social reform.[16] The strategy might work again.

In response to protests from Henry Grider, the House Judiciary Committee endorsed the strategy when it reviewed the first amendment to prohibit states and the United States from reimbursing anyone for a free person, proposed by Ohio Republican William Lawrence in March.[17] The committee was chaired by George S. Boutwell, a Republican from Massachusetts. Boutwell's own views on compensation had evolved throughout the war. Early on, he favored compensating loyal enslavers in the border states; by 1864, however, he denied that any enslaver had a claim to property in people or therefore compensation for them.[18] The committee compared Lawrence's amendment to other wartime acts of Congress regarding emancipation. Members worried that a joint resolution or other state action might support former enslavers' claims to compensation, citing the 1864 Enrollment Act's provision to pay border state enslavers for enlisted men. However, the committee concluded that prior legislation did not give "any just claim to compensation for slaves, since no State acted on the faith of it." Slave states—those that remained in the United States and those that did not—had forfeited their right to compensation by failing to take advantage of it when it was offered.

To be safe, the Committee recommended, and Lawrence added, a clause to except any compensation promised by law before January 1, 1865.[19]

The committee gave Congress the authority to use a constitutional amendment to invalidate all claims for compensation, but considerable confusion remained in Congress about whether eligible enslavers would still receive the payments promised in the 1864 Enrollment Act for enlisted men. There would be no clarity regarding Lawrence's amendment because Border state congressmen helped stall it on March 28.[20] Nevertheless, the discussion revealed that paying enslavers for emancipation, once a fairly moderate compromise position, was increasingly unpopular in Congress.

Compensation, the National Debt, and the Bloody Shirt

With the legal authority to invalidate claims for compensation, Republicans continued to devise an amendment that would gain political support over border state congressmen's objections. Throughout March, Congress proposed a number of policies that would become the Fourteenth Amendment. On April 21, the Joint Committee on Reconstruction approved a version of the amendment that combined into section 4 three issues: the validation of the national debt, the invalidation of Confederate debts, and the invalidation of "claims of compensation for loss of involuntary service or labor."[21] By combining compensation with the issue of the national debt, Republicans leveraged loyalty as a political tool to gain support for the amendment.

These issues fit together because attitudes toward compensation, the national debt, and Confederate debt were barometers of loyalty, not just fiscal politics. The United States had accumulated an unprecedented amount of debt to finance the war by issuing government bonds. By 1866, the war debt was well over $2.8 billion, over forty-one times larger than it had been before the war. The United States had taken on national debt to finance wars since the American Revolution, but Americans' experiences with antebellum state debts aggravated postwar anxieties over the extraordinary size of the debt. In the 1840s, a number of states had defaulted on their debts after the Panic of 1837, damaging investors' confidence in each state's government and electorate, which stymied investments and lowered a state's income. After the Civil War, many believed that the United States could pay its debt, but those who managed the largest national debt in history worried that increasing it by compensating enslavers or paying Confederate state debts could alarm investors in the United States and abroad.[22]

So, too, was the reach of the debt unprecedented. Previously, elites in the United States funded national wars. During the Civil War, government-appointed financiers marketed bonds to a wide range of investors—from everyday Americans to international financiers—selling the promise of Union victory. People purchased more bonds when the US Army was victorious and when the Thirteenth Amendment passed in Congress. During Reconstruction, their wartime investments became entwined with the legacies of the Civil War: paying off the debt was a symbol of patriotism and sound fiscal policy, as typified by the Republican Party, which had led the United States through new financial policies, the war, and emancipation. As historian Eric Foner observes, "Most . . . viewed the sanctity of the national debt as a moral legacy of the war second only to emancipation itself."[23] Thus, Republicans often pursued policies to preserve the national debt alongside policies to preserve the legacy of immediate, uncompensated emancipation.

Republicans feared for the national debt despite public support for it because they knew that the composition of Congress would change once former Confederate states were admitted. Before the war, three-fifths of enslaved people in the South had counted toward a state's total representation in Congress. After emancipation, freed people would count fully for total representation, but since they did not have the franchise to vote, white Southerners would gain a sizable majority in Congress without being accountable to a large segment of their states' populations. With that majority, they could elect Democrats who might implement policies unfavorable to freed people and the United States. In Southern states, Democrats ran for state and federal offices on promises to repeal the Confederate debt, reject payments for the United States' debt, and reimburse former enslavers once they were restored to political power.[24]

To garner support for the proposed amendment, Republicans in the House and Senate repeated Democratic congressmen's threats that "when" Democrats were restored to power, they would "demand payment for emancipated slaves or the repudiation of our national debt."[25] If a sovereign state or nation, company, or individual repudiated a debt, they disputed the validity of the contract they had entered into and refused to honor terms for payment. Republican campaigners and policymakers took Democrats' promises seriously because the sanctity of the debt represented the success of the Union war effort, including emancipation. Most Northerners were willing to assume the national debt, but they refused to pay for or legitimate former Confederate states' debts, accumulated in a treasonous war against them. Unionists in the South, especially those who had not purchased Confederate bonds, also supported the repudiation of the Confederate debt. Like Northerners, they saw the repudiation of rebel debt as a punishment for treason. So, too, was uncompensated emancipation to be defended at the risk of defaulting on the national debt. One Connecticut paper warned its readers that should Democrats gain control in Congress and reimburse former enslavers, claims for the value of enslaved people freed by the war would "double at least our present national debt."[26] The author was probably correct.

Any compensation scheme would also impose a huge tax burden on Americans, Republicans worried. Economic historians estimate the value of enslaved people in 1860 to be anywhere between $2.7 billion and $3.059 billion, or well over half the market value of all the goods and services produced in the United States that year. Paying that sum would have required borrowing additional money. Assuming the United States bought enslaved people with 6 percent bonds paid over a thirty-year period, the tax rate to refund them would have been between $6.30 and $9.66 per person in 1860, depending on whether the United States levied taxes on white Southerners as well as freed people—a per capita figure that was about 5 percent of what the average American earned in that year. For comparison, the British government borrowed so much money to compensate enslavers for the Slavery Abolition Act of 1833 that it was not paid off until 2015.[27] Furthermore, the wartime debt held by Confederate states and the Confederacy was over $1.4 billion. If Democrats assumed the Confederate debt and secured reimbursements for former enslavers, then the national debt would more than double, perhaps increasing the chance that the United States would default.[28]

Few strategies were more effective for preserving Republican power than waving the bloody shirt. Historians have identified this Reconstruction-era campaign strategy, in which Republicans positioned their party as the victors of the war and defenders of its legacies, and the compensation debates helped Republicans establish it. The Republican Party mobilized these economic fears in national and regional elections in late 1860s alongside statements like that made by Broomall, who reminded Congress that Confederates "murdered" hundreds of thousands of Americans.[29] Republicans argued that the human cost of emancipation was too great to pay former enslavers, and the deaths of thousands of men legitimized immediate, uncompensated abolition. Notably, Republicans were preoccupied with the number of lives lost and the financial cost of reimbursing enslavers in these debates, while no congressman calculated the value of the loss and labor that generations of enslaved people had sacrificed.

In the former Confederacy, too, Republicans emphasized southern politicians' intentions to pay former enslavers to gain white working-class Southerners' votes and divide them from white elites. In North Carolina, the party published a broadside warning "working men" that "the men who involved you in war did so in the interest of, and for slavery. They lost their slaves, and now they want to tax you to make good their loss.... They now want to tax you to pay for their slaves." The party distinctly appealed to white North Carolinians by threatening that a "tax of this sort would make slaves of" *them*, a tactic to separate lower-class white men from former enslavers. The Republican appeal to these "working men" was well targeted. Working-class North Carolinians historically opposed policies that benefited enslavers financially, and this had resulted in a division between Confederates and Unionists in western and central North Carolina, the latter having loathed the enslaving aristocracy who had led the Confederacy.[30]

On the one hand, Democrats in Congress ridiculed Republicans who panicked over repudiating the national debt and paying the rebel debt. Carl Schurz, a Republican himself, suggested in his report on conditions in the South in 1865 that there was more reason to expect white Southerners to claim compensation than ask for "help paying the expenses of the whipping they have received." Schurz believed they were more likely to obey the federal government and repudiate the Confederate debt than end calls for compensation.[31]

On the other hand, framers of the Fourteenth Amendment did have legitimate reasons to believe these threats that some states would reimburse enslavers and honor the Confederate war debt. South Carolina's provisional governor had told President Johnson that his state's debt was "inconsiderable" and should be paid off. Mississippi and South Carolina had refused to repudiate their war debt in their constitutional conventions. North Carolina and Georgia only did so after President Johnson intervened.[32] White Southerners also balked at being taxed to pay the US debt, accrued in conflicts against them. Their reluctance to sanction what many Northerners believed were the legacies of the war fed Republican concerns that Democrats and white Southerners would force the United States to recognize and repay the Confederate debt and pay enslavers once they returned to Congress. Along with the joint committee's findings and Democratic politics in the South, all parties in Congress had plenty of evidence to believe these outcomes were likely. In any case, the issue effectively mobilized voters—and Congress.

By emphasizing the financial and human cost of emancipation, Republicans played up associations of disloyalty and gained overwhelming support for section 4, which became the least controversial part of the Fourteenth Amendment. These arguments swayed other Republicans in the House and Senate who suggested that compensated emancipation was an issue so specific to the war that it should not be included as a lasting clause in the Constitution. Republican Senator Luke Poland of Vermont approved of section 4's "sound propositions," but he questioned "the propriety or necessity of incorporating them into the fundamental law."[33] Others downplayed the significance of white Southerners' claims for compensation or even the controversy of the section. Samuel Randall, a Democrat from Pennsylvania, thought an amendment to nullify compensation was so obviously warranted that he need not discuss it. On May 10, he explained that if the "proposition was presented to this House as a simple proposition it would be almost unanimously adopted." Even when said in support of the amendment, these were attempts to discredit Republicans' assertions that there was urgent political and economic need for the Fourteenth Amendment as a whole.[34]

Ultimately, congressmen across the political spectrum agreed that incorporating section 4 into the Constitution would at least "save disputes and wrangling hereafter" and preserve the country's financial system.[35] Broomall's arguments about loss and loyalty, as well as the possibility that Democrats could return to power, reverse the country's financial policies, and reimburse enslavers was enough to convince the House that section 4 was a modest but necessary constitutional change to secure the outcomes of the war. The House passed the Fourteenth Amendment after the last day of debate on May 10.[36]

Compensation and the Limits of Constitutional Change

Republicans opposed paying enslavers and successfully mobilized uncompensated emancipation as a political tool; however, their stance on emancipation and eminent domain remained ambiguous. When the Senate debated the amendment, one potentially significant change in the language went unexplained. Members of the Joint Committee on Reconstruction and other senators proposed a number of changes, often in private caucus. One of those changes modified the language concerning enslaved people. The original phrasing of section 4 included language about labor, not property in people, stating that "claims of compensation for loss of involuntary service or labor shall not be paid by any state, or by the United States." On June 4, the Senate edited the section to invalidate any claim for the "loss or emancipation of any slave" and add that "all such debts, obligations, and claims shall be forever held illegal and void." The Thirteenth Amendment included the word "slavery," but the Fourteenth Amendment became the first to directly name the status of "slave."[37]

Considering how often Congress had debated the status of enslaved people under the law before and during the war, its neglect of the topic during congressional debates over the Fourteenth Amendment is notable. Supporters of paying enslavers insisted that enslaved people were property, which implied that no government could seize them without "just compensation" under the Fifth Amendment's takings clause. However, the Fugitive Slave Clause, the Confiscation Acts, the 1862 DC Emancipation Act, and the 1864 Enrollment Act all described enslaved people as persons "held to service or labor," as did the initial drafts of the Fourteenth Amendment.[38] The distinction suggested that enslavers had no unending, unlimited right to claim an enslaved person themselves as property, only their labor. The phrase originated in English and early American law, which characterized workers' labor as a "kind of property" held by their master under contract, in the words of historian Robert J. Steinfeld. After gradual abolition in Northern states, some lawmakers began to distinguish between owning property in people and owning their labor. As we have seen during debates about abolishing slavery in the national capital in the 1830s, antislavery congressmen had told pro-slavery factions that the takings clause did not apply to government-sponsored emancipation because the Constitution spoke of enslaved people not as property but as persons held to service.[39] These arguments did not have much doctrinal or political support.

During the Civil War, antislavery congressmen likewise emphasized that an enslaved person was not actually property; what an enslaver owned was the right to their labor. As historian Silvana R. Siddali describes, Republicans argued in debates about the Confiscation Acts that they could subject an enslaved person's labor to the same confiscation procedures as other forms of property. It could be said, then, that the DC Emancipation Act and the 1864 Enrollment Act rewarded or reimbursed former enslavers up to $300 for some of the future *labor* of an enslaved person rather than their property in a person. Furthermore, Republicans suggested that the value of enslaved people's future labor was, unlike physical property, impossible to guarantee and therefore subject to confiscation. Antislavery congressmen used this logic to respond to their pro-slavery opponents who insisted that an enslaved person represented a unique form of property with which no government could interfere without due process of law.[40]

That Republicans included and rephrased section 4 suggests that they were cautious about relying on this and other antislavery legal arguments in peacetime. Throughout the war, Republicans had held that federally sponsored emancipation was a noncompensable regulation enabled by police powers and the war. Yet despite wartime policies, some policymakers and judges, including Judge Advocate General Joseph Holt, repeatedly referred to enslavers' rights to compensation based on the public taking of private *property*. Without records from private caucuses, it is difficult to determine why Senate Republicans changed the phrasing of section 4 to prevent compensation for any slave. Given the purpose of the section, it is likely that they changed the language to "slave" to preserve the outcome of the war.

Republican senators probably aimed to suppress the familiar argument that the Fifth Amendment guaranteed enslavers compensation in the event of legislated emancipation. Even if they incorporated the category of "slave" into the Constitution, the section reflected radical abolitionists' long-held stance that people could not be property under the law by denying enslavers compensation. At the same time, section 4 distinguished enslaved people from other kinds of property without clarifying their status, ensuring that no one could apply the principles of uncompensated emancipation to other forms of permanent property confiscation.

Section 4 thus helped Republicans abolish property in people without creating precedents to abolish all property. Congress had acted similarly when it wrote the Second Confiscation Act. Then, Congress built the legal framework to legislate confiscation in disloyal areas but rejected its own power to broadly confiscate property as punishment for disloyalty to unite radical, moderate, and conservative wings of the Republican Party around the legislation. Similarly, section 4 created a new framework to abolish property rights in people without interfering with increasingly conservative views that the United States could not permanently confiscate private property in peacetime.[41]

Republicans may also have changed the language to avoid further conflict with border state senators. The phrasing of the 1864 Enrollment Act suggested that the United States was compensating enslavers for the service or labor that enlisted men owed them, and the Maryland Slave Claims Commission of 1864 did allow some compensation for formerly enslaved enlisted men as well as apprentices based on the length of service yet owed.[42] During congressional debates about the Fourteenth Amendment, Kentucky congressmen anticipated and protested the new language's implications for border state enslavers' claims, but Senate Republicans outmaneuvered Kentucky senator Garrett Davis when he attempted to amend section 4 to preserve them.[43]

In any case, by avoiding public debate about the legal status of slaves, Republicans successfully focused the question of compensation on loyalty rather than property law. Border state congressmen and other opponents of section 4 could not critique the amendment openly at the risk of being accused of disloyalty. Congress passed the Fourteenth Amendment on June 13, 1866. A few days later, Kentucky representative Lawrence Trimble submitted a speech that contested the constitutionality of section 4. Trimble objected to the idea that enslavers were traitors, especially because Kentucky enslavers never seceded. He reprimanded Congress for "robbing Kentucky and the South of $4,000,000,000 of property" and "trampling beneath their unhallowed feet the Constitution they have sworn in the presence of God to support, protect, and defend." He contested the validity of the wartime emancipation, telling his fellow congressmen, "If you have a right by constitutional amendment to take my private property without compensation, either for public use or not . . . then I fear indeed the Union is gone, our liberties forever lost."[44] Trimble was one of the only congressmen who publicly alluded to the Fifth Amendment's takings clause in recorded discussions of the Fourteenth Amendment in the spring of 1866.

Trimble insisted that the United States had pledged leniency and a return to the rule of the Constitution as it was before the war when former Confederate states rejoined the Union. He commended white Southerners for the "alacrity and unanimity" with which they accomplished this and reproached Congress for going back on that pledge. However, white Southerners had not in fact willingly relinquished their claims to profit from enslaved people, and their questionable loyalties only worried Republicans. As Congress saw it, white Southerners' and enslavers' behavior after the war proved their continued disloyalty to the United States and resistance to the federal government's demands for emancipation. Trimble and anyone else who resisted the immediate, uncompensated abolition of slavery proved the need for section 4 and the Fourteenth Amendment.

Trimble also objected to this conflation of loyalty and acquiescence to emancipation. Slavery was a national crime, he reminded Congress. "Did not the New England and northern ship-owners and capitalists receive rich and solid tribute from this trade they then so zealously protected, and now so unanimously denounce and condemn?" Since slavery was connected to national and international markets, the whole nation should have to pay the price of emancipation by reimbursing enslavers. Trimble echoed British abolitionists who had made similar arguments in the first decades of the nineteenth century and secured reimbursements for enslavers there.[45] The country should bear the cost of emancipation and compensate enslavers, they had argued, to acknowledge that the entire country had profited from and been complicit in the institution.

Of course, a key difference between enslavers in the United States and those in Britain discredited Trimble: The vast majority of enslavers in the United States had waged war against the nation. By connecting compensation and repudiation to the legacies of the war and condemning their opponents as treasonous, Republicans made it difficult to oppose section 4 of the proposed Fourteenth Amendment and discouraged debates about the constitutionality of property rights in people. During the war, many Americans imagined those who relinquished their property rights in people to be loyal, potentially deserving of compensation. By the spring of 1866, anyone who would defend enslavers' property rights in humans would have failed because their appeals sounded like those of rebels. As Pennsylvania senator Edgar Cowan pointed out when debating section 3 of the amendment, Republicans called men "loyal" only if they were abolitionists.[46] As this criticism made clear, by conflating loyalty to the United States with the rejection of slave ownership, Republicans had cast slavery as a distinctly Southern problem and associated all border state enslavers who would seek federal compensation with rebels.

Republicans had successfully associated paying enslavers with treason by defending future measures to invalidate claims for compensation on political and economic rather than legal grounds. Americans had come to believe that paying enslavers would betray the legacies of US victory, and Republicans enshrined in section 4 a constitutional framework for uncompensated emancipation and the idea that loyalty to the Union meant relinquishing the right to own and profit from property in people. By refusing to acknowledge even loyal enslavers' property rights in people in their debates and celebrating uncompensated emancipation as an outcome of the Civil War, Congress delimited and narrowed slavery to a Confederate, or Southern, issue.

Compensation and the 1866 Congressional Elections

On June 18, 1866, Congress submitted the Fourteenth Amendment to the states for ratification. Outside Congress, the amendment served important political purposes. Border state politicians knew that the Fourteenth Amendment would prevent the federal government from paying their constituents for the partial value of enlisted men as soon as it was ratified, and they continued to press Congress to make the payments promised in the 1864 Enrollment

Act. However, Republicans' tactics cemented the bind that border state politicians often found themselves in during the war. Not only would pushing for compensation to border state enslavers appear disloyal, but it would ally them politically with former Confederates. Americans had come to believe that paying enslavers would betray the legacies of US victory, and even border state enslavers and politicians could not avoid the taint of treason when they, like former Confederates, sought reimbursements for former enslavers.

Nevertheless, a number of them scrambled to secure the payments promised by the Enrollment Act before the Fourteenth Amendment could be ratified. In 1866, there were 829 outstanding approved claims worth $242,583 that remained to be paid from Maryland and Delaware. Kentucky, Tennessee, West Virginia, and Missouri had not yet had the opportunity to present claims, despite their eligibility. In 1866, Stanton had reported to Congress that payments had been paused in 1865 because the money was needed to pay troops and supplies. Commenting on the claims, one newspaper concluded, "It will probably be some time before the debt is paid." Though the federal government could pay Maryland and Delaware claimants and more in 1866, the War Department continued to stall.[47]

In Congress, Republicans avoided opposing the promised payments outright to increase the chances of ratification and avoid alienating voters in the upcoming November congressional elections. As one Maryland Republican pointed out that summer, the looming elections would be seen as a referendum on the Fourteenth Amendment and Republican Reconstruction policy. He worried that stalling or nullifying payments for former enslavers would give border states a reason to reject the amendment.[48] Republicans also sought to maintain political alliance with the border states. Rejecting their claims to compensation would risk breaking with border state politicians, who, in turn, could create new coalitions with former Confederate states in and outside Congress as Reconstruction continued. Furthermore, the votes of former Whigs; War Democrats; and members of the Constitutional Union Party, the Unconditional Union Party, and the National Unionist Party were still up for grabs. These men had opposed secession and supported the Union war effort but did not call themselves Republicans. President Johnson hoped to unite them and rebuild the National Union Party with conservative Republicans and moderate Democrats to challenge Radical Republican control of Reconstruction.[49]

To avoid charges of disloyalty in open debates, many border state politicians mobilized new tactics to secure payments before the amendment became law: congressional procedure and bureaucratic maneuvering. In and outside Congress, border state politicians pressured the United States to collect necessary records of the enlisted men and assist former enslavers in receiving compensation.[50] In Congress, some Republicans and border state politicians tried to fund payments through appropriations bills, created over the summer of 1866 to outline a budget for the next fiscal year. If enslavers' constitutional claims for compensation no longer existed, they insisted that Congress owed border state enslavers the payments as a contractual obligation created by the Enrollment Act.[51]

Republicans thus capitulated to the creation of the Slave Claims Commissions to review border state enslavers' claims. Nevertheless, border states' ostensible allies in Congress suggested new hurdles to delay payments, including a loyalty test. Congress passed an appropriations bill on July 28, 1866, that allocated funds for payments to border state enslavers from the commutation funds, stipulated that only "loyal" enslavers qualified for payments, defined loyalty for the commissions, and indicated that all payments were to be postponed until each commission filed a report concluding their investigation. But as border state politicians pointed out, who knew how long that would take?[52]

These tactics may have helped Republicans maintain their coalitions with former Unionists and conservative factions of their party as the congressional elections approached. While Republican papers presented the Fourteenth Amendment as a "binding contract or treaty of peace," conservative Republicans and Democrats campaigned in the summer and fall against it and urged Congress to admit loyal representatives from seceded states.[53] Southern politicians vehemently protested the privileges and immunities clause, the reduction of congressional representation for states that denied the vote to any group of men, and the third section, which denied the right to vote to former Confederate officeholders. But Southern politicians did not often protest section 4. Governors in the former Confederate states received some advice from constituents about how to respond to or change section 4, but petitioners were more concerned with the clauses that repudiated the Confederate debt than with the rejection of claims for compensation.[54]

Conservatives' silence on section 4 was probably calculated, like Republicans' bloody shirt campaigning. That summer, Southern politicians, many of whom had attended the 1865 presidential Reconstruction constitutional conventions in their state, attended the July National Union Convention in Philadelphia. There, President Johnson and other political leaders hoped to unite Southern Unionists, moderate Republicans, and Northern Democrats against the Fourteenth Amendment. The convention accepted the end of slavery and the repudiation of the Confederate war debt, but its journal said nothing about compensation.[55] One Tennessee newspaper worried that the convention's silence on the subject reflected Unionists' desire to secure compensation at a later date.[56] However, the 1866 elections, along with the New Orleans massacre in late July, dashed conservative hopes. In New Orleans, white rioters slaughtered Black demonstrators at the Mechanics' Institute in a contest over the legitimacy of the 1864 state constitutional convention, which Republicans reconvened to eliminate the Black Codes and extend suffrage to Black men. The massacre proved to many Americans that radicals in Congress, not moderates or conservatives, needed to lead Reconstruction. Republicans achieved a massive congressional majority in the November election, and their electoral success signified public approval of the Fourteenth Amendment.[57]

Supporting the Slave Claims Commissions had helped Republicans position themselves as the reasonable compromisers, especially after ten Southern states' legislatures rejected the Fourteenth Amendment between October 1866 and January 1867. But after their electoral victories, Republicans in Congress moved more decisively to curtail the work of the commissions. After three months of drafting different resolutions to postpone payments, suspend the commissions' work, or dissolve the commissions altogether, Congress finally succeeded at the end of March 1867. New Reconstruction policy accelerated that process. Southern intransigence throughout 1866 convinced many congressmen to impose stricter measures on former Confederate states and force them to accept congressional policies. As the last session of the 39th Congress ended, Congress passed the first Reconstruction Act of 1867. Among other things, the act stipulated that former Confederate states must ratify the Fourteenth Amendment to rejoin the United States, which in effect decreased the window of time for border state politicians to secure payments. In that moment, Radical Republicans renewed their attack on the commissions. On March 2, the penultimate day of the session and the same day that Congress passed the Reconstruction Act, Illinois Republican senator Lyman Trumbull revived a joint resolution from the House that would suspend them. Garrett Davis successfully moved to end debate, and the 40th Congress would take up the resolution when it convened at the end of the month.[58]

The debates that ensued echoed prior arguments, with one important exception. As before, Republicans emphasized the disloyalty of former enslavers, and Davis accused the Senate of repudiating its contract with former enslavers and violating "the plighted faith of the Government." Foreseeing defeat, Willard Saulsbury—another border state senator and former enslaver—offered new reasons for conservatives to end the commissions. Though Saulsbury agreed with Davis that the United States had enlisted enslaved men for public use, which would otherwise require the federal government to pay enslavers, he pointed out that it abolished slavery for humanitarian reasons. And it was the latter goal that Saulsbury had protested in the 1864 Enrollment Act: "They were going to elevate a degraded race and make the negro equal to the white man. I then uttered my feeble voice against it as an outrage upon my constitutional rights." Saulsbury was more concerned about racial equality than his wallet. He told his colleagues, "Having taken that position, I shall never vote one single dollar to reimburse myself or anybody else situated as I am." Saulsbury advised his colleagues to do the same. "Let it go. . . . You say you have restored the Union; so be it. Then we can all unite and thank God in one common voice."[59]

Saulsbury, a Democrat, was intimating and beginning to articulate a strategy that the Democratic Party would advance for the next five years: Accept the losses of the war and emancipation in order to regain political power and thereby block efforts to secure Black Americans' civil rights. Saulsbury's speech also reveals one reason why many border states began to align themselves with former Confederates in Reconstruction. For Saulsbury, Union victory over the Confederacy meant defeat for border state enslavers, their compensation claims, and white supremacy.[60]

Shortly after Saulsbury spoke, the Senate voted to approve the resolution and end the Slave Claims Commissions—and, with them, the promise of compensation to any more former enslavers. The resolution passed overwhelmingly but split along regional and party lines. No Democrat except Saulsbury voted to suspend the commissions, and the only other border state senator who agreed to forfeit payments on behalf of their constituents came from Missouri. President Johnson signed the resolution into law on March 30, and Secretary of War Stanton disbanded the commissions in April. The commissions had received 11,600 new claims from the border states, awarded 1,217 claims, and rejected 382 through the fall of 1866 and winter of 1867. Ten thousand were never reviewed.[61]

A few states refused to relinquish their claims quietly. Throughout 1867, Kentucky's and Maryland's legislatures passed resolutions to count the number of freed people the US government "owed" to their states in compensation and censured what the Kentucky Senate called the repudiation of debts for the value of enlisted men. Politicians in Kentucky and Maryland, where the state paid at least some former enslavers $100 for enslaved men who enlisted, continued to demand federal payments, and their attempts continued to mobilize Republicans. It is unlikely that any enslavers other than twenty-five Maryland claimants received payments from the US based on the 1864 Enrollment Act's promise.[62]

WHEN IT WAS ADOPTED on July 9, 1868, the Fourteenth Amendment could have ended all conversation of compensating former enslavers for the value of enslaved people. Confederate resistance to wartime emancipation helped convince Republicans and other Americans that compensated emancipation was an unacceptable compromise that necessitated additional constitutional change to proscribe. Republicans, Black and white, celebrated uncompensated emancipation as a dividend of US victory and a promise for Black freedom. By incorporating uncompensated emancipation into section 4, Republicans wanted to prevent planters' economic and political ascendance and national financial calamity by promoting their party's Reconstruction policies. Their support for section 4 painted slavery as a Confederate problem, forcing ostensibly loyal border state politicians to accept immediate, uncompensated emancipation.

Though defeated, former enslavers' claims for compensation continued to animate Reconstruction politics. If Republicans avoided financial calamity nationally, the South still faced it regionally. Immediate, uncompensated emancipation toppled the financial base of the Southern economy: the value of enslaved people. White Southerners had bought and sold enslaved people on credit and mortgaged them throughout the war. As early as 1863, individuals who still owed money for an outstanding debt based on the value of an enslaved person asked whether they should have to pay their creditors for a person whom the law no longer considered property. White Southerners who owed debts for the value of enslaved people continued to seek other avenues for relief. Their creditors took them to court for payments, and debtors begged their states, President Johnson, and Congress for relief. A few suggested that section 4 of the Fourteenth Amendment invalidated both claims for compensation and outstanding debts for the value of slaves.

Although these Southerners contested private contracts rather than public claims for property takings, the compensation debates shaped their fight for relief. Some litigation resulted from the lack of clarity about compensation. Notably, both President Johnson and Congress avoided intervening. Even as

Republicans continued to campaign as the party of emancipation, the Republican-controlled Congress refused to extend its power to invalidate both claims for compensation and outstanding debts for slaves. Federal inaction led to inconsistent policies and judicial rulings across the former slaveholding South. White Southerners eventually forced the issue before the Supreme Court, where the court had a chance to comment on the extent and meaning of section 4.

CHAPTER FIVE

Debt Relief and Repudiation
The Legal and Economic Consequences of Uncompensated Emancipation

No State shall... pass any Bill of Attainder, ex post facto Law, or Law impairing the Obligation of Contracts.
—US Constitution, Article I, Section 10, Clause 1

In the early 1870s, Frederick Douglass and his colleagues warned Americans in the *New National Era*—his postwar paper based in Washington, DC—that many white Southerners wanted to repeal the Fourteenth Amendment to secure compensation for formerly enslaved people. Few people in the South and none in the North were "bold enough" to speak about this aloud, but Douglass worried that "very little attention ha[d] been given to the subject." He made it a mission to publicize white Southerners' claims for compensation. In its four-year lifespan the *New National Era*, named after antebellum abolitionist newspaper the *New Era*, accused Southern newspaper editors of disingenuously professing "an acquiescence in the reconstruction measures of Congress." But white Southerners, Douglass insisted, missed "no opportunity, lawful or unlawful, peaceable or violent, to show their contempt for such teachings and their undying animosity to the Government." They continued to hope for compensation.[1]

Americans, who had long turned to the law for national stability, recognized that Reconstruction rested on untested legal foundations. The United States determined that enslaved people were no longer a species of property and repudiated any claim for illegal takings. Congressional Republicans specified that no enslaver would receive compensation based on principles of loyalty and citizenship, rather than on foundations of property law. As legal historian Cynthia Nicoletti found, some Americans worried that "they had allowed a violent conflict to provide the final determination of the most divisive legal issue in their society." The Civil War and Radical Reconstruction had supplanted the nation's "ordinary legal process," which was apparently too limited to resolve the most contentious legal disputes in the country.[2]

Though Nicoletti addressed these ideas in Americans' debates about secession, a similar process unfolded in debates about emancipation. It remained to be seen how states and courts would respond to Congress's directives and section 4 of the Fourteenth Amendment. How much did the war and section 4 change traditional federalist relationships—if at all? If the courts had determined the rules of property and contracts before the war, did military emancipation and Reconstruction grant states or other branches of government the authority to change long-standing practices relating to slavery? How would courts define the meaning of section 4?

Americans resolved these questions in a long and winding debate over the private laws of slavery—laws of contracts, property, inheritance, marriage, and more. During and after the war, most debate over reimbursing former enslavers referred to public takings, asking whether enslaved people were property wrongfully seized by a state or the federal government without "just compensation." At the same time, many Southerners sought relief from private debts for the value of enslaved people. Consider Nannie Durman, a widow from Mississippi who had purchased land and enslaved people in 1860 and still owed money at the time of the war. She asked her governor whether she would be compelled to pay for the value of enslaved people for whom she had made a valid contract but who had been freed by the war. She wondered, Did emancipation retroactively destroy the vested right to claim property in people *and* a contract for their sale?[3] Others added, Was a contract for the sale of a person ever valid?

Though Durman's questions rested on different legal principles than emancipation—the private laws of contracts rather than property and public law—Americans based their answers on their understandings of the history of slavery, the legality of uncompensated takings of property, and the legality of emancipation as it happened. Historians such as Giuliana Perrone and Andrew Kull have explored how jurists reconciled antebellum legal practices with the realities of emancipation.[4] This chapter joins these conversations, adding perspectives outside the courtroom to understand how Americans interpreted the effects of section 4 of the Fourteenth Amendment. Some suggested that section 4 extended beyond compensation from federal and state governments to private contracts. Some debtors and judges (but many more debtors, comparatively) argued that the last clause of that section—"all such debts, obligations and claims shall be held illegal and void"—expanded the amendment's power to private debts for slaves as well as public debts. A few went so far as to say that the repudiation of private debts for enslaved people counted as compensation for those debtors.

This chapter argues that some contract litigation resulted from the intentional lack of clarity about compensation and the ongoing popular belief that it should be forthcoming. Congress, President Johnson, and the courts avoided the messy political, legal, and economic debates that outstanding contracts for the value of enslaved people created in part to forestall legal challenges to uncompensated emancipation. Debtors and their allies pleaded with Johnson, Congress, and their states to intervene. They felt that military emancipation was a taking or loss beyond their control that absolved debtors from any contractual obligation to their creditors. They suggested, probably erroneously, that debt relief from property in people became all the more important in the absence of compensation. Repudiating outstanding contracts might relieve debtors of *some* of the financial burden of emancipation, if not return to them the value of the formerly enslaved. However, it was no substitute for direct reimbursements.

As legal scholars have argued, state politicians prevaricated because repudiating contracts for the value of enslaved people would retroactively violate the US Constitution's contracts clause, which stipulated that "no state shall pass any law impairing the obligations of contracts."[5] Yet legislative and executive inaction enabled Southerners to force the issue into the courts through unanticipated avenues. Uncertain of which level or branch of government to turn to after political and legal upheaval, debtors and their allies forced politicians and, eventually, the Supreme Court to consider whether section 4 enabled states to nullify outstanding contracts despite the Constitution's contract clause. They mobilized self-interested, often spurious interpretations of uncompensated emancipation's effects on the law and economy. They portrayed all debtors as former enslavers who were loyal and innocent victims of uncompensated emancipation or their creditors, who they argued were disloyal human traffickers. In this political discourse, debtors and their allies often conflated a number of complicated financial transactions and legal rules—from the sale or hire of enslaved people to traded promissory notes to mortgages—to emphasize the widespread loss of uncompensated emancipation. Such dubious arguments helped politicians, judges, and US Army generals justify their own interventions into murky legal territory.

As conflicting solutions emerged across the South, creditors continued to take debtors to court as a way to recover their money. These cases wound their way into the US Supreme Court in 1871. In *White v. Hart, Osborn v. Nicholson*, and its 1873 decision, *Boyce v. Tabb*, the court rejected debtors' arguments, preserving a relatively conservative vision of emancipation based on contract law. Focusing on antebellum financial rules and economic order, it avoided postwar legal arguments that contested the legitimacy of slave law in retrospect. Particularly, the court would not substantiate debtors' broad interpretation of section 4 of the Fourteenth Amendment that would have repudiated outstanding private contracts for the value of enslaved people.

Historians and legal scholars alike have already explored what the court's decision meant for abolition, freed people's rights, and American law. By examining contract debates outside the courtroom, this chapter shows that many white Southerners would not stop agitating for compensation in some form. Political movements about compensated emancipation continued to shape Reconstruction politics and law after the ratification of the Fourteenth Amendment in 1868. Southerners mobilized the power of new Reconstruction governments in attempt to develop unique interpretations of section 4 and shape the process of rebuilding the New South after the economic devastation of the war. Their continued agitation forced the Supreme Court to specify—albeit indirectly—that section 4 applied only to the repudiation of public takings, not to private debts for slaves.

Seeking Relief outside the Courts

While Congress drafted the Fourteenth Amendment in 1866, Southerners continued to grapple with the economic consequences of emancipation. The Southern economy was in shambles. Before emancipation, many white Southerners bought and sold Black people on credit or mortgaged enslaved people to rapidly expand their plantation enterprise. White Southerners regularly borrowed from neighbors, friends, families, and businesses called factorage firms, which were financial agents or private bankers. Buyers often contracted with sellers or third-party creditors using a promissory note. Promissory notes were IOUs, legal contracts in which the purchaser promised to pay back the seller or creditor at a stipulated time after receiving the property they had purchased. The notes could be traded like cash. Creditors often used them to pay off their own debts, and the original signer was still liable to the new note bearer for the note's value. If the original signer could not pay their creditor or the note bearer, the bearer seeking repayment could initiate legal proceedings, which could lead to confiscation of the debtor's property, including enslaved people.[6] Without cash or capital (in human property or not), many debtors could not make good on their contract.

Immediate, uncompensated emancipation threatened to topple the financial base on which debts for the value of enslaved people rested. For example, Nannie Durman had been a widow for twelve years when she wrote to her state's provisional governor, William Sharkey, for advice. She had purchased 1,000 acres of land and forty enslaved people in 1860 for $80,000. Though she paid $30,000 that year, she still owed $50,000 to be paid over four years. Then the war came. Durman did not elaborate how the war affected her operations and finances, but she implied that she had not paid her debts during that time. In her letter, she pointed out that "all bills of sale guarantees a negroe slave for life," referring to the written or unwritten warranty that usually accompanied the purchase of an enslaved person. Then she appealed to Sharkey's pity rather than his legal knowledge, telling him that "to be forced to give up my home and all I had will be too hard." Durman's predicament was quite typical, both for widows specifically and for former enslavers generally. If the debtors could no longer leverage the value and bodies of enslaved people against their obligations, they petitioned their states and the federal government to invalidate contracts for the purchase of enslaved people through legislation.[7]

Debtors and creditors also turned to the courts during and immediately after the war. Southern courts heard a number of disputes regarding outstanding contracts for the value of freed slaves. However, it took time for legal disputes regarding these contracts to percolate into formal politics and governance. For one thing, Reconstruction state governments faced a crisis of legitimacy that delayed arbitration regarding any kind of debt. Between 1861 and 1869, most former Confederate states had at least three different governments. Each new constitution required a new state court system to adjudicate alongside US military tribunals and Freedmen's Bureau courts. Each system's jurisdictions overlapped, and the federal government's shifting Reconstruction policy exacerbated the uncertainty surrounding state courts' scope and powers.

The overwhelming need for debt relief—for all kinds of debts—made it a popular political platform but precarious law and economic policy. No one in state government or the federal government was sure how to proceed. When Southern legislatures reconvened in late 1865 and 1866, they passed a series of laws to alleviate the war's toll on debtors. They halted the collection of debts for a period with stay laws, scaled old debts to new values, suspended court proceedings for debt collection, lowered property values, and exempted certain types and quantities of land and personal property from seizure. States also passed crop lien laws in hopes of securing credit for planters and increasing agricultural production. These initiatives, referred to broadly as repudiation, had wide support among both large and small property holders. The platform also had a sectional bent. Former Confederates avoided paying prewar loans to Northern merchants, who tended to oppose relief laws alongside Southern governors and courts. These groups all feared stymieing outside investment and undermining the availability of credit, which would further impede economic growth.⁸

Given the main legal impediment to state-sponsored debt relief—the Constitution's contracts clause—some politicians doubted that repudiation measures could effectively cancel debts altogether. Ever since the Constitution had been ratified, US courts had been overseeing state debt relief laws using the contracts clause, which prevented states from interfering with valid contracts, with little public opposition. Before the Civil War, the Supreme Court under Chief Justice Roger Taney began to articulate the doctrine that neither legislatures nor courts could impair contracts, and suggested that the laws in existence when a contract was made formed part of the contract itself. As long as both contracting parties received due consideration—for example, money from the buyer and the enslaved person from the seller—the contract was valid. Legislatures could not pass laws that retroactively broke or changed a contract for any kind of property; they could, however, change the remedies available to debtors to complete their contracts, postpone the time of payment, or restrict access to the courts where creditors could seek legal redress. The Supreme Court's decisions reflected a predominant legal interpretation of the mid-1800s: legal formalism. Judges turned to precedent to establish a system of objective rules that created the assurance of certainty and predictability, which, in turn, helped ensure market stability. Maintaining the integrity of contracts was essential for minimizing market conflicts and encouraging business; and, the logic went, these principles strengthened commerce nationally and regionally.⁹

After the war, Southerners offered popular legal understandings as alternatives to formalist interpretations to address the debt crisis. Debtors were desperate, but they also believed in the need and legal justification for compensation, particularly in absence of clear policy. All Southerners felt the economic effects of the war and emancipation, and many blamed uncompensated emancipation for the debt crisis.¹⁰ In and outside the courts, debtors claimed that emancipation was a taking or a loss that caused a failure of consideration for outstanding contracts for the value of enslaved people because one party, the slave buyer, could no longer claim the property in people promised by the seller or creditor. One writer, under the name "Roscoe," outlined the problem debtors faced in a widely reprinted letter to the editor of the *Richmond Whig* in August 1866: "Four-fifths of the people" of Virginia were debtors, and emancipation had deprived them of their most secure form of collateral and income—enslaved people. The value of the enslaved and their labor would have been sufficient to pay off the majority of Southern debtors' obligations,

Roscoe wrote, but now their land and livelihoods were at stake.[11] Debtors would struggle to pay their debts without forfeiting land and other capital required to sustain themselves. If uncompensated emancipation was to blame for the South's economic troubles, Roscoe suggested, then repudiating debts for the value of slaves was a logical consequence and a just outcome of uncompensated emancipation.

Sympathetic Southern politicians tried to respond to their constituents, but the contracts clause prevented widespread reform. At least one state, South Carolina, had attempted to address outstanding debts for enslaved people in its legislature in 1865 and 1866. The legislature's House Judiciary Committee reviewed a petition from six citizens from Clarendon County that demanded that the assembly "take some action" to relieve those who owed debts for the purchase of enslaved people.[12] The assembly dismissed it on December 18, 1865, adding that the question of whether to enforce contracts for the purchase of enslaved people after emancipation belonged "to the courts."[13] Knowing that the contracts clause would circumscribe states but not Congress, some South Carolina senators attempted to appeal to Congress to relieve these kinds of debts in a series of unsuccessful resolutions.[14]

Southern courts overwhelmingly upheld outstanding contracts for slaves, even though some judges agreed that uncompensated emancipation represented a loss, and one that might warrant some sort of relief. The 1867 North Carolina Supreme Court likened emancipation to the legal and political death of enslaved people, emphasizing the sense of loss that debtors and former enslavers expressed. There is little evidence to suggest that its framers meant loss as a euphemism for death, but as historian Daina Ramey Berry argues, enslaved people had a "ghost value" after death for legal and insurance purposes. Such language was consistent with antebellum financial norms as well as Southern legal culture. An enslaved person's value often extended beyond their lifetime, and enslavers expected courts to understand these norms. As historian Ariela Gross shows, enslavers developed and performed a culture of mastery in antebellum courtrooms that led them to expect that the law would side with them if they could demonstrate their "good business sense" in a legal conflict. This is one reason why many debtors stressed that emancipation, and therefore their debts, came at no fault of their own.[15]

Even the most sympathetic judges denied that debtors' sense of loss justified a change in contract law; however, one did argue that it justified federal compensation. In two 1865 Kentucky Supreme Court cases regarding the escape of an enslaved man, Marshall, and an enslaved woman, Milly,

Chief Justice George Robertson told enslavers and those contracting to hire Marshall and Milly that emancipation without "just compensation" was unconstitutional. Nevertheless, any such hiring contract remained valid. Even before emancipation, jurists recognized that financial loss was sometimes a risk of investment. Without a warranty, the escape, death, or loss of an enslaved person and their labor did not retroactively invalidate a contract for their sale or hire.[16] Robertson would not nullify an outstanding contract, but he did recognize the hirer's and enslaver's financial loss. The courts were not the right avenue for these claims, he advised; instead, enslavers "must look alone to the government for reparation." Even though he upheld the hiring contract, Robertson wrote what most courts did not—that the United States owed enslavers for emancipation.[17]

Between 1865 and 1871, most courts, with two exceptions, concluded that creditors could not be expected to bear the financial burden of emancipation and upheld outstanding debts for slaves. Enslavers' conflation of their emotional and financial loss did not help them. Courts interpreted emancipation as akin to an act of God or the general government or to an enslaved person's death and thus beyond the scope of ordinary legal exceptions. According to the courts, the contracts' connections to slavery did not disqualify them. Emancipation had invalidated their rights to own property in people but not to *contract* for the sale of an enslaved person. To many judges, the contracts were, in the words of Giuliana Perrone, "matters of established commercial law doctrine (law related to business and trade, including contracts) and they treated them like any other contract." As long as sellers or creditors to whom money was owed had performed their end of the bargain by delivering an enslaved person to the buyer (or debtor), the contracts remained valid because they were consistent with laws in effect when they were executed. Some judges even pointed out that purchasers of enslaved people could have protected themselves from this contingency by writing a warranty into the contract that provided for indemnity in the event of government-sponsored emancipation. Their failure to do so meant that the contract was still valid and that the buyer was liable for their debt.[18]

Judges upheld these contracts, too, because contracts represented for many the foundation of American freedoms. Americans extolled the inviolability of contracts not only out of financial interest and adherence to the Constitution but also because many believed that a person's ability to enter into a contractual relationship was constitutive of their liberty as an American citizen. Creditors and their allies insisted that outstanding contracts for the value of enslaved people be paid, and they also pointed out (probably correctly) that repudiating such contracts would exacerbate, not solve, Southern indebtedness.[19]

If states could not violate the contracts clause and courts would not remedy their losses, debtors reasoned, perhaps the federal government would. In August 1865, a group of forty-five petitioners calling themselves "Louisiana Citizens" had written to President Andrew Johnson, informing him that local courts were upholding outstanding contracts for the mortgage or sale of Black people and thus recognizing "a right to that kind of property." Legal arguments based in contract law were clearly failing debtors, so the Louisiana Citizens emphasized their loyalty to the United States. They had complied with all federal policies regarding emancipation, they insisted, and cast courts and creditors as disloyal. They accused the courts of ignoring "the proclamations and laws of Congress declaring slaves free and no longer property." The petitioners implied that Johnson should do something to nullify outstanding debts for enslaved people because the federal government had already abolished slavery.[20] By distancing themselves from rebellion and disloyalty, the Louisiana Citizens suggested they were worthy of federal support and aligned all creditors with the rebellious Confederacy.

The Louisiana Citizens also tried to convince Johnson that he had the authority to nullify outstanding debts for slaves as an extension of the war powers that had ended slavery. They pointed out that the military, at the bidding of the president, had destroyed slavery by war, and so, too, should the president destroy all monetary obligations yet owed for the value of freed people. However, President Johnson was no more certain than state officials that he could or should respond to debtors' petitions. He avoided any action and referred the Louisiana petition to the War Department, and on October 12, 1865, Judge Advocate General Joseph Holt replied. The "military authorities can neither legally nor with any justice or propriety afford any remedy," Holt recommended, implying that Johnson could take no further action because courts had jurisdiction over questions regarding contracts. Holt's determination prevented the executive branch from intervening in these cases, even under the pretense of war powers.[21]

But when Congress passed the first Reconstruction Act in March 1867, it gave debtors new and unexpected avenues for relief. After Southern states refused to ratify the Fourteenth Amendment, Congress split the former Confederacy into five military districts and established a plan to reorganize the states' civil governments through military occupation. One new avenue for relief was the US military. Between November 1867 and February 1869, two generals of the Second Military District of the Carolinas issued orders intervening in cases regarding debts for the value of the enslaved. On April 11, 1867, in General Orders No. 10, General Daniel Sickles introduced several debt relief measures to North and South Carolina and prevented courts from hearing cases regarding debts for the value of enslaved people sold after South Carolina's secession in December 1860. When Sickles was removed from his position as commander of the Second Military District for unrelated reasons, his successor, General Edward Canby, announced that he would maintain General Orders No. 10. On December 31, 1867, Canby issued a modified version, General Orders No. 164, and stipulated that courts could not hear cases about debts for enslaved people sold after January 1, 1863, when the Emancipation Proclamation went into effect.[22] The orders created more confusion than resolution. Many denounced them, including North Carolina's governor, and military headquarters received numerous letters pleading for both relief and clarification of how the orders would play out.[23]

Debtors hoped for more help from the federal government than Sickles, Canby, or President Johnson gave. Without it, they turned to a second avenue for relief: the upcoming state constitutional conventions. Under the Reconstruction Acts, each former Confederate state (except Tennessee, which had already been admitted to the Union) would convene a second constitutional convention, and unlike the 1865 conventions, Black men could vote for delegates and serve as delegates themselves. When a state ratified its new constitution and the Fourteenth Amendment, Congress would lift the occupation and readmit the state into the Union. Debtors took advantage of new opportunities to undermine the courts and invalidate outstanding contracts for the value of enslaved people. Like the Louisiana citizens, they used these opportunities to portray all debtors as loyal victims of rebel creditors and forward new arguments that section 4 of the Fourteenth Amendment invalidated both public claims for compensation and private contracts for the value of enslaved people.

With broad support for repudiation in these congressional Reconstruction conventions, each state considered invalidating outstanding contracts for the value of enslaved people. When they convened between early November 1867 and February 1869, six of the ten states that held conventions produced constitutions that contained provisions or ordinances denying the enforceability of contracts for property in humans and preventing courts from hearing cases regarding outstanding debts for enslaved people (Alabama, Arkansas, Florida, Georgia, Louisiana, and South Carolina). The constitutions of Virginia, North Carolina, Mississippi, and Texas did not contain such measures, although with the exception of North Carolina, each did consider resolutions or ordinances on the topic that made it to the floor of each state's convention.[24]

To justify delegates' intervention, debtors and their allies worked hard to align the project of financial relief with antislavery and Republican principles. Convention delegates in Alabama, Arkansas, Florida, Georgia, Louisiana, and South Carolina succeeded in nullifying outstanding debts for the value of the enslaved, even as the effort failed elsewhere, because many delegates favored extensive debt relief measures in general. Particularly in state conventions such as South Carolina's, where moderates and Republicans allied to win the support of white citizens who owned small pieces of land and extend the legacies of emancipation, delegates overwhelmingly supported constitutional measures to invalidate outstanding contracts for the value of enslaved people along with other debt relief measures. In comparison to other states, South Carolina's delegation lacked any organized conservative or factional opposition, and delegates had a diverse mix of socioeconomic perspectives. South Carolina's interracial alliance succeeded in invalidating these contracts partly with appeals to natural law. Black delegates and white allies born in the North, especially, understood repudiating these contracts as a transformation of US law more than a violation of the Constitution's contracts clause. Echoing antebellum abolitionist arguments rooted in natural law, they held that despite legal customs that defined them as property, enslaved people had always been subjects and it had always been immoral and thus illegal to contract for their sale.[25]

Debt repudiation, particularly invalidating contracts for the value of enslaved people, served both moderate white Southerners' and Black politicians' purposes. As regards the first group, the new state governments and Republicans shaped economic legislation to win the support of the white upcountry, where people were very indebted. Many Southern politicians held out the promise of canceling debts to entice indebted white voters to participate in the elections for convention delegates and, later, to ratify the new state constitutions themselves.[26] As regards the second group, repudiation of contracts for the value of enslaved people satisfied many Black voters and politicians and white abolitionists, who declared that enslaved people *should never have been* property under the law. Other Republicans joined Black politicians to support repudiating outstanding contracts for the value of slaves as one policy that would help fulfill the promise of emancipation. Since debtor relief was a major part of the Republican Party platform, Black politicians supported relief from these outstanding contracts to strengthen the party, even

Delegate Jonathan J. Wright would become the first Black justice on the Supreme Court of South Carolina in 1870, having defeated fellow delegate William J. Whipper in the election. *Harper's Weekly*, March 5, 1870. Harp Week.

though few Black constituents benefited directly. Black delegates often had their own diverse agendas, and many hoped to realize them by allying with white politicians and supporting their priorities, such as halting reprisals against Confederates and other relief measures that protected landowners.[27]

Some of South Carolina's delegates also insisted that the Reconstruction Acts and the Fourteenth Amendment required them to invalidate outstanding contracts for the value of enslaved people despite the contracts clause. South Carolina delegates cited General Orders No. 10 as a precedent for the nullification of these contracts, albeit a shaky one that critics decried as the mandate of a despotic "military chieftain."[28] Section 4 of the Fourteenth Amendment held particular interpretive promise. Delegate Jonathan J. Wright, a lawyer from Pennsylvania who had made his name in the Colored Conventions and the American Missionary Association, read extensive power into section 4, holding that it already "repudiates all claims for slaves" because it voided "any debt or obligation incurred in aid of" the Confederacy and stipulated that "all such debts, obligations and claims shall be held illegal and void." Since Congress required former Confederate states to ratify the amendment, Wright wanted delegates to believe that they had to invalidate these contracts in order to receive congressional approval for their new constitution. That congressional approval would, in turn, enable the state to bypass the Constitution's contracts clause, which only applied to the states.[29]

Delegates could mobilize section 4 of the Fourteenth Amendment as the mechanism by which the United States prevented enslavers from receiving compensation to unite their legal and economic claims. Many viewed repudiation as a necessary consequence of uncompensated emancipation, insisting that section 4 applied to private debts. Landon S. Langley, for example, a Black Vermonter who worked for the Freedmen's Bureau in Beaufort County, argued that South Carolina had to nullify contracts for the value of enslaved people precisely *because* the federal government had not reimbursed enslavers. He acknowledged that "both seller and purchaser are equally guilty" of trading in people, and that it was once legal to do so. Presumably, if the federal government had reimbursed enslavers, then debtors would have been able to pay back their debts and would not require relief. Therefore, uncompensated emancipation was unjust unless former enslavers' outstanding debts for slaves were also repudiated. A few other delegates across the former Confederacy shared Langley's view. A delegate in Mississippi, former planter Joseph W. Field, encouraged his fellow delegates to void all indebtedness for property in people because the actions of Mississippi and the United States—beyond the buyer's or seller's control—had abolished slavery. A failed Virginia resolution was proposed on the same grounds that the federal government might have compensated enslavers, but since it did not, the financial burden of emancipation was now unfairly falling on debtors.[30]

Pulling from section 4 allowed delegates to offer a new interpretation based in constitutional law that did not fit within the traditional rules of contract law. There was fundamental disagreement about the meaning of the last sentence of section 4, but delegates nevertheless mapped the contract question onto constitutional law to challenge the validity of debts for enslaved people based on principles of justice or fairness. Nevertheless, this new interpretation did not garner widespread support. Mississippi's finalized constitution did not contain a provision to nullify contracts for the value of enslaved people, but it did void claims for compensation, determining that Mississippi would never "in any manner claim from the United States, or make any allowance or compensation for slaves emancipated or liberated in any way whatever since the 9th day of January, 1861." The Virginia convention's Judiciary Committee denied the convention's authority to interfere with such contracts.[31] The Virginia and Mississippi conventions ultimately limited the scope of emancipation to enslavers' property rights alone and endeavored to end the conversation there.³²

Relief measures succeeded in South Carolina and five other states not in arguments over legal doctrine but because repudiationists managed to convince enough people that debtors were loyal, innocent victims of uncompensated emancipation. In South Carolina, many repudiationists imagined all creditors as evil human traffickers or rebels and all debtors as innocents. By these arguments, the enslaver was transformed into the debtor and the two identities were set in spurious opposition to each other. Many South Carolina delegates fashioned all creditors as disloyal slave traders who took advantage of Southern Christians. William J. Whipper, a Philadelphia-born Black lawyer from a prominent abolitionist family, explained that a debt for the value of an enslaved person should not "be paid to the men who traded all his life in slave property, who made their money by it." Delegate Whipper said that to assist these slave traders "in recovering their property" (or, more specifically, the value of their property), did not "comport with" his "idea of Christianity."³³

Arguments about slave traders also played into the sectional conflict over slavery. Wright told South Carolina delegates that slave traders were not Southerners but "came from the Northeast and the West," sailed into Southern ports "with vessels bringing a cargo of slaves, sold them to the people of the South, put what money they could in their pockets, and went back where they belonged." These politicians suggested that while buying a person was a neutral business act, trading in humans for a profession was immoral. Elsewhere, including in Congress, debtors and their allies accused creditors of being traitors to the Union who deserved to "pay the penalty of their rebellion." Such arguments implied that slave traders had caused the war by perpetuating the trade in Black bodies.³⁴ They also referenced the same wartime conceptions of loyalty that section 4 of the Fourteenth Amendment reinforced. Politicians aligned private debts for the value of enslaved people with debts that aided rebellion—a kind of public debt prohibited from repayment by section 4. No loyal person, they implied, would seek to profit from property in people.

This vilification of creditors and slave traders was effective because it echoed the same accusations that abolitionists and enslavers had leveled at them before the war. Abolitionists and evangelical Christians of the Upper South had both protested that slave traders separated families, kidnapped free people, and raped or enabled the rape of enslaved women. This discourse highlighted the inhumanity of the slave trade and fabricated a sectional divide that hid non-slave states' complicity in the vast entangled economy of human bondage. Even enslavers could distance themselves from those evils. Slave buyers often accused traders of tricking them during a sale by disguising an enslaved person's diseases, criminality, and history of rebellion.[35]

During Reconstruction, opponents of repudiation were skeptical that buyers were somehow less complicit in the slave trade than sellers. The Southern institution of slavery was a complex local economy. The debtors and creditors negotiating the postwar economy were probably all enslavers, and they may well have been the same people. As historians Bonnie Martin and Richard Kilbourne have shown, other local enslavers, not solely banks or professional traders, provided significant sources of credit for those who purchased enslaved people. After the Civil War, the same neighbors and families who had lent money to each other to purchase enslaved people now had no cash and few means to pay off their own outstanding debts.[36] Opponents also noted the hypocrisy of slave buyers in stories of slave traders' corruption. Manuel Simeon Corley, a former Confederate soldier who opposed repudiation, asked a key question: "Is there any difference between the seller and buyer in a moral sense?" He elaborated, "If the act of the speculator in the bones and muscles of man was criminal, that of the purchaser was equally, and even more so." Corley concluded that there was "no good reason" to deny the seller's right to collect the debt, notwithstanding that enslavers' "pious clamor now denounces the contract as an outrage upon justice and right."[37]

To create the impression of moral difference, the South Carolina delegates also gendered all debtors as women to portray them as worthy innocents who deserved financial relief. Delegate Whipper feared that enforcing the payment of outstanding debts for the sale of enslaved people "would only distress, in great part, the young or helpless women and children who had no control or hand in this business, who had nothing left but their homes, and who, if these executions are enforced, will be thrown out of doors upon the cold charities of the world." Whipper and his colleagues suggested that women and children who claimed ownership over enslaved people were exempt from the sins of their husbands and fathers and argued that the state had a duty to void these contracts to protect widows and orphans from creditors.[38]

However, these arguments were as misleading in 1868 as they were when they were introduced in the 1865 conventions during debates over compensation. A white delegate, James M. Rutland, opposed repudiation and was befuddled. He thought the appeal on behalf of widows and orphans "would come more properly from my side."[39] Rutland was correct—many white widows and orphans were more likely to be owed money for the value of an enslaved person than owe money *for* them. Families claiming enslaved people often sold up to 80 percent of those they claimed ownership over after a patriarch died. Consequently, executors of estates and family members were prominent as creditors in cases concerning debts for the enslaved. And since the 1840s in some of the states considering repudiation, the property that women brought into a marriage—often enslaved people—had both informal and formal legal protection from their husbands' debt obligations. Many Southern households protected their investments by buying enslaved people with a wife's dowry to insulate them in case of a patriarch's bankruptcy. If the patriarch found himself in financial trouble, no creditor could collect on enslaved people claimed by his wife or children because the patriarch did not legally own them. Therefore, many white women might have had substantial investments in enslaved people after emancipation that would be worthless if the convention repudiated outstanding contracts for the value of enslaved people. As in the 1865 conventions, delegates mobilized these moral arguments to conform to the politics of dependency. By appearing to support dependents, the delegates legitimized their own political mission and the convention as a whole.[40]

Though specious, these moral arguments echoed the conversations Southerners had about compensating former enslavers. They helped delegates establish the need for measures invalidating contracts for the value of enslaved people, despite the convention's questionable authority to do so. The South Carolina convention approved a new constitution with a measure invalidating these outstanding contracts, which voters ratified on March 17, 1868. However, the conventions only had so much power. Congress, not Southern voters, had the final say on the state's constitution. A few months later, Congress debated whether it would accept the constitutions of North Carolina, South Carolina, Louisiana, Georgia, and Alabama and readmit those states into the Union with an omnibus bill.

Congress had little to say about these measures. It was not clear from public debates on section 4 of the Fourteenth Amendment whether its framers intended to void outstanding debts for slaves. In 1868, congressmen found Georgia's constitution particularly vexing because its debt relief clauses were far-reaching, nullifying most debts contracted before July 1, 1865. To the extent that Congress addressed the measure repudiating contracts for the value of enslaved people, many congressional Republicans adopted the natural law argument that enslaved people never should have been property under the law. Republicans tended to oppose debt relief measures, but they supported this and other repudiation measures because they, like some Georgians, agreed that they would help dissatisfied Georgians accept universal manhood suffrage.[41]

Congressional Republicans also modified Georgia's debt relief measure to maintain one goal of section 4: to ensure that disloyal Georgians shouldered the costs of emancipation. Savvy Southern creditors had often appealed to federal politicians to enforce outstanding contracts for the value of enslaved people based on their loyalty. North and South Carolina creditors had denounced General Sickles's General Orders No. 10 and went over Sickles's head to protest the measures, claiming that they and many "others, who are guiltless, and who had no hand in causing and carrying on the late 'wicked rebellion,'" were unfairly maligned by them.[42] In 1868, Georgians wrote to Congressman Thaddeus Stevens, urging him to reject the debt relief clauses because most creditors in Georgia were Unionists. Consistent with Congress's use of loyalty claims during the drafting of the Fourteenth Amendment, Congress added new language to the Georgia measure that repudiated contracts for the value of enslaved people. The measure now ensured that debts due to "any person who, during the whole time of the rebellion, was loyal to the United States and opposed secession" were paid.[43]

By editing only Georgia's constitution to exempt loyal creditors, Congress showed surprising restraint. As South Carolina delegates had argued and the Georgia Supreme Court would later, Congress's approval of the new state constitutions' measures invalidating outstanding contracts for the value of enslaved people could override the US Constitution's contracts clause, which applied only to states, because an act of Congress ultimately made them law. Furthermore, Congress could have passed a law invalidating these contracts altogether. Senator Charles Sumner tried in 1869. He proposed a bill in the Senate that would have nullified any promissory note for the value of an enslaved person or enforcement of a contract for their value but preserved the value of a note held by a third party who did not know its value was based on the value of a formerly enslaved person. The bill also stipulated that any court that heard a case regarding an obligation for the value of an enslaved person had to dismiss the suit and repealed all acts that conflicted with the bill. As legal scholar Andrew Kull found, the bill was referred to the Judiciary Committee and "never heard from again."[44]

Without additional records, it is difficult to say definitively why Congress or other federal officials did not act. Many viewed the repudiation debates as a matter of Union versus Confederate, and Congress expected disloyal Southerners to bear the financial burden of emancipation. Section 4 of the

Fourteenth Amendment was proof of congressmen's stance on that sectional divide.[45] Still, Congress did not address Southerners' suggestions that Section 4 could apply to private debts as well as public, which would have had ramifications for any American who held a debt for an enslaved person, including Northerners and loyalists. Furthermore, Sumner's bill would have been difficult to enforce, especially the measure preserving the value of a note for an unaware third party, and the section repealing all conflicting acts was unpredictable. In theory, Congress could have justified the bill with section 2 of the Thirteenth Amendment, which gave it the power to enforce emancipation with "appropriate legislation." Even the Supreme Court had recently acknowledged the power of Congress to exercise legislative power to "give full effect to the abolition of slavery" under this section in *United States v. Rhodes* (1866).[46]

Likely, Congress chose to leave these questions to the courts. Republican ideology rested on the idea that a person's liberty rested on their right to sell their labor in fair and voluntary contracts, a right that the United States had defended throughout the Civil War and Reconstruction as a constitutional right protected by the due process clause. Though the validity of contracts and the freedom to contract were distinct legal theories recognized by different sections of the Constitution, these ideas remained fundamental to nineteenth-century politicians' worldviews. For many moderates in the Republican and Democratic Parties, Reconstruction meant expanding the freedom to contract to freed people, not necessarily challenging legal traditions or notions of liberty. However, Republicans pursued repudiation for outstanding contracts for the value of enslaved people at the state level because the platform helped them build interracial, class-based coalitions that contributed to the Republican Party's electoral successes in the former Confederacy.[47] Rather than clarify legal questions surrounding uncompensated emancipation, their efforts created new conflicts between state and federal law.

Adjudicating Section 4 of the Fourteenth Amendment

When it avoided a debate about outstanding contracts for the value of enslaved people, Congress opened section 4 of the Fourteenth Amendment to judicial scrutiny. The six state constitutions' measures invalidating these contracts created more confusion than they resolved. With different precedents across the South, creditors challenged the new measures in state courts. They also challenged debtors' arguments about uncompensated emancipation's effects on such contracts and lawmakers' interpretation of the Fourteenth

Amendment. By 1870, the highest courts of Georgia, Florida, Arkansas, Louisiana, and South Carolina had heard cases that contested their constitutional provisions. In three of those five states (Arkansas, Florida, and South Carolina), high courts rejected sections of the states' 1868 constitutions that nullified contracts for the value of enslaved people. Around the same time, West Virginia's Supreme Court considered whether a creditor could seize their debtor's land to collect on a debt for an enslaved person. In many of their rulings, judges considered not only the legality of repudiation but also slave law and uncompensated emancipation. Although the ratification of the Fourteenth Amendment on July 9, 1868, had already made compensation unconstitutional when these cases were handed down, a few judges used former enslavers' earlier claims for compensation to justify their judgments for or against the repudiation of outstanding contracts for the value of enslaved people.[48]

The state-level cases were the first to consider the validity of section 4. Whether or not they favored repudiation, some Southern judges suggested—similar to Judge Robertson in Kentucky—that uncompensated emancipation violated eminent domain. A dissenting judge in Arkansas, John McClure, argued that wartime emancipation in Arkansas invalidated contracts for the value of enslaved people, and he asked how else advocates of the Thirteenth Amendment could explain that the state could abolish property rights in people without just compensation if "the same power, in the same manner, is without authority to destroy all right of property in *notes* founded upon the *sale or purchase of slaves*?" Another judge revived the argument that the Fifth Amendment's takings clause should have guaranteed that those who claimed ownership over humans received compensation upon emancipation. Though he upheld the validity of the disputed contracts, Justice James H. Brown of West Virginia suggested that former enslavers could pay off their debts by claiming compensation from their state, "whose constitution authorizes no act of legislation which impairs the obligation of contracts nor the taking of private property for public use without just compensation."[49]

Postwar conceptions of loyalty once again proved to be important factors for decision-makers. Both Brown and McClure were Unionists at the outbreak of the war. Brown was a Virginia Democrat who nevertheless opposed secession. He became one of the leaders in the formation of West Virginia, served as a delegate to the 1861 Wheeling Convention and in the legislature of the Restored Government of Virginia, and, in 1863, was elected to the West Virginia Supreme Court. McClure had defended the United States as a former army officer and agent of the Freemen's Bureau. During Reconstruction, Brown echoed Unionist Southerners of 1865 who sought direct compensation from the federal government, while McClure argued that voiding outstanding contracts for the value of enslaved people was a logical outcome of uncompensated emancipation. Their decision and dissent dodged any outright opposition to wartime emancipation as it unfolded yet maintained their commitment to federal authority as Unionists.[50] They sought a resolution to the legal questions at hand that acknowledged the financial losses of white Southerners while reconciling the legal irregularities and postwar realities of wartime emancipation.

Georgia's supreme court was eager to challenge federal emancipation under Chief Justice Joseph E. Brown, whose loyalties were notoriously slippery. Throughout the Civil War and Reconstruction, Brown consistently supported pro-debtor policies. A pro-slavery Democrat before the war, he supported small farmers and championed many relief measures. He became governor of Georgia in 1857 and continued in that office until the collapse of the Confederacy in 1865. He had favored secession but resisted the centralized authority of the Confederate government during the war and clashed with Confederate president Jefferson Davis over many policies, most notably the draft, the army's impressment of goods and services, and, in particular, enslaved laborers. He believed that a centralized government should protect, not tax or impress, citizens' property. In the immediate aftermath of the war, Brown played a prominent role in bringing Georgia back into the United States and crafting a white supremacist political strategy. He joined the Republican Party after a brief stint as a political prisoner and hoped to realign Southern politics by appealing to centrist voters.[51]

Brown continued to advocate for repudiation in his role as Georgia's chief justice and wrote the opinion for an 1869 case, *Shorter v. Cobb*, which was one of the few cases to uphold its state constitution's repudiation measures. In *Shorter*, Brown argued that the state's constitutional measure invalidating outstanding contracts for the value of slaves did not violate the US Constitution's contracts clause because it was created after secession and approved by an act of Congress. His argument depended on his view of secession. The Confederacy, he argued, as Radicals in Congress did, had legally seceded but became conquered territory after Confederate defeat. Therefore, the state did not exist under the stipulations of the US Constitution until it was readmitted by Congress. Ironically, Brown concluded that Georgia's secession actually gave it the legal authority to override the contracts clause.[52]

Using this theory of secession, Brown challenged the federal government to maintain the validity of outstanding contracts for the value of enslaved people without paying enslavers the value of freed slaves. He applauded

Georgians—inaccurately—for abolishing slavery at federal demand without asking for compensation. He asked whether uncompensated emancipation would be legal if Georgia had remained, theoretically, in the Union and "the property of the slave-holder in his slave was guaranteed by the Constitution and laws of the United States." If Georgia could abolish slavery without compensating enslavers, then couldn't its government invalidate outstanding contracts for the value of now-freed people? Brown evoked no specific constitutional clause, such as the Fifth Amendment's takings clause; however, he suggested that Georgia was not bound to respect the validity of contracts for human property if it was not bound to respect enslavers' property rights in people.[53]

Even while embracing Radical ideas about secession, Brown challenged Congress's loyalty litmus tests to determine postwar law and policy. He rejected Congress's changes to Georgia's constitution ensuring that debtors met their obligations to loyal creditors. Loyal enslavers' property rights, Brown insisted, were no more or less "legally sacred" than other creditors' rights to recover debts. It would be unjust, he argued, to reward some for loyalty and punish others who nevertheless abolished slavery without compensating enslavers.[54] Though willing to confront the inconsistencies of wartime emancipation policy and claim state authority to regulate these contracts, Brown also wanted to end what he viewed as erroneous and politically charged legal decisions based on wartime categories for citizenship, like loyalty.

Another judge offered more comprehensive legal arguments on section 4 of the Fourteenth Amendment, suggesting that it justified repudiation. In the federal circuit court of the eastern district of Arkansas, Judge Henry Clay Caldwell upheld the state's constitutional measure invalidating contracts for the value of enslaved people on the grounds that the Thirteenth Amendment destroyed property rights in people and the Fourteenth Amendment invalidated any debt or obligation for freed people. In *Osborn v. Nicholson*, Caldwell determined that Congress had added section 4 to prevent any legislature from appropriating funds to reimburse those who claimed to own people. He acknowledged that there was ambiguity about whether section 4 applied to individuals or states; however, he insisted, "the spirit of the constitution" was clear, which meant that the fourth section enabled Arkansas to repudiate outstanding contracts for the value of enslaved people. To do otherwise, he said, would be to make the Constitution as much a "violation of right, reason, and justice" as the slave codes themselves.[55] As clear as the spirit of the amendment was to Caldwell and South Carolina delegates who argued similarly in their constitutional convention, he was one of the only judges to interpret section 4 this way.

Why was Caldwell one of the only jurists to interpret the Fourteenth Amendment so broadly? The related US Supreme Court cases offer some answers. Like Congress and the presidency before it, the Supreme Court was wary of making any legal decision that could change the settled outcomes of the war. But it was also wary of allowing wartime policies and practices to change practiced law and federalism. The Supreme Court rejected Caldwell's interpretation of section 4 as it applied to outstanding contracts, but not his interpretation of uncompensated emancipation. While convention delegates and some Southern judges tried to make sense of the effects of the war on the law, the Supreme Court suggested that the federal government carried out emancipation with temporary wartime powers. The court tried to peel away from its determination anything outside the letter of preexisting antebellum law and the Reconstruction amendments. As Cynthia Nicoletti put it, the court upheld the "verdict" of the war—including uncompensated emancipation—but not much else.[56]

The US Supreme Court took up three cases regarding outstanding debts for the value of enslaved people. In 1871, the court struck down the clauses in Georgia's and Arkansas's 1868 constitutions that nullified contracts for the value of enslaved people in its *White v. Hart* and *Osborn v. Nicholson* decisions. In its 1873 decision, *Boyce v. Tabb*, the court also overturned Louisiana's provision nullifying such contracts.[57] These cases rejected arguments that section 4 of the Fourteenth Amendment enabled states to invalidate such contracts.

Justice Noah Haynes Swayne mobilized not only the contracts clause but also the principle of eminent domain to argue that emancipation affected only the title to an enslaved person. He reasoned in *Osborn*, as many Southern judges had before him, that enslavers' claims to own enslaved people "were lost . . . by the paramount act of the State, which neither party anticipated, and in regard to which the contract was silent." He compared emancipation to eminent domain. He argued that "contracts are inherently subject to the paramount power of the sovereign" and that sellers were not liable for subsequent acts of the state, such as eminent domain or emancipation. "Emancipation and the eminent domain work the same result as regards the title and possession of the owner," he concluded. "Both are put an end to."[58]

By comparing emancipation and eminent domain, Swayne suggested that an existing legal precedent—eminent domain—could direct the court's decision in an unprecedented wartime event—emancipation. However, Swayne did not say that emancipation transferred the title for a slave to the federal government, nor did he argue that the Constitution's takings clause gave former enslavers a right to compensation. Nor did Swayne mention section 4 of the Fourteenth Amendment, which would have invalidated enslavers' claims even if Swayne had affirmed their right to them. Instead, Swayne avoided a conversation about section 4 and wrote in *Osborn* that emancipation was an act of the state justified for public ends during the war. His determination was consistent with early-nineteenth-century interpretations of regulatory takings at the state level, which held that all property was retained at the sufferance of the sovereign government, as well as Republican emancipation policy during the war.[59] The decision maintained that the United States could abolish slavery without compensating former enslavers for their property in people as an outcome of the war and Reconstruction.

Swayne also intimated in *White* that former enslavers in rebelling states had little recourse to challenge immediate, uncompensated emancipation. Swayne said that residents of Confederate states were still citizens, but they were "guilty" of offending the sovereign government. Therefore, their "political rights may be put in abeyance or forfeited." This reasoning overruled Georgia chief justice Joseph Brown's assertion that Georgia's secession granted the state or debtors the right to impair contracts because Georgia was not beholden to the laws of the United States. It also reinforced Congress's actions punishing enslavers for their rebellion, such as forcing former Confederate states to ratify the Fourteenth Amendment. By seceding, residents of former Confederate states forfeited any rights now prohibited by the new constitutional amendments. If former enslavers once had a right to compensation, they no longer did.[60]

Swayne otherwise avoided the sectional politics that influenced the repudiation debate. In response to moralizing arguments made by many state politicians about what debtors or creditors deserved, he added, "Whatever we may think of the institution of slavery viewed in the light of religion, morals, humanity, or a sound political economy, as the obligation here in question was valid when executed, sitting as a court of justice, we have no choice but to give it effect." Swayne evaded the legality of military emancipation measures, adding, "This opinion decides nothing as to the effect of President Lincoln's emancipation proclamation." While avoiding all these questions and issues, Swayne did stipulate that the decision to uphold contracts for the value of enslaved people was "necessary to the repose and welfare of all communities." However, here he vacillated. After suggesting that the moral and political-economic questions surrounding the institution of slavery were beside the point, he nevertheless insisted that upholding contracts was necessary for economic stability. Swayne pushed aside debtors' financial concerns in favor of what he called the "repose and welfare" of their communities.[61]

Citing economic stability helped the court describe immediate emancipation as a noncompensable act for the public welfare and justify its decisions, but the economic outcomes of the repudiation debates were far from certain. Southerners were plagued by debt, but retroactively invalidating contracts and shifting the obligation to creditors would have merely shifted the financial losses of uncompensated emancipation. Whether or not paying their debt for the value of a person was legally required, it is unlikely that most debtors could pay their creditors, regardless of any court decision.[62] Instead, Swayne and the court hoped to build creditors' confidence in the Southern economy. They speculated that validating outstanding contracts for the value of enslaved people would stabilize the economy by reinforcing the sanctity of contracts and thus encourage investment.

Although the court's action reinforced the main objective of section 4, Chief Justice Salmon P. Chase's dissent suggested, like Caldwell, that section 4 should be interpreted more broadly to include debts for the value of slaves. Chase dissented on the grounds that Swayne's opinion contradicted the principles of the Fourteenth Amendment. Considering his long antislavery career, it is unsurprising that Chase interpreted the Thirteenth and Fourteenth Amendments much more broadly than Swayne. He held that contracts for the sale of property in people "were and are against sound morals and natural justice" and that the Thirteenth Amendment voided them when it abolished slavery itself: By that action, it annulled all the piecemeal laws that had made the trade in human property possible. Chase also asserted that section 4 "can be vindicated only on these principles." In declining health while he wrote the dissent, Chase gave little further explanation for why he interpreted section 4 that way, and his dissent left unexplored his legal rationale regarding the Fourteenth Amendment. Nevertheless, his dissent echoed his prewar writings. Before the Civil War, Chase and Charles Sumner advocated for federal antislavery policies on the basis that the Fifth Amendment superseded any pro-slavery clauses in the Constitution and state laws by restricting Congress from depriving *any person* of life, liberty, or property without due process of law. Chase argued that enslaved people never were property under the law; therefore, enslavers had no right to compensation and all contracts for the value of enslaved people had always been invalid. Thus, no debt for the value of an enslaved person should be paid.[63]

Chase's view was a radical one, and Swayne and the court majority were unwilling to allow the Thirteenth and Fourteenth Amendments to change most federalist traditions. As the court majority ruled, section 4 of the Fourteenth Amendment worked exactly as the framers of the Fourteenth Amendment intended: to forestall any claims to reimburse enslavers. The majority defended immediate, uncompensated emancipation, but nevertheless maintained that enslaved people had always been property recognized by federal law, even during the war. The court's *White* and *Osborn* decisions effectively limited the powers of the Thirteenth and Fourteenth Amendments to titles for enslaved people, and not to contracts for their sale and value. Like debtors and their allies, historians, too, have regretted that Swayne's decision limited abolition to the legal destruction of property rights in people, not the system in contracts and commerce that undergirded those property rights. As historians such as Perrone have argued, the court's decisions avoided the complicated and often contradictory political arguments at hand.[64]

However, when we place these court cases in the political contexts of Reconstruction and the compensated emancipation debates, the historical picture is more complex than this denunciation of justices' limited moves. The scope of justices' decisions was already circumscribed by Americans' concerns about the economic effects of uncompensated emancipation on the Southern economy (as opposed to the opportunities and challenges freed people faced). Uncertain of which level or branch of government to turn to after political and legal upheaval, Southerners mobilized carefully crafted, often self-interested interpretations of uncompensated emancipation's effects on the law for financial gain. Many debtors and their allies portrayed themselves as victims of uncompensated emancipation at the same time that they mobilized the natural law argument of abolitionist opponents of compensated emancipation. Based on antebellum legal norms and postwar realities, these arguments were internally contradictory and clashed with formalistic legal reasoning. Nevertheless, politicians, judges, and US Army generals who sought to legitimize their own power grasped them to justify their own authority to avoid or address the postwar repudiation debates.

In the *White* and *Osborn* decisions, the Supreme Court rejected repudiationists' inconsistent arguments and determined that the federal judiciary would resolve the questions that uncompensated emancipation had caused. Even while it ruled according to the basic text of the Thirteenth Amendment and section 4 of the Fourteenth Amendment, the court and other branches of the federal government refused to legitimize any alternative reading that could change how the private right to contract—the bedrock of American liberty—was regulated in the federalist system. Arguably, this is what congressional Republicans had intended when they added section 4 to the Constitution: that the amendment could deflect any challenges to immediate, uncompensated wartime emancipation in the courts and ensure that the financial burden of emancipation fell on the former Confederacy.[65] By refusing to intervene in political debates about outstanding contracts for the value of enslaved people, delimiting the meaning of section 4, and upholding the validity of these contracts, the court and US policymakers bet that immediate, uncompensated emancipation, with support for industry through a stable contract law regime, would reconstruct the Southern economy.

NEITHER THE FOURTEENTH AMENDMENT nor the Supreme Court rulings silenced political movements for compensation. As the *New National Era* warned, white Southerners never relinquished their desire for compensation. Take, for example, the relationship between Harriet Berry, a freed woman from North Carolina who applied for a federal widow's pension in 1878, and her former enslaver, Martha Burgess. Berry had married her husband, Joseph, in 1863 with the permission of those who enslaved them, celebrating with a party thrown by a relative of Harriet's enslaver. Shortly thereafter, the couple escaped enslavement by running to freedom behind US Army lines in Norfolk, Virginia. There, Joseph enlisted in the United States Colored Troops, dying after only a year in service. When Harriet applied for her pension almost fifteen years later, the clerk of court who reviewed her application contacted her former enslaver to sign a statement corroborating her wartime history and relationship with Joseph. Burgess refused to cooperate, replying, "I don't know why I should sign anything for her to get money [from the government], she run away from me and I never got anything for her."[66] Despite Burgess's attempts to thwart the pension application, Berry did receive a pension after other former enslavers in her community corroborated her story and cast suspicion on Burgess's testimony. Nevertheless, Burgess's refusal to testify on behalf of Berry reflected not only her desire to be reimbursed for the value she once claimed over Berry but also the relationship between white supremacist political rhetoric and compensation: Former enslavers viewed compensated emancipation as an entitlement that they should receive before Black people gained any of the rights of citizenship and aid from states or the federal government—everything from public education to widows' pensions.

Most Southern families who had claimed enslaved people recovered their financial losses within one generation after emancipation, but this sense of loss and entitlement lingered.⁶⁷ Even as the immediate economic need for compensation dwindled, white Southerners only abandoned their claims when they became politically inexpedient. White Southern politicians soon realized that their attempts to secure compensation and recoup the losses of uncompensated emancipation attracted unwanted attention to the national legacies of slavery and the Civil War in national politics. Hamstrung by Republicans waving the bloody shirt, they needed to reconsider their claims in order to face regional and national challenges to the Democratic Party. Chapter 6 explains why white Southerners eventually relinquished their claims for compensation and how historians minimized their claims in the historical record.

CHAPTER SIX

Writing Uncompensated Emancipation into the Lost Cause

By the early 1900s, historians began to downplay white Southerners' claims for compensation. In his 1901 history of Reconstruction in Mississippi, James Wilford Garner acknowledged that some Mississippians had hoped the United States would eventually compensate former enslavers. However, he qualified, "Few... allowed themselves to be seduced by such a hope, and even the most hopeful soon abandoned it." In 1915, historian C. Mildred Thompson quoted but did not discuss Georgia's 1865 constitutional amendment abolishing slavery while maintaining former enslavers' right to compensation. According to historian Joseph Grégoire de Roulhac Hamilton, a committee in North Carolina's legislature tasked with reporting on the Fourteenth Amendment called section 4 "useless." Writing in 1914, he said, "In regard to compensation for the slaves, the committee thought it injustice, but declared that the people of the South had never expected to be paid for them." Benjamin B. Kendrick, historian of the Fourteenth Amendment, called section 4 unnecessary "political buncombe."[1]

These historians who dismissed or denied white Southerners' desire for payments for the value of freed slaves were students of William Archibald Dunning. Dunning was a professor of history at Columbia University now known for training a generation of pro-Confederate historians who whitewashed the history of the Civil War and Reconstruction era. They argued that debates over slavery had not caused the war, explaining that slavery was an unprofitable institution that would have ended on its own had the Civil War not interfered. After Confederate defeat, their story went, white Southerners readily relinquished their property in people. Modern historians have debunked their interpretations, but these scholars' insistence that white Southerners accepted the immediate, uncompensated abolition of slavery maintained the long-standing myth that slavery was unprofitable.[2]

The Dunning School's pro-Confederate histories substantiated the Lost Cause myth that Confederate veterans and women perpetuated. In memoirs, travel journals, veterans' reunions, and the press, Confederate veterans debated the causes and consequences of the war. They fostered a "separate sectional identity," writes historian Caroline Janney, as a reaction and rebuke to

Reconstruction and a national memory that celebrated US victory as a just cause for the Union and freedom.[3] Confederates insisted their Lost Cause was also just. They defended secession and slavery, insisted that the Constitution protected slavery, and emphasized the entire nation's complicity with the institution. Some revived antebellum arguments that slavery was a positive good for both enslavers and the enslaved. Many Lost Cause advocates professed that the United States had violated the Constitution by inhibiting the expansion of slavery and secession, equating the right to own people with states' rights.

These histories also served an important political purpose in the early twentieth century: to legitimize the Lost Cause cultural narrative that maintained Democratic Party power throughout the South. Many historians have shown how Democrats used the Lost Cause as one of many tools of white supremacy to secure one-party rule by the beginning of the twentieth century.[4] This chapter adds that downplaying the question of compensating enslavers was integral to Lost Cause mythology. When they disregarded white Southerners' claims for compensation during and after the Civil War, Dunning School historians bolstered an already-existing narrative among former Confederate veterans that white Southerners never wanted or needed compensation.

However, it was not until the late 1890s that Confederate veterans developed the narrative that former enslavers never wanted compensation. Veterans began to articulate this narrative in response to growing political challenges to the Democratic Party. Even after the ratification of the Fourteenth Amendment, Republicans won national elections in the late 1860s and early 1870s by threatening that the Democratic Party would compensate enslavers. Southern Democrats relinquished their claims for compensation to avoid this bloody shirt campaigning on the national stage. White Southerners' claims for compensation diminished in the late 1870s and 1880s, but they never entirely disappeared. In the early 1890s, some third-party candidates revived plans to compensate enslavers, sometimes alongside the formerly enslaved, to challenge Democrats regionally. Though these politicians were part of a vocal minority, they emerged during hard economic times and at the same time that Black Southerners—some of whom were themselves the subjects of property claims by enslavers, or their relatives were—articulated complex relationships to enslavers' calls for compensation. One of these third-party politicians, John Williamson, even campaigned for Congress on a platform to reimburse both former enslavers and the formerly enslaved. Somewhat counterintuitively, former enslavers' claims for compensation supported Black activists' contention that the US government had protected enslavers' property rights in people, thereby enabling the nation as a whole to profit from slavery. The United States, they argued, owed the formerly enslaved for their stolen labor, if not also former enslavers for the harm of uncompensated emancipation.[5]

These seemingly diametrically opposed ideas came together in the 1890s. Proposals to pay enslavers and the formerly enslaved aimed to unite Southerners across racial and class lines and provide an influx of government funding when the region desperately needed economic stimulus. Though some Democrats supported calls for compensation to the formerly enslaved or former enslavers in order to build political alliances, most realized that they had to relinquish claims for compensation—and other wartime issues—to win national elections and stave off threats from third parties regionally. In a time of rapid economic and social change, they tried to downplay class divisions among white Southerners that would have threatened the Democratic Party's political control over the region.[6]

By 1900, Confederate veterans and white Southerners who celebrated Lost Cause traditions rewrote the failed history of compensated emancipation in the US South to elide the possibility that the war was fought to preserve the means of wealth of the planter class. Former Confederates insisted that they had fought the war to preserve their constitutional rights and that white Southerners never wanted or needed reimbursements for the value of freed people. To acknowledge otherwise would have implied that they had fought the Civil War to protect slavery, a suggestion they had come to vigorously deny. Instead, they insisted that states' rights, not slavery, had caused the Civil War.

By downplaying the profitability of slavery, former Confederates and Democrats diminished class antagonism among white Southerners in contemporary political movements and undermined Black Southerners' calls for payments for slavery. In turn, Lost Cause mythology helped Democrats win votes from elite and non-elite white Southerners and consolidate Democratic Party rule in the so-called Solid South. Assisted by pro-Confederate historians, Confederate veterans succeeded in deeply planting the fabrication that white Southerners never sought compensation in US history books for another half century and more. The persistence of compensation claims well beyond Confederate defeat in the Civil War and into the twentieth century corrects almost a century of forgetting.

No Reunion with Compensation

To understand the dilemmas facing Southern Democrats in the 1890s, we turn first to the presidential election of 1872, when white Southerners learned firsthand that they could no longer wield compensation to former enslavers as a political tool. Although some Southerners continued to propose paying former enslavers after the Fourteenth Amendment was ratified in 1868 and the *White* and *Osborn* decisions came down in 1871, only a few outlined specific plans for reimbursing former enslavers publicly. By 1869, conservative "Redeemers" began to take over Southern state governments. These politicians galvanized white Southerners and intimidated Republican officeholders, voters, and particularly Black Southerners to secure Democratic control of the South county by county. The Democratic Party initiated the "New Departure" in 1870, a platform that accepted the Reconstruction Amendments in an attempt to burnish their image and recapture the political center by concentrating on issues such as lower taxes and political reform. In turn, Republicans emphasized economic policy rather than social reforms, such as civil and political rights for African Americans.[7]

In the former Confederacy, Democrats grappled with Republicans for control of Black voters and centrist voters, who were often former Whigs and Unionists. Former Whigs and Unionists were still receptive to federal payments to former enslavers, and a few conservatives and Democrats wielded the promise of federal reimbursements for enslaved people in order to woo them. However, the tactic had its costs. In national elections, Republicans hoped to alienate centrists from the Democrats by threatening that Democrats would compensate former enslavers.[8]

These threats helped galvanize the Republican Party's base. Waving the bloody shirt, or blaming the white South for the war and reminding voters which party won it, Republicans insisted again that American taxpayers should not be accountable for the price of emancipation. Republicans acknowledged that the "South has financially paid very dearly for its rebellion," but they blamed white vigilante violence, rather than uncompensated emancipation, for the South's continuous economic woes. White Southerners terrorized Black citizens for exercising their political rights. Vigilantes targeted politically active and economically independent community members. Republicans learned from Black Southerners who testified in Congress that white violence traumatized them, jeopardized their financial futures, and stymied the Southern economy.[9]

These tensions between Democrats and Republicans, Black and white voters, and former Whigs and Unionists came to a head in the presidential election of 1872. The Liberal Republicans, a group of conservative Republican detractors, emerged as a centrist option for voters. Unlike Republicans, Liberal Republicans spoke out against the patronage and the spoils system, favored broad civil service reforms, and opposed currency reforms and protective tariffs, which they believed stemmed from the patronage system because they advantaged "special interests."[10] They disputed the first Grant administration's use of federal military power to confront white violence, and worried that Grant was pursuing military despotism in the South. After winning a few state-level elections during and after the Civil War, they started the national phase of their movement by nominating *New York Tribune* editor Horace Greeley to run against incumbent Ulysses S. Grant. Greeley, who had positioned himself as a "spokesman for the spirit of reunion" and amnesty since 1867, according to historian David Blight, promised to peacefully settle turmoil in the South and reinstate upright, legal state governments. Most realized that restoring legitimate state governments in the South meant granting amnesty to former Confederates and local self-government to white Democrats, who backed Liberal Republicans by nominating Greeley as their presidential candidate in July.[11]

The Democratic Party's support of Greeley disappointed those remaining Whigs and Unionists in the South, who sought alternative coalitions. In August, shortly after the Democrats endorsed Greeley, the *Richmond Whig*, a conservative paper, disparaged Democrats for aligning with Northerners. Southerners, the *Whig* claimed, had "common interests" in Southern unity. Its prime example was compensation for slavery—for both enslavers and the enslaved. The *Whig* estimated that the market value of enslaved people was $3 billion at the start of the war, and argued that property in people was a "constitutional and vested" right that must be paid for. Half the sum might "redress the whites, the other half would console the blacks." The *Whig* understood that US occupation of the South must end first, but it believed that allying with a Northern party would jeopardize any hope of future compensation.[12]

As Northern papers pointed out, the *Whig*'s plan was a transparent attempt to challenge the Republican Party in the South by uniting Black and white Southerners under one party. Northern papers largely mocked the plan. The *New National Era* reprinted much of the article and commented that the *Whig* "mistakes the character" of Black citizens "as Democrats always have" by assuming they could buy off Black voters and "aid in fastening the chains of slavery upon their limbs once more." The *Era* advised its readers to unite behind the Republican Party instead and pressure the party to support their calls for land redistribution. The *Tribune*, Greeley's paper, reprinted the article with the heading "Honorable and frank avowal of what is to be attempted when the Democrats come in power—southern slaves to be paid for, and the money divided with the conservative colored voters." The *Whig* responded by explaining that its plan was "a direct bid to Gen. Grant, or Mr. Greeley, or any other Presidential aspirant who will deal with us justly and liberally. *We are in the market.*"[13]

Such tactics put both Liberal Republicans and Democrats on the defensive. The Republican Party positioned itself as the one that had won the war and abolished slavery. According to Republican campaigners, Greeley and his supporters were Confederate sympathizers who would use federal funds to reimburse former enslavers. A vote for Horace Greeley, US general Benjamin Butler warned, was "a vote to burn school-houses; a vote for murder and the violating of women, a vote to pay for emancipated slaves, and for the payment of pension to the rebel soldiers."[14] Few campaigners addressed the *Whig*'s suggestion to also pay the formerly enslaved.

Greeley's wartime record only confirmed Republicans' points. When the US Army and Northern support for the war faltered, Greeley supported abolishing slavery with reimbursements to former enslavers. In December 1862, he proposed to President Lincoln that the United States should assume Confederate debts and compensate border states for freed slaves. At the nadirs of Northern support for the war in 1863 and 1864, Greeley suggested that Lincoln should signal flexibility to the Confederacy concerning his Emancipation Proclamation. His persistence led to his national embarrassment. At the 1864 Niagara Peace Conference, Greeley discussed peace with up to $400 million in federal compensation to all slave states with unauthorized Confederate commissioners, who turned their correspondence with Greeley over to the press. The documents revealed that Lincoln had reaffirmed his commitments to the Union and emancipation, while Greeley had waffled on abolition. To the Northern public in 1864, Greeley appeared at worst a traitor and at best a fool.[15]

Backed into another corner in 1872, Greeley's campaign tried to have it both ways. On the one hand, the *New York Tribune* defended his actions at Niagara Falls and his stance on compensated emancipation during the war. It explained that the Confederate commissioners were impostors and Greeley had proposed to compensate only loyal citizens, though seceded and loyal states alike could be eligible for reimbursements. On the other hand, Liberal Republicans and Democrats reminded constituents that the Republican accusations were absurd, insofar as the Fourteenth Amendment made compensation for former enslavers impossible.[16]

Liberal Republicans and Democrats had hoped that their alliance would win white voters and that Greeley's reputation as an abolitionist might attract Black voters, but they rejected Greeley in the election. Republican accusa-

"RED HOT!"

Greeley eats his past words and deeds in this July 13, 1872, *Harper's Weekly* cartoon by Thomas Nast. Harp Week.

tions that Greeley would reimburse former enslavers had the intended effect of splitting the vote. Liberal Republicans scrambled to reassure Black and Northern voters that white Southerners accepted emancipation to uncertain effect. Ever vigilant, the *New National Era* reminded its readers that with or without an alliance with Liberal Republicans, a vote for Greeley meant a vote for the Democratic Party. Unlike many Republican papers, the *Era* conceded that Greeley "mildly repudiated" any design to compensate enslavers or pay the rebel debt, but warned that his alliance with the Democrats would nonetheless lead to both. They would pay the rebel debt, compensate former enslavers, distribute pensions to rebel soldiers, and "practically restore slavery." Democrats would find the Reconstruction Amendments "a very trifling obstacle," especially if they controlled the White House and Congress in the near future, as the paper predicted two vacancies could open up on the US Supreme Court.[17]

The 1872 election had two long-term effects: realigning white Southern voters and casting doubt on the Fourteenth Amendment. First, Democrats had to rethink claiming federal reimbursements for enslavers. Republican campaigning persuaded many voters that Democrats would challenge Reconstruction policy, even with the New Departure platform. Grant defeated Greeley in the election, winning all but six states. Both campaigns' discourses about compensating former enslavers functioned in sometimes contradictory ways. Republican accusations wedged the Liberal Republicans and Democrats along sectional lines but also gave some white Southerners incentive to vote for Greeley by advertising his wartime support for compensated emancipation. At the same time, the New Departure campaign emphasized that white Southerners accepted emancipation as it happened as well as the Reconstruction Amendments. This strategy worked for former Whigs and Unionists in the South, who had disavowed the Republican Party and embraced white Democrats. Most Northerners, however, did not want to subsidize emancipation beyond what they had already paid by lives lost during the war.[18]

Greeley's loss, along with other regional elections, taught a growing group of Southern Democrats that there would be no end to Reconstruction if they continued to push for federal compensation to former enslavers and financial relief. Greeley's loss discredited the Democratic and Liberal Republican alliance and the New Departure, and partnering with moderates gained Democrats little. Any claims for compensation were politically inexpedient and also economically unnecessary.

The Panic of 1873 exacerbated these trends regionally. In September, nearly a year after the election, a financial panic initiated an economic downturn that aggravated both the national and regional economies, necessitating different political strategies. In Virginia, an 1874 Senate race revealed that many white Southerners no longer viewed federal compensation for former enslavers as an economic booster but as a deterrent to Northern investment. For example, Virginian Robert M. T. Hunter—former Confederate secretary of state, former Confederate senator of Virginia, and president pro tempore of the Confederate Senate—returned to politics after a long hiatus when he ran for one of Virginia's senate seats in 1874. Before the war, Hunter was a Whig senator turned states' rights Democrat. During Reconstruction, he was a member of Virginia's Conservative Party. In October 1873, Hunter proposed a plan to secure federal grants that would both compensate former enslavers and, he promised, conform to section 4 of the Fourteenth Amendment.[19]

Hunter's reasoning was very similar to that of the *Richmond Whig*. Hunter suggested that Black Americans as well as white recognized the Fifth Amendment property claim the United States created when it abolished slavery, and that white Southerners still had a right to compensation. Section 4 of the Fourteenth Amendment did not supersede the Fifth Amendment's guarantee of "just compensation" for freed slaves. Hunter hoped to sidestep the Fourteenth Amendment's restrictions by securing a federal loan to former slave states for $400 million. The money, which could come from surplus tax revenue, would alleviate the depression in Southern states, enable them to contribute to common taxes, promote interstate trade, and "repay before very long to the whole Union the expenses of the original outlay." At a time when racial violence in the South was at the forefront of American news, Hunter claimed the loan would "restore peace between" white and Black Southerners by relieving Black Southerners' fears, unfounded though he thought they were, that white Southerners wanted to re-enslave them. Black Southerners would "feel that the claim of his former master had been satisfied, if not paid or compensated by the money of the United States." Similar to the argument that slavery was a positive good, Hunter suggested that reimbursing enslavers was helpful to formerly enslaved people.[20]

Despite Hunter's assurances, Black Americans did not respond positively. The *New National Era* insisted that the United States pay former enslavers in worthless Confederate bonds and pay "back pay" to the formerly enslaved instead.[21] Many white Southerners also rejected the plan. By proposing compensation, Hunter had recalled the issues of the war. A rising group of Democratic politicians in Virginia and elsewhere wanted to avoid bloody shirt politics. Hunter's opponents denounced his age and traditionalism, calling him and other candidates who had wartime political careers "old fogies." The Virginia legislators who elected their senators were afraid to send an old Confederate to Congress at the risk of losing Northern and Midwestern politicians' cooperation, and Hunter lost his Senate bid. Calls for compensation would contradict the new guard's goals, especially if papers like the *New National Era* continued to criticize them nationally.[22]

Greeley's and Hunter's defeats contributed to and demonstrated the shifting political boundaries of the Reconstruction South. The Liberal Republican critique of Grant and federal Reconstruction policy nourished the growing Lost Cause mythology that white Southerners were beginning to use to dignify Confederate defeat, justify counter-Reconstruction policies, and unite with white Northerners across wartime political divides. Many white Americans were persuaded that genuine harmony between the sections could come only from peace and "home rule." White Southerners' pursuit of compensation would only instigate sectional strife.[23]

Like many conservatives of the time, Hunter failed to realize that the Panic of 1873 had reshaped both national and regional politics. Southerners had blamed their region's economic distress on uncompensated emancipation, but the Panic of 1873 and national labor unrest created new enemies for politicians to blame. Elite Republican and Democratic Party leaders alleviated intraparty factions among centrists like former Whigs, former Unionists, and conservatives by defending property interests against labor. White voters began to turn against Republicans nationally, leading to a Democratic majority in the House after the 1874 congressional elections. In seven Southern states throughout the 1870s, Democrats amassed enough votes to hold conventions and rewrite their state constitutions for the third time during Reconstruction. Their new constitutions demolished the congressional Reconstruction governments that states had created under Republican control, pruning the power (and expense) of government and protecting planter interests.[24]

Democrats also needed to appeal to voters nationwide. Southern Democrats could not estrange Northern Democrats, who remained less likely to support compensation than their Southern counterparts. Plans to reimburse former enslavers only rekindled the bloody shirt campaigning that Democrats had spent years deflecting. Former abolitionists and US Army veterans suffering from economic reversals still carried their commitments to racial reform or Unionism, but the majority of Northerners had embraced a sentimental memory of the war, allowing the Lost Cause to eventually eclipse Unionist memories. Sectional reconciliation reunited North and South. Compensating former enslavers would hardly demonstrate to moderate Northerners that the Southern Democratic Party had acquiesced to emancipation and Reconstruction.[25]

Many Democrats also avoided wartime issues to position themselves as the party of the "New South," poised to attract outside investment and bring new prosperity to the region. New South politicians understood that reconciliation facilitated their pursuit of Northern investment. Alliances with Northern businessmen would secure funds for improvements and investments, and advocating for compensation by Southern Democrats would more likely than not expose them to attacks from within and outside their own party. Business and reunion went together. The South no longer needed capital from property in people or federal funds, they reasoned; new industry and low taxes would bring that.[26]

The second major effect of Greeley's campaign was to cast doubt on the stability of the Fourteenth Amendment. Even if Republicans and Democrats were merely fearmongering to win elections, platforms for compensated emancipation caused a number of Americans to question the legitimacy of section 4 throughout the last decades of the nineteenth century. Hunter had suggested that a federal loan to Southern states could bypass section 4's restrictions. Similarly, during the 1872 presidential election, Washington, DC's *Morning Chronicle* editor James Harlan, who had served in President Andrew Johnson's cabinet, argued that there was only a "constitutional inhibition" against paying *individual* enslavers. According to Harlan, section 4 prohibited states and the federal government from paying individuals for enslaved people freed by the war, but there was nothing to prevent a Democratic Congress from paying Southern *states* $400 million for freed people.[27]

Harlan probably overemphasized the possibility and likelihood that Congress could or would pay states the value of freed slaves. Section 4 prohibited both the United States and states from paying "any claim for the loss or emancipation of any slave." Even if Congress tried to bypass the amendment by paying states for individual claims, it would arguably violate the clause. More importantly, at a time when most federal spending went to the North, it was unlikely that the United States would have sent the significant sum of federal money that compensation would have required, whether that money was called compensation for former enslavers or appropriated under other pretenses.[28]

Nevertheless, such questions about the meaning of section 4 contributed to the Democratic Party's rise in the early 1870s by adding white Unionists to the fold. Republican bloody shirt campaigning alienated white voters in the South, revealing Southern Unionists' growing disillusionment with the Republican Party and Black men's suffrage. George W. Paschal, one of the Texas politicians who had warned his governor in 1865 that white Texans would secure compensation for formerly enslaved people during the state's presidential Reconstruction convention, challenged Harlan's interpretation of the amendment in an open letter. Paschal, a lawyer and former Unionist who had joined the Republican Party by 1869, insisted that the Fourteenth Amendment was a stronger provision against slavery and federal reimbursement for former enslavers than the Thirteenth. He chided Harlan and other Grant supporters for agitating the public over a constitutionally impossible policy and accused them of manipulating Black voters by teaching them that "they owe their emancipation, not to Providence and the blood and treasure of every class, but to what remains of the Republican organization as it now is." Paschal managed to criticize the Republicans' bloody shirt politics while denying Black voters' agency. He was indignant that Grant's supporters would interfere in Southern politics by, as he saw it, exploiting Black voters and discrediting Southern Unionists like himself, who had advocated for the Reconstruction Amendments and sacrificed their lives, property rights in people, plantations, and financial futures to support the Union without any compensation or reward.[29] Like many Southern Unionists, Paschal abandoned Republicans for the Liberal Republicans and Democrats in 1872, believing that the legacies of the war that he valued were secure. Although he blamed Republicans, he was also frustrated that many Black Southerners supported and promoted the policies that estranged him from his former party.

Paschal was confident that the Fourteenth Amendment protected uncompensated emancipation and other legacies of the war, but others worried as the Supreme Court began to chip away at the gains of Reconstruction. A few white Southerners appealed for compensation throughout the 1870s and 1880s, as monitored and reported by the Black and white press.[30] Despite their recurrence in national politics, no related policy materialized, and Republicans and Democrats alike began to abandon the issue. However, the US Supreme Court began to pick apart the Fourteenth Amendment, while Democratic Party leaders attempted to downplay the legacies of the war and slavery in the 1870s and 1880s. From the *Slaughterhouse Cases* (1873) to the *Civil Rights Cases* (1883), the court dismantled civil rights protections guaranteed by the amendment. In this context, section 4 seemed precarious.[31]

However, historians have not recovered a case that challenged section 4 of the amendment in the 1880s. The Supreme Court focused on the first section's Equal Protection Clause as it applied to contract law, civil rights, and voting rights, continuing to delimit the meaning of emancipation in constitutional law.[32] Nevertheless, some white politicians, although far fewer than in previous years, reprised the argument that the Fifth Amendment guaranteed former enslavers federal reimbursements and made claims based on the United States' wartime policies. For example, former Maryland congressman Benjamin G. Harris called on the United States to pay some enslavers based on the 1864 Enrollment Act. As a disgraced wartime congressman, convicted of harboring two Confederate soldiers, Harris had long defended Maryland enslavers' constitutional guarantee of property rights in humans, and in 1884 he claimed that the Fourteenth Amendment could not "be construed to refer to the border states." Contrary to Southern jurists who had played up the loss of emancipation in the 1860s and 1870s, Harris insisted that "in no sense were their slaves lost, but were taken and held openly by the Government for its own use," declaring that the enslaved men the US Army enlisted in the border states "became the property of the United States, of course, for a fair consideration due to their owners." According to Harris, the United States owed border state enslavers "just compensation" according to the Fifth Amendment's takings clause, exactly $26,156,700 to Maryland and $129 million total to the border states.[33]

In an environment where the Supreme Court was chipping away at other elements of the Fourteenth Amendment, some Black Americans worried that Democrats could mobilize Harris's argument and challenge section 4 in court. A reporter for the *Cleveland Daily Herald* interviewed George Washington Williams about Harris's claim. At the time, Williams was working on two major historical works about Black history in the United States and the Civil War: *A History of the Negro Troops in the War of the Rebellion* and *The History of the Negro Race in America* from 1619. Williams had fought in the US Army during the Civil War, in Mexico to remove Emperor Maximilian from power, and in the US wars against Native Americans in the West. During Reconstruction, he enrolled at Howard University and Newton Theological Institution, where he was ordained as a Baptist minister. He studied law in Cincinnati, Ohio, and was the first African American elected to the Ohio General Assembly. There, he served for one year, 1880–81. In 1884, Williams told the *Daily Herald* reporter that he had "long been expecting" such claims as Harris's. Even with the Thirteenth and Fourteenth Amendments, Williams believed that property rights in people so pervaded the US legal system that the courts would overturn section 4 of the Fourteenth Amendment if the question ever came to them.[34]

In his writings, Williams criticized US wartime emancipation policies for their ambiguity, which opened the nation up to former enslavers' reimbursement claims. He thought that General Benjamin Butler's contraband of war theory implied that people could be property under the law, since it categorized Black people who came "into the hands of Union troops . . . with wages, horses, cotton and other property." Likewise, the DC Emancipation Act gave former enslavers precedent to claim compensation for the enslaved whom they called property, and Williams questioned whether section 4 could ever manage to "reach backwards and destroy the position of the Government, previously taken on the question of property in man"—the position, that is, of the United States and proponents of compensation alike: that enslavers had legally held Black people as property.[35]

Despite the immediate failure of compensated emancipation, Williams worried that the Fourteenth Amendment was insufficient to prevent the federal government from paying former enslavers in the long run. He agreed with Republicans of the 1870s, suggesting that the only way to prevent the threat was to "keep the Democratic party from National control."[36] Yet Harris was an outlier who had continuously lobbied for the payments promised to border state enslavers. By the 1880s, there were few on the national stage who wanted to change section 4 or sincerely feared for it. Even Republicans often diminished the role slavery played in the Civil War. Nearly twenty years after serving in Congress during Reconstruction, Maine congressman James G. Blaine concluded that the decision to deny compensation to former enslavers had been primarily financial. He reasoned that the "public credit might be fatally impaired" if the national treasury were forced to pay "from two to three thousand millions of dollars to the slaveholders of the South." Congress prohibited compensation, he recalled, because "the burden would be so great that the Nation which had survived the shock of arms might be engulfed in the manifold calamities of bankruptcy." Writing in 1886, Blaine, a proponent of reconciliation, downplayed the war over slavery as a war between heroic white Americans to preserve national stability, deemphasizing contemporary Republicans' offense against treasonous, slaveholding rebels.[37]

Regionally, Democrats no longer needed to entice voters with the possibility of compensation. By the late 1870s, opponents of Reconstruction had already absorbed many of the South's moderate white voters. True, from the late 1870s through the 1890s, independent factions and fusion parties composed of Black and white Southerners threatened Republican and Democratic victories in each Southern state and in many localities. Throughout the South, parties such as the Readjusters in Virginia forced the established parties to respond to their causes—debt readjustment and election reform—to varying degrees of success. Democrats weathered these electoral threats by avoiding decisive or divisive policies, such as compensation for former enslavers. They refused to take a hard stance on any issue, consolidated political power by reducing the function of government, and united their base with the rallying cry of white supremacy when all else failed. Claiming federal compensation to former enslavers, Democrats reasoned, was more likely than not to provoke sectional antagonisms and exacerbate class divisions among white voters. Yet Williams's legal interpretations of emancipation, section 4, and Fifth Amendment property claims would continue to influence Black and white politicians and activists in the following decade.[38]

Who Is Owed?

In part because of all the independent parties, the issue of compensation to former enslavers ebbed and flowed in the national press throughout the 1870s and into the 1890s. The attention paid to the legality of compensation diminished in the 1880s, reemerging during presidential elections and periodic economic downturns. In presidential elections in the 1880s, Republicans continued to warn that the Democratic candidates would pay former enslavers, and Democrats denied the charge. Many Americans were disillusioned with their political system, and some Southerners still protested that uncompensated emancipation had destroyed their prewar economy.[39]

When discussion of paying former enslavers emerged again in the 1890s, it did so in a new political context. Southern politicians and the press began to combine compensation for white Southern enslavers with compensation for the enslaved and their descendants. Once again, compensation became a compromise measure to unite disparate political factions. This time, however, claims to compensate enslavers accompanied (or discredited) various plans to pay the formerly enslaved. Americans, particularly abolitionists, had long connected these ideas. Throughout the history of enslavers' claims for compensation, some opponents suggested that the formerly enslaved, not enslavers, deserved remunerations instead. Similar to remarks made at Elihu Burritt's 1857 National Compensated Emancipation Convention, where abolitionist William Watkins pushed the convention to remember the enslaved, and in the *New National Era*'s reporting in the 1870s, Black activists attempted to widen the scope of the debate and challenge the idea that enslavers were entitled to compensation—alone or at all. In these moments, proponents of paying enslavers did not often take efforts to secure compensation for the enslaved seriously. However, the emerging ex-slave pension movement changed the tenor of these debates.

In 1890, the idea of compensating the formerly enslaved began to eclipse that of paying former enslavers. Then, Walter Vaughan, a white Democrat and former newspaper editor of the *Nebraska Daily Democrat*, promoted a bill to provide pensions to freed people, many of whom were by then elderly and unable to work for wages. Proposed in multiple sessions of Congress throughout the 1890s and modeled after pensions for disabled Civil War veterans and their families, the bill stipulated that the United States would provide for a one-time payment and a monthly pension for freed people on a sliding scale based on their age. The bill required only that a claimant had been enslaved and assumed that any Black person alive before 1861 was enslaved in the South unless documentation proved otherwise.[40] Vaughan framed the bill as tax relief. He believed that freed people were burdens on white Southerners, especially since former enslavers had been "deprived of their property without recompense." Vaughan reasoned that the South needed money, and that freed people with pensions would purchase goods and services from whites and thus help reinvigorate the economy. His proposal stayed alive through 1903, when two Republicans introduced a version of the bill for the last time.[41]

Throughout the 1890s, Southern politicians and activists, Black and white, transformed the meaning of Vaughan's bill to their own ends. Failed by both Republican and Democratic Parties, a few Black and white politicians across the South hoped to create new political coalitions to break the Democrats' hold over the region and recover the faltering Southern economy in the 1892 congressional elections. Instead of fighting against enslavers' claims for compensation, some embraced paying former enslavers—and sometimes the formerly enslaved as well. Independent and fusion parties sometimes mobilized the promise of compensation to the formerly enslaved and former enslavers toward their own political goals.[42]

The emergence of the Populist Party created opportunities for such alliances. Throughout the nation, organized labor and Populists challenged the two-party system's cronyism and anti-labor practices. As populism gained national prominence in the early 1890s after regional success in the 1880s, the party emphasized that class, not section, divided Americans, and urged them to reunite for "the masses." Under the leadership of Joseph C. Manning, the People's Party in Georgia and Alabama reportedly added federal payments to former enslavers for freed slaves to their platform. This platform was not common among Populists regionally and might have even been considered anti-Populist elsewhere. After all, compensating former enslavers may have resulted in government payments for the region's former landholding elites, as opposed to supporting small farmers. It could also have antagonized sectional conflict as much as it could represent reconciliation among white Northerners, Westerners, and Southerners. However, Populists in Georgia and Alabama differed from those in other states. Many were upcountry whites who refused to join the Republican Party after the war. By the 1890s, their interests conflicted with the Democratic Party. Petitioning for compensation would have further distinguished these Populists from Democrats who gave up on compensation, attracting white voters who would not have voted either Republican or Democrat.[43]

Others recognized, as the *Richmond Whig* once had, that their campaigns could attract interracial support. In 1892, John H. Williamson, the editor of the *Gazette*—a Black newspaper in Raleigh, North Carolina—ran for Congress on the platform that he would compensate the formerly enslaved as well as those who had claimed ownership over them. Born enslaved in Georgia, Williamson became a prominent state politician and editor after the Civil

HON. JOHN H. WILLIAMSON.

John H. Williamson had a varied career in local and state politics, serving as a state legislator, a justice of the peace, and a member of the Franklin County Board of Education. In 1881, he founded his first newspaper. Penn, *Afro-American Press, and Its Editors*, 181.

War. He was a delegate to the state Freedmen's Convention and served six terms in North Carolina's legislature. Throughout his career, he advocated for equal rights and racial uplift through education. In the early 1880s, he founded two newspapers, *The Banner* and the *North Carolina Gazette*, which became one of North Carolina's leading Black newspapers.[44] When he announced his campaign, he told audiences that even Abraham Lincoln had stated that enslaved people were lawful property and proposed to pay former enslavers $300 for each freed person, plus 6 percent interest. He suggested that money appropriated for the measure should be equally divided between the former enslavers and the formerly enslaved (or their heirs). Beyond these details, there is little evidence to further explain the proposal. Williamson voted to ratify the Fourteenth Amendment as a member of the North Carolina General Assembly in 1868, so he likely knew that section 4 would restrict him. Realistic or not, the proposal successfully drew attention to his campaign.[45]

Constituents were reportedly receptive to Williamson's campaign, although he did not win the election. Writing about Williamson, a white correspondent from Raleigh's *News and Observer* used racist rhetoric to describe him. He referred to all candidates by their last name except Williamson, whom he referred to by his first. Though his disparaging remarks call his reporting into question, he described one Black audience's reaction to the idea: The audience's initial disappointment that Williamson supported compensation to former enslavers turned to excitement when he announced that the money would be equally divided. Papers reported that Williamson himself claimed that "letters from all parts of the country commend his views." Indeed, other Black newspapers, like the Indianapolis *Freeman*, criticized anyone who supported compensating former enslavers for emancipation without paying freed people for their labor under slavery.[46]

At first, both Republicans and Democrats deflected such campaigns. Republicans responded by parading the party's support of Civil War veterans' pensions to attract voters to whom populism might have otherwise appealed. Democrats sought to downplay class tensions between white Southerners, which undermined their race-based campaigning. Because US military pension spending, which benefited only US veterans, was higher than ever, some Democratic papers responded sarcastically: Paying formerly enslaved people was only fair to add cash into the Southern economy (as if pension recipients only lived in the North or were not also formerly enslaved). Where third parties were less organized or allied with Democrats, Southern Democrats dismissed any desire for payments to enslavers, rejecting any economic need for it.[47]

It became more difficult to downplay a financial need for compensation after the Panic of 1893 aggravated the already difficult economic conditions many Southerners faced. Then, several different groups emerged on the national scene proposing payments for former enslavers, the formerly enslaved, or both, including some Democrats. Like earlier proponents, they sought political support and legal solutions. For example, Guy C. Sibley, a solicitor from Alabama running for Congress against a Democratic incumbent, advocated both causes on the grounds that the US Constitution recognized property rights in people and thus the federal government sanctioned both the uncompensated use of enslaved labor and uncompensated emancipation. In 1894 he proposed a bill that would appropriate $400 million for freed people or their heirs, and in 1896 he proposed a sixteenth amendment to repeal section 4 of the Fourteenth Amendment and replace it with a provision to split the value of people freed by the Emancipation Proclamation between former enslavers and the formerly enslaved.[48] One newspaper called Sibley a Jeffersonian Democrat, a Republican, and a Populist; indeed, Sibley sought alliances wherever he could find them. He contacted prominent Virginia Democrat William E. Bibb, who had led failed efforts to create the National Adjustment Society in Virginia, which was to be dedicated to changing the Constitution to pay former enslavers.[49]

These efforts to repeal section 4 appeared to have garnered little support in their states or even among like-minded advocates like Sibley and Bibb. They failed to unite Black or white voters behind upstart politicians. On the other hand, the idea that former enslavers could claim compensation for the value of the formerly enslaved animated support for the growing ex-slave pension movement.

A much larger group of Black Americans transformed the meaning of Vaughan's bill beyond these legal and economic rationales and political pragmatism. Organizers of the National Ex-Slave Mutual Relief, Bounty and Pension Association (MRB&PA) wanted to pay the formerly enslaved for their years of coerced labor and service to their country. The MRB&PA was organized in 1897 in Nashville and led by the Reverend Isaiah H. Dickerson and Callie D. House, and since its founding had lobbied for federal pensions for the formerly enslaved. It also operated as a mutual aid society for its members. Inspired by the extensive federal pension program for US Civil War veterans and their dependents, the MRB&PA aimed to compensate those who "served" the country and "worked as slaves for the development" of its "great resources and wealth."[50] The association hoped to pass a bill that would pension the formerly enslaved based on their age. Each pensioner would be paid a onetime sum and monthly payments that escalated over time. If a pensioner was too elderly or ill to care for themselves, then their caretakers would be compensated.

Disillusioned with calls for Black self-improvement in a world that had failed to make good on the promises of Reconstruction, the MRB&PA arose out of a long tradition of Black activism for some form of payment or reparations for enslavement to the formerly enslaved. Before and after emancipation, freed people sued former enslavers' families for money and property promised to them in enslavement.[51] During and immediately after the Civil War, many expected to own land and have full access to citizenship rights. When they did not receive land, activists such as Sojourner Truth pushed Congress in 1870 to provide land for freed people in and around Washington, DC. In 1872, Benjamin Singleton created a company to acquire land and create a Black territory in Kansas.[52] Claims like these could both compensate the formerly enslaved for their unpaid labor and redress some of the material damages suffered by the formerly enslaved and their descendants as a result of generations of enslavement. Claimants also hoped to create opportunities for self-determination, economic power, and full political participation.

The MRB&PA used economic ideas and claims similar to those of proponents of compensation for former enslavers. If uncompensated emancipation had destroyed the Southern economy, leaving thousands of people impoverished, including the formerly enslaved, then paying former enslavers and the enslaved alike would in theory revitalize the economy. However, economic hardship and devastation were not distributed equally: By the 1880s, most descendants of former enslavers had recovered their families' pre-emancipation income and wealth. Black Southerners would indeed benefit from an influx of cash through reparations, but former enslavers and their descendants no longer needed the money to revitalize their personal finances and increase their purchasing power.[53]

Whether they sought personal gain, political backing, or mutual aid, politicians and organizers like Williamson, Sibley, and the association's representatives sometimes supported or acknowledged enslavers' legal claims to compensation for property in people to justify their own claims for the formerly enslaved's uncompensated labor. While former enslavers' claims were rooted in property rights, enabling them to claim a constitutional right to compensation under the Fifth Amendment, freed people's claims for payments were rooted in labor rights and the idea that their uncompensated, coerced work should be retroactively paid. If enslavers' rights to profit from property in people were constitutional or otherwise valid, they suggested, then freed people should be paid for their labor, which had made property in people so valuable.

Though the MRB&PA did not promise it, its members sometimes mobilized arguments in support of payments for enslavers to garner support for and defend their own efforts. In fact, in September 1899 the US Post Office issued a fraud order against the MRB&PA for allegedly swindling formerly enslaved people through the mail. Federal agents in the Bureau of Pensions, the Post Office Department, and the Department of Justice investigated House, Dickerson, and other members of the movement on the grounds that they were swindling donors because the proposed pension bill would never pass. They accused the association of "arousing false hopes" in formerly enslaved people, and the Post Office issued its fraud order against them. The order, which permitted the US government to intercept the association's mail, made it difficult for the MRB&PA to circulate newsletters or collect the membership dues that supported its lobbying efforts and local community work.[54]

To challenge the fraud order, the MRB&PA hired Robert Abraham Lincoln Dick in November 1901. Named for the Great Emancipator, Dick was an attorney who specialized in pension law. He told the US Post Office that the association's goals were reasonable because if Lincoln had lived, Southern enslavers might have been paid for those they claimed ownership over as a condition of Reconstruction. If that were the case, Dick argued, then there was no reason that the association could not advocate for the payment of freed people.[55]

The similarities between organizations like the MRB&PA and campaigns like Sibley's stopped there. Williamson's and Sibley's suggestions to combine payments for former enslavers and the formerly enslaved echoed the 1857 Compensated Emancipation Convention, where more radical abolitionists tried to convince the moderate majority that money, land, and consideration to the formerly enslaved should accompany any plan to abolish slavery with compensation to former enslavers. However, in the 1890s, politicians thought they could gain votes by suggesting that former enslavers and the formerly enslaved could share the profits of slavery. These later campaigns were less about reparative justice, redress, and self-determination than about economic relief, and many commenters—often Democrats—viewed them cynically.

More often than not, such comparisons between compensation for enslavers and pensions for freed people worked against ex-slave pension organizers. In 1896, another group—the United States Ex-Slave Owners Registration Bureau—emerged in the national press. The organization claimed to be collecting a record of all enslaved people freed by the Emancipation Proclamation and enslavers or their heirs in order to secure "reasonable compensation" for former enslavers from the United States. The bureau had been operating for at least three years out of Washington, DC, and Savannah, Georgia, and sending circulars across the South, which read: "History shows that no civilized nation has ever emancipated her slaves and failed to compensate their owners." The circular instructed former enslavers to mail a registration form to indicate how many people they claimed and provide a scaling fee from $1 for one to ten enslaved people up to $5 for more than fifty—the equivalent of between $37 and $188 in 2024. Northern newspapers denounced the bureau as a scam and used it as another opportunity to condemn Democrats, both North and South, for seeking compensation for former enslavers. Though the US Postal Service shut down the bureau for mail fraud that spring, a few newspapers played up the scam's success, renewing concerns that a number of white Southerners still sought compensation for freed slaves.[56]

Commenters discussed the US Ex-Slave Owners Registration Bureau, ex-slave pension claims, and Sibley's campaign in the same columns and made the bureau a symbol of the futility of payments for former enslavers and the formerly enslaved. Newspapers acknowledged that multiple bills had been introduced in Congress to compensate the formerly enslaved, but they maligned Black Americans' efforts at the same time that they mocked those on behalf of former enslavers.[57] Many called both the bureau and the bills for ex-slave pensions swindles. When Sibley circulated pamphlets for his amendment in Congress that summer, some commenters referenced the "Pay for Our N—" party, a secret political party that met in Washington, DC, in the early 1890s. After much speculation, it turned out to be a joke by a group of "waggish newspaper correspondents."[58] Whether they wanted a laugh, sought to discredit politicians, or sincerely thought that payments to freed people or enslavers were impossible, journalists repeatedly condemned any pursuit of joint compensation for white Southerners and Black Americans.

Despite the successes of the MRB&PA, the Black press, too, condemned its efforts. Between 1897 and 1899, the association had enrolled at least 34,000 new members, suggesting that its ideas appealed to Black Americans. Yet Black politicians and the regional and national press remained skeptical about ex-slave pensions and compensation to former enslavers alike. One paper, the *National Reflector*, concluded that neither were likely to happen.[59] National Black leaders derided both the MRB&PA and Vaughan as unrealistic or fraudulent.[60] Others emphasized that Black Americans did not require payments from the United States, almost construing them as handouts rather than as compensation for labor performed: Their race had come up from slavery on their own, and they celebrated their uplift. Similarly, a good number of other Black political leaders, such as Virginia congressman John Mercer Langston, prioritized greater protections for the right to vote or state and federal resources for education over reparations. Black Americans who were more economically secure and who had more formal education believed ex-slave pension bills were nonstarters, as they distracted from the education and voting rights initiatives for which Langston and other Black politicians sought white politicians' support.[61]

Perceiving scams, upstart politicians, and skepticism from national Black leaders, the press had a hard time reconciling payments to any—but especially to both—groups. By the end of the 1890s, it became clear that by abandoning and dismissing compensation to former enslavers as a political issue, Democrats had dragged down compensation to the formerly enslaved as well. And without support from the Black press or more powerful politicians, the conflation of payments for enslavers and freed people hindered both causes. The press's dismissal of Williamson, Sibley, and the Ex-Slave Owners Registration Bureau made it easy in turn to ridicule the MRB&PA.

Furthermore, the press's growing attention to the material, profit-making elements of slavery in Southern history, with its focus on compensation for property and compensation for the labor of the enslaved, made Confederate veterans increasingly uneasy about their image in national history. If Confederates had fought to secure white Southerners' rights to claim ownership over Black people and profit from slavery, they wondered, then how would future generations remember them? George Washington Williams, Abraham Dick, and other Black organizers emphasized that the United States had sanctioned property rights in people, and they demanded remedies for enslavement on those grounds. Their arguments clashed with those of a growing number of white Southerners who sought to obscure and diminish the centrality of slavery to Southern secession and the war.

Hampton Roads and Compensation in Confederate Memory

There is little evidence to suggest that Confederate veterans directly responded to the ex-slave pension movement or campaigns such as Williamson's. Nonetheless, after claims to compensate former enslavers damaged Democratic campaigns, and while Black activists campaigned for ex-slave pensions and compensation during these decades, Confederate veterans began to write a new history of the Civil War that discredited former enslavers' claims for compensation and freed people's claims for payments in turn. When Confederate veterans wrote histories that denied the profitability of slavery to the region and nation, they necessarily undermined the work of Black leaders like House and Williams. Former Confederates reinterpreted the history of former enslavers' demands for compensation as one element of the Lost Cause cultural project that rewrote the history of the Civil War and Reconstruction.

Concerned over the role that slavery played in the secession crisis and the Civil War, Confederate veterans called into question whether white Southerners had ever wanted compensation. Historically, as other chapters have shown, they certainly did. But in the late 1890s, Confederate veterans crafted an alternative narrative by scrutinizing one event in particular: the Hampton Roads Conference of February 1865, where President Lincoln purportedly offered to pay Confederate states for freed slaves if they surrendered to the United States.

The Hampton Roads Conference elicited a great deal of debate in the 1890s because few knew for certain what transpired there. Events after the conference suggest that Lincoln offered compensation as a condition for Confederate surrender that February. As we have seen, shortly after the meeting, Lincoln presented to his cabinet a joint resolution to Congress that would authorize him to pay $400 million to Confederate states and border states in government bonds in proportion to a state's 1860 enslaved population. His cabinet unanimously opposed the resolution, and Lincoln abandoned the plan.[62] However, no one took notes during the meeting, and the only existing accounts were published by three Confederate commissioners three to ten years after it ended. By the 1890s, all attendees had died and thus could not speak to the veracity of any account.[63]

Beginning in 1895 with a speech by Henry Watterson, editor of the Louisville, Kentucky, *Courier-Journal*, Southern papers eagerly circulated debates about whether Lincoln offered to pay Confederate states the value of former slaves at Hampton Roads. Throughout the South, papers printed Confederate veterans' and officials' take on the question, often accompanied by reprinted evidence from Civil War memoirs and federal records.[64] While some applauded Lincoln's genius and generosity to Confederates, regretting that they rejected his terms, others asked, "If such an offer was made," why did they not accept it? The debate lasted in the press for five years without any evidence-based conclusion.[65]

Instead, the debate culminated in Confederate veterans ultimately denying that Lincoln proposed to pay a $400 million indemnity for freed people and the restoration of the Union in a resolution presented during the Ninth Annual Meeting of the United Confederate Veterans (UCV), held in Charleston, South Carolina, in 1899. The resolution, presented by the Tennessee delegation, cited the same documents that had been circulating in the press for years. It was absurd to think that Lincoln would have offered compensation, the resolution stated, because Northerners would "not have tolerated" such a move when "federal arms were in the full tide of success, and final victory was so near at hand." The Tennessee veterans insisted that the South, not the North, "had always been the party of compromise and peace." According to one reporter covering the event, the resolution sparked much debate among the veterans and looked like it would be defeated until it was referred to the Committee on History for the next year's meeting.[66]

While the UCV debated the historical accuracy of the controversy, the United Daughters of the Confederacy (UDC) debated whether to petition Congress to pay for enslaved people freed by the war. At the UDC's November 1899 annual meeting, Georgia delegates hoped to appeal for federal compensation, but Virginia and Kentucky delegates rejected the petition, burying the issue. The *American Citizen*, a Black newspaper, reported from Kansas that the UDC was "too proud to favor compensation."[67] Indeed, the UDC worked to distinguish white Southern women from the violence of plantation slavery, portraying mistresses as benevolent caretakers, divorced from the masculine economic activities of slave trading and plantation management.[68] Supporting appeals for federal compensation to former enslavers would have drawn attention to their financial interests in property in people.

At its meeting the following year, the UCV also buried the issue of compensation after UCV's Committee on History discredited the idea that Lincoln offered Confederate states indemnities for emancipation. The UCV adopted the committee's report unanimously, and the 1899 resolution was passed.[69] Most veterans willingly admitted that controversy over the future of slavery had caused the Civil War, but, in the words of one veteran attending a state-wide meeting between the 1899 and 1900, many worried that Union-sympathizing historians would remember them to be "actuated by no higher motive than the desire to retain the money value of slave property." They feared that "the world" would hold them "degraded rather than worthy of honor," and that their children would be ashamed of their fathers. This fear was also central to the previous newspaper debates.[70]

The UCV resolution represented important changes in the organization. Along with some white Northerners, Confederate veterans embraced a heroic view of Southern military men that focused on military accomplishments rather than a legacy of slavery and racial violence in the South. Their stories responded to the growing political importance of a white professional class who had never claimed ownership over enslaved people. Democrats and veterans alike shifted away from honoring Confederate leadership or elite planters and toward honoring ordinary soldiers to speak to a wider base of support. As third-party campaigning showed, calling attention to reimbursing enslavers would have played up the class divisions that Confederate veterans and Democrats sought to avoid.[71] Invested in painting a sympathetic picture of their cause for posterity, Confederate veterans denied that white Southerners wanted or needed federal compensation for freed slaves.

The debate over the Hampton Roads Conference offered former Confederates a way to deny that slaveholding states wanted, needed, or were ever offered compensation, and to remove the question of the profitability of slavery from the historical debate altogether. With these two facts denied, it was not a far stretch to say that the institution of slavery did not cause the war. As one veteran put it, with the Hampton Roads Conference report, the UCV eliminated "from the history of the conflict of 1861–65 the side issue of slavery."[72] Except for the Louisville *Courier-Journal*, the Southern white press rapidly adopted the UCV's version of events.[73]

A few Black newspapers and organizations commented on the debate, suggesting that white men of the South would not support pensions for the formerly enslaved because they were not themselves compensated for property in people. Cutting to the heart of the politics of the past decade, the editor of the *Richmond Planet*, John Mitchell, reminded readers that despite some politicians' suggestions, paying former enslavers would not solve the problems of the Democratic-controlled "Solid South."[74]

MITCHELL WAS CORRECT. Paying former enslavers would not solve the problems of the Solid South, in part because claims for compensation were less a realistic economic policy than political tools. Politicians used the claims throughout the end of Reconstruction and into the Jim Crow era to discredit opponents, cast doubt on the legitimacy of the Fourteenth Amendment, and build political coalitions to challenge the two-party system. When claims for compensation damaged Democrats' and former Confederates' political aims, they abandoned them.

The UCV's debate over the Hampton Roads Conference gave historical weight to Democrat's goals and political power. Not only did the white press adopt the UCV's version of events, but so too would the white academy. One academic, Walter B. Hill—a lawyer and the chancellor of the University of Georgia—explained the UCV's logic in a letter discussing the Hampton Roads debate in 1905. He observed, "The South is exceedingly and justly sensitive and proud in maintaining the position that the war between the states was not fought for slavery." If Lincoln had actually offered the Confederacy reimbursement for freed slaves, he conjectured, then Confederate president Jefferson Davis's rejection of the hypothetical offer, he admitted, "adds great force" to the idea that the South did not secede over slavery. He elaborated, "Even as late as February 1865, when the doom of the Confederacy was sealed and when full compensation for the slaves might have been obtained on condition of surrender, the South . . . refused to entertain the suggestion." Though Confederate leaders could not have known that Confederate armies would begin to surrender to the United States only two months later, Hill nevertheless concluded, "This is [a] complete demonstration that no mercenary consideration of property had been the cause of the war or was then a ground for its practically hopeless continuance." In search of a way to absolve white Southerners from perpetuating a war for slavery, Hill summarized the teleological thinking of many white Southerners and Americans generally: Because the Confederacy acquiesced to immediate, uncompensated emancipation, white Southerners had recognized slavery as unprofitable, and the white South did not secede to protect it.[75]

Historians followed suit. They dismissed white Southerners' postwar claims for federal compensation, if they acknowledged them at all. These conclusions also discredited Black Americans' movements to redress the history and the material and economic damages of slavery. The same historians who insisted that white Southerners never wanted or needed federal compensation spurned the ex-slave pension movement as well. Walter Fleming—a member of the Dunning School and a professor of history at Louisiana State University—wrote a twelve-page article in 1910, "Ex-Slave Pension Frauds." The article dismissed the MRB&PA as a swindle, writing that Vaughan's original fund was "the more honest part of the slave pension movement."[76]

Fleming's article bolstered the US Post Office's fraud charges against the MRB&PA. Callie House paid for her efforts to redress the national history of slavery: She served eleven months in a Missouri state prison after being charged for mail fraud by an all-white jury in 1917. Over the same period, historians like Fleming ensured that the UCV's version of events was woven into historical memory and scholarship. Rather than acknowledge the profitability of slavery, white historians denied that white Southerners ever claimed compensation for enslavers. Such an acknowledgment that former Confederates sought compensation for freed people would have contradicted the assumptions on which they rested their histories of the Civil War and on which Democrats rested Jim Crow laws.

Conclusion

The idea that white Southerners never wanted or expected compensation for the value of enslaved people continues to shape American memory and historiography despite the fact that historians have long discredited the Dunning School of Reconstruction History and other whitewashed histories of the war. This view was so prominent in twentieth-century historiography that even the Dunning School's detractors expressed ambivalence about white Southerners' claims for compensation.[1] By the second half of the century, revisionist historians argued that white Southerners accepted immediate, uncompensated emancipation after Confederate surrender. A few explored how white Southerners' claims for compensation contributed to political realignments in the postwar South, concluding that white Southerners quickly relinquished them to recoup political power and control Black labor.[2]

This book corrects the long-standing view that white Southerners accepted immediate, uncompensated emancipation. Before the Civil War, enslavers in the antebellum United States wanted to preserve and expand slavery at almost any cost, and pro-slavery Americans believed their ability to claim ownership over people was a fundamental right for which individuals or states deserved to be compensated in the event of emancipation. They designed state governments and laws to preserve the value of enslaved people, and many believed the federal government should do so, too. After emancipation and Confederate defeat, many white Southerners thought compensation was possible because they believed the Constitution supported their claims. They felt that emancipation was a financial and social loss for which they were entitled to remuneration. They described their claim to profit from property in people as a constitutional right protected by the Fifth Amendment's takings clause; as a reward for accepting the end of slavery; as a necessary economic protection for dependent white widows and orphans; and as a natural right that only courts, not military force, could revoke.

In 1866, Republicans defeated former enslavers' compensation claims by passing section 4 of the Fourteenth Amendment, which was ratified in 1868. Although US policymakers routinely proposed compensated emancipation schemes in different places until the end of the war, Republicans successfully defeated them during Reconstruction because Americans questioned whether enslavers, who had perpetuated a violent civil war, deserved compensation. When pro-slavery advocates refused to relinquish slavery, Republicans determined that anything other than the immediate, uncompensated abolition of slavery was treasonous and justified further intervention with the Fourteenth Amendment.

Section 4 of that amendment ended the possibility that former enslavers would be remunerated for emancipation. As a result, emancipation in the United States looks much more progressive than other nations by the 1860s at first glance. The United States' refusal to compensate enslavers after the Civil War was an important departure from previous moments of emancipation in other nations. As historian Steven Hahn writes, "Like the Haitian Revolution before it, the Civil War broke the logic of gradualism and slaveholder compensation and made a new and different country."[3] In the years immediately after the Civil War, Black Americans gained some rights of citizenship that other nations denied freed people upon emancipation—notably the vote for Black men. The United States refused to pay enslavers directly or indirectly despite international precedents, and historians came to understand both the illegality of secession and the legality of uncompensated emancipation as a "verdict of Appomattox," an unquestioned fact of military victory.[4] By the end of the nineteenth century, white Americans recast uncompensated emancipation as a moral victory determined by the outcome of the Civil War rather than a contingent political process that punished pro-slavery advocates for resisting immediate, uncompensated emancipation and departed from existing national and international precedents.

Such conclusions, however, overlook that the United States did compensate some enslavers during the Civil War, and that enslavers and their political allies continued to mobilize constitutional and other legal arguments for compensation after the Civil War and ratification of the Thirteenth Amendment. Thanks in part to the Dunning School's histories and the Lost Cause, Americans forgot that it took a concerted effort *not* to pay enslavers, and the United States came to uncompensated emancipation through a series of wartime policy decisions. In accordance with two of those policies, the United States paid 930 petitions for compensation in part or in full to enslavers in Washington, DC, and 25 claims in Maryland. Meanwhile, enslavers in the border states and the former Confederacy continued to advocate for compensation.[5] After decades of debates over whether the Constitution protected property rights in people, congressional Republicans incorporated section 4 into the Fourteenth Amendment to void any claim for compensation, suggesting that many policymakers believed—or at least were uncertain whether—the Constitution required compensation to former enslavers even after civil war.

The United States broke the logic of gradualism but maintained much of the logic of slave law and the political culture that had enabled enslavers to profit from property rights in people in the first place. Republicans and their allies knew that the constitutionality of uncompensated emancipation would be determined by the party in power, so they altered the Constitution to achieve major social reforms and secure uncompensated emancipation as a legacy of the US war effort. But the Thirteenth and Fourteenth Amendments did not "signal a clear, fundamental shift in constitutional ideology," as historian Michael Vorenberg argues. I argue alongside Vorenberg and other historians that even after the Emancipation Proclamation and the Thirteenth Amendment, freedom and slavery interacted in complex ways at the state and federal levels because of existing property and contract regimes that preserved enslavers' rights to profit from property in people. This process unfolded long after the Civil War because policymakers and the Supreme Court did not want to create mechanisms that could justify the abolition of all property, only property rights in people. Section 4 of the Fourteenth Amendment created a constitutional framework that retroactively expanded federal authority for immediate, uncompensated emancipation without suggesting that the United States could permanently confiscate other forms of private property.[6]

This history went overlooked because as early as 1866, Democrats minimized former Confederate resistance to uncompensated emancipation and the significant constitutional change that section 4 represented. The Dunning School followed. A central tenet of the Dunning School and Lost Cause narratives as they emerged in the early 1900s was that Radical Republicans unduly punished white Southerners during Reconstruction. True, Republican congressmen routinely referred to punishing traitors in congressional debates over the Fourteenth Amendment using bloody shirt rhetoric. But federal Reconstruction policy only appears disproportionate if historians do not record white Southerners' resistance to immediate, uncompensated emancipation as it happened. The Dunning School and Lost Cause propagandists minimized white Southerners' resistance and the profitability of slavery, dismissed section 4 as unnecessary, and rebranded the debate over whether the federal government protected enslavers' "property rights in people" as a constitutional debate over "states' rights."[7] I argue in contrast that section 4 of the Fourteenth Amendment was imperative to secure immediate, uncompensated emancipation against white Southerners' opposition after Confederate surrender.

WHY SHOULD WE CARE about failed demands to pay enslavers? Obscuring them shaped how Americans and historians understood emancipation. Ever since the Dunning School denied white Southerners' claims for compensation and slavery's profitability, the moral and ethical dimensions of quantifying slavery and its profitability have suffused the study of American slavery. US historians and other scholars have generally discussed slavery and emancipation in terms of the monetary profits and losses for enslavers to understand the extent to which it instigated the Civil War, shaped the modern American economy, and what modern Americans owed for slavery.

Over the course of the twentieth century, historians asked whether slavery profited the enslavers who claimed ownership over people. If slavery were profitable, it was an efficient and perhaps even capitalist economic system, suggesting that it was foundational to the US economy. In the era of cliometrics, economic historians quantified enslaved people's labor, food, reproduction, and other pieces of their lives to understand slavery as an economic institution; to define profitability under the economic conditions of the nineteenth century's slave system; and to reconsider whether slavery contributed to the growth of US capitalism. These studies also shaped historians' understandings of the causes of the Civil War. Why else, they asked, would the South fight a war for slavery unless it was profitable?[8]

Most recently, new historians of capitalism, Black digital slavery studies, and popular works of history like "The 1619 Project" have revived the economic debates, concluding that the North's free-labor-based, capitalist economy depended on Southern slavery, a different kind of capitalist economy built on enslaved labor and the value of property in people. Many of these critics challenge a neoliberal celebration of capitalism, arguing that slavery was the foundation of the US economy—North and South—and that slavery's legacies continue to perpetuate economic inequities for Black Americans that need to be redressed.[9] Although these histories debunked the Dunning School's tenet that slavery was unprofitable, they tend to end before the Civil War, obscuring what we can learn from white Southerners' attempts to recoup the lost value of enslaved people after emancipation.

By recovering the Civil War and Reconstruction-era compensation debates, this book suggests that it is not enough to analyze slavery and emancipation from the lens of economic profitability or individual financial gain. Whether they profited from slavery or received remuneration, enslavers and pro-slavery advocates wanted to protect slavery so badly that they devised many ways to defend and maintain it before the Civil War using the law, political maneuver, and economic and financial tools. During and after the war, they devised ways to retain or echo slavery, though their claims for compensation failed. The most vocal proponents of compensation often would not have benefited personally, suggesting that more was at stake than personal profit. When they demanded compensation and later obscured those claims, enslavers and their political allies also shaped conversations about regional identity politics and complicity for slavery.

Contemporary politicians and writers, too, understood emancipation policy in terms of financial and moral absolution. During the war, Abraham Lincoln echoed British abolitionists of the 1820s and 1830s who viewed reimbursing enslavers as a national sacrifice for the sin of slavery. As it turned out, the English paid in money, the United States in blood. When Confederate armies surrendered, Republican congressmen denied enslavers compensation but continued to play up the nation's sacrifice. They insisted that the only loyal enslavers were those who willingly relinquished their profits in human property for the benefit of a nation that had offered up the lives of countless men to end slavery. Loyal Americans would not pay more.[10]

These national conversations had important effects on American politics. Republicans and Northerners blamed all enslavers for the war over the protests of border state politicians, which, this book suggests, led to another regional political realignment. The border states became Confederate in part because former enslavers there did not receive reimbursements for freed slaves. Most historians who have explained how border states abandoned Unionist parties for Democrats and became Southern after the Civil War dismissed the idea that enslavers there sought federal reimbursements for freed people after the Emancipation Proclamation. But it is clear that many desired and petitioned for the bounties for formerly enslaved enlisted men promised in the 1864 Enrollment Act long after the war ended. They had remained in the Union because they believed property rights in people would be best protected under the US Constitution. When Congress passed section 4 and refused to compensate border state enslavers, they felt betrayed by the federal government and the Republican Party. White border state Unionists rejected Republican accusations that pursuing reimbursements for freed slaves made an enslaver disloyal and soon allied with Democrats in former Confederate states.[11]

Southerners, too, resented Republican accusations and insisted that the North was complicit in perpetuating slavery in the United States in fiscal terms. In 1866, Kentuckian Lawrence Trimble reminded his colleagues of Northern complicity in the slave trade and related industries to protest section 4 and uncompensated emancipation.[12] Dunning School historians and popular media like *Birth of a Nation* blamed slave traders for bringing slavery to the United States and accused Northern merchants of profiting from slavery and products produced by enslaved laborers. The sin of slavery, they admitted, did not belong solely to the South. Later, Robert Penn Warren, a writer, literary critic, and Southerner, criticized Northerners for imagining themselves detached from the history of American slavery and the contemporary civil rights violations that were slavery's legacies. In 1961, during the centennial of the Civil War and the civil rights movement, he wrote that the Northerner "feels redeemed by history, automatically redeemed." According to Warren, Northerners—ostensibly white Northerners—remembered the Civil War as a "consciously undertaken crusade" to abolish slavery. As a result, they conveniently forgot that emancipation happened incrementally and haphazardly, or that "racism and Abolitionism might, and often did, go hand in hand." Instead, they remembered the war as "an indulgence, a plenary indulgence, for all sins past, present, and future, freely given by the hand of history." Warren called this indulgence the "Treasury of Virtue." When they abolished slavery in a bloody civil war, Warren accused, Northerners imagined that they absolved themselves of any involvement in slavery and, by extension, Jim Crow.[13]

We see echoes of debates about regional complicity for slavery in twenty-first century conversations about slavery and reparations. In 2019, "The 1619 Project" reminded a new generation of Americans that slavery was not a Southern problem but a national problem requiring national redress. With these conversations at hand, *Counting the Cost of Freedom* suggests that the fiscal debate over complicity—stemming from the political and economic interests of politicians in different moments across the nineteenth century—rarely resulted in moral clarity and obscured more about the history of slavery and its legacies than it resolved. If immediate, uncompensated emancipation granted the United States a treasury of virtue, few had to imagine what debts the nation had accrued for slavery.[14]

For most of the nineteenth century, it was easier for Americans to imagine that emancipation created a national debt to enslavers than it was for them to consider that slavery created a debt to the formerly enslaved. As historian Tera Hunter reminded *New York Times* readers in 2019, "It is important to remember that slaveowners, far more than enslaved people, were always the primary beneficiaries of public largess."[15] Although African Americans long claimed reparations, most Americans took enslavers' claims for compensation more seriously throughout the nineteenth century because of international precedents and the legal protections that enslavers enjoyed for their property rights in people. It was so much easier for Americans to understand their debt to enslavers that leaders of the National Ex-Slave Mutual Relief, Bounty and Pension Association mobilized former enslavers' claims for compensation to justify ex-slave pensions and their mutual aid efforts well after the Fourteenth Amendment had invalidated them.

But measuring the monetary value of slavery and the cost of emancipation led to unexpected and muddy convergences. When 1890s congressional candidates like John Williamson and Guy Sibley suggested paying former enslavers alongside the formerly enslaved, they combined two seemingly diametrically opposed ideas: one, that enslavers deserved compensation for the lost value of property in people, and two, that the formerly enslaved deserved payment for generations of forced labor. Intended to unite disparate constituencies, their proposals did not make for successful politics. Such comparisons enabled slavery apologists to posit the equivalence of the harm emancipation caused enslavers to the harm slavery caused the enslaved. While the literal accounting might have added up, the political principles did not. To reimburse one group without reimbursing the other, they suggested, would be impossible; yet some detractors recognized that to reimburse one group while reimbursing the other would be unfair.[16]

Focused on debates about compensation to former enslavers during the Civil War era, this book only scrapes the surface of nineteenth-century African Americans' conversations about debt, slavery, and the law; however, it is clear that African Americans, such as the editors of the *New National Era* and George Washington Williams, participated in and had their own conversations about these ideas in the years following the Civil War and Reconstruction for different ends.[17] We need more research on how they mobilized ideas about finance, law, and debt—both monetary and metaphorical—before and after the war to express the country's moral obligations to the enslaved and their descendants in order to better understand these complicated politics.[18]

This book does show that when calls to pay enslavers began to hurt their political goals, former Confederates and Southern Democrats abandoned and then lied about them to bolster their political prominence and national legacy. By obscuring their own claims for compensation and denying slavery's profitability, white Southerners undermined Black Americans' claims for reparations, as well as any remaining compensation claims after the nineteenth century. The Lost Cause narratives and Warren's Treasury of Virtue suggested there was nothing left to repair and nothing owed to enslavers or freed people. Emancipation had already been won, and Americans had already paid the price of freedom—but not the costs of slavery.

Acknowledgments

Writing this book has been my great privilege, and I could not have done it without the support of many family, friends, colleagues, and institutions. Thank you to the staff at the University of North Carolina Press, including Mark Simpson-Vos, Debbie Gershenowitz, Thomas Bedenbaugh, Erin Granville, and Abigail Michaud for making this book a reality. Aaron Sheehan-Dean has been a generous editor and reader, encouraging me across the finish line. I must also thank the anonymous reviewers: I am grateful for your constructive feedback, which helped me frame this story and its contributions to the field.

This book began at Northwestern University. In my time there, and ever since, Kate Masur has mentored me, inspired me, and pushed me. She has always given generous and incisive feedback. I view her as the standard for writing complex histories simply and clearly. I am especially grateful to her for fostering a supportive community among my fellow students and providing flexibility when life required it, and for her continuing feedback and mentorship since I left Northwestern. Dylan Penningroth, Caitlyn Fitz, Joanna Grisinger, and scholars at the American Bar Foundation offered critical questions and insights that helped me begin this manuscript.

I am lucky to be a member of a community of scholars who are so generous with their time and expertise. Cynthia Nicoletti has read many versions of these chapters since 2020, shared the intricacies of nineteenth-century legal history, and talked me through my ideas. I hope this published version positively reflects her efforts. Ed Ayers, Abena Boakyewa-Ansah, Robert Colby, Laura Edwards, Sally Gordon, Robert Kenzer, Anne Kerth, Jacob Lee, Kirsten Lee, Jessica Levy, Thomas Mackey, Caleb McDaniel, Giuliana Perrone, Reuel Schiller, Rachel Sheldon, Nina Silber, Michael Vorenberg, and Kid Wongsrichanalai have all read parts of the manuscript and improved it immeasurably. Marie Stango and Tyler Sperrazza read early drafts of some of my most difficult chapters in a Society for Civil War Historians writing group, and Dr. Stango pointed me to resources on colonization. Pamela Haag helped me prepare the book for review, and Amron Lehte prepared the index.

A contingent of historians based in or focused on Kentucky—including Jacob Lee, Patrick Lewis, Thomas C. Mackey, Amy Murrell Taylor, and Chuck Welsko—have pointed me in the direction of Kentucky sources and historiographies. Leslie Rowland and Joseph Reidy have shared archival sources, research advice, and feedback that shaped my work on the border states. Caleb McDaniel shared newspaper articles related to claims to pay enslavers and the formerly enslaved, many of which appear in chapter 6. Amy Fluker and Kelly Mezurek provided great insights on the border states and Black enlistment.

Due to wonderful friends and colleagues, I was never lonely writing this book. Giuliana Perrone has been my friend since we connected over Zoom in 2020. Particular thanks go to Giuliana for reading my work, sharing her unpublished manuscript, and helping me navigate the tenure track and publishing process. I also thank Sandra Berjan, Stephanie Brehm, Misty De Berry, Myisha Eatmon, Meaghan Fritz, Jessica Levy, Laura McCoy, Lucy Newton,

Brittnay Proctor, Vanda Rajcan, Ana Rosado, Leigh Soares, Angela Tate, and LaCharles Ward for feedback that stuck with me, engaging conversations, and writing dates that motivated and inspired at every stage of the process.

I am grateful for a number of opportunities for feedback, training, library access, and networking. The American Society for Legal History's 2019–20 Wallace Johnson First Book Program gave me the springboard I needed to begin this book. Reuel Schiller built our cohort, ensured that we remained connected after COVID-19 forced us all into quarantine, demystified the publishing process, and guided us as we wrote book proposals and sample chapters. Thank you to Reuel, Sally Gordon, Cynthia Nicoletti, and my fellow authors—Pedro Cantisano, Marie-Amelie George, Kalyani Ramnath, Evan Taparata, and Adnan Zulfiqar—for your advice and support.

As a faculty fellow at the Gilder Lehrman Center for the Study of Slavery, Resistance, and Abolition at Yale University (GLC) in spring 2020, I was given the resources to complete chapter 6. I made lasting friendships and received encouraging feedback that helped shape the book. Thank you to David Blight, Lorena Chambers, Lou deBaca, Lena Gotteswinter, Melissa McGrath, Lisa Monroe, Stephanie Redden, Ed Rugemer, Thomas Thurston, and Michelle Zacks. It's been a pleasure staying connected with Stephanie and Michelle through Zoom as we've navigated life and career transitions since.

A number of workshops provided invaluable feedback on this project. The Malgeri Modern American Society and Culture Seminar at the Massachusetts Historical Society in October 2020 allowed me to reconnect with scholars from across the country. Thank you to Nina Silber for her generous feedback on an initial draft of chapter 6. Thanks to Kid Wongsrichanalai for organizing the workshop and for your feedback. In April 2023, I presented a first draft of my introduction to the Southern Historical Association's Junior Scholars Workshop at the invitation of Kelly Kennington, K. Steven Prince, and Selena Sanderfer Doss. Thank you to Caleb McDaniel and Michael Vorenberg for commenting and for your continued engagement with my work. Rachel Shelden invited me to the George and Ann Richards Civil War Era Center's workshop in October 2023, where she helped me frame chapter 4. Thanks to each workshop attendee for their comments and suggestions.

This book took shape at the Massachusetts College of Liberal Arts (MCLA), where I had supportive colleagues who made space for our research alongside our teaching focus. Thank you to the History and Political Science Department for supporting my leave for the Gilder Lehrman fellowship and thereby jump-starting my book. Thank you to the librarians at Freel Library for making my research possible through their extraordinary support, including patient instruction. Thank you especially to Kate Flower, as well as Emily Alling, Alishia Alther, Danielle Christenson, Pamela Contakos, and Glenn Lawson. Victoria Papa invited me to the 2021–2022 *Mind's Eye* Faculty Works-in-Progress Colloquium, where I tested out new ideas for the book's conclusion. Jenna Sciuto and Liz Hartung provided mentorship and friendship in my time at MCLA and after, as did other new faculty and friends: Caren Beilin, Kate Gigliotti, Guangzhi Huang, Michael Petrovich, Jerome Socoloff, and Eric Uthus.

When I moved to Elon University in the fall of 2022, I returned to the South and gained a host of outstanding new colleagues. Elon and the History and Geography Department provided funding and mentoring. In particular, Mike Carignan, Peter Felton, Mary Jo Festle,

Evan Gatti, Waseem bin Kasim, and Michael Matthews provided sage advice and energizing conversations about writing a book and pursuing a research agenda at Elon. Outside the department, Clare Callahan, Kristie Ellison, and Erin Pearson collectively read the entire manuscript. Cora Wigger shared her expertise in economics and the histories of racial inequality. Teresa LePors and the rest of Belk Library provided essential research support.

I received generous funding to complete this book, from the research to production stages. I traveled to many archives thanks to research support from librarians and archivists, as well as funding from Northwestern University; the American Bar Foundation; the Littleton-Griswold Research Grant from the American Historical Association; a Congressional Research Grant from the Dirksen Congressional Center; the Archie K. Davis Fellowship from the North Caroliniana Society; the Governor Thomas Gordon McLeod and First Lady Elizabeth Alford McLeod Research Fellowship from the South Caroliniana Library; the Lawrence T. Jones III Research Fellowship from the Texas State Historical Association; and the William and Madeline Welder Smith Endowed Travel Award from the Dolph Briscoe Center for American History. A summer stipend from the National Endowment for the Humanities along with the faculty fellowship from the Gilder Lehrman Center for the Study of Slavery, Resistance, and Abolition granted me more time to write this book. Elon University and the William Nelson Cromwell Foundation Early Career Scholar Fellowship provided funding that helped produce this book.

Perhaps one of the greatest privileges is a supportive family. The women in my family have modeled for me so many different ways to pursue a career and a life, and I am so grateful that they created room for me to explore. I would not be a historian, or have known it was possible to be one, if it weren't for them. My grandmothers Romaine and Wilma, and Beverley, have given me so much in their own ways and have always supported me as I pursued my career goals, even if that meant living far away from them. My mom, Lisa Laury-Kleintop—a scientist by training—tolerated and even encouraged trips to historic sites that inspired my interest in history and taught me how to be a woman in academia. Lizabeth Kleintop shared her love of history with me by teaching me everything she knows about the Civil War, giving me a solid grounding in the era well before I began this book.

I met Jeremy Needle at Northwestern around the same time that I began research for this project. Thank you for being there all along.

Notes

Abbreviations

CWAL	*Collected Works of Abraham Lincoln*, 8 vols. (Ann Arbor: University of Michigan Library Digital Collections, 1953)
LaRC	Louisiana Research Collection, Tulane University Special Collections, New Orleans, LA
LOC	Library of Congress
MDAH	Mississippi Department of Archives and History, Jackson, MS
NARA	National Archives and Records Administration, Washington, DC
OR	*The War of the Rebellion: A Compilation of the Official Records of the Union and Confederate Armies*, 128 vols. (Washington, DC: Government Printing Office), 1880–1901
PAJ	Andrew Johnson, *The Papers of Andrew Johnson*, ed. Paul H. Bergeron, LeRoy P. Graf, and Ralph W. Haskins, 16 vols. (Knoxville: University of Tennessee Press, 1967–2000)
SANC	State Archives of North Carolina, Raleigh, NC
SCDAH	South Carolina Department of Archives and History, Columbia, SC
TSLAC	Texas State Library and Archives Commission, Austin, TX

Introduction

1. This book cites estimated values relating to slavery and the Southern economy to provide a scale of the enormous wealth invested in slaves before the US Civil War. However, these numbers are exactly that—estimates—and can range widely. Economic historians have long debated how to measure the value of enslaved people to the US and Southern economies and whether uncompensated emancipation negatively affected the southern economy. New histories of capitalism have reaffirmed the significance of slavery to the US economy and reconsidered the relationship between slavery and capitalism, exploring slavery's regulatory regimes, plantation technology, financial practices, and more, to show how slavery was central to and even created modern capitalism. See D. R. Berry, *Price for Their Pound of Flesh*; Baptist, *Half Has Never Been Told*; Beckert, *Empire of Cotton*; W. Johnson, *River of Dark Dreams*; Beckert and Rockman, *Slavery's Capitalism*; Olmstead and Rhode, "Cotton, Slavery, and the New History of Capitalism"; Sinha, "Problem of Abolition in the Age of Capitalism." For explanations of how economic historians measured and estimated these values, see Wright, *Slavery and American Economic Development*, 2, 7–11; Williamson and Cain, "Measuring Slavery in 2020 Dollars"; Goldin, "The Economics of Emancipation," 74–75; Roger L. Ransom, "The Economics of the Civil War,"; Huston, *Calculating the Value of the Union*, chap. 2; Hornbeck and Logan, "One Giant Leap."

2. Historians explain how unusual immediate, uncompensated emancipation was in the nineteenth century by pointing to the US South and Haiti as exceptions. However, these comparisons overlook Haiti's colonial relationship to France, the complicated circumstances of emancipation there, and the French indemnity. Dubois, *Haiti*, 76–104; L. M. Alexander, *Fear of a Black Republic*, chap. 2.

3. For histories of emancipation in the regions listed, see Hodges, *Slavery and Freedom in the Rural North*, 171; Bierck, "Struggle for Abolition in Gran Colombia"; Blanchard, *Under the Flags of Freedom*; Draper, *Price of Emancipation*; Araujo, *Reparations for Slavery and the Slave Trade*; Scalan, *Slave Empire*; Drescher, "British Way, French Way." According to Bierck, compensated emancipation in Gran Colombia was not universally carried out as legislated because enslavers' heirs resisted the taxation plan established to pay enslavers. The breakup of the republic in 1829–30 further complicated administrative efforts to pay them.

4. US Const. amend. V. This book is indebted to the following comparative histories for contrasting the US South with those areas of the world that did compensate enslavers directly or indirectly. Hahn, *Political Worlds of Slavery and Freedom*; Sinha, *Slave's Cause*; Kolchin, "Some Thoughts on Emancipation in Comparative Perspective"; Kolchin, "South and the World"; Holt, "'Empire over the Mind'"; Hahn, "Class and State in Postemancipation Societies"; Engerman, "Emancipation Schemes"; Fladeland, "Compensated Emancipation"; de la Fuente and Gross, *Becoming Free, Becoming Black*; Scott, *Degrees of Freedom*; Scott and Hébrard, *Freedom Papers*; Cooper et al., *Beyond Slavery*; Foner, *Nothing but Freedom*; Manajpra, *Black Ghost of Empire*.

5. Vorenberg, *Final Freedom*; Gross, *Double Character*; Siddali, *From Property to Person*; Hamilton, *Limits of Sovereignty*; Downs, *After Appomattox*; Foner, *Fiery Trial*; Oakes, *Freedom National*.

6. Quote from Berlin et al., "Destruction of Slavery," 4. See also Fields, *Slavery and Freedom on the Middle Ground*; A. M. Taylor, *Embattled Freedom*. Regarding the contingencies and complexities of emancipation on the ground, I've also been influenced by the Freedmen and Southern Society Project and the following books: Jackson, *Force and Freedom*; Sinha, *Slave's Cause*; Ayers, *In the Presence of Mine Enemies*; T. Hunter, *To 'Joy My Freedom*; T. Hunter, *Bound in Wedlock*.

7. The following historians have identified claims for compensation in the former Confederacy, though they often described them as unrealistic or inevitably doomed endeavors that distracted from efforts to control Black labor after emancipation. Bright, "Radicalism and Rebellion"; Carter, *When the War Was Over*, 82–85; Roark, *Masters without Slaves*, 104–5, 134; Perman, *Reunion without Compromise*, 87; Breese, "Politics in the Lower South during Presidential Reconstruction," 139–40, 145; Wolfe, "South Carolina Constitutional Convention of 1865," 26. Other historians argue that the Lincoln administration dropped all schemes to compensate former enslavers after 1863, when President Lincoln issued the Emancipation Proclamation. However, this book shows how debates over compensation continued well past the Proclamation, the Thirteenth Amendment, and US victory. For a few of these arguments, see Du Bois, *Black Reconstruction in America*, 150; Foner, *Fiery Trial*; Oakes, *Freedom National*; Finkelman, "Lincoln and the Preconditions for Emancipation," 13–44.

8. US Const. amend. XIV, § 4.

9. Federal sources often filled in gaps across the former Confederacy. Federal military presence and freedom seekers changed the circumstances of emancipation in different places, and the archival information available in every state is diverse. All former Confederate states published records of their presidential and congressional Reconstruction constitutional conventions; however, the level of detail ranges from direct transcripts of the debates to summaries of the measures proposed. In addition, the papers of state politicians and judges are less well-preserved than those of federal politicians. For example, one historian reported that a goat ate the majority of Louisiana Supreme Court justice James B. Taliaferro's papers. Other state politicians were less prolific, or their descendants did not preserve their papers. Further, while governors' papers could offer a lens into constituents' views on emancipation, each state kept different records. For example, Louisiana did not keep official records of governors' papers until the twentieth century, while South Carolina not only kept detailed indexes of the letters received by the governor's office but kept the letters themselves. Personal papers of state politicians and enslavers proved less informative than I had hoped when embarking on this project. As historian James Huston has found, manuscript collections often contain personal correspondence about partisan political movements but not about policy issues. I share his sense that politicians put most of their policy thinking into formal speeches and public statements rather than reiterate them in their letters. Similarly, former enslavers may not have written about political issues in their personal correspondence except in shorthand. Business records like account books did not provide much information either, likely because the purpose of those documents was to track transactions, not record the political machinations that would change those balances. Huston, *Calculating the Value of the Union*, xvi; Mills, "James Govan Taliaferro (1798–1896)."

10. Digitized newspaper databases including Newspapers.com; Readex's America's Historical Newspapers; Gale's Nineteenth Century US Newspapers; Readex's African American Newspapers, Series 1; and Accessible Archives helped me explore the extent of claims for compensation when archival research was restricted by the COVID-19 pandemic; however, many papers available digitally were from the North or had a Republican bent. Southern papers were more difficult to access online. Thank you to Caleb McDaniel, who shared with me relevant articles from Newspapers.com, which I wouldn't have had access to otherwise. While many historians have successfully recovered Black peoples' voices from state governors' papers, I had less success finding Black Southerners' discussions of and opinions on debates over remuneration for former slaveowners during and immediately after the war in those archives. Digitized records of the Colored Conventions Project showed little discussion among African American communities of payments to enslavers. I had more success finding freed people's voices discussing compensation and the value of enslaved people in digitized Black newspapers rather than government-produced sources after 1870. This book attempts to incorporate their perspectives by expanding beyond Reconstruction. See Colored Conventions Project: Digital Records, https://omeka.coloredconventions.org.

11. Cherokee who sided with the United States during the war negotiated emancipation with the US government in the winter of 1863. They attempted to secure for loyal Cherokee enslavers reimbursements for freed slaves but quickly dropped their claims for compensation. The 1866 treaty between the Cherokee Nation and the United States provided that no Cherokee would receive compensation. After siding with the Confederacy, both the Choctaw and Chickasaw Nations hoped to secure compensation from the United States for enslavers

when negotiating a joint peace treaty in 1866. Such payments would have accounted for a substantial number of people, given that at least 14% of the population of Choctaws were enslaved and Chickasaws enslaved 18% of their population. The United States' refusal to compensate Cherokee, Choctaw, and Chickasaw enslavers while eventually allotting land to the formerly enslaved people of those nations reflected the nation's dual goals of defending Black freedom while separating Natives from their land. Miles, *Ties That Bind*, 349, 353; Saunt, "The Paradox of Freedom," 64–65, 79; Krauthamer, *Black Slaves, Indian Masters*, 10–11, 108, 113; Roberts, *I've Been Here All the While*, 47–48. Miles cites a work-in-progress by Melinda Miller and Rachel Smith Purvis, "'No Rights of Citizenship': The 1863 Emancipation Acts of the Loyal Cherokee Council," which discusses the negotiations between pro-Union Cherokee and the US in 1863.

12. Huston, *Calculating the Value of the Union*, 52; Vorenberg, *Final Freedom*, 6. Many historians and legal scholars have described the characteristics of US slave law, concluding that the laws of slavery were groups of laws and legal practices embedded within different areas of law, including property law, commercial law, and contract law. Tushnet, *American Law of Slavery, 1810–1860*; Morris, *Southern Slavery and the Law, 1619–1860*; Wahl, *Bondsman's Burden*; Simard, "Slavery's Legalism"; W. Johnson, "Inconsistency, Contradiction, and Complete Confusion"; Axtell, "Towards a New Legal History of Capitalism and Unfree Labor"; Morris, "Chattel Mortgages of Slaves." They've also shown how Southern politicians and enslavers sustained these practices in legal and political culture, working to ensure that localities, states, and the federal government would protect their investments in human property and help enslavers expand their planation enterprises across the United States. W. Johnson, *Soul by Soul*; A. J. Gross, *Double Character*; Fehrenbacher, *Slaveholding Republic*; Finkelman, *Imperfect Union*; Genovese and Genovese, "Slavery, Economic Development, and the Law"; Stohler, "Slavery and Just Compensation in American Constitutionalism." Because this book investigates the legal category of "slave," I have tried to be careful of the language I use to refer to the systems and people that this book describes. Over the past decade and more, historians of slavery have moved away from the words "slavery" and "slave" to emphasize the identities and humanity of the enslaved. In this book, I use the new terminology to refer to enslaved people in the aggregate or when discussing individuals. I use the words "slave" and "slavery" in quotes from historical documents, as adjectives to describe legal or economic systems, and when emphasizing the legal and economic nature of a person's actions and transactions, such as "slaveowner" or "slave trader." My choices have been informed by debates in public history, descendant communities, and the following historians: Miles, *All That She Carried*, 287–89; Penningroth, "Race in Contract Law," 1205n13; P. Gabrielle Foreman et al., "Writing about Slavery/Teaching about Slavery: This Might Help," community-sourced document, accessed December 29, 2024, https://docs.google.com/document/d/1A4TEdDgYslX-hlKezLodMIM71My3KTN0zxRvoIQTOQs/mobilebasic.

13. George Potter, Robert Brown, and William Yerger, 1860 US census, slave schedule, Ancestry.com.

14. US Const. amend. XIV, § 4.

15. Graber, *Punish Treason, Reward Loyalty*, xxxi, 3. Those historians who dismissed section 4 include Kendrick, *Journal of the Joint Committee of Fifteen on Reconstruction*, 350; James, *Framing of the Fourteenth Amendment*, 160, 180, 194; J. G. Clark, "Historians and the

Joint Committee on Reconstruction," 348–61; Flack, *Adoption of the Fourteenth Amendment*, 133–13. The following histories of the Fourteenth Amendment focus on section 1 and related civil rights struggles: Maltz, "Moving beyond Race," 306–7; Curtis, *No State Shall Abridge*; Aynes, "Unintended Consequences of the Fourteenth Amendment and What They Tell Us about Its Interpretation," 318–21; Foner, *Reconstruction*, 257; W. E. Nelson, *Fourteenth Amendment*, 8; Masur, *Until Justice Be Done*; M. S. Jones, *Birthright Citizens*.

16. The value of human property played a significant role in the Southern economy before and after the Civil War, though economic historians have not always agreed on whether the lost value of slaves negatively affected it. They have also disagreed over the strength of and total wealth in the antebellum slave economy, and have used different methods to determine the economic effects of slavery and emancipation. Some, such as Roger Ransom and Richard Sutch, concluded that as long as Black Southerners continued to work in Southern agriculture as sharecroppers and tenant farmers, the Southern economy retained the value of their labor and did not suffer from the lost value of enslaved people as capital. Although enslavers lost the ability to leverage the value of the future labor of their slaves as credit, they no longer paid for enslaved people's upkeep, which offset their lost value. In contrast, Gavin Wright argued as early as 1986 that the lost value of slaves crippled the Southern economy because enslaved people represented invaluable credit. That value disappeared with the abolition of slave labor, as did the value of slaves as credit and collateral in the economy. Recent studies of slavery's legal and financial systems support Wright's supposition. More recently, Richard Hornbeck and Trevon Logan have argued that emancipation gained the United States more economically than previously estimated because economists had not considered the high costs of slavery to the enslaved. Emancipation decreased output but also decreased inputs on the costs of labor. See Kilbourne, *Debt, Investment, Slaves*, 12, 50, 63–64, 73, 75–76; Martin, "Slavery's Invisible Engine"; W. Johnson, *Soul by Soul*, 25–26; Ransom and Sutch, *One Kind of Freedom*, 52; Wright, *Old South, New South*, 87–89; E. L. Thompson, *Reconstruction of Southern Debtors*; Hornbeck and Logan, "One Giant Leap"; Bleakley and Rhode, "Economic Effects of American Slavery." For other studies on slavery's financial systems, see Coclanis, *Shadow of a Dream*, 102–3; Menard, "Financing the Lowcountry Export Boom"; Follett, *Sugar Masters*, 30–31; D. R. Berry, *Price for Their Pound of Flesh*; Hartman, *Scenes of Subjection*.

17. Vorenberg, *Final Freedom*, 6; Hamilton, *Limits of Sovereignty*, 9; Siddali, *From Property to Person*, 6, 81–83. For a conversation about the lack of consensus on the meanings of the Reconstruction amendments, see Edwards, *Legal History of the Civil War and Reconstruction*, chap. 5; Foner, *Reconstruction*; Du Bois, *Black Reconstruction in America, 1860–1880*; Richardson, *Greatest Nation of the Earth*.

18. Perrone, *Nothing More Than Freedom*; Nicoletti, *Secession on Trial*; Nicoletti, "William Henry Trescot, Pardon Broker"; Kull, "The Enforceability after Emancipation of Debts Contracted for the Purchase of Slaves"; Klein, "Paying Eliza"; J. C. Williams, "Slave Contracts and the Thirteenth Amendment"; Brandwein, *Rethinking the Judicial Settlement of Reconstruction*.

19. Mathisen, *Loyal Republic*; Lee, *Claiming the Union*; Blair, *With Malice toward Some*; Inscoe and Kenzer, *Enemies of the Country*, introduction. This book describes how the meaning of moderate and conservative political ideology in the compensation debates shifted alongside notions of loyalty during the war. In her study of slavery and emancipation

in Maryland, Barbara Fields critiqued nineteenth-century statesmen's use of the word "moderate" on the eve of the Civil War, noting that it is "nearly always a term of approval" that betrayed moderate's relatively conservative efforts to maintain and protect slavery. She held that "border-state moderates in the growing sectional discord of the mid-nineteenth century enjoyed a prestige wholly at variance with their effectiveness." While I emphasize that moderates' views were distinct from secessionists' and fire eaters', who would have denied the federal government's ability to interfere with slavery, we will see in the following chapters how some anti-secessionist politicians in the border states and former Confederacy coalesced around compensated emancipation after Confederate surrender, ineffectively. While they may have been understood as moderates before the war, by 1866, supporting federal compensation for freed people made them conservatives in the eyes of many moderate and Radical Republicans. Fields, *Slavery and Freedom on the Middle Ground*, xii, 93.

20. Today, reparations for slavery describe local, national, and international programs that acknowledge, redress, and provide closure for injustices against enslaved African Americans and their descendants. Monetary compensation is only one of many conditions for various reparations plans. Reparations activists ask us to consider that slavery was a collective wrong that needs to be not only paid for but also repaired, healed, and righted. With that in mind, I never refer to claims to pay enslavers as "reparations for enslavers," and I do not call claims to pay the enslaved "reparations" when they were paired with compensation to enslavers. In this book, most people who called for payments to the formerly enslaved and former enslavers were not trying to repair the harms of slavery or restore political rights to the enslaved and their descendants; instead, they were seeking political support or economic stimulus for the South, not the harmed group. Darity and Mullen, *From Here to Equality*, 7; Araujo, *Reparations for Slavery and the Slave Trade*, 90–95; Biondi, "Rise of the Reparations Movement," 5–18; Chisolm, "Sweep around Your Own Front Door"; Westley, "Many Billions Gone: Is It Time to Reconsider the Case for Black Reparations?"; Manajpra, *Black Ghosts of Empire*; "The Global Reparations Movement," Caricom Reparations Commission, https://caricomreparations.org/the-global-reparations-movement; "What Are Reparations," National Coalition of Blacks for Reparations in America (N'COBRA), www.officialncobraonline.org/home-page; G.A. Res. 60/147, Basic Principles and Guidelines on the Right to a Remedy and Reparation for Victims of Gross Violations of International Human Rights Law and Serious Violations of International Humanitarian Law (Dec. 16, 2005), www.ohchr.org/sites/default/files/2021-08/N0549642.pdf.

21. Many historians, notably David Blight, Caroline Janney, and Adam Domby, have explored how Confederate veterans, their families, and white Southern politicians reinterpreted the history of the Civil War as a "lost cause" to justify their losses, regain political power in the South, and redeem their moral legacies. Blight, *Race and Reunion*; Janney, *Remembering the Civil War*; Domby, *False Cause*; Foster, *Ghosts of the Confederacy*; Silber, *Romance of Reunion*.

Chapter One

1. Bennett et al., *Debates in the Convention for the Revision and Amendment of the Constitution of the State of Louisiana*, 313.

2. Report of the Committee on Emancipation, 1864, M-451, LaRC; Bennett et al., *Debates in the Convention for the Revision and Amendment of the Constitution of the State of Louisiana*, 97, 152, 153, 313.

3. Hodges, *Slavery and Freedom in the Rural North*, 171; Bierck, "Struggle for Abolition in Gran Colombia"; Blanchard, *Under the Flags of Freedom*; Draper, *Price of Emancipation*; Drescher, "British Way, French Way"; Holt, "'Empire over the Mind'"; Hahn, "Class and State in Postemancipation Societies"; Engerman, "Emancipation Schemes"; Cooper et al., *Beyond Slavery*; Foner, *Nothing but Freedom*; Manajpra, *Black Ghost of Empire*; Fladeland, "Compensated Emancipation."

4. Sinha, *Slave's Cause*; Blanchard, *Under the Flags of Freedom*; Dubois, *Avengers of the New World*.

5. Ely, *Contract Clause*, 54–55.

6. Sinha, *Slave's Cause*, 25–33; Dyer, *Natural Law and the Antislavery Constitutional Tradition*, Prologue; A. L. Brophy, *University, Court, and Slave*, 67–71, 248–49; Zilversmit, *First Emancipation*, chaps. 4–5, 169–75, 227–28.

7. Zilversmit, *First Emancipation*, 145; Steinfeld, *Invention of Free Labor*, 99–107, 138–46, 159–60; Van Cleve, *Slaveholder's Union*, 73. At least one group used the logic that the enslaved owed their labor, not their person, to their enslaver during the Civil War to argue that emancipation was merely the "confiscation of debts," not property. See Final Report of the American Freedmen's Inquiry Commission to the Secretary of War, Office of the American Freedmen's Inquiry Commission, May 15, 1864, *OR*, Ser. 3, vol. 4, 342–47; Price, *Property Rights*, 61–65.

8. Quote from *New Jersey Gazette*, February 14, 1781, in Zilversmit, *First Emancipation*, 146; see also 139, 145, 176–77. Melish, *Disowning Slavery*, 58–75.

9. Melish, *Disowning Slavery*, 58–59; Van Cleve, *Slaveholder's Union*, 72; Engerman, "Emancipation Schemes," 273.

10. The question of whether government-legislated emancipation was an act of eminent domain is difficult to answer conclusively in part because of disagreements among contemporaries and legal scholars regarding the regulatory powers of state and federal governments. Traditionally, accounts of nineteenth-century American history framed government regulation as invisible and limited. In the rare case that government confiscated or destroyed property, policymakers needed convincing reasons for public use and to compensate property owners. Since the 1990s, legal historians and scholars have debated the extent to which this was true. According to William Novak, early American law gave more power to state and local governments to confiscate and destroy property for the public interest and to defend others' personal liberty without compensation. Americans often avoided government confiscation under eminent domain and recognized that all property owners held property at the "sufferance of the sovereign," as legal historian Morton J. Horwitz wrote and Novak premised. After the ratification of the Constitution, states performed the majority of takings, and those takings typically involved extensive development efforts for mills, canals, turnpikes, railroads, and other infrastructure. Courts tended to reject most claims for compensation, even while state constitutions added provisions requiring reimbursement for property confiscated for public use.

On the other hand, some legal scholars have argued that governments routinely compensated property owners under eminent domain. James Ely Jr. held that legislatures "routinely extended compensation when property was taken for large-scale public works," and he and others found that the principle of compensated takings by legislatures existed in and was often applied by English common law long before the US Constitution was ratified. Other legal scholars have emphasized that courts discouraged legislative interference with private property. Many judges defended property ownership as a natural right and feared frequent government enactment of eminent domain, while others have emphasized the ubiquity of the principle of confiscation with "just compensation" in British common law and early American law. However, few legal histories consider how rules about regulation and compensation applied to slavery, and most doctrine on eminent domain in the nineteenth century is at the state level. There is little consensus among legal scholars about the consistency with which the federal government, in particular, applied eminent domain in the early nineteenth century. The origins and applications of compensation clauses in state constitutions and the takings clause of the US Constitution have been difficult for legal scholars to establish, though it is clear that different states inserted takings clauses into their own constitutions in order to clarify and mobilize that power. Novak, *The People's Welfare*, 16; Horwitz, *Transformation of American Law, 1780–1860*, 66, 260–61; Price, *Property Rights*, 66; Treanor, "Original Understanding of the Takings Clause and the Political Process"; Stohler, "Slavery and Just Compensation in American Constitutionalism"; Ely, "'That Due Satisfaction May Be Made,'" 14; Ely, *Contract Clause*, 54; Stoebuck, "General Theory of Eminent Domain"; Fischel, *Regulatory Takings*, 77–80. Legal scholars have continued these conversations about the distinction between eminent domain and state police or regulatory powers into the twentieth century. Though theoretically informative, their examples apply mainly to the post–Civil War era and do not consider slavery. See Stoebuck, "Police Power, Takings, and Due Process"; Ackerman, *Private Property and the Constitution*, 190n55; Epstein, *Takings*, 162–64.

11. Van Cleve, *Slaveholder's Union*, 71–79, 311n49; Zilversmit, *First Emancipation*, 139, 145, 176–77, 182, 192–93, 228–29; Engerman, "Emancipation Schemes," 271–72; Fogel and Engerman, "Philanthropy at Bargain Prices"; Nash and Soderlund, *Freedom by Degrees*, 102.

12. Fogel and Engerman, "Philanthropy at Bargain Prices"; Gellman, *Emancipating New York*, 154–83; Tucker, *Dissertation on Slavery*; Irons, *Origins of Proslavery Christianity*, 60; Gronningsater, "Born Free in the Master's House," 123–50.

13. White, *Somewhat More Independent*; Engerman, "Emancipation Schemes"; Berlin, *Many Thousands Gone*, 233–39; Melish, *Disowning Slavery*, 74, 101–2; Gellman, *Emancipating New York*, 183; Hodges, *Slavery and Freedom in the Rural North*, 149–50; Zilversmit, *First Emancipation*, 181–84.

14. Seeley, *Race, Removal, and the Right to Remain*, 9, 174–83; Magness and Page, *Colonization after Emancipation*, 1–3; Sinha, *Slave's Cause*, 160–71, 196–227; Fladeland, "Compensated Emancipation," 176.

15. Seeley, *Race, Removal, and the Right to Remain*, 41, 193.

16. James Madison to Robert Evans, June 15, 1819, James Madison Papers, Series 1, General Correspondence, 1723–1859, Library of Congress, https://tile.loc.gov/storage-services/service/mss/mjm/19//19_0220_0230.pdf; Treanor, "Original Understanding of the Takings Clause and the Political Process," 839; Fladeland, "Compensated Emancipation," 173–80.

17. Witt, *Lincoln's Code*, 29, 70–77; Fehrenbacher, *Slaveholding Republic*, 92; Jasanoff, *Liberty's Exiles*, 330; Winks, *Blacks in Canada*, 114–15; Ostdiek and Witt, "Czar and the Slaves."

18. Jasanoff, *Liberty's Exiles*, 330.

19. Bierck, "Struggle for Abolition in Gran Colombia," 365–86; Blanchard, *Under the Flags of Freedom*, 165–81.

20. Draper, *Price of Emancipation*, 100; Engerman, "Emancipation Schemes," 269, 271. Two British colonies, Bermuda and Antigua, granted immediate emancipation without compensation to former owners. Planters in Antigua argued that the island's high population density meant that freed people would remain on plantations without legal coercion, and planters in both colonies did not need or receive cash reimbursements.

21. Draper, *Price of Emancipation*, 77, 83, 91; Price, *Property Rights*, 61; Melish, *Disowning Slavery*, 58–59.

22. Draper, *Price of Emancipation*, 87–92; James Madison to Robert Evans, June 15, 1819.

23. Draper, *Price of Emancipation*, 89, 101.

24. Draper, *Price of Emancipation*, 137.

25. Engerman, "Emancipation Schemes," 270–71.

26. Fladeland, "Compensated Emancipation," 183; Sinha, *Slave's Cause*, 42–43, 413; Rugemer, *Problem of Emancipation*.

27. L. M. Child, *Right Way, the Safe Way*, quotes from 8, 93 (emphasis original); see also 8–10, 38, 69–70, 89–90, 93. Venet, *Neither Ballots nor Bullets*, 23. Child's argument is one of many that US abolitionists wrote about emancipation in the British empire, particularly Jamaica. For more on how US abolitionists responded to British emancipation leading up to the Civil War, see Rugemer, *Problem of Emancipation*, 133–36, 153, 290.

28. Stroud, *Sketch of the Laws Relating to Slavery in the Several States of the United States of America*, 143; Goodell, *American Slave Code in Theory and Practice*, 34–35. For more examples of this antislavery argument against compensation, see Wythe, "Power of Congress over the District of Columbia."

29. Kellow, "Conflicting Imperatives," 203; Stauffer, "Frederick Douglass and the Politics of Slave Redemptions," 215–16; Bernier, "'Never Be Free without Trustin' Some Person.'"

30. Fitz, *Our Sister Republics*, chap. 3; Rugemer, *Problem of Emancipation*, 182; Fladeland, "Compensated Emancipation," 173–83.

31. Morris, *Southern Slavery and the Law*, 430–32; Price, *Property Rights*, 62.

32. W. Johnson, *Soul by Soul*, 31–34; Morris, "Chattel Mortgages of Slaves," 147–52; Wahl, *Bondsman's Burden*, 29.

33. Murphy, *Investing in Life*, chap. 7; Ryder, "'To Realize Money Facilities'"; D. R. Berry, *Price for Their Pound of Flesh*, 54–56, 88–89, 115–19, 142, 210–11; Levy, *Freaks of Fortune*, 88–97.

34. Wheeler, *Practical Treatise on the Law of Slavery*, 310, 387; Stroud, *Sketch of the Laws Relating to Slavery in the Several States of the United States of America*, 51–57, 145–54; Goodell, *American Slave Code in Theory and Practice*, 63–68; Morris, *Southern Slavery and the Law*, 388–92.

35. Northup, *Twelve Years a Slave*, chap. 8; D. R. Berry, *Price for Their Pound of Flesh*.

36. Northup, *Twelve Years a Slave*, 127–28; Kilbourne, *Debt, Investment, Slaves*, 50.

37. Stohler, "Slavery and Just Compensation in American Constitutionalism"; Price, *Property Rights*, 65–67.

38. For the most recent treatment of the rebellion, see Holden, *Surviving Southampton*.

39. Wolf, *Race and Liberty in the New Nation*, 199–200, 213–14; Stohler, "Slavery and Just Compensation in American Constitutionalism," 18.

40. Van Cleve, *Slaveholders' Union*, 196; Brophy, *University, Court, and Slave*, 26–27, 30; Wolf, *Race and Liberty in the New Nation*, 214–19; "Speech by James H. Gholson to the House of Delegates (January 12, 1832)," *Encyclopedia Virginia*, www.encyclopediavirginia.org/Speech_by_James_H_Gholson_to_the_House_of_Delegates_January_12_1832. Another Virginian and enslaver, John Robertson—former state attorney general and congressman from 1834 to 1839—argued, in accordance with Gholson, that eminent domain prevented states and the federal government from abolishing slavery because emancipation did not involve public use. See Fehrenbacher, *Slaveholding Republic*, 364–65n144; 1850 US census, slave schedules, Judge John Robertson, Ancestry.com.

41. Thomas Marshall, quoted in Brophy, *University, Court, and Slave*, 28; *The Speech of Thomas Marshall . . . January 14, 1832*, 4.

42. Price, *Property Rights*, 63; "The Speech of Charles Jas. Faulkner, (of Berkeley) in the House of Delegates of Virginia, on the Policy of the State with Respect to Her Slave Population. (January 14, 1832)," *Encyclopedia Virginia*, https://encyclopediavirginia.org/primary-documents/the-speech-of-charles-jas-faulkner-of-berkeley-in-the-house-of-delegates-of-virginia-on-the-policy-of-the-state-with-respect-to-her-slave-population-january-14-1832.

43. Stohler, "Slavery and Just Compensation in American Constitutionalism," 15–19.

44. Since Northern states abolished slavery, Americans still had not come to any predominant agreement over whether emancipation represented a government taking, let alone for public use. Between the Panic of 1837 and the 1850s, apprehension grew that governments could use eminent domain to redistribute wealth, and this apprehension united most legal opinion in favor of compensation to the owner of any property taken for public use. At the same time, states developed practices to limit the amount of compensation paid to landowners and to define narrowly what constituted a government taking. Some legal scholars suggest that courts defined "public use" narrowly in order to limit a government's ability to confiscate property. How eminent domain applied to property in people was also unclear. There are no examples for state-sponsored emancipation, but many states reimbursed individual enslavers for at least part of the value of an enslaved person executed by the state for criminal offenses. On the other hand, federal courts denied enslavers' claims for reimbursement for enslaved people seized and jailed by the federal government for committing a crime because they were not taken for public use. Such doctrinal ambiguities enabled politicians to make different arguments about the relationship between emancipation and eminent domain. See Horwitz, *Transformation of American Law, 1780–1860*, 66; Price, *Property Rights*, 61–67; Epstein, *Takings*, 162–64; Ackerman, *Private Property and the Constitution*, 190n55; Allen, *Origins of the Dred Scott Case*, 109–10, 114; Morris, *Southern Slavery and the Law*, 253–56; Wahl, *Bondsman's Burden*, 105, 171, 259n157; Stohler, "Slavery and Just Compensation in American Constitutionalism," 27–29; Treanor, "Original Understanding of the Takings Clause and the Political Process," 854; see also 837–55.

45. Brophy, *University, Court, and Slave*, 35–47; Faust, *Ideology of Slavery*, 15–16.

46. Dew, "Abolition of Negro Slavery," 40.

47. Dew, "Abolition of Negro Slavery," 29, 40.

48. Dew, "Abolition of Negro Slavery," 30, 49.

49. Slade, *Speech of Mr. Slade, of Vermont, on the Abolition of Slavery*, 21; "Am I Gagged, or Am I Not?" Treasures of Congress: Struggles over Slavery: The "Gag" Rule. NARA, www.archives.gov/exhibits/treasures_of_congress/text/page10_text.html.

50. Crallé, *Works of John C. Calhoun*, 169, 174–75; Fladeland, "Compensated Emancipation," 182. For other instances of congressmen arguing that the Fifth Amendment protected property in people, see Fehrenbacher, *Slaveholding Republic*, 5, 80, 268. Calhoun's view of emancipation was consistent with the trends legal scholars have identified regarding eminent domain and legal formalism, particularly Morton Horwitz. After the Panic of 1837, Horwitz writes, jurists revealed a "growing reluctance to rationalize" redistributive acts by the state "as an exercise of public domain, since any legislative authorized taking could then be upheld simply because it contributed to economic improvement." Similarly, Calhoun sought to protect vested property rights against constitutional interference. See: Horwitz, *The Transformation of American Law, 1780–1860*, 259–61.

51. Clay, *Speech of the Hon. Henry Clay*, 27–28.

52. Clay, *Speech of the Hon. Henry Clay*, 12, 29. For one example of abolitionists who took up Clay's challenge, see Hasted, "Copy of the Letter, Written to the President of the United States." See also Fladeland, "Compensated Emancipation," 184–85.

53. Stauffer, *Black Hearts of Men*, 177–79.

54. *Liberator*, November 24, 1843; Minardi, "'Centripetal Attraction' in a Centrifugal World," 176–91; Tolis, *Elihu Burritt*, 236–51; Curti, *Learned Blacksmith*, 131–38.

55. Burritt, *Plan of Brotherly Copartnership of the North and South for the Peaceful Extinction of Slavery*, 31; *New York Times*, August 28 and August 31, 1857.

56. Burritt, *Plan of Brotherly Copartnership*, 24, 31, 34, 40–42; *New York Times*, August 28, 1857.

57. *National Anti-Slavery Standard*, September 5, 1857; *New York Times*, August 28, 1857; *New York Daily Tribune*, August 31, 1857.

58. *New York Daily Tribune*, August 31, 1857; *New York Times*, August 28, 31, 1857; Stauffer, *Black Hearts of Men*, 142–44.

59. *National Anti-Slavery Standard*, September 5, 1857; *New York Daily Tribune*, August 31, 1857.

60. Fladeland, "Compensated Emancipation," 183–84; *New York Times*, May 15 and June 9, 1858; *Liberator*, March 15, June 28, and November 22, 1844; July 18 and August 8, 1845; August 21, September 4, September 11, September 18, September 25, and October 2, 1857; *National Anti-Slavery Standard*, August 22, September 26, October 31, and December 26, 1857; June 26 and August 28, 1858; August 18, 1860; July 6, 1861; *New York Daily Tribune*, August 31, 1857; *New York Times*, June 9, 1858 and January 19, 1859; Stampp, *America in 1857*, 128–29.

61. Finkelman, *Imperfect Union*, 15, 278–84; Price, *Property Rights*, 64; *Dred Scott v. Sanford*, 60 US 393 (1857); Huston, *Calculating the Value of the Union*, 204–5; Baptist, *Half Has Never Been Told*, 369.

62. Huebner, *Liberty and Union: The Civil War Era and American Constitutionalism*, 57–58.

63. Reuben Davis, quoted in Huston, *Calculating the Value of the Union*, 210; Albert Gallatin Brown, quoted in Huston, *Calculating the Value of the Union*, 208. See Huston, chap. 7 for more on debates about property rights in people, *Dred Scott*, and the Presidential Election of 1860.

64. "Constitution of the Confederate States; March 11, 1861," The Avalon Project: Documents in Law, History and Diplomacy, Lilliam Goldman Law Library, Yale Law School, https://avalon.law.yale.edu/19th_century/csa_csa.asp.

Chapter Two

1. Dew, *Apostles of Disunion*, 74–81; Freehling, *The Road to Disunion*, 369–72; Hahn, *Nation under Our Feet*, 13–16; Christopher Beagan, "Freedom's Fortress: Fort Monroe National Monument," National Park Service, last updated September 6, 2024, www.nps.gov/articles/featured_stories_fomr.htm.

2. Masur, "'Rare Phenomenon of Philological Vegetation,'" 1054, 1066; Randall, *Constitutional Problems under Lincoln*, 355–56.

3. Hamilton, *Limits of Sovereignty*, 3–4; Siddali, *From Property to Person*, 12, 98; *Chicago Tribune*, quoted in *National Anti-Slavery Standard*, August 3, 1861; *National Anti-Slavery Standard*, August 24 and 31, 1861; *National Anti-Slavery Standard*, September 7, 1861.

4. Crofts, *Reluctant Confederates*, chap. 5; Inscoe and Kenzer, *Enemies of the Country*, 1–17; Lee, *Claiming the Union*.

5. "The Great Speech: Frederick Douglass on the War," *Christian Recorder*, January 18, 1862; Masur, "'Rare Phenomenon of Philological Vegetation,'" 1054, 1066; Dilbeck, *Frederick Douglass*, 102–5.

6. W. E. Nelson, "Impact of the Antislavery Movement upon Styles of Judicial Reasoning in Nineteenth Century America," 532–33; "To the Honorable Senate and House of Representatives in Congress Assembled from the Women of the North," July 16, 1861, folder 66, Francis Lieber Papers, South Caroliniana Library, Columbia; Foner, *Fiery Trial*, 182–83.

7. "The Great Speech: Frederick Douglass on the War," *Christian Recorder*, January 18, 1862.

8. Child, *Rights and Duties of the United States Relative to Slavery under the Laws of War*, 22–24; Whiting, *War Powers of the President and the Legislative Powers of Congress in Relation to Rebellion, Treason and Slavery*, 20–23, 49, 57, quote on page 59; Randall, *Constitution Problems under Lincoln*, chap. 15; McPherson, *Struggle for Equality*, 67–74.

9. Hamilton, *Limits of Sovereignty*, 38, 80; Whiting, *War Powers of the President and the Legislative Powers of Congress*, iv, 138; *National Anti-Slavery Standard*, August 3, 1861.

10. Whiting, *War Powers of the President and the Legislative Powers of Congress*, 130–33; Child, *Rights and Duties of the US Relative to Slavery under the Laws of War*, 39–44; Simon Cameron, Washington, DC, to Benjamin Butler, Commanding Department of Virginia, Fortress Monroe, August 8, 1861, *OR*, series 2, vol. 1, 761–62; Hamilton, *Limits of Sovereignty*, 40; *Douglass' Monthly*, January 2, 1863; *National Anti-Slavery Standard*, August 24, 1861.

11. *Cong. Globe*, 37th Cong., 2d Sess. 1516–18, 1520, 1616–18 (1862).

12. *Cong. Globe*, 37th Cong., 2d Sess. 1285–86, 1336–38, 1497, 1638 (1862); Sumner, *Ransom of Slaves at the National Capital*, 9; Kurtz, "Emancipation in the Federal City," 255–56; Masur, *Example for All the Land*, 23–25. "Purchasing Power Today of a US Dollar Transaction in the Past," MeasuringWorth, 2024, www.measuringworth.com/ppowerus.

13. Nunley, *At the Threshold of Liberty*, 168–72; Kurtz, "Emancipation in the Federal City," 260–64; Emancipation in the District of Columbia, 38th Cong., 1st sess. (1864), H.R. Exec. Doc. No. 42. Appointed commissioners heard former enslavers' claims and made recommendations for payments to Congress. Whenever contested claims arose, the commission awarded some compensation to all parties. The commissioners withheld reimbursements only if evidence existed that claimants had borne arms against the United States or given other aid to the rebellion. The commission even recommended that Congress pay the wife of a Confederate soldier because the enslaved people she claimed had been signed over to a

loyal citizen to secure a debt. Congress did, but it was less generous to the enslaved who claimed freedom under the act. In cases where enslavers claimed compensation for a freedom seeker, the commissioners granted emancipation to the enslaved person and compensation to the person who claimed ownership over them only if they lived in DC or the enslaved person claimed to live there. For example, if an enslaved person from Maryland or Virginia ran away from their enslaver, followed the US Army, or went North after the DC Emancipation Act was passed, the commissioners did not free them but nevertheless compensated the owner a reduced amount, with some exceptions.

14. Waldrep, "Garrett Davis and the Problem of Democracy and Emancipation," 363–402; Cong. Globe, 37th Cong., 2d Sess. 1334–37, 1474–75, 1496–1503 (1862).

15. Kurtz, "Emancipation in the Federal City," 252–55; Cong. Globe, 37th Cong., 2d Sess. 1192, 1335, 1645–46 (1862); Waldrep, "Garrett Davis and the Problem of Democracy and Emancipation," 382. For a counterargument, see Whiting, *War Powers of the President and the Legislative Powers of Congress*, 20–23. In the House, Kentucky representative William Henry Wadsworth opposed the DC Emancipation Act on the grounds that emancipation was an act of eminent domain, and Congress could not deprive loyal or disloyal enslavers of their right to just compensation (Cong. Globe, 37th Cong., 2d Sess. 1644 [1862]).

16. Waldrep, "Garrett Davis and the Problem of Democracy and Emancipation," 382–83; Hamilton, *Limits of Sovereignty*, 4, 47–56; Siddali, *From Property to Person*, 157; Blair, "Friend or Foe," 27–51. When challenged, Davis sometimes denied that he believed the right to property was a natural right; however, many scholars have characterized his beliefs as consistent with a natural right to property ownership. Cong. Globe, 37th Cong., 2d Sess. 1378 (1862). Also see Crittenden's commentary on property in people during the DC Emancipation Act debates in Cong. Globe, 37th Cong., 2d Sess. 1635 (1862).

17. Waldrep, "Garrett Davis and the Problem of Democracy and Emancipation"; Cong. Globe, 37th Cong., 2d Sess. 1191–92, 1333–39, particularly 1336, 1523, 1524 (1862); Siddali, *From Property to Person*, 157.

18. Hamilton, *Limits of Sovereignty*, 11–12, 57–59; Siddali, *From Property to Person*, 81–82.

19. Hamilton, *Limits of Sovereignty*, 38.

20. Hamilton, *Limits of Sovereignty*, 58.

21. Cong. Globe, 37th Cong., 2d Sess. 1903 (1862); Siddali, *From Property to Person*, 157; Hamilton, *Limits of Sovereignty*, 38–40, 47–48, 50, 53, 58, 68, 74; Randall, *Constitution Problems under Lincoln*, 358–63.

22. Message to Congress, March 6, 1862, *The Collected Works of Abraham Lincoln* (hereafter cited as *CWAL*), 5:145–46; Appeal to Border State Representatives to Favor Compensated Emancipation, July 12, 1862, *CWAL*, 5:318–19, 319n1; Foner, *Fiery Trial*, 208–30; Oakes, *Freedom National*, 285–93; Waldrep, "Garrett Davis and the Problem of Democracy and Emancipation," 385–87; Cong. Globe, 37th Cong., 2d Sess. 1371 (1862).

23. Waldrep, "Garrett Davis and the Problem of Democracy and Emancipation," 386–87; Border state congressmen to Abraham Lincoln, Monday, July 14, 1862 (Response to Lincoln's proposal for compensated emancipation), Abraham Lincoln Papers: Series 1, General Correspondence, 1833–1916, LOC, http://hdl.loc.gov/loc.mss/mss00001.mss30189a.1708800.

24. Border state congressmen to Abraham Lincoln, Monday, July 14, 1862 (Response to Lincoln's proposal for compensated emancipation), Abraham Lincoln Papers: Series 1, General Correspondence, 1833–1916.

25. Appeal to Border State Representatives to Favor Compensated Emancipation, July 12, 1862, *CWAL*, 5:318–19, 319n1; Foner, *Fiery Trial*, 208–30; Oakes, *Freedom National*, 285–93; Waldrep, "Garrett Davis and the Problem of Democracy and Emancipation," 374, 381, 388.

26. Hamilton, *Limits of Sovereignty*, 76–78; Foner, *Fiery Trial*, 217–19; Fladeland, "Compensated Emancipation," 184–86.

27. Annual Message to Congress, December 1, 1862, *CWAL*, 5:519–37; Preliminary Emancipation Proclamation, September 22, 1862, *CWAL*, 5:433–36; Foner, *Fiery Trial*, 231–40; Siddali, *From Property to Person*, 6.

28. Annual Message to Congress, December 1, 1862, *CWAL*, 5:519–37; Preliminary Emancipation Proclamation, September 22, 1862, *CWAL*, 5:433–36; Foner, *Fiery Trial*, 231–40; Fehrenbacher, *Slaveholding Republic*, 314; Berlin et al., "Destruction of Slavery," 4, 29–30.

29. Annual Message to Congress, December 1, 1862, *CWAL*, 5:519–37.

30. Like the DC Emancipation Act and others, Lincoln's plan to pay enslavers included a mechanism to colonize freed people "with their own consent," within and outside the United States. White politicians continued to attempt colonization schemes during the war to ease the process of wartime emancipation on a reluctant white populace and spread US influence abroad, particularly in the Caribbean. The Lincoln administration pursued a number of colonization schemes in the early war years, including a diplomatic and commercial effort with the British that lasted through the end of the war. Such plans might transport formerly enslaved refugees with some reimbursement from the federal government. However, Lincoln's cabinet tended to oppose colonization schemes after the Emancipation Proclamation because, they recognized, formerly enslaved men who were refugees made good soldiers, and colonization schemes tended to perpetuate racist arguments that detractors made against Black enlistment. Nevertheless, the administration pursued colonization schemes through the end of the war. While some historians suggest that these schemes helped convince conservatives to support other emancipation policies, Mark Neeley disagrees. He argues that historians' interpretation of white Americans' views on colonization—particularly Lincoln's—are the result of a lack of archival evidence on Lincoln's views and historians' indictment of a people "hopelessly steeped in an ineradicable racism." See Magness and Page, *Colonization after Emancipation*; Seeley, *Race, Removal, and the Right to Remain*, 331, Sinha, *Slave's Cause*, 579–80; Vorenberg, "Abraham Lincoln and the Politics of Black Colonization," 35–56; Neeley, "Colonization and the Myth That Lincoln Prepared the People for Emancipation," 45–74, quote from page 69.

31. Foner, *Fiery Trial*; Oakes, *Freedom National*; Finkelman, "Lincoln and the Preconditions for Emancipation," 13–44; Blair and Younger, 1–11; Finkelman, "Lincoln, Emancipation, and the Limits of Constitutional Change"; Berlin, "Who Freed the Slaves? Emancipation and Its Meaning."

32. The 1862 Militia Act, 12 Stat. 597.

33. J. Holt to Stanton, August 20, 1863, *OR*, series 3, vol. 3, 694–96; Hamilton, *Limits of Sovereignty*, 11–13. Holt's history and politics demonstrate how enslavers' allegiance to the United States became a condition of their receiving compensation. Holt was an unconditional Unionist who had worked to prevent Kentucky's secession and opposed its early war policy of neutrality. Neutrality was tantamount to disloyalty, he believed, and he was eager to not only punish rebels but also those who did not actively defend the Union. Though he had struggled to reconcile his support of slavery and Union during the secession crisis,

Holt threw his support behind Lincoln's emancipation policies. Holt publicly acknowledged that slavery and the Union could not both be saved, and he accused not only seceded Southerners but also Peace Democrats (aka Copperheads)—who sought to end the war and restore the Union with slavery intact—of conspiracy. Leonard, *Lincoln's Forgotten Ally*, 146–47, 160–63.

34. Lieber, *Instructions for the Government of Armies of the United States in the Field*, arts. 32, 38, 40–43, 155–57; Witt, *Lincoln's Code*, 240–42.

35. J. M. Schofield, Headquarters of the Department of the Missouri, Saint Louis, to Col E. D. Townsend, Assistant Adjutant-General, Washington, DC, September 29, 1863, *OR*, series 3, vol. 3, 847–49.

36. General Orders No. 329, October 3, 1863, *OR*, series 3, vol. 3, 860–61; Report by Edwin M. Stanton, October 1, 1863, *OR*, series 3, vol. 3, 855–56.

37. Major General J. M. Schofield, St. Louis, MO, to HM Stanton, November 12, 1863, *OR*, series 3, vol. 3, 1022; General Orders No. 135, Headquarters of the Department of the Missouri, Saint Louis, MO, November 14, 1863, *OR*, series 3, vol. 3, 1034–36.

38. Blassingame, "Recruitment of Colored Troops in Kentucky, Maryland and Missouri," 540–42.

39. Siddali, *From Property to Person*, 4–6.

40. Full text of Lincoln's Amnesty oath: "I,———, do solemnly swear, in presence of Almighty God, that I will henceforth faithfully support, protect and defend the Constitution of the United States, and the union of the States thereunder; and that I will, in like manner, abide by and faithfully support all acts of Congress passed during the existing rebellion with reference to slaves, so long and so far as not repealed, modified or held void by Congress, or by decision of the Supreme Court; and that I will, in like manner, abide by and faithfully support all proclamations of the President made during the existing rebellion having reference to slaves, so long and so far as not modified or declared void by decision of the Supreme Court. So help me God." M. P. Johnson, *Abraham Lincoln, Slavery, and the Civil War*, 272–75.

41. Abraham Lincoln to Nathaniel P. Banks, December 24, 1863, Abraham Lincoln Papers, LOC, http://hdl.loc.gov/loc.mss/mss000001.mss30189a.2888000; Nathaniel Banks to James Bower, Provost Marshall General, December 26, 1863, Nathaniel P. Banks Letterpress Copybook, Louisiana State University Special Collections, Hill Memorial Library, Baton Rouge; Nathaniel P. Banks to Abraham Lincoln, January 11, 1864, Abraham Lincoln Papers, LOC, http://hdl.loc.gov/loc.mss/mss000001.mss30189a.2934700; To the People of Louisiana, January 11, 1864, in *OR*, series 3, vol. 4, 22–23; Nathaniel P. Banks to Abraham Lincoln, January 22, 1864, Abraham Lincoln Papers, LOC, http://hdl.loc.gov/loc.mss/mss000001.mss30189a.2971000; Hyman, *Era of the Oath*, 41–44; Vorenberg, "'Deformed Child,'" 242–43.

42. *Daily Picayune*, February 5 and February 17, 1864; McCrary, *Abraham Lincoln and Reconstruction*, 222–30.

43. *Daily Picayune*, March 5, 1864; McCrary, *Abraham Lincoln and Reconstruction*, 234–36.

44. Nathaniel P. Banks to Abraham Lincoln, January 22, 1864, Abraham Lincoln Papers, LOC, http://hdl.loc.gov/loc.mss/mss000001.mss30189a.2971000; Christian Roselius to Abraham Lincoln, January 12, 1864, Abraham Lincoln Papers, LOC, http://hdl.loc.gov/loc.mss/mss000001.mss30189a.2939800; Abraham Lincoln to Nathaniel P. Banks, January 31,

1864, Abraham Lincoln Papers, LOC, http://hdl.loc.gov/loc.mss/mss00001.mss30189a
.3000100; *Daily Picayune*, March 5, 1864; McCrary, *Abraham Lincoln and Reconstruction*,
207–8, 234–236; Wilson and Fiske, "Roselius, Christian," 325–26; Havrylyshyn, "Free for a
Moment in France," 108–9.

45. McCrary, *Abraham Lincoln and Reconstruction*, 244–53, 371. It is possible that up to twenty-four delegates claimed ownership over enslaved people, but I could not definitively match ten delegates to the 1860 census record. US census, Louisiana, slave schedule, Ancestry.com; Bennett et al., *Debates in the Convention for the Revision and Amendment of the Constitution of the State of Louisiana*, 13, 19, 20, 34–35.

46. Report of the Committee on Emancipation, 1864, M-451, LaRC.

47. Report of the Committee on Emancipation, 1864, M-451, LaRC; McCrary, *Abraham Lincoln and Reconstruction*, 250, 252; Cooper et al., *Beyond Slavery*. Later in the convention, two other delegates also proposed apprenticeship systems that sought to retain slave labor, give slaveowners the opportunity to recoup their financial losses, and divest themselves from their investments in slaves. Antonio Mendiverri, a lawyer from New Orleans, proposed a plan that would keep slavery intact, even while it prohibited the slave trade, legitimized slave marriages, protected slaves from punishment from their masters, and provided education for slaves. During the convention, Mendiverri suggested that Louisiana abolish slavery over a period of ten years, with compensation to loyal owners, and "let a generation" of freed people be "educated" while masters kept them laboring on plantations to "prepare" them for freedom. Delegate C. H. L. Gruneberg of Lafourche Parish, a sheriff who said he was elected to the convention "without any distinct pledge to vote for immediate, unconditional emancipation," recommended another plan that would force freed people to return to their former master's plantation to work. Under his plan, the state would tax their wages to raise money "to indemnify the owners" for the gradual emancipation of human property. Gruneberg, who represented a parish populated by over 10,000 slaves, announced that he became a delegate to "secure the welfare of the now enfranchised portion of Louisiana," and to adopt a plan to gradually abolish slavery by 1900. Bennett et al., *Debates in the Convention for the Revision and Amendment of the Constitution of the State of Louisiana*, 165, 197–98, 605.

48. Report of the Committee on Emancipation, 1864, M-451, LaRC; Bennett et al., *Debates in the Convention for the Revision and Amendment of the Constitution of the State of Louisiana*, 152, 166, 187; US Const. art. I, § 3; art. IV, § 1; art. V; "Death of Judge Edmund Abell," *Times-Picayune*, August 10, 1884.

49. Bennett et al., *Debates in the Convention for the Revision and Amendment of the Constitution of the State of Louisiana*, 36, 165; see also 551 for another reference to Rome and the Bible. For a brief history of historical, classical, and religious defenses of slavery, see Finkelman, *Defending Slavery*, 29–32.

50. Bennett et al., *Debates in the Convention for the Revision and Amendment of the Constitution of the State of Louisiana*, 174, 180, 245.

51. Bennett et al., *Debates in the Convention for the Revision and Amendment of the Constitution of the State of Louisiana*, 169, 171, 177–78, 551. Many delegates argued that the war had already ended slavery. See also pages 153, 158, 160–61, 172, 177–78.

52. Bennett et al., *Debates in the Convention for the Revision and Amendment of the Constitution of the State of Louisiana*, 172, 179.

53. Bennett et al., *Debates in the Convention for the Revision and Amendment of the Constitution of the State of Louisiana*, 553.

54. Bennett et al., *Debates in the Convention for the Revision and Amendment of the Constitution of the State of Louisiana*, 175.

55. Bennett et al., *Debates in the Convention for the Revision and Amendment of the Constitution of the State of Louisiana*, 35, 157, 168, 177, 183, 189; McCrary, *Abraham Lincoln and Reconstruction*, 247.

56. Bennett et al., *Debates in the Convention for the Revision and Amendment of the Constitution of the State of Louisiana*, 183.

57. Bennett et al., *Debates in the Convention for the Revision and Amendment of the Constitution of the State of Louisiana*, 189.

58. Bennett et al., *Debates in the Convention for the Revision and Amendment of the Constitution of the State of Louisiana*, 35, 184, 187, 189, 192, 193, 196.

59. Bennett et al., *Debates in the Convention for the Revision and Amendment of the Constitution of the State of Louisiana*, 189, 196–97. Abell's plan was rejected on May 6 in a vote of 71 to 19.

60. Bennett et al., *Debates in the Convention for the Revision and Amendment of the Constitution of the State of Louisiana*, 200–205; *Daily Picayune*, May 10, 1864.

61. Bennett et al., *Debates in the Convention for the Revision and Amendment of the Constitution of the State of Louisiana*, 224. The final vote for the emancipation measure was 72 for and 13 against.

62. 1860 US census, Louisiana, slave schedule, Robert W. Taliaferro, M. R. Ariail, and James M. Wells, Ancestry.com.

63. Bennett et al., *Debates in the Convention for the Revision and Amendment of the Constitution of the State of Louisiana*, 313–14. The convention accepted the report with a vote of 42–7 and ordered that 200 copies be printed and sent to Congress. The petition is printed in the debates of the convention, which did not indicate whether the Committee on Compensated Emancipation sent the report to Congress, and I did not find the petition in records of the 38th Congress accessible in ProQuest Congressional or in records of the 38th Congress's House Committee on Claims, the House Select Committee on Emancipation, the House or Senate Petitions and Memorials, or the Senate Committee on Slavery.

64. *National Anti-Slavery Standard*, December 17, 1864; Lord and Parkhurst, *Debates of the Constitutional Convention of the State of Maryland*; Smith and Willis, "The Maryland Constitution," 142–43; Randall, *Constitutional Problems under Lincoln*, 402–3; Md. Const. of 1864, art. III, § 36; An Act to Aid and Encourage Enlistments into the Maryland Regiments in Service of the United States, chap. 15, sec. 3, in *Laws of the State of Maryland*, 20–23; Papers Concerning the Payment of Maryland Bounty to Enoch H. Fohner and the Settlement by the US Board of Claims of a Claim by John Marshall for the Enlistment of William H. Green, a Man He Had Formerly Enslaved, 1864–1865, Charles F. Meadows Jr., Collection, 1864–1865, NARA; Christopher Haley, "Legacy of Slavery in Maryland: 'Slave Statistics.'" *Journal of Slavery and Data Preservation* 5, no. 2 (2024): 41–45. https://doi.org/10.25971/2pkv-dp96. Bearss, "Restored and Vindicated," 169–70; *Journal of the Missouri State Convention*, 145, 265. Missouri's 1865 constitution prevented its general assembly from making compensation for freed people.

65. Cong. Globe, 38th Cong., 2d Sess., 120–24 (1864); *Cleveland Daily Herald*, October 9, 1865.

66. Vorenberg, "'Deformed Child'"; Final Report of the American Freedmen's Inquiry Commission to the Secretary of War, Edwin M. Stanton, Office of the American Freedmen's Inquiry Commission, New York City, May 15, 1864, *OR*, series 3, vol. 4, pt. 1, 289–382; see also 366–68.

Chapter Three

1. Andrew Johnson, "May Proclamations," May 29, 1865, in Prince, *Radical Reconstruction*, 42–44.

2. Interview with South Carolina delegation, June 24, 1865, in Johnson, *PAJ*, 8:280–83, quote on 283.

3. Delegates' status as enslavers (or not) influenced but did not dictate their support for compensated emancipation in two presidential Reconstruction conventions—Louisiana in 1864 and Mississippi in 1865. In Louisiana, at least fourteen of the ninety-six delegates had claimed ownership over enslaved people in 1860. Two enslavers, Robert W. Taliaferro and Thomas M. Wells, were sons of Unionist planters and local political leaders. While eleven of these delegates enslaved fewer than 10 people, R. V. Montague of Madison, Louisiana, claimed ownership over as many as 104 people. Regardless of whether or not they still claimed slaves at the time of the convention, the majority of these enslavers supported immediate emancipation; only two voted against it. Yet about 85 percent of non-slaveholding delegates supported petitioning Congress to compensate loyal slave owners, which suggests that the delegates wanted to raise support for emancipation in the convention and reward loyal men as much as they wanted to emancipate enslaved people. Furthermore, the most vocal supporter of gradual, compensated emancipation—Edmund Abell—did not claim ownership over anyone in 1860. Of the ninety-nine Mississippi delegates who attended the convention, sixty-one claimed enslaved people in 1860. Half of those delegates had claimed 16 or fewer people; one as many as 240. Yet two of the most vocal supporters of compensation for enslavers—George Potter and Robert Brown—had not claimed ownership over anyone, while the most vocal opponent of the policy—William Yerger—did. Potter and Brown owned no slaves; Yerger owned at least 11. The median number of slaves owned by Mississippi delegates in 1860 was 15; 75 percent of the delegates owned less than 26 slaves, meaning that the delegate who owned 240 slaves was a significant outlier. Of course, enslavers and non-enslavers alike could see the economic benefits of federal compensation, but ensuring that the spokespeople of the policy did not directly benefit added a veneer of necessity. To find these numbers, I compared the delegates at Louisiana's and Mississippi's 1864 and 1865 constitutional conventions to records in the 1860 US census, slave schedule, Ancestry.com.

4. Interview with South Carolina delegation, June 24, 1865, in *PAJ*, 8:280–83; Vorenberg, *Final Freedom*, 227–30. Some discrepancy exists among historians over how Johnson wanted former Confederate states to abolish slavery. While Eric McKitrick wrote in 1960 that Johnson required former Confederate states to ratify the Thirteenth Amendment abolishing slavery, Michael Vorenberg noted that Johnson's first proclamations on Reconstruction said nothing about the Thirteenth Amendment, and Johnson entreated the pro-

visional governors to encourage their states to endorse ratifying the amendment at the constitutional conventions. Michael Perman has noted that Congress stipulated that state legislatures rather than the state conventions should ratify the amendment. Other sources, like Andrew Johnson's interview with South Carolina delegates on June 24, 1865, support Vorenberg's assertion. McKitrick, *Andrew Johnson and Reconstruction*, 161; Vorenberg, *Final Freedom*, 227; Perman, *Reunion without Compromise*, 87.

5. Bright, "Radicalism and Rebellion"; Carter, *When the War Was Over*, 82–85; Roark, *Masters without Slaves*, 104–5, 134; Perman, *Reunion without Compromise*, 87. Breese, "Politics in the Lower South during Presidential Reconstruction," 139–40, 145; Wolfe, "South Carolina Constitutional Convention of 1865," 26.

6. Hahn, *Nation under Our Feet*, 135, 137, 141, 156; Schurz, *Report on the Condition of the South*; Joshua Hill, Madison, GA, to President Andrew Johnson, May 10, 1865, in *PAJ*, 8:55–56; J. B. Lake to Gov. William L. Sharkey, July 4, 1865, series 771, box 955, folder 8, Mississippi Governors' Papers, Mississippi Department of Archives and History. Other letters expressing similar sentiments of confusion about national and state emancipation policy include George T. Swann to Gov. William L. Sharkey, June 29, 1865, series 771, box 954, folder 4, Mississippi Governors' Papers; George S. Gaines to Gov. William L. Sharkey, July 17, 1865, series 771, box 955, folder 6, Mississippi Governors' Papers; John W. Ford to President Andrew Johnson, June 29, 1865, in *PAJ*, 8:312–31; Orville Eastland to President Andrew Johnson, September 3, 1865, in *PAJ*, 9:16–17; Christopher C. Andrews to President Andrew Johnson, May 11, 1865, in *PAJ*, 8:59.

7. Holt, *Problem of Freedom*; Rugemer, *Problem of Emancipation*; Christopher G. Memminger to President Andrew Johnson, September 4, 1865, in *PAJ*, 9:25.

8. Schurz, *Report on the Condition of the South*; Pleasant W. Yell to Andrew Jackson Hamilton, August 10, 1865, box 2, folder 34, Andrew Jackson Hamilton Governor's Papers, Texas State Library and Archives Commission (hereafter cited as TSLAC). For analyses of the proslavery ideology on Black labor, see Finkelman, *Defending Slavery*; Faust, *Ideology of Slavery*; C. W. Buckley to Gov. Alexander Hamilton, August 22, 1865, box 3, folder 39, Andrew Jackson Hamilton Governor's Papers, TSLAC; Rable, *Confederate Republic*, 50.

9. John J. Seibels to Abraham Lincoln April 14, 1865, in *PAJ*, 7:694–96; Christopher C. Andrews to President Andrew Johnson, May 11, 1865, in *PAJ*, 8:59; Joseph M. S. Rogers to Gov. William Holden, September 17, 1865, GP 189, Governors' Papers, Holden Correspondence, State Archives of North Carolina; James Russell to President Andrew Johnson, September 30, 1865, in *PAJ*, 9:158. See also S. R. Frierson to Gov. William L. Sharkey, July 5, 1865, series 771, box 955, folder 7, Mississippi Governors' Papers; George S. Gaines to Gov. William L. Sharkey, July 17, 1865, box 955, folder 6, Mississippi Governors' Papers.

10. Foner, *Nothing but Freedom*; Holt, "Essence of the Contract"; Rugemer, *Problem of Emancipation*; Gronningsater, "Born Free in the Master's House," 123–50.

11. Foner, *Reconstruction*; Hahn, *Nation under Our Feet*; A. M. Taylor, *Embattled Freedom*, 211–21; Ochiai, "Port Royal Experiment Revisited," 94–117.

12. The Confederacy did not accept or create any compensated emancipation plans. By the end of the war, the Confederacy had considered a scheme to enlist and free enslaved soldiers. Earlier acts had employed enslaved men in the army and compensated enslavers for their labor and persons if they died in service. However, the Confederate enlistment policy, according to historian Ervin L. Jordan, encouraged enslavers to free men for national

defense so that the policy to arm them was not "misinterpreted as abolitionism" (235). See General Orders No. 32 in *General Orders from the Adjutant and Inspector General's Office, Confederate States Army*, 59–61; General Orders No. 14, Adit. and Insp. General's Office, Richmond, VA, March 23, 1865, *OR*, series 4, vol. 3, pp. 1161–62. Lincoln to the Senate and House of Representatives, February 5, 1865, *CWAL*, 8:260–61; Lincoln to the House of Representatives, February 10, 1865, *CWAL*, 8:274–85; *Boston Daily Advertiser*, February 11, 1865; *Daily Evening Bulletin*, March 10, 1865; W. C. Harris, "Hampton Roads Peace Conference," 30–61; Vorenberg, "Spielberg's *Lincoln*," 566; Rable, *Confederate Republic*, 292; Vorenberg, "'Deformed Child.'"

13. *Journal of the Proceedings and Debates in the Constitutional Convention of the State of Mississippi*, 50, 52, 82, 92. One exception is Maryland, which passed a law on February 6, 1864, to pay some enslavers $100 for an enslaved man who enlisted in the US Army. See An Act to Aid and Encourage Enlistments into the Maryland Regiments in Service of the United States, chap. 15, sec. 3, in *Laws of the State of Maryland*, 20–23.

14. B. F. Moore Jr. to Gov. William Sharkey, July 28, 1865, series 771, box 955, folder 5, Mississippi Governors' Papers; John Pratt, *Address to the voters of the Fourth Congressional District, 1865*, broadside, Louisiana State University Special Collections, Hill Memorial Library, Baton Rouge, LA.

15. Cutler, *Address of Hon. R. King Cutler*, 7.

16. K. Rayner to Gov. William L. Sharkey, August 21, 1865, series 776, box 960, Mississippi Governors' Papers.

17. Cantrell, *Kenneth and John B. Rayner and the Limits of Southern Dissent*, 116, 120, 137, 151; Dew, *Apostles of Disunion*, 74–81. Rayner himself owned over 200 slaves on plantations in North Carolina and Arkansas in 1860. After the surrender, he was in financial straits, and soon after, he bought land in Mississippi. At the time of his letter to Governor Sharkey, he did not own that land, though he sought money from investors to purchase it. He did so in 1867, and his wife also purchased land in DeSoto County, Mississippi, in 1869. See 1860 US census, slave schedule, Kenneth Rayner, Ancestry.com; Cantrell, *Kenneth and John B. Rayner and the Limits of Southern Dissent*, 56, 153–54, 155.

18. Byrne, *Becoming Bourgeois*, 53, 123–26; Storey, *Loyalty and Loss*, 23; Myers, *Rebels against the Confederacy*, 20–33, 229; Kruman, *Parties and Politics in North Carolina*; Inscoe and Kenzer, *Enemies of the Country*, 1–17; Taliaferro, *A Protest against the Ordinance of Secession*.

19. It is difficult to quantify and describe these Whiggish Unionists' influence on Civil War era Southern politics. The products of not only the Whig Party but also the American and Constitutional Union parties, they failed to create cohesive inter- and intrastate political coalitions during the secession crisis and, later, during congressional Reconstruction. Without a formal party spanning slaveholding states, they left no organized bureaucratic records. Their pro-slavery and pro-Constitution ideology has more recently been confined to biography and state-level studies of Southern Unionists in both former Confederate and border states. T. B. Alexander, "Persistent Whiggery in the Confederate South," 305–29; Mering, "Persistent Whiggery in the Confederate South," 124–43; Rable, *Confederate Republic*; Crofts, *Reluctant Confederates*; McCrary et al., "Class and Party in the Secession Crisis," 429–57; Inscoe and Kenzer, *Enemies of the Country*, 3–14; Holt, *The Rise and Fall of the American Whig Party*, chap. 26.

20. *Journal of the Proceedings and Debates in the Constitutional Convention of the State of Mississippi*, 17, 33–38, 43, 220–21. The two delegates who challenged the illegality of secession wrote a minority report that invalidated the ordinance of secession but sustained its jurisdiction from 1861 to 1865. On August 22, the convention delegates officially invalidated the ordinance of secession by a vote of 81 to 14. Though their outcome was similar, the state suicide theory and the conquered province theory were distinct. Proponents of the state suicide theory argued that secession was illegal, and therefore states willfully ended their statehood and transformed into territories. The conquered province theory accepted secession but viewed Confederate states as belligerents. Military defeat led them to become conquered territories. Americans continued to contest whether secession had been constitutional, to no legal resolution. Instead, their conclusions usually reflected their postwar political needs and expediency. Historians, too, have debated these various views of secession to understand the break between presidential and congressional Reconstruction. See Nicoletti, *Secession on Trial*, 14–19, 105n55, 172–81; Les Benedict, *Preserving the Constitution*, 8–10; Perrone, *Nothing More Than Freedom*, 117–18; Les Benedict, "Preserving the Constitution," 65–90. Greg Downs suggests that military occupation after the Civil War enabled federal politicians to wield the authority to direct Reconstruction, not the legal status of seceded states. However these legal theories of state status still had important ramifications for emancipation. Downs, *After Appomattox*, 65–87, chap. 5.

21. US Const. amend. V; *Journal of the Proceedings and Debates in the Constitutional Convention of the State of Mississippi*, 55–56, 82, 92.

22. K. Rayner to Gov. William L. Sharkey, August 21, 1865, series 776, box 960, Mississippi Governors' Papers.

23. Cimprich, *Slavery's End in Tennessee*, 105–6; Martha Deery Churchwell to Andrew Johnson, July 17, 1865, in *PAJ*, 8:416; Sam Milligan to Andrew Johnson, July 10, 1865, in *PAJ*, 8:386.

24. Report of the Joint Committee on Reconstruction, H.R. Rep. No. 39-30, at X (1866) and pt. 2, at X, 8, 124; *Journal of the Convention of Delegates of the People of Arkansas*; Foner, *Reconstruction*, 45.

25. Ben H. Procter, "Reagan, John Henninger," Handbook of Texas Online, Texas State Historical Association, updated July 6, 2021, www.tshaonline.org/handbook/online/articles/fre02; John H. Reagan to the People of Texas, August 11, 1865, John H. Reagan Letters, 1864–1896, TSLAC.

26. Hughes v. Todd, 63 Ky. 188 (1865); Corbin v. Marsh 63 Ky. 193 (1865); Perrone, *Nothing More Than Freedom*, 79–80; Pincus, "Virginia Supreme Court, Blacks, and the Law," 21–25.

27. The US Court of Claims evolved from the functions of the claims and judiciary committees of the House and Senate. During the Civil War, these committees sometimes worked with the War Department. There is evidence that border state and other loyal enslavers petitioned army offices and congressmen for compensation for the value of enslaved people freed during the war. These petitions or letters made their way to the House Committee on Claims, Memorials and Petitions and the Senate's Committee on Claims for compensation for the value of enslaved people. In these cases, Congress either discharged the relevant committees from considering a claim or rejected it. I found little evidence of enslavers in the Confederacy petitioning Congress during or immediately after the war, but

legislative records are voluminous and such petitions were scattered throughout the branches of the federal bureaucracy. More research can be done. See Smith Minor, H.R. Rep. No. 37-58 (1863); F. A. Lewis, Jefferson Co., [West] Virginia, to Hon H. B. Anthony, February 12, 1866, box 50, Various Subjects, Tabled, SEN 39A-J3, RG 46: Records of the US Senate, NARA; "Petition of F. A. Lewis," February 2, 1866, Senate Committee on Claims, Serial 1240, Senate Report 6, 39th Cong. 1st sess; The Petition of Miss Lydia A. Hershey, Miss Christiann Hershey, Mrs. Kate Hershey, and Mrs. Susan Emmett, sisters, 1863 (?), Records of the Committee on Claims, Memorials and Petitions, House of Representatives, 38th Congress, 38A-G2.1, NARA; *Journal of the House of Representatives of the United States: Thirty-Eighth Congress*, 373. Bowman, "Brief History of the Courts of Claims"; Wiecek, "Origin of the United States Court of Claims," 387–406; G. H. Williams, *Civil War Suits in the US Court of Claims*, 3–7; Neff, *Justice in Blue and Gray*, 222–44; United States v. Klein, 80 US 128 (1871).

28. See Perrone, *Nothing More Than Freedom*, 106–7, for a comprehensive chart of state court cases commenting on the legality of emancipation. In chapter 3, Perrone asks when jurists set the date of emancipation for contract disputes and other private law issues and how they justified their decisions. Notably, most cases were heard months after the presidential Reconstruction conventions, while Congress passed the Fourteenth Amendment, or after, suggesting that white Southerners could not get into the courts to challenge immediate, uncompensated emancipation quickly enough to circumvent Congress's measures against compensated emancipation.

29. For observations about resistance to emancipation and the amnesty oath in Texas in Andrew Jackson Hamilton Governor's Papers at the TSLAC, see Charles Amos to Governor Andrew Jackson Hamilton, August 23, 1865, box 3, folder 50; A. K. Foster to Governor Andrew Jackson Hamilton, July 11, 1865, box 1, folder 3; A. A. Devalon to Governor Andrew Jackson Hamilton, July 10, 1865, box 1, folder 3; John Nobel to Governor Andrew Jackson Hamilton, July 18, 1865, box 1, folder 4; J. R. Morris to Governor Andrew Jackson Hamilton, July 27, 1885, box 1, folder 8; J. C. Rushing to Governor Andrew Jackson Hamilton, August 12, 1865, box 2, folder 32; R. A. McGee and Ralph Hughes to Governor Andrew Jackson Hamilton, August 14, 1865, box 2, folder 34; Nathaniel Hart Davis to Governor Andrew Jackson Hamilton, August 1865, box 3, folder 62; J. M. McAlpine to Governor Andrew Jackson Hamilton, August 1865, box 3, folder 63; petition from Meridian, Bosque County, September 6, 1865, box 3, folder 68; J. D. Dewberry to Andrew Jackson Hamilton, August 1, 1865, box 1, folder 13; petition, August 1, 1865, box 1, folder 14; anonymous to Andrew Jackson Hamilton, August 11, 1865, box 2, folder 30.

30. From "Four Texans" (James Bell, Thomas Duval, Elisha Pease, and Francis White) to Andrew Johnson, August 30, 1865, microfilm reel 17, Andrew Johnson Papers, LOC.

31. Proclamation by the governor, Austin, August 19, 1865, Executive Records Collection, Reel 6, TSLAC; Andrew Jackson Hamilton to Andrew Johnson, August 30, 1865, in *PAJ*, 8:674–78; anonymous to Governor Andrew Jackson Hamilton, August 10, 1865, box 2, folder 29, Andrew Jackson Hamilton Governor's Papers, TSLAC; Downs, *After Appomattox*, 143–45; Hahn, *Nation under Our Feet*; K. E. Williams, *They Left Great Marks on Me*.

32. Andrew Jackson Hamilton to Andrew Johnson, August 30, 1865, in *PAJ*, 8:674–78; proclamation by the governor, Austin, September 11, 1865, Executive Records Collection, Reel 6, TSLAC. We might also understand Hamilton's actions from his later writing. In

1868, Hamilton delivered the dissent to Texas's Emancipation Proclamation Cases during his tenure on the Texas Supreme Court. The concurring justices determined that the Emancipation Proclamation was a war measure that did not actually free enslaved people when it was issued. Hamilton disagreed. He said the proclamation had legal power, deriving from President Lincoln's authority as commander in chief. As provisional governor, Hamilton could use his political power to enforce emancipation and postpone the convention, even if doing so left Texas's statehood in a liminal status. Hamilton's view of the Emancipation Proclamation matched that of abolitionists and freedom seekers early in the war. Emancipation meant that policymakers could mobilize their power to guarantee Black freedom and protect the rights and lives of Black people. For analysis of the Emancipation Proclamation cases, see Perrone, *Nothing More Than Freedom*, 93–96, 104, 107, 132; Emancipation Proclamation Cases (*Hall v. Keese* and *Dougherty v. Cartwright*), 31 Tex. 504 (1868).

33. Philip Holbert to Andrew Jackson Hamilton, October 14, 1865, box 4, folder 101, Andrew Jackson Hamilton Governor's Papers, TSLAC; Cohen-Lack, "Struggle for Sovereignty," 76–77; Andrew J. Hamilton to Andrew Johnson, November 27, 1865, in *PAJ*, 9:436–37. For further reports of white violence at this time, see also D. J. Baldwin to Andrew Jackson Hamilton, November 7, 1865, box 5, folder 116, Andrew Jackson Hamilton Governor's Papers, TSLAC.

34. Drake, "Mississippi Reconstruction Convention of 1865," 225–56.

35. Carter, *When the War Was Over*, 65–67; Foner, *Reconstruction*; "Tabular View of Mississippi State Convention, Which Assembled in Jackson, August 14, 1865," Certificate of Election of Delegates, box 29401, Series 472, General Records of the State of Mississippi, Mississippi Department of Archives and History.

36. Les Benedict, "Preserving the Constitution"; *Journal of the Proceedings and Debates in the Constitutional Convention of the State of Mississippi, August, 1865*, 17, 33–8, 220–21.

37. Drake, "Mississippi Reconstruction Convention of 1865," 229–30; Garner, *Reconstruction in Mississippi*, 82–88; *Journal of the Proceedings and Debates in the Constitutional Convention of the State of Mississippi, August, 1865*, 70–71.

38. *Journal of the Proceedings and Debates in the Constitutional Convention of the State of Mississippi, August, 1865*, 55–56, 65–68, 82, 92.

39. Jasanoff, *Liberty's Exiles*, 330; Witt, *Lincoln's Code*, 29, 70–77; *Journal of the Proceedings and Debates in the Constitutional Convention of the State of Mississippi*, 69; Preliminary Emancipation Proclamation, September 22, 1862, *CWAL*, 5:433–36. The congressional resolution that Potter referred to is likely the Joint Resolution declaring that the United States ought to cooperate with, affording pecuniary Aid to any State which may adopt the gradual Abolishment of Slavery, Pub. L. No. 37-26, 12 Stat. 617; "Great Britain and Slaves Taken in War," *New York Times*, September 16, 1861; Fehrenbacher, *Slaveholding Republic*, 92–98; Mason, "Battle of Slaveholding Liberators," 676–77.

40. *Journal of the Proceedings and Debates in the Constitutional Convention of the State of Mississippi*, 55–56, 73, 83, 152.

41. *Journal of the Proceedings and Debates in the Constitutional Convention of the State of Mississippi*, 55–56, 70, 91–93; *Journal of the Proceedings of the Convention of the People of Georgia*, 139. In Louisiana's 1864 conventions, Edmund Abell, a proponent of compensation, also appealed to delegates' sympathies for white widows and orphans. See *Debates in the Convention for the Revision and Amendment of the Constitution of the State of Louisiana*, 143, 154, 166.

42. Nannie Durman to Gov. William Sharkey, Jackson, MS, July 14, 1865, series 771, box 955, folder 1, Mississippi Governors' Papers. See also Martha Deery Churchwell to Andrew Johnson, July 17, 1865, in *PAJ*, 8:416; Annie E. Hutchcroft to Andrew Johnson, July 25, 1865, in *PAJ*, 8:471; Ann H. Kincheloe to President Andrew Johnson, January 8, 1866, in *PAJ*, 9:578; *Journal of the Proceedings of the Convention of the People of Georgia*, 139.

43. Downs, *Declarations of Dependence*, 4; A. J. Gross, *Double Character*, 98–99, 120. In Louisiana's 1864 convention, Edmund Abell, a proponent of compensation, also appealed to delegates' sympathies for white widows and orphans. See *Debates in the Convention for the Revision and Amendment of the Constitution of the State of Louisiana*, 143, 154, 166.

44. *Journal of the Proceedings of the Convention of the People of Georgia*, 139; McCurry, *Confederate Reckoning*, 86–87, 103, 239; Clay, *Speech of the Hon. Henry Clay*, 27–28; Draper, *Price of Emancipation*, 90n56. In the 1864 Louisiana convention, opponents of compensation echoed these ideas. There, one delegate scoffed, "Talk not to me of the tears of slaveholders. Who were the husbands of these widows? Who are to be robbed, as the gentleman calls it, of their slaves? . . . There is every reason to believe the greater portion of them fell on the field of battle in deep-dyed, bloody rebellion." *Debates in the Convention for the Revision and Amendment of the Constitution of the State of Louisiana*, 169. See also Draper, *Price of Emancipation*, 89–92, for further discussion of British appeals to protect insolvent widows and orphans in the event of emancipation.

45. L. F. Edwards, *Scarlett Doesn't Live Here Anymore*, 66–70, 71–84, 97–99; McCurry, *Confederate Reckoning*, 214–15; McCurry, *Women's War*, 35–54; Witt, *Lincoln's Code*; Lieber, *Instructions for the Government of Armies of the United States in the Field*, arts. 155–57.

46. Chemerinsky, *Constitutional Law*, 663.

47. Witt, "From Loss of Services to Loss of Support," 736–37, 744; Witt, "Toward a New History of American Accident Law."

48. Benson, "*Fisher v. Allen*: The Southern Origins of the Married Women's Property Acts," 97–122; Holton, "Equality as Unintended Consequence," 313–40; Jones-Rogers, *They Were Her Property*, 25–56; L. F. Edwards, *Scarlet Doesn't Live Here Anymore*, 28–31, quote on 29; Wood, *Masterful Women*.

49. Goodman, "Emergence of Homestead Exemption in the United States," 472, 487–89, 495. Goodman concludes that although widespread in the nineteenth century, homestead exemptions fell short of "providing an effective safety net" (496); Ely, *Contract Clause*, 122.

50. L. F. Edwards, *Scarlet Doesn't Live Here Anymore*, 91–92, 120–21; J. L. Gross, "'And for the Widow and Orphan,'" 217–23.

51. McClintock, "Civil War Pensions and the Reconstruction of Union Families." To understand the racialized dimensions of US widows' pensions, see Brimmer, *Claiming Union Widowhood*.

52. *Debates in the Convention for the Revision and Amendment of the Constitution of the State of Louisiana*, 154; *Journal of the Proceedings and Debates in the Constitutional Convention of the State of Mississippi*, 122.

53. Downs, *Declarations of Dependence*, quotes on 2, 6; see also 27, 32–33.

54. McCurry, "Reconstructing Belonging," 19–40; Gordon, *Pitied but Not Entitled*, 7, 11–12.

55. *Journal of the Proceedings and Debates in the Constitutional Convention of the State of Mississippi*, 91–93; Report of the Committee on Emancipation, 1864, M-451, LaRC.

56. Interview with South Carolina Delegation, June 24, 1865, in *PAJ*, 8:280–83; *Journal of the Proceedings and Debates in the Constitutional Convention of the State of Mississippi*, 92–95, 155; *New York Times*, "Sixth Day," September 30, 1865.

57. *Journal of the Proceedings and Debates in the Constitutional Convention of the State of Mississippi*, 71–72; Drake, "Mississippi Reconstruction Convention of 1865," 239; *Journal of the Convention of the People of South Carolina*, 12, 59–60.

58. Nicoletti, "American Civil War as a Trial by Battle," 76.

59. *Journal of the Proceedings and Debates in the Constitutional Convention of the State of Mississippi*, 99.

60. *Journal of the Proceedings and Debates in the Constitutional Convention of the State of Mississippi*, 100, 112–14, 162–63, 230; Drake, "Mississippi Reconstruction Convention of 1865," 229.

61. *Journal of the Proceedings and Debates in the Constitutional Convention of the State of Mississippi*, 91–95, 124–26.

62. *Journal of the Proceedings and Debates in the Constitutional Convention of the State of Mississippi*, 61–62, 73, 164–65. The convention journal does not stipulate how many delegates supported tabling Hudson's substitute.

63. Ga. Const. of 1865, art. I, § 20; *Journal of the Proceedings of the Convention of the People of Georgia*, 45.

64. *Journal of the Proceedings and Debates in the Constitutional Convention of the State of Mississippi*, 99–102.

65. Message to Congress, December 4, 1865, in *PAJ*, 9:472; Oakes, *Freedom National*, 484–85; Vorenberg, *Final Freedom*, 231–32.

66. Report of the Joint Committee on Reconstruction, H.R. Rep. No. 39-30, pt. 3, at 146, 150 (1866); S. Wright to Andrew Jackson Hamilton, January 23, 1866, box 6, folder 148, Andrew Jackson Hamilton Governor's Papers, TSLAC; William W. Holden to Andrew Johnson, August 1, 1866, in *PAJ*, 11:6.

Chapter Four

1. Foner, *Reconstruction*, 251–52; James, *Framing of the Fourteenth Amendment*, 53; Downs, *After Appomattox*, 129.

2. Cong. Globe, 39th Cong., 1st Sess. 2499 (1866). See also Republican representative Shelby Cullom's speech on the Fourteenth Amendment in Cong. Globe Appendix, 39th Cong., 1st Sess. 910–12 (1866). Broomall was not an outlier. As Mark Graber shows, Republicans feared and were determined to prevent "rebel rule." Graber, *Punish Treason, Reward Loyalty*, chap. 2; see also 62, 299n22, and 299n23 for other instances of congressmen discussing former Confederate desire for compensation.

3. Cong. Globe, 39th Cong., 1st Sess. 2499 (1866); Downs, *After Appomattox*, 114; Graber, *Punish Treason, Reward Loyalty*, 36. See Graber, chap. 3, for further explanation of legal theories of secession.

4. There is little historical research on section 4 of the Fourteenth Amendment, and what research there is reflects past historians' decidedly pro-Confederate sympathies. Exacerbating the lack of research on section 4 is the fact that there is little evidence of the joint committee's work in the archives. The few existing histories argued that section 4 was an

unnecessary peculiarity because white Southerners had given up slavery willingly. These historians generally concluded that Republicans added the section to punish white Southerners for the war. See Kendrick, *Journal of the Joint Committee of Fifteen on Reconstruction*, 350; James, *Framing of the Fourteenth Amendment*, 160, 180–81, 194; J. G. Clark, "Historians and the Joint Committee on Reconstruction," 348–61; Flack, *Adoption of the Fourteenth Amendment*, 133–36.

5. With a few exceptions, historians and legal scholars have neglected section 4, focusing instead on the equal protection and due process clauses of section 1, which have been so significant to the expansion of civil rights since the ratification of the Fourteenth Amendment. Focused on national finance, section 4 does not fit into this rights framework. See Maltz, "Moving beyond Race," 306–7; Curtis, *No State Shall Abridge*; Aynes, "Unintended Consequences of the Fourteenth Amendment and What They Tell Us about Its Interpretation," 318–21, quote from 319; Foner, *Reconstruction*, 257; W. E. Nelson, *Fourteenth Amendment*, 8. A few have investigated section 4 to understand modern debates about the United States' national debt but largely neglected the debate over compensation. See McCommas, "Forgotten but Not Lost"; Charles, "Debt Limit and the Constitution." More recently, Mark Graber has argued persuasively that sections 2–5 were the most significant sections of the amendment. Republicans who drafted the amendment sought to prevent "rebel rule," punish treason, and reward loyalty. This book agrees with his interpretation, adding that compensated emancipation was another important political tool to direct Reconstruction of the South's political systems and economy. Graber, *Punish Treason, Reward Loyalty*. See also Blair, *With Malice towards Some*, 269.

6. When they avoided a direct debate about slavery and the law, congressional Republicans acted similarly to other lawmakers of the time who hoped to align the revolutionary outcomes of the war with US law without fundamentally changing the Constitution. See Vorenberg, *Final Freedom*, 6; Nicoletti, *Secession on Trial*, 5.

7. On debates regarding compensated emancipation and the Thirteenth Amendment, see Vorenberg, *Final Freedom*, 108–109. Cong. Globe, 38th Congress, 2nd sess., 158–167, 181–83, 297, 380–81, 404, 425, 616–17, 838 (1864); Cong. Globe Appendix, 38th Cong., 2d Sess. 99–101 (1864); Chattanooga *Daily Gazette*, January 29, 1865. On February 6, 1865, Missouri senator and Constitutional Unionist James Sidney Rollins proposed another amendment to the Constitution to secure compensation for loyal enslavers in the border states and rebellious states "who are, have always been, or may be willing to again become faithful to the Government of the United States." Any enslaver living in the Confederacy could claim compensation as long as they pledged allegiance to the United States and had never served in the Confederate military. Rollins also justified federal compensation as an economic boost and reward for slaveowners' willingness to give up their property in people. The amendment died as a result of unsympathetic senators' maneuvers.

8. *National Anti-Slavery Standard*, November 18, December 2, and December 9, 1865; *National Anti-Slavery Standard*, April 21, 1866; *Connecticut Courant*, November 7, 1865; Thomas Shankland to Thaddeus Stevens, September 29, 1865, box 2, Thaddeus Stevens Papers, LOC, Washington, DC; R. W. Flournoy to Thaddeus Stevens, November 20, 1865, box 3, Thaddeus Stevens Papers; Cong. Globe 39th Cong., 1st Sess. 93(1865)Abney, "Reconstruction in Pontotoc County," 234.

9. Petition of Citizens of the US, undated, ordered to lie on the table on Feb. 13, 1866, Petitions and Memorials, RG 233.8: Records of the Committee Relating to Claims, National Archives and Records Administration (hereafter cited as NARA). Emphasis in original.

10. James, *Framing of the Fourteenth Amendment*; Schuckers, *Life and Public Services of Salmon Portland Chase*, 526–27; *National Anti-Slavery Standard*, May 26, 1866; *Tribune* (New Orleans), June 18, August 9, September 20, and October 31, 1865.

11. Kendrick, *Journal of the Joint Committee of Fifteen on Reconstruction*, 282. Though Kendrick writes that three witnesses replied to the question in the negative, I write two here because one witness replied in the negative and immediately contradicted himself by mentioning instances when he had heard people saying that they wanted compensation. See testimony of Colonel Orlando Brown in Report of the Joint Committee on Reconstruction, H.R. Rep. No. 39-30, pt. 2, at 124 (1866).

12. Report of the Joint Committee on Reconstruction, H.R. Rep. No. 39-30, pt. 3, at xvii, 124, 150, and pt. 4, at 128 (1866); Downs, *After Appomattox*, 129. The Senate Committee on Claims also reviewed and rejected a Virginia claim for the value of property and enslaved people. Henry Bowen Anthony, Report of the Committee on Claims, S. Rep. No. 39-6 (1866); F. A. Lewis, Rippon Post Office, Jefferson County, VA, to Hon H. B. Anthony, February 12, 1866, 39th Congress, box 50, Various Subjects, Tabled, SEN 39A-J3, RG 46: Records of the US Senate, NARA.

13. Schurz, *Report on the Condition of the South*, 14.

14. C. W. Foster, Assistant Adjutant General Volunteers, and Bvt. Maj. Gen. E. D. Townsend, Assistant Adjutant General, US Army, Washington, DC, to Edwin Stanton, Washington DC, October 20, 1865, *OR*, series 3, vol. 5, 139–40.

15. Annual Report of the Secretary of War, 1864, House Exec. Doc. No. 83, 38th Cong., 2d sess. (1865), 27–28; C. W. Foster, Assistant Adjutant General Volunteers, and Bvt. Maj. Gen. E. D. Townsend, Assistant Adjutant General, US Army, Washington, DC, to Edwin Stanton, Washington DC, October 20, 1865, *OR*, series 3, vol. 5, 139–40; Edwin M. Stanton to Hannibal Hamlin, January 25, 1865, Letter of the Secretary of War, *OR*, series 3, vol. 4, part 2, 1075–76; Edwin M. Stanton to Schuyler Colfax, January 9, 1866, Letter of the Secretary of War, H.R. Exec. Doc. No. 39-22 (1866). See also Letter of the Secretary of War, communicating in compliance with a resolution of the Senate of the 8th instant, information in regard to the appointment of commissioners under the 24th section of the act of February 24, 1864, entitled "An act to amend an act entitled 'An act for enrolling and calling out the national forces, and for other purposes,' approved March 3, 1863, and the awards made by the said commissioners, and why payments on awards have been suspended. S. Exec. Doc. No. 39-9 (1866). As of time of publication, the author has found confirmation of the twenty-five paid claims in Reports of the Board for the Assessment of Claims Arising Under Provisions of Adjutant General's Office General Order 329 of 1863, UD 181, RG 94, NARA. No other claims are similarly categorized as "Rec'v ck" or "check received" in the reports or other related records. Sebastian F. Streeter to Major C. W. Foster, May 11, 1864, Letters Received by the Disbursing Office, 1864–1867, Box 2, UD 177, RG 94, NARA.

16. Vorenberg, *Final Freedom*, 6.

17. H.R. 43, 39th Cong., 1st Sess; *Journal of the House of Representatives of the United States: Thirty-Ninth Congress.*

18. Boutwell, *Speeches and Papers Relating to the Rebellion and the Overthrow of Slavery,* 120, 126, 129, 178, 290–91, 294.

19. Report from the Committee on the Judiciary on Amendment to the Constitution [To accompany H. Res. No. 43], H.R. Rep. No. 39-33 (1866); Cong. Globe, 39th Cong., 1st Sess. 1367, 1605, 1695–6 (1866); Joint Resolution Declaring That the United States Ought to Cooperate with, Affording Pecuniary Aid to Any State Which May Adopt the Gradual Abolishment of Slavery, Pub. L. No. 39-26, 12 Stat. 617.

20. Cong. Globe, 39th Cong., 1st Sess. 1695–6 (1866).

21. James, *Framing of the Fourteenth Amendment,* 92–93, 100–110; Report of the Joint Committee on Reconstruction, H.R. Rep. No. 39-30, IV; Kendrick, *Journal of the Joint Committee of Fifteen on Reconstruction,* 103.

22. Thomson, *Bonds of War,* 3, 17–18, 159, 198; Holton, *Unruly Americans and the Origins of the Constitution,* 214–15, 267; Noll, "Repudiation!," 11; English, "Understanding the Costs of Sovereign Default," 268–70.

23. Thomson, *Bonds of War,* 85, 113, 121, 126; Lawson, *Patriot Fires,* chap. 2; Noll, "Repudiation!," 3–15; Foner, *Reconstruction,* 22–24, quote on 311; Barreyre, "Politics of Economic Crises," 411; Richardson, *Greatest Nation of the Earth,* 64–65; Barreyre, *Gold and Freedom,* trans. Arthur Goldhammer, part II. As Thomson describes, by the 1870s, investors had purchased most war bonds. Everyday Americans no longer held investments in the nation's war effort; however, the future of the national debt remained a salient political issue throughout Reconstruction. See Thomson, *Bonds of War,* chap. 6.

24. Eder, "Forgotten Section of the Fourteenth Amendment," 5; McCommas, "Forgotten but Not Lost," 1295, 1312–16; John Pratt, *Address to the Voters of the Fourth Congressional District, Composed of the Parishes of Natchitoches, Sabine, Rapides, Calcasieu, St. Landry, Vermilion, Lafayette, Avoyelles, Pointe Coupee, St. Martin, West Baton Rouge, Iberville, Assumption and St. Mary,* 1865, broadside, Louisiana State University Library Special Collections, Hill Memorial Library, Baton Rouge; Schurz, *Report on the Condition of the South;* Grider, *Speech of Hon. Henry Grider, of Kentucky, on Reconstruction,* 6.

25. Cong. Globe, 39th Cong., 1st Sess. 2499, 3169 (1866); see also Cong. Globe, 39th Cong., 1st Sess. 257, 2510, 3171 (1866); Jacob Merritt Howard, Reconstruction Report of the committee, 1866, Small Manuscript Collections, Rubenstein Library, Duke University, Durham.

26. Lawson, *Patriot Fires*; Aynes, "Unintended Consequences of the Fourteenth Amendment and What They Tell Us about Its Interpretation," 316–21; Blair, *With Malice toward Some,* 287–88; *Journal of the House of Representatives of the United States: Being the First Session of the Thirty-Ninth Congress,* 335, 357; *Cleveland Daily Herald,* March 26, 1866; *Connecticut Courant,* November 7, 1865.

27. David Olusoga, "The Treasury's Tweet Shows Slavery Is Still Misunderstood," *Guardian,* February 12, 2018, www.theguardian.com/commentisfree/2018/feb/12/treasury-tweet-slavery-compensate-slave-owners.

28. James, *Framing of the Fourteenth Amendment,* 94; Cong. Globe, 39th Cong., 1st Sess. 1631–32 (1866); Goldin, "The Economics of Emancipation," 74–75; Ransom and Sutch, "Who Pays for Slavery?," 39–40; Bailey-Williams, "Appraisal of the Estimated Rates of

Slave Exploitation," 56–63. These numbers are not definitive and should be treated as a range of possibilities; they are based on different economic models that use many different variables to estimate the costs.

29. Cong. Globe, 39th Cong., 1st Sess. 2499 (1866); Blight, *Race and Reunion*, 51–53.

30. North Carolina Republican State Executive Committee(?) *Address to the white working-men of North-Carolina*, between 1865 and 1869, broadside, Wilson Library, University of North Carolina, Chapel Hill; *Cleveland Daily Herald*, October 9, 1865; Merritt, *Masterless Men*; Rable, *The Confederate Republic*; Hartford *Courant*, November 7, 1865. Republicans also feared that former Confederates would stop paying widows' pensions for their husbands' service to the US and appealed to the insecurity of impoverished widows, similar to how Potteries appealed to their colleagues to protect widows and orphans to gain support for compensation in Mississippi. See Graber, *Punish Treason, Reward Loyalty*, 15, 62.

31. Schurz, *Report on the Condition of the South*, 14.

32. McCommas, "Forgotten but Not Lost," 1295; Charles, "Debt Limit and the Constitution," 1234–40; Eder, "Forgotten Section of the Fourteenth Amendment," 6–10; James, *Framing of the Fourteenth Amendment*, 24–27; Blair, *With Malice toward Some*, 286–87. By the summer of 1866, all former Confederate states except South Carolina and Mississippi repudiated their war debts. "Laws of the Late Insurgent States," June 18, 1866, House Ex. Doc. 131, 39th Cong., 1st Sess.

33. Cong. Globe, 39th Cong., 1st Sess. 2964 (1866).

34. Cong. Globe, 39th Cong., 1st Sess. 2530 (1866). Also see Cong. Globe, 39th Cong., 1st Sess. 2801–2 (1866). Joint Committee on Reconstruction, *Report of the Joint Committee on Reconstruction, Minority Report*, 24. Future historians would use a similar tactic to suggest that section 4 was inconsequential or politically motivated. Kendrick, Journal *of the Joint Committee of Fifteen on Reconstruction, 39th Cong., 1865–1867*, 350.

35. Cong. Globe, 39th Cong., 1st Sess. 2964 (1866).

36. James, *Framing of the Fourteenth Amendment*, 125–31.

37. Kendrick, *Journal of the Joint Committee of Fifteen on Reconstruction*, 84; *Senate Journal*, 39th Cong., 1st sess. 489; Cong. Globe, 39th Cong., 1st Sess. 1426, 2896, 2941 (1866). In the Senate on March 13, Henry Lane of Kansas proposed that the Committee on the Judiciary review a version of the new amendment that would have prohibited "the General Government or any State government from paying for any slave property." It did not move forward. Cong. Globe, 39th Cong., 1st Sess. 1350 (1866).

38. US Const., art. IV, § 2, clause 3.

39. This characterization of labor is called the chose in action theory. Steinfeld, *The Invention of Free Labor*, 66–93, 138–46, 147–81; Slade, *Speech of Mr. Slade, of Vermont, on the Abolition of Slavery and the Slave Trade in the District of Columbia*, 21; Owen, *Wrong of slavery, the right of emancipation, and the future of the African race in the United States*, 141.

40. Siddali, *From Property to Person*, 81–82, 157.

41. Republicans' use of compensated emancipation as a political tool during Reconstruction helps explain why, as historian Daniel Hamilton argues, Americans came to take for granted that the government could not permanently seize private property without just compensation despite antebellum legal practices that enabled government seizure without compensation. As William Novak wrote, immediate, uncompensated emancipation represented the "new regime" of centralized federal power and authority to abolish slavery even

as it demarcated what federal power could and could not do with individual property rights more broadly. See: Hamilton, *Limits of Sovereignty*, 9; Siddali, *From Property to Person*, 6, 81–83; Novak, *The People's Welfare*, 243–44.

42. The War Department vacillated over whether to compensate enslavers for apprentices bound to service for a number of years, as opposed to life. It decided that for enlisted men who owed three to five years' service, enslavers would receive $100; five to ten years', $200; ten or more years, $300. Assistant Adjutant General C. W. Foster to P. F. Streeter, December 24, 1863, January 11, 1864, Maryland Slave Claims Commission Correspondence, 1864–1865, UD 176, RG 94, NARA. Sebastian F. Streeter to Captain Le Grand Benedict, May 10, 1864, Colonel C. W. Foster to James K. Mills, November 23, 1866, Letters Received by the Disbursing Office, 1864–1867, Box 2, UD 177, RG 94, NARA.

43. After the House approved the Senate's changes, one Kentucky congressman protested section 4 as an "open repudiation" of the Enrollment Act. Cong. Globe, 39th Cong., 1st Sess. 3041, 3147 (1866). James, *Framing of the Fourteenth Amendment*, 103, 149–52.

44. Cong. Globe Appendix, 39th Cong., 1st Sess. 269–72 (1866).

45. Cong. Globe Appendix, 39th Cong., 1st Sess. 269–72 (1866); Draper, *The Price of Emancipation*, 87–92.

46. Cong. Globe, 39th Cong., 1st Sess. 2989 (1866).

47. Cong. Globe, 39th Cong., 1st Sess. 212–13, 3845 (1866); "Letter of the Secretary of War, communicating in compliance with a resolution of the Senate of the 8th instant, information in regard to the appointment of commissioners under the 24th section of the act of February 24, 1864 . . . ," January 11, 1866, 39th Cong., 1st sess., Senate Ex. Doc. No. 9; "Commissioners of Claims for Maryland and Delaware," January 9, 1866, House Ex. Doc. No. 22, 39th Cong., 1st. sess.; Quote from *Daily News and Herald*, February 22, 1866; *Loyal Georgian*, January 27, 1866.

48. Cong. Globe, 39th Cong., 1st Sess. 3845, 4027–29 (1866). Kentucky congressman Sam McKee attempted to stop all payments to former enslavers in the Border States while preserving the promised bounties to enlisted men on June 25, 1866. Cong. Globe, 39th Cong., 1st Sess. 3402–3 (1866).

49. Shelden and Alexander, "Dismantling the Party System: Party Fluidity and the Mechanisms of Nineteenth-Century US Politics," 17; Vorenberg, *Final Freedom*, 4–5; Blair, *With Malice toward Some*; A. I. P. Smith, *Stormy Present*, 218–25.

50. Legislative Document No. 23: Report of the State Agent for Kentucky, in Regard to Credits on Drafts and Certificates for Slaves Muster into the US Service by James P. Flint, Kentucky Documents (Frankfort, Ky.: State Printing Office, 1866): 1–8; Cong. Globe, 39th Cong., 1st Sess. 3845 (1866); Cong. Globe Appendix, 39th Cong., 1st Sess. 271–72 (1866).

51. Cong. Globe, 39th Cong., 1st Sess. 3134, 3893, 3927, 3931 (1866); An Act Making appropriations for sundry civil expenses of the government for the year ending June thirty, eighteen hundred and sixty-seven, and for other purposes, HR 737, 39th Cong., 1st Sess. (1866); An Act Making appropriations for the legislative, executive, and judicial expenses of the government for the year ending the thirtieth of June, eighteen hundred and sixty-seven, HR 213, 39th Cong., 1st sess., (1866).

52. Cong. Globe, 39th Cong., 1st sess., 3964–65, 4027–29; An Act: Making appropriations for sundry civil expenses of the government for the year ending June thirtieth, eighteen hundred and sixty-seven, and for other purposes, *Statutes at Large*, vol. 14, Ch. 296, 321.

53. *Washington Reporter*, October 10, 1866.

54. B. S. Hendrick to Governor Worth, April 29, 1866, North Carolina Governors' Papers, Worth Correspondence, SANC; Horace H. Day to Governor Orr, October 1, 1866, box 4, folder 4, Governor Orr Letters Sent and Received, SCDAH; Governors Orr and Scott, Abstract of Letters Received, SCDAH; Moran W. Day to Governor Charles Jenkins, October 15, 1866, box DOC-2803, Gov. Charles Jenkins, 1865–1868, Governors' Subject Files, Georgia State Archives, Morrow, GA.

55. National Union Convention Executive Committee, *The Proceedings of the National Union Convention, Held at Philadelphia, August 14, 1866* (Washington: National Union Executive Committee, 1866).

56. *Nashville Journal*, November 1, 1866.

57. Du Bois, *Black Reconstruction in America*, 315–21; Foner, *Reconstruction*, 260–62.

58. Cong. Globe, 39th Congress, 2nd Sess. 26, 55, 301–2, 319, 328, 431–32, 1049, 2004 (1867); Foner, *Reconstruction*, 271–80.

59. Cong. Globe, 40th Congress, 1st Sess. 196–97, 248–50 (1867).

60. Astor, *Rebels on the Border*; Marshall, *Creating a Confederate Kentucky*.

61. The Senate vote was thirty-two to seven. Cong. Globe, 40th Congress, 1st sess., 250; An Act suspending the Payment of Moneys from the Treasury as Compensation to Persons claiming the Service or Labor of colored Volunteers or drafted men, and for other Purposes, *Statutes at Large*, vol. 14, Ch. 8, 1867, 376–377; Joint Resolution suspending all Proceedings in Relation to Payment for Slaves drafted or received as Volunteers in the military Service of the United States, *Statutes at Large*, Joint Resolution 31, vol. 15, 29; Cong. Globe, 40th Cong., 1st Sess. 193, 196, 250, 460 (1867); *New National Era*, April 24, 1873; Annual Report of the Adjutant General's Office, Bureau for Colored Troops, October 20, 1867, F. W. Taggard, 1st Lieutenant US Army in charge of Bureau of Colored Troops, Colored Troops Division, Annual Reports of the Adjutant General Relating to the Colored Troops Division, 1864–65, 1867, RG 94, entry 388, NARA.

62. Archival evidence suggests that the War Department intended to pay more claims reviewed and awarded in 1864. The Compiled Military Service records of formerly enslaved soldiers whose enslavers filed approved claims sometimes contain duplicates of vouchers for the awarded dollar amount, with signatures from an officer of the Bureau of Colored Troops in the Adjutant General's Office and the enslaver. However, I have not yet seen such a voucher that includes a date of payment or other archival evidence that any other claims were paid. Furthermore, the payments of the twenty-five paid claims from Maryland are also confirmed in the Register of Vouchers and Disbursements, 1863–1864, RG 94, entry 387, NARA. Despite the record's catalog title, the register includes entries from 1864–1867 of accounts owed by the Colored Troops Division of the Adjutant General's Office, which oversaw the 1864–1865 and 1866–1867 Boards of Claims and Slave Claims Commissions. The register tracks debts owed for the business of the commissions from 1864–1867, such as commissioners' salaries and expenses, and awards made to former enslavers in 1864 and 1865. Whereas commission salaries, expenses, and the twenty-five paid claims are listed with dates of payment, all former enslavers' claims except the twenty-five paid Maryland claims are listed without date of payment and sometimes marked "suspended" or, in one case, "returned." Therefore, the author infers that awarded claims without dates of payment were not paid. In light of the debates and reports cited in this chapter,

it is unlikely that awards made under the 1864 Enrollment Act, reviewed during or after the war, were paid. See, for example: "Enoch Reed—9th US Colored Infantry," *Compiled Service Records of Volunteer Union Soldiers Who Served with the United States Colored Troops: Infantry Organizations, 8th through 13th, including the 11th (new)*, Microfilm Serial M1821, Microfilm Roll 34, NARA, accessed on Ancestry.com. Lowell *Daily Citizen*, January 26, 1867; *North American*, February 8, 1867; *New Orleans Tribune*, June 12, 1867; *National Anti-Slavery Standard*, January 5, June 29, and August 3,1867; "Kentucky Wants Pay for Her Slaves," *Cleveland Daily Herald*, December 12, 1867; Cincinnati *Daily Gazette*, February 7, 1867; *Journal of the Senate of the Commonwealth of Kentucky* (1867), 56–57, 158; *Proceedings and Acts of the General Assembly of Maryland, January 2—March 23, 1867*, vol. 133, images 852, 4115–19, 4559–62, Archives of Maryland Online, http://aomol.msa.maryland.gov/megafile/msa /speccol/sc2900/sc2908/000001/000133/html/index.html; Assistant Adjutant General C. W. Foster, Special Orders, November 26, 1866, RG 94, Letters Received by the Office of the Adjutant General, Roll 0528, page 35, Fold3.com; Annual Report of the Adjutant General's Office, Bureau for Colored Troops, October 20, 1867, F. W. Taggard, 1st Lieutenant US Army in charge of Bureau of Colored Troops, Colored Troops Division, Annual Reports of the Adjutant General Relating to the Colored Troops Division, 1864–65, 1867, RG 94, entry 388, NARA. The Ohio House of Representatives responded to Maryland and Kentucky's resolutions by passing its own resolution protesting such payments. *Journal of the House of Representatives of the State of Ohio, 1868*, 30, 135.

Chapter Five

1. Quotes from *New National Era*, August 31, 1871, and November 2, 1871. Also see: *New National Era*, February 9, 1871, March 9, 1871, August 24, 1871, June 18, 1874.

2. Nicoletti, *Secession on Trial*, 5, 10–11.

3. Nannie Durman to Gov. William Sharkey, July 14, 1865, box 955, folder 1, Mississippi Governors' Papers, Series 771, MDAH.

4. Perrone, *Nothing More Than Freedom*; Simard, " Citing Slavery," 90; Simard, "Slavery's Legalism"; Soifer, "Status, Contract, and Promises Unkept"; L. F. Edwards, *People and Their Peace*; Kull, "Enforceability after Emancipation of Debts Contracted for the Purchase of Slaves"; Klein, "Naming and Framing the 'Subject' of Antebellum Slave Contracts"; J. C. Williams, "Slave Contracts and the Thirteenth Amendment," 1009–29.

5. Stanley, *From Bondage to Contract*, 1–2; Ely, *Contract Clause*; Ely, "Contract Clause during the Civil War and Reconstruction," 257–74; US Const. art. I, § 10; E. L. Thompson, *Reconstruction of Southern Debtors*, 17; Kull, "Enforceability after Emancipation of Debts Contracted for the Purchase of Slaves."

6. Pomeroy, *People's Law Book*, 40, 42–44, 59; Beadle, *American Lawyer and Business-Man's Form-Book*, 40–41, 98–100; Kilbourne, *Debt, Investment, Slaves*, 3–4.

7. Nannie Durman to Gov. William Sharkey, July 14, 1865, box 955, folder 1, Mississippi Governors' Papers, Series 771, MDAH. See also Martha Deery Churchwell to Andrew Johnson, July 17, 1865, in *PAJ*, 8:416; Annie E. Hutchcroft to Andrew Johnson, July 25, 1865, in *PAJ*, 8:471; Ann H. Kincheloe to President Andrew Johnson, January 8, 1866, in *PAJ*, 9:578. For further research on outstanding debts for the value of enslaved people, see Perrone, *Nothing More Than Freedom*.

8. Foner, *Reconstruction*, 212–14, 326–27; L. F. Edwards, *Gendered Strife and Confusion*, 165; E. L. Thompson, *Reconstruction of Southern Debtors*, 15–18; Woodman, *New South, New Law*, 4; Ely, *Contract Clause*, 120–21.

9. Perrone, *Nothing More Than Freedom*, 22–24; Ely, *Contract Clause*, 88–89, 103; Horwitz, *The Transformation of American Law, 1780–1860*, 253–55.

10. James, "Southern Reaction to the Proposal of the Fourteenth Amendment," 477–97; *Cincinnati Daily Gazette*, February 7, 1867; *Cleveland Daily Herald*, December 12, 1867; *Crisis*, March 3, 1869; *Daily Globe*, March 9, 1870; *Bangor Daily Whig and Courier*, September 5, 1871; *Milwaukee Daily Sentinel*, September 8, 1871; *New National Era*, April 24, 1873, and November 13, 1873; *Augusta Chronicle*, October 18, 1866.

11. *Richmond Whig*, August 21, 1866.

12. Citizens of Clarendon District, Petition Asking That Relief Be Granted to Debtors in the Purchase of Slaves Now Set Free by the US Government, November 25, 1865, South Carolina Legislative Papers, Petitions, South Carolina Department of Archives and History (hereafter cited as SCDAH).

13. Report on the Petition from Clarendon District, December 18, 1865, S165006, #00213, South Carolina Legislative Papers, Judiciary Committee, Committee Reports, SCDAH; Report on the Liability of Admors. and Other Trustees for Monied Transactions during the War and the Liability of Parties for the Sale and Purchase of Negro Property since 1860, December 18, 1865, S165005, #46, Judiciary Committee, Committee Reports, SCDAH. See also Resolution to Have the Judiciary Committee Inquire into the Liability of Admors., Executors, Guardians, and Trustees for Monied Transactions during the War and the Liability of Parties for the Sale and Purchase of Negro Property during and since 1860, No Date [c. 1865], S165018, #1242, Resolutions of the General Assembly, SCDAH. The South Carolina House of Representatives also considered the liability of administrators and trustees who sold or purchased slaves since 1860 for estates they controlled.

14. US Const. art. I, § 10; E. L. Thompson, *Reconstruction of Southern Debtors*, 17; Resolutions concerning Fees Due Owners of Slaves Sold on Credit then Emancipated prior to the Payment of Debt, c. 1866, S165018, #377, South Carolina Legislative Papers, Resolutions of the General Assembly, SCDAH; *Journal of the Senate of South Carolina, 1866*, 229–30.

15. A. J. Gross, *Double Character*, chap. 4; D. R. Berry, *Price for Their Pound of Flesh*, 7. See Wahl, *Bondsman's Burden*, chaps. 4 and 5, for further discussion of how the law treated the death or injury of an enslaved person in various scenarios.

16. Fede, "Legal Protection for Slave Buyers in the US South"; Kull, "Enforceability after Emancipation of Debts Contracted for the Purchase of Slaves," 507–12; Morris, *Southern Slavery and the Law*, 108–11, chap. 6.

17. Woodfin v. Sluder, 61 N.C. 200 (1867); Banks v. Shannonhouse, 61 N.C. 284 (1867); Corbin v. Marsh, 63 Ky. 193 (1865); Hughes v. Todd, 63 Ky. 188 (1865); Perrone, *Nothing More Than Freedom*, 83–90, 151–58.

18. Perrone, *Nothing More Than Freedom*, 15; Kull, "Enforceability after Emancipation of Debts Contracted for the Purchase of Slaves," 494–95, n2; Soifer, "Status, Contract, and Promises Unkept," 1929, 1938; Scott v. Scott, 59 Va. 150 (1868); Haskill v. Sevier, 25 Ark. 152 (1867), aff'd, 26 Ark. 133 (1868), error dismissed, 81 US 12 (1872); Hand v. Armstrong, 34 Ga. 232 (1866); Walker v. Gatlin, 12 Fla. 9 (1867); Bradford v. Jenkins, 41 Miss. 328 (1867); Hall v. Keese, 31 Tex. 504 (1868); Corbin v. Marsh, 63 Ky. 193 (1865); Thomas v. Porter, 66 Ky. 177 (1867).

19. Stanley, *From Bondage to Contract*, 1–2; Ely, *Contract Clause*; Ely, "Contract Clause during the Civil War and Reconstruction," 257–74; US Const. art. I, § 10; E. L. Thompson, *Reconstruction of Southern Debtors*, 17.

20. Louisiana Citizens to Andrew Johnson, August 12, 1865, in *PAJ*, 8:572–76.

21. Louisiana Citizens to Andrew Johnson, August 12, 1865, in *PAJ*, 8:572–76. See footnote 4 on page 576, which cites the Holt letter, Letters Received, EB12 President 3006 (1865), RG 107, NARA.

22. Why Canby changed the date is unknown. See Perrone, *Nothing More Than Freedom*, chap. 3, for a discussion of how judges decided when emancipation happened. *Tri-Weekly Standard*, September 10, 1867; "Destitution in the South: Measures of Relief for the People of the Second District—Order by Gen. Sickles," *New York Times*, April 15, 1867; Bradley, *Bluecoats and Tarheels*, 137–39; *Executive Documents Printed by Order of the House of Representatives during the Second Session of the Fortieth Congress*, 20:82; Foner, *Reconstruction*, 373–74.

23. J. F. G. Mittag to Andrew Johnson, April 27, 1867, in *PAJ*, 12:242–43; Bradley, *Bluecoats and Tarheels*, 139. Letters sent from the Department of the Carolinas to Alfred Dantridge, Rocky Mount, NC, December 2, 1867, vol. 2, pp. 454–55; to William Rollins, Charleston, SC, December 17, 1867, vol. 3, p. 11; to Fanny S. Covington, Rockingham, Richmond Co., NC, December 17, 1867, vol. 3, p. 11; to J. H. Matthews, 56 Broad St., Charleston, SC, December 24, 1867, vol. 3, p. 73, Letters Sent, March 1867–August 1868, RG 393.14: Records of Military (Reconstruction) Districts, Department of the Carolinas, NARA. Letters written to the Department of the Carolinas from Whaley, Mitchell, Clancy, and Dunkin, Solicitors, October 1867, vol. 8, p. 469; from Alfred Dantridge, Rocky Mount, NC, November 10, 1867, vol. 8, p. 108; from A. J. Magrath, Charleston, SC, November 25, 1867, vol. 9, p. 278; from M. Maner, Haw River, NC, November 26, 1867, vol. 9, p. 279, Register of Letters Received, RG 393.14: Records of Military (Reconstruction) Districts, Department of the Carolinas, NARA.

24. Alabama Constitutional Convention, Ordinance No. 38, § 3 (December 6, 1867), 1868 Ala. Acts 185, 186; Ark. Const. of 1868, art. XV, § 14; Fla. Const. of 1868, art. XVII, § 26; Ga. Const. of 1868, art. V, § 7; La. Const. of 1868, tit. VI, art. 128; SC Const. of 1868, art. IV, § 34. In Texas, three different delegates introduced failed resolutions that would void all obligations for slaves made after the Emancipation Proclamation. *Journal of the Reconstruction Convention*, 1:247–48, 921–22, and 2:116–17. North Carolina delegates tabled an ordinance that would prohibit the collection of debts contracted for the purchase or hire of slaves, and other similar ordinances did not leave the Judiciary Committee. "An Ordinance to Prohibit the Collection of All Debts Contracted for the Purchase or Hire of Slaves, or in Aid of the Late Confederate Government," 1865, SS. 14, North Carolina Department of State Files, Constitutional Conventions, 1868—Petitions, Committees, State Archives of North Carolina (hereafter cited as SANC); *Journal of the Constitutional Convention of the State of North Carolina*, 45. See Kull, "Enforceability after Emancipation of Debts Contracted for the Purchase of Slaves," Appendix, for a full list of proposed or enacted constitutional and statutory provisions prohibiting the enforcement of debts for slaves.

25. *Proceedings of the Constitutional Convention of South Carolina*, 239; Kull, "Enforceability after Emancipation of Debts Contracted for the Purchase of Slaves"; Memorial of Citizens of Bladen Co., asking that obligations incurred in the purchase of slaves be annulled, Hollow District, Bladen County, North Carolina, to A. W. Fisher and F. F. French, Janu-

ary 15, 1868, SS. 14, North Carolina Department of State Files, Constitutional Conventions, 1868—Petitions, Committees, SANC.

26. *Daily Constitutionalist*, December 18, 1867; *Weekly Georgia Telegraph*, December 20, 1867; Foner, *Reconstruction*, 373–74; Memorial of Citizens of Bladen Co., asking that obligations incurred in the purchase of slaves be annulled, Hollow District, Bladen County, North Carolina, to A. W. Fisher and F. F. French, January 15, 1868, SS. 14, North Carolina Department of State Files, Constitutional Conventions, 1868—Petitions, Committees, SANC; Hume and Gough, *Blacks, Carpetbaggers, Scalawags*, 122.

27. Hume and Gough, *Blacks, Carpetbaggers, Scalawags*, 169–70, 172; Foner, *Reconstruction*, 374; Hahn, *Nation under Our Feet*, 209–10.

28. *Proceedings of the Constitutional Convention of South Carolina*, 215, quote from 221.

29. *Proceedings of the Constitutional Convention of South Carolina*, 218; Kull, "Enforceability after Emancipation of Debts Contracted for the Purchase of Slaves," 517n85.

30. *Proceedings of the Constitutional Convention of South Carolina*, 224–25; Holt, *Black over White*, 102; *Journal of the Proceedings in the Constitutional Convention of the State of Mississippi*, 197–98, 402–3; *Debates and Proceedings of the Constitutional Convention of the State of Virginia*, 210–11; *Journal of the Constitutional Convention of the State of Virginia*, 37, 50–51.

31. *Journal of the Proceedings in the Constitutional Convention of the State of Mississippi*, 652; *Debates and Proceedings of the Constitutional Convention of the State of Virginia*, 50.

32. *Debates and Proceedings of the Constitutional Convention of the State of Virginia*, 37; *Journal of the Proceedings in the Constitutional Convention of the State of Mississippi*, 739.

33. *Proceedings of the Constitutional Convention of South Carolina*, 124–25.

34. *Proceedings of the Constitutional Convention of South Carolina*, 215, 219, 224, 231; *Journal of the Proceedings of the Constitutional Convention of the People of Georgia*, 136. For similar rhetoric, see Louisiana Citizens to Andrew Johnson, August 12, 1865, in *PAJ*, 8:572–76.

35. W. Johnson, *Chattel Principle*, 5; Gudmestad, *Troublesome Commerce*, 2–4;

36. Martin, "Neighbor-to-Neighbor Capitalism," 107–21; Kilbourne, *Debt, Investment, Slaves*.

37. *Proceedings of the Constitutional Convention of South Carolina*, 199; "Corley, Manuel Simeon, 1823–1902," Biographical Dictionary of the United States Congress: 1774–Present, http://bioguide.congress.gov/scripts/biodisplay.pl?index=C000778.

38. *Proceedings of the Constitutional Convention of South Carolina*, 124, 219.

39. *Proceedings of the Constitutional Convention of South Carolina*, 221, also see Delegate DeLarge on 219–20.

40. Kull, "Enforceability after Emancipation of Debts Contracted for the Purchase of Slaves," 528; The statistic that slave-owning families sold up to 80 percent of their slaves after a patriarch died pertains to Maryland, as determined Calderhead, "How Extensive Was the Border State Slave Trade?," 47; Kilbourne, *Debt, Investment, Slaves*, 99–100; Chused, "Married Women's Property Law," 1398–1400, 1399n207–209; Jones-Rogers, *They Were Her Property*, 25–56, 197; Downs, *Declarations of Dependence*, 2, 6.

41. An initial draft of section 4 did not include the last clause at all, suggesting that its framers did not consider whether it would apply to outstanding debts for slaves. However, one historian called the senator who added the clause, Jacob Merritt Howard of Michigan, a "stickler for constitutional regularity" with "deep respect for the structure of federalism." Presumably, he would support a narrower reading of the contracts clause regarding the states' constitutional measures. Cong. Globe, 39th Cong., 1st Sess. 2941 (1866); James, *The*

Framing of the Fourteenth Amendment, 103–104; Kendrick, *Journal of the Joint Committee of Fifteen on Reconstruction*, 86–87, 91; Maltz, " Radical Politics and Constitutional Theory," 25.

42. J. F. G. Mittag to Andrew Johnson, April 27, 1867, in *PAJ*, 12: 242–43; Bradley, *Bluecoats and Tarheels*, 139.

43. *Daily Republican*, June 5, 1868, at 2, col. 1, in Kull, "Enforceability after Emancipation of Debts Contracted for the Purchase of Slaves," 498, see also 498–501; Cong. Globe, 40th Cong., 2nd Sess. 2433 (1868); E. M. Keister to Thaddeus Stevens, May 18, 1868, box 5, Thaddeus Stevens Papers, LOC, Washington, DC. See also J. W. Stewart to Thaddeus Stevens and W. D. Kelly, May 15, 1868; Thomas Gunn to Thaddeus Stevens, May 26, 1868; and a Northern Bill Holder to Thaddeus Stevens, June 4, 1868, all in box 5, Thaddeus Stevens Papers, LOC, Washington, DC; Cong. Globe, 40th Cong., 2d Sess. 2445 (1868); Amos T. Akerman to Benjamin Conley, April 10, 1868, and May 23, 1868, box 2, folder 19, Benjamin Conley Papers, 1839–1875, Georgia Archives.

44. Kull, "Enforceability after Emancipation of Debts Contracted for the Purchase of Slaves," 538. A Bill to Prevent the Courts of the United States from Enforcing Tracts concerning Slaves, S. 254, 41st Cong. (1869); Cong. Globe, 41st Cong., 1st Sess. 492 (1869).

45. One exception to this is the 1867 Bankruptcy Act, which, Elizabeth Lee Thompson argues, benefited elite white Southerners and former planters who otherwise opposed federal power. E. L. Thompson, *Reconstruction of Southern Debtors*.

46. United States v. Rhodes, 27 F. Cas. 785 (No. 16,151) (C.C. Ky. 1866); Perrone, *Nothing More Than Freedom*, 253; Kull, "Enforceability after Emancipation of Debts Contracted for the Purchase of Slaves," 538.

47. Ely, *Contract Clause*, 5; Stanley, *From Bondage to Contract*; Foner, *Reconstruction*.

48. McNealy v. Gregory, 13 Fla. 417 (1870); Jacoway, admx., v. Denton, 25 Ark. 625 (1869); Calhoun v. Calhoun, 2 SC 283 (1870); Palmer v. Marston, 81 US 10 (1872); Shorter v. Cobb, 39 Ga. 285 (1869); White v. Hart, 80 US 646 (1871); Kull, "Enforceability after Emancipation of Debts Contracted for the Purchase of Slaves," 494–95, n2. As a newly elected justice to the South Carolina Supreme Court, former convention delegate Jonathan J. Wright concurred with Chief Justice Moses in *Calhoun v. Calhoun*, where the South Carolina Supreme Court struck down the state constitution's measure repudiating outstanding debts for slaves. For further discussion, see Jaffe, "Obligations Impaired," 485–88.

49. *Jacoway*, 25 Ark. 625; Matthews v. Dunbar, 3 W. Va. 138 (1869).

50. Bailey, "Test Oaths, Belligerent Rights, and Confederate Money," 1–22; "Finding Aid for the John McClure Collection," Butler Center for Arkansas Studies, http://cdm15728.contentdm.oclc.org/cdm/ref/collection/findingaids/id/3788; "James H. Brown of Kanawha County, W. Va." *West Virginia History on View*, West Virginia & Regional History Center, West Virginia University, https://wvhistoryonview.org/catalog/037984; Callahan, *History of West Virginia, Old and New*, 207–8.

51. Perman, *Road to Redemption*, 9–10; Kull, "Enforceability after Emancipation of Debts Contracted for the Purchase of Slaves," 521.

52. Perrone, *Nothing More Than Freedom*, 24, 112–29; Nicoletti, *Secession on Trial*, 92.

53. *Shorter v. Cobb*, 39 GA 285 (1869).

54. *Shorter*, 39 GA 285; Ga. Const. of 1865, art. 1, § 20. Brown's view was also shared by a South Carolina lawyer, William Whaley, who argued on behalf of a debtor that Congress

had already impaired the obligations of contracts for the value of enslaved people with section 4 of the Fourteenth Amendment, permitting South Carolina to do so as well. Whaley, *Argument of William Whaley*, 11–12, 17, 19–23.

55. *Jacoway*, 25 Ark. 625; *Matthews*, 3 W. Va. 138; *Osborn v. Nicholson*, 18 F. Cas. 846 (1870). Giuliana Perrone writes that Caldwell's opinion of the fourth section was unique. I am grateful to her for drawing my attention to it. Perrone, *Nothing More Than Freedom*, 28.

56. Perrone, *Nothing More Than Freedom*; Nicoletti, *Secession on Trial*, 19.

57. Louisiana continued to follow the precedent of Wainwright v. Bridges, 19 La. Ann. 234 (1867), which nullified outstanding contracts for the value of enslaved people. Articles 128 and 129 of Louisiana's 1868 constitution both invalidated claims for compensation and reaffirmed the *Wainwright* decision by adopting a measure that voided contracts for the sale of persons and made them unenforceable in state courts. *Constitution Adopted by the Constitution Convention of the State of Louisiana*, 17. Boyce v. Tabb did not overturn *Wainwright*. *Palmer*, 81 US 10; *White*, 80 US 646; *Osborn v. Nicholson*, 80 US 654 (1871); *Boyce v. Tabb*, 85 US 546 (1873); Kilbourne, *Debt, Investments, Slaves*, 96–99.

58. *Osborn*, 80 US 654.

59. *Osborn*, 80 US 654; Garland, *Henry T. Osborn, Plaintiff in Error, vs. Young A. G. Nicholson et al., Defendants*, 44, 73; Horwitz, *Transformation of American Law, 1780–1860*, 66; Novak, *People's Welfare*, 16; Treanor, "Original Understanding of the Takings Clause and the Political Process."

60. *Osborn*, 80 US 654; *White*, 80 US 646. For further discussion of the court's rulings regarding secession and former Confederate states' relationship to the federal government, see Perrone, *Nothing More Than Freedom*, 241–47.

61. *Osborn*, 80 US 654; Perrone, *Nothing More Than Freedom*, chap. 2.

62. Kilbourne, *Debt, Investments, Slaves*, 99.

63. *Osborn*, 80 US 654; Ely, *Contracts Clause*, 114; Perrone, *Nothing More Than Freedom*, 252. I have found no additional primary source materials about Justice Chase's dissent. According to his journal, Chase wrote to Supreme Court reporter John William Wallace about his dissent on June 11, 1872, but I have not found that letter in his published papers or in the Salmon P. Chase Papers, LOC Digital Collections. Niven, *Salmon P. Chase Papers*, 688–89; Oakes, *Freedom National*.

64. Kull, "Enforceability after Emancipation of Debts Contracted for the Purchase of Slaves"; Soifer, "Status, Contract, and Promises Unkept"; Perrone, *Nothing More Than Freedom*; Klein, "Naming and Framing the 'Subject' of Antebellum Slave Contracts," 243–83; J. C. Williams, "Slave Contracts and the Thirteenth Amendment," 1009–29.

65. It is possible that creditors and debtors outside the Confederacy also bore the financial results of these decisions; however, I am unaware of any studies that explore the interregional slave financial system during or after the Civil War. For a recent study of the slave trade during the Civil War, see Colby, *Unholy Traffic*.

66. Harriet Berry pension claim, Martha Burgess affidavit, April 3, 1884, in Regosin, *Freedom's Promise*, quote on 36, 194n31. For Harriet Berry's biography and pension claim, see Regosin, chap. 1.

67. Ager et al., "Intergenerational Effects of a Large Wealth Shock."

Chapter Six

1. Garner, *Reconstruction in Mississippi*, 90; C. M. Thompson, *Reconstruction in Georgia*, 150–52; De Roulhac Hamilton, *Reconstruction in North Carolina*, 170; Kendrick, *Journal of the Joint Committee of Fifteen on Reconstruction*, 350. One exception is a 1905 master's thesis from the University of Nebraska by Margaret Davis. However, the thesis does not extend beyond 1865 to incorporate section 4 of the Fourteenth Amendment, exacerbating the tendency to downplay post-war debates about compensation.

2. Du Bois, *Black Reconstruction in America*, chap. 17; Fogel, *Slavery Debates, 1952–1990*; Ransom and Sutch, "Capitalists without Capital," 134; Stampp, "Introduction," in *Reckoning with Slavery*, 12–13.

3. Janney, *Remembering the Civil War*, 134.

4. Foster, *Ghosts of the Confederacy*; Janney, *Remembering the Civil War*; Blight, *Race and Reunion*; Cox, *Dixie's Daughters*.

5. Sources obtained through Newspapers.com, Nineteenth Century US Newspapers, and Readex's America's Historical Newspapers and African American Newspapers, Series 1 and 2. Search terms included "compensation for former slaveowners," "the Hampton Roads Conference," and "payments for slaves." I reviewed each article from these searches, not all of which referred to debates over compensation for property in humans. This chapter utilizes 273 of the articles from this initial search, including articles that I followed up on based on information from the original search, as well as additional articles about 1890s claims for compensation to enslavers and the enslaved from Dr. Caleb McDaniel.

6. Foster, *Ghosts of the Confederacy*, 6–7, 80–90; Silber, *Romance of Reunion*, 149, 172; Janney, *Remembering the Civil War*, 134, 145–47, 181, 207; Blight, *Race and Reunion*; Domby, *False Cause*.

7. Foner, *Reconstruction*, 505–9; Michael Perman, *Road to Redemption*; Ayers, *Promise of the New South*, 8.

8. Perman, *The Road to Redemption*. The following papers discussed white Southerners' calls for compensation after Congress passed the Fourteenth Amendment: *Ripley Bee*, August 28, 1867, and September 9, 1868; *Milwaukee Daily Sentinel*, November 11, 1867, and September 15, 1868; *Bangor Daily Whig and Courier*, February 4, 1870; *Morning Republican*, November 10, 1870; *New National Era*, February 9. For commentary that ex-Confederates did not expect compensation, see: *New National Era*, September 7, 1871.

9. K. E. Williams, *They Left Great Marks on Me*, 29–39, 48–50; Rosen, *Terror in the Heart of Freedom*; *Report of the Joint Select Committee to Inquire into the Condition of Affairs in the Late Insurrectionary States*, 1; *Daily Times*, February 19, 1872; *Cincinnati Daily Gazette*, February 20, 1872; *Providence Press*, February 22, 1872; *Weekly Louisianan*, March 31, 1872; *Daily Evening Bulletin*, February 29, 1872; *New National Era*, October 5, 1871.

10. Slap, *The Doom of Reconstruction*, 30, 98, 111.

11. Blight, *Race and Reunion*, 50.

12. *Richmond Whig*, August 17, 1871.

13. *New National Era*, August 24, August 31, and November 2, 1871; *New York Tribune*, August 18, 1871; *Richmond Whig*, August 21, August 22, August 24, August 28, and August 29, 1871.

14. Slap, *Doom of Reconstruction*, 91–102, 164–201; Foner, *Reconstruction*, 505–9; Edward Bates, quoted in R. C. Williams, *Horace Greeley*, 254; *Bangor Daily Whig and Courier*, July 8,

1872; *Boston Daily Advertiser*, July 30, 1872; *Milwaukee Daily Sentinel*, May 2, May 10, August 14, August 27, and September 12, 1872; *Morning Republican*, August 1 and August 3, 1872; *Vermont Watchman*, August 7 and September 4, 1872; *New National Era*, September 12, 1872; *St. Alban's Messenger*, August 16, 1872; *Cleveland Daily Herald*, September 16, 1872.

15. Lundberg, *Horace Greeley*, 133–39, 215n72; R. C. Williams, *Horace Greeley*, 251–54; Vorenberg, "'Deformed Child,'" 246. Correspondents would repeat $400 million as the expected sum for compensation to former enslavers in the following decades. Not only is this the number reported from the Niagara Peace Conference, but it is also the sum that President Lincoln proposed to pay Confederate states after the 1865 Hampton Roads Conference. Likely, this number is $100 times 4 million, the number of enslaved people in the South on the eve of civil war.

16. *New York Tribune*, July 25, 1872; Sumner, "Greeley or Grant?" (speech intended to be delivered at Faneuil Hall, Boston, September 3, 1872), in *Charles Sumner: His Complete Works*, 20:209–54; *North American*, August 1, 1872; *St. Alban's Messenger*, August 16, 1872; *Georgia Weekly Telegraph and Georgia Journal and Messenger*, August 20, 1872.

17. Slap, *Doom of Reconstruction*, 203; *Milwaukee Daily Sentinel*, August 27, 1872; *Vermont Watchman*, September 4, 1872; *New National Era*, September 12, 1872.

18. Perman, *Road to Redemption*, 131; Foner, *Reconstruction*, 509–11; Slap, *Doom of Reconstruction*, chap. 9.

19. *New York Times*, November 9, 1873; Barreyre, "Politics of Economic Crises"; Barreyre, *Gold and Freedom*, 202–10.

20. *New York Times*, November 9, 1873.

21. *New National Era*, October 23, 1873; *Connecticut Courant*, November 15, 1873; *Milwaukee Daily Sentinel*, November 6, 1873; *Georgia Weekly Telegraph and Georgia Journal and Messenger*, November 18, 1873.

22. Maddex, *Virginia Conservatives, 1867–1879*, 288–89, quote from 288; Foner, *Reconstruction*, 535–53; Barreyre, *Gold and Freedom*, 204, 210.

23. Perman, *Road to Redemption*, 131; Foner, *Reconstruction*, 509–11; Slap, *Doom of Reconstruction*, 199; Silber, *Romance of Reunion*, 45.

24. Foner, *Reconstruction*, 512–24; Barreyre, "Politics of Economic Crises"; Perman, *Road to Redemption*, 149–92.

25. *Galveston Daily News*, June 12, 1875; Silber, *Romance of Reunion*, 56–63, 82, 95–96, 108; Janney, *Remembering the Civil War*, 9–10.

26. *St. Louis Globe-Democrat*, December 8, 1883; *Galveston Weekly News*, December 13 and December 20, 1883; Barreyre, "Politics of Economic Crises"; Perman, *Road to Redemption*, 213–20; Silber, *Romance of Reunion*, 93–108.

27. Paschal, *Compensation for Emancipated Slaves*, Dolph Briscoe Center for American History, University of Texas at Austin.

28. Ayers, *Promise of the New South*, 49.

29. Paschal, *Compensation for Emancipated Slaves*, Dolph Briscoe Center for American History, University of Texas at Austin; Handbook of Texas Online, Amelia W. Williams, "Paschal, George Washington," accessed April 7, 2020, www.tshaonline.org/handbook/online/articles/fpa46. Black suffrage had long split white Southern Unionists. See Foner, *Reconstruction*, 270. Many Southern Unionists agreed with Paschal that they had sacrificed property for the Union cause. In 1871, President Grant established the Southern Claims

Commission to hear their claims for reimbursement for property losses from the war. Though the Commissions would not pay for enslaved people freed during the war, some Northern newspapers picked up on Unionists' attitudes and warned that the Commission came one step too close to compensating former enslavers. See *North American*, April 7, 1873; *Daily Evening Bulletin*, August 15, 1874; *Daily Inter Ocean*, February 11, 1875.

30. The following articles report white Southerners claiming compensation for freed slaves. They follow similar themes discussed in this section. *Cleveland Daily Herald*, May 20, 1874; *Daily Inter Ocean*, November 2 and November 20, 1874, May 24 and June 12, 1876, March 30, 1888; *Alexandria Gazette*, March 3, 1875; *Weekly Louisianan*, June 12, 1875; *Commoner*, September 4, 1875; *Colored Radical*, October 12, 1876; *Georgia Weekly Telegraph and Georgia Journal and Messenger*, June 18, 1878; *Milwaukee Daily Sentinel*, October 26, 1874, and August 31, 1880; *New York Times*, August 8 and September 17, 1875; *Chicago Times*, reprinted in the *Courier-Journal*, October 4, 1876; *New York Herald*, October 25, 1876; *St. Louis Globe Democrat*, November 1, 1876; *Daily Evening Bulletin*, October 27, 1876; *Wisconsin State Register*, November 4, 1876; *Topeka Tribune*, October 7, 1880; *New York Times*, July 24, 1880; *Independent Statesman*, September 2 and October 13, 1880; *Bangor Daily Whig and Courier*, September 2 and October 13, 1880, and December 25, 1883; *News and Observer*, June 18, 1884; *Georgia Weekly Telegraph and Georgia Journal and Messenger*, June 18, 1878; *North American*, December 28, 1878; *Territorial Enterprise*, June 9, 1878; *Cincinnati Daily Gazette*, July 31, 1878; *Oregonian*, April 13, 1888.

31. *Slaughterhouse Cases*, 83 US 36 (1872); *Civil Rights Cases*, 109 US 3 (1883). For a full discussion of the Fourteenth Amendment in Reconstruction-era jurisprudence and the judicial and political abandonment of Reconstruction, see Brandwein, *Rethinking the Judicial Settlement of Reconstruction*.

32. Brandwein, *Rethinking the Judicial Settlement of Reconstruction*; Perrone, *Nothing More Than Freedom*.

33. *Cleveland Daily Herald*, May 4, 1884. It is unclear what Harris based these values on. As of January 1866, the War Department indicated that it owed $223,850 for unpaid claims based on the Enrollment Act in Maryland, which would have amounted to much less than Harris's claim in 1884. Likely, Harris is claiming the value of all enslaved people in Maryland and the border states. "Letter of the Secretary of War, communicating in compliance with a resolution of the Senate of the 8th instant, information in regard to the appointment of commissioners under the 24th section of the act of February 24, 1864 . . . ," January 11, 1866, 39th Cong., 1st sess., Senate Ex. Doc. No. 9; "Commissioners of Claims for Maryland and Delaware," January 9, 1866, House Ex. Doc. No. 22, 39th Cong., 1st. sess.; Annual Report of the Adjutant General's Office, Bureau for Colored Troops, October 20, 1867, F. W. Taggard, 1st Lieutenant US Army in charge of Bureau of Colored Troops, Colored Troops Division, Annual Reports of the Adjutant General Relating to the Colored Troops Division, 1864–65, 1867, RG 94, entry 388, NARA. Other papers brought up the issue of compensating loyal enslavers in the 1880s: *Galveston Daily News*, February 19, 1886; *Daily Evening Bulletin*, March 3, 1888; *News and Observer*, June 18, 1884. The House censured Harris for "treasonable utterances" in April 1864, and a military court in Washington, DC, tried him for harboring two paroled Confederate soldiers. After he was sentenced to three years' imprisonment and banned from holding any office in the US government, President Johnson remitted his sentence. "Harris, Benjamin Gwinn (1805–1895)," *Biographical Directory of*

the United States Congress, https://bioguideretro.congress.gov/Home/MemberDetails?memIndex=H000232.

34. *Cleveland Daily Herald*, May 4, 1884.

35. *Cleveland Daily Herald*, May 4, 1884.

36. *Cleveland Daily Herald*, May 4, 1884. Four years later, Williams wrote another book on the history of Black soldiers during the US Civil War, in which he emphasized that Congress, US military officials, and President Lincoln secured federal reimbursements for loyal slave owners on multiple occasions. For his conversation on Black enlistment and compensation, see G. W. Williams, *History of the Negro Troops in the War of the Rebellion*, 115–16, 137–38, 147–50; "George W. Williams," *Ohio History Central*, https://ohiohistorycentral.org/w/George_W._Williams; Franklin, *George Washington Williams*.

37. Foner, *Reconstruction*, 251–52; Blaine, *Twenty Years of Congress*, 191–92.

38. Perman, *Road to Redemption*, 263, 275–77; Kousser, *Shaping of Southern Politics*, chap. 1; Dailey, *Before Jim Crow*.

39. *Galveston Daily News*, June 12, 1875; *Independent Statesman*, June 24, 1875; *Georgia Weekly Telegraph and Georgia Journal and Messenger*, November 1, 1875; *Austin Weekly Statesman*, August 29, 1878; *Greensboro Patriot*, September 8, 1880; *Ottawa Daily Republic*, September 13, 1880; *Ellis County Star*, September 20, 1880; *Memphis Daily Appeal*, October 1, 1880; *News and Observer*, June 18, 1884; *Choctaw Herald*, June 2, 1885; *Boston Globe*, August 13, 1886; *Daily Inter Ocean*, March 30, 1888; *Oregonian*, April 13, 1888; *Mississippian*, November 18, 1891.

40. M. F. Berry, *My Face Is Black Is True*, 34–46, 107.

41. M. F. Berry, *My Face Is Black Is True*, 46; Vaughan, *Vaughan's "Freedmen's Pension Bill*," 184; Araujo, *Reparations for Slavery and the Slave Trade*, 95–99; Darity and Mullen, *From Here to Equality*, 11.

42. Janney, *Remembering the Civil War*, 187; Kelly, "Election of 1896 and the Restructuring of Civil War Memory"; Skocpol, *Protecting Soldiers and Mothers*, 128–39; Kousser, *Shaping of Southern Politics*, chap. 1; Dailey, *Before Jim Crow*; Ayers, *Promise of the New South*; *Emporia Daily Gazette*, April 19, 1892.

43. *Messenger and Intelligencer*, March 17, 1892; *Times and Democrat*, April 13, 1892; *Emporia Daily Gazette*, April 19, 1892; *Watchman and Southron*, October 23, 1895; Ayers, *Promise of the New South*, 280; Hahn, *Nation under Our Feet*, 431–32; Silber, *Romance of Reunion*, 99–101; Blight, *Race and Reunion*, 294; Janney, *Remembering the Civil War*, 187. On the other hand, one Democratic paper in North Carolina noted that the popularity of the Farmers Alliance forced Republicans to end bloody shirt campaigning and discredited their threats that Democrats would try to secure compensation. *Morning Star*, February 3, 1891.

44. *Fayetteville Observer*, February 11, 1892. "John Williamson," North Carolina Highway Historical Marker Program, North Carolina Department of Cultural Resources, accessed December 30, 2024, www.ncmarkers.com/Markers.aspx?MarkerId=E-114. Sources differ over when Williamson began the *Gazette*, but it likely began as the *North Carolina Gazette* in 1884 or 1885 and continued into the 1890s as the official paper of the North Carolina Industrial Association (NCIA), a Black civic organization to promote African American education and involvement in industry and agriculture. A lack of extant issues in 1892 obscures the history of Williamson's run. "About *The Gazette*," Chronicling America: Historic American Newspapers, LOC, https://chroniclingamerica.loc.gov/lccn/sn83027097; "About

North Carolina Gazette," Chronicling America: Historic American Newspapers, LOC, https://chroniclingamerica.loc.gov/lccn/sn92073076; "The Gazette [1891-1898] (Raleigh, N.C.), Digital NC, www.digitalnc.org/newspapers/north-carolina-gazette-raleigh-n-c/; www.digitalnc.org/newspapers/the-gazette-raleigh-n-c/).

45. *Journal of the House of Representatives of the General Assembly of the State of North Carolina,* 12–15. This was not the first time that Williamson sought Black economic progress while aligning with a white supremacist project—that of settler colonialism. According to historian Alaina E. Roberts, in the 1880s Williams advocated a Black settlement in the West to avoid white violence and create space for Black self-determination. He argued that Black people could better civilize the land than Native Americans. Roberts, *I've Been Here All the While,* 81–82.

46. *Cleveland Gazette,* February 13, 1892; *Fayetteville Observer,* February 11, 1892; *News and Observer,* September 18, 1892; *Freeman,* June 24 and September 16, 1893.

47. Janney, *Remembering the Civil War,* 187; Kelly, "Election of 1896 and the Restructuring of Civil War Memory"; Skocpol, *Protecting Soldiers and Mothers,* 128–39; Kousser, *Shaping of Southern Politics;* Dailey, *Before Jim Crow;* Ayers, *Promise of the New South; Emporia Daily Gazette,* April 19, 1892; *Morning Star,* February 3, 1891; *Messenger and Intelligencer,* March 17, 1892; *Times and Democrat,* April 13, 1892; *Watchman and Southron,* October 23, 1895.

48. *Linden Reporter,* October 12, 1894; *Courier-News,* June 4, 1896; *Atchison Globe,* June 5, 1896.

49. *Roanoke Times,* February 7, 1896; *Rutland Daily Herald,* February 7, 1896; *Linden Reporter,* October 12, 1894; *Baldwin Times,* June 11, 1896; *Greenville Advocate,* February 2, 1898; Guy C. Sibley to W. E. Bibb, February 7, February 22, and April 14, 1896, and William M. Fitch to Bibb, April 1, 1896, folder "1894–1896, Bibb, W. E.: Political Correspondence," and Elmer Dovers to Bibb, Louisa, Virginia, February 20, 1903, folder, "1898–1904, Bibb, W. E.: Political Correspondence," box 14, Papers of W. E. Bibb and Other Louisa County, Virginia, Families, accession 4171, Albert and Shirley Smalls Special Collections, University of Virginia; *Journal of the Senate of the Commonwealth of Virginia,* 370, 510, 557.

50. "Petition to Congress," cited in M. F. Berry, *My Face Is Black Is True,* 62–63.

51. Enslaved and freed people had extensive experience with the law in the antebellum era and after emancipation and sometimes claimed damages or redress from former enslavers and their families. See Penningroth, *Before the Movement,* chaps. 1–2; Jones, *Birthright Citizens;* L. F. Edwards, *People and Their Peace;* A. J. Gross, *Double Character;* Morris, *Southern Slavery and the Law;* Kennington, *In the Shadow of Dred Scott;* Twitty, *Before Dred Scott;* VanderVelde, *Redemption Songs;* Welch, *Black Litigants in the Antebellum American South;* Penningroth, *Claims of Kinfolk;* Regosin, *Freedom's Promise;* Milewski, *Litigating across the Color Line;* Brimmer, *Claiming Union Widowhood;* Perrone, "Rehearsals for Reparations," 132–50; Eatmon, "From the 'Legal Culture of Slavery' to Black Legal Culture."

52. Araujo, *Reparations for Slavery and the Slave Trade,* 90–95; Biondi, "Rise of the Reparations Movement," 5–18; Chisolm, "Sweep around Your Own Front Door"; Darity and Mullen, *From Here to Equality.*

53. Ager et al., "Intergenerational Effects of a Large Wealth Shock."

54. Ex-Slave Pension Correspondence and Case Files, 1892–1922, Ancestry.com, 2011 (original data: Correspondence and Case Files of the Bureau of Pensions Pertaining to the

Ex-Slave Pension Movement, 1892–1922, Microfilm M2110, 1 roll, RG 15: Records of the Department of Veteran Affairs, NARA; M. F. Berry, *My Face Is Black Is True*, 122.

55. M. F. Berry, *My Face Is Black Is True*, 147; Miranda Booker Perry, "No Pensions for Ex-Slaves: How Federal Agencies Suppressed Movement to Aid Freedpeople," *Prologue* 42, no. 2 (2010), www.archives.gov/publications/prologue/2010/summer/slave-pension.html.

56. *New York Tribune*, April 14, 1896; *Milwaukee Journal*, April 15, 1896; *National Tribune*, April 16, 1896; *Ness County News*, April 4, 1896; *Times-Democrat*, April 13, 1896; *Sioux City Journal*, May 6, 1896; United States Ex-Slave Owners Registration Bureau, 1896, and Affidavit for United States Ex-Slave Owners Registration Bureau, David M. Rubenstein Rare Book & Manuscript Library; Onion, "The Vault: A Letter Promising Compensation to Former Owners of Slaves, 1893," https://slate.com/human-interest/2013/04/ex-slave-owners-registration-bureau-broadside-sent-to-former-slave-owners-promised-compensation.html; "Purchasing Power Today of a US Dollar Transaction in the Past," MeasuringWorth, 2024, www.measuringworth.com/ppowerus/.

57. *Courier-News*, June 4, 1896; *Pine Bluff Daily Graphic*, March 23, 1897.

58. *Atchison Globe*, June 5, 1896; *Ness County News*, April 4, 1896.

59. *National Reflector*, August 14, 1897.

60. M. F. Berry, *My Face Is Black Is True*, 82–91, 131–32; *Freeman*, July 17 and September 4, 1897, and March 5, 1898; *Colored American*, March 11, 1899.

61. M. F. Berry, *My Face Is Black Is True*, 42, 60–61, 79; Araujo, *Reparations for Slavery and the Slave Trade*, 99–108.

62. Lincoln to the Senate and House of Representatives, February 5, 1865, *Collected Works of Abraham Lincoln*, 8:260–61; *New York Times*, November 1, 1885.

63. Stephens, *Constitutional View of the Late War between the States*, 592–618; Campbell, *Reminiscences and Documents Relating to the Civil War during the Year 1865*, 17; R. M. T. Hunter, "Peace Commission of 1865," 168–76.

64. Stephens, *Constitutional View of the Late War between the States*, 610–17; Davis, *Rise and Fall of the Confederate Government*, chap. 50; *Daily News and Herald*, May 18, 1867; *Daily Herald*, May 3, 1874; *Courier-Journal*, June 10, 1870, April 25 and May 7, 1874; *Atlanta Constitution*, May 10, 1874; Pendleton, *Alexander H. Stephens*, 331; Vorenberg, "'Deformed Child,'" 256–57; W. C. Harris, "Hampton Roads Peace Conference," 51; Margolies, *Henry Watterson and the New South*, 8, 11–16.

65. *Courier-Journal*, February 13, March 14, May 8, May 20, and July 21, 1895; *Galveston Daily News*, March 29 and May 27, 1895, and July 25, 1896; *Denver Evening Post*, May 8, 1895; *News and Observer*, May 10, 1895; *Daily Inter Ocean*, May 11, 1895.

66. *Charleston Tri-Weekly Courier*, May 17, 1899; *Minutes of the Ninth Annual Meeting and Reunion of the United Confederate Veterans*, 181–83.

67. Foster, *Ghosts of the Confederacy*, 157, 260–61n29; *American Citizen*, November 24, 1899; "Minutes of the Annual Meeting," November 7, 1899, United Daughters of the Confederacy, Grand Division of Virginia Records, Virginia Museum of History & Culture, Richmond, VA ; *Minutes of the Sixth Annual Meeting of the United Daughters of the Confederacy*.

68. Glymph, *Out of the House of Bondage*, 4–6; Jones-Rogers, *They Were Her Property*; Hale, *Making Whiteness*, 61–62, 86; Cox, *Dixie's Daughters*, chap. 6.

69. *Minutes of the Tenth Annual Meeting and Reunion of the United Confederate Veterans,* 45–46, 73–74.

70. *Proceedings of the Twelfth Annual Meeting of the Grand Camp Confederate Veterans,* 22; *Courier-Journal,* June 23, 1897; Foster, *Ghosts of the Confederacy,* 119; Janney, *Remembering the Civil War;* Silber, *Romance of Reunion.*

71. Blight, *Race and Reunion,* chap. 8; Silber, *Romance of Reunion,* 172–78; Janney, *Remembering the Civil War,* chap. 6; Foster, *Ghosts of the Confederacy,* 88–95, chap. 8.

72. *Minutes of the Tenth Annual Meeting and Reunion of the United Confederate Veterans,* 73–74.

73. *Courier-Journal,* May 2, June 20, June 23, September 4, and December 23, 1916; Lively, "Payment for Negroes Suggested," 120.

74. *Cleveland Gazette,* May 22, 1901, August 16, 1902; *Freeman,* August 20, 1904; *New York Age,* February 22, 1906.

75. Walter B. Hill to Lyman J. Bailey, May 25, 1905, "Correspondence concerning the Hampton Roads Conference," Lyman J. Bailey Papers, 1905, Dolph Briscoe Center for American History, University of Texas at Austin; Walter B. Hill, "Lincoln in the South," Walter B. Hill Papers, Hargrett Rare Book and Manuscript Library, University of Georgia, originally published in *Youth's Companion* 79, no. 6 (1905); Barnhart, "Apostles of the Lost Cause," 388, 391, 407–8; Nolan, "Anatomy of the Myth," 14–17; Carmichael, "New South Visionaries," 113, 119, 123; Foster, *Ghosts of the Confederacy,* 116–17, 119, 180–83; Araujo, *Reparations for Slavery and the Slave Trade,* 11–12, 29–33, 42–43; Starnes, "Forever Faithful."

76. Nolan, "Anatomy of a Myth," 16; Fleming, "Ex-Slave Pension Frauds," 3, 6. Notably, Fleming did acknowledge if not analyze in his history of Alabama the role of one Alabama "loyalist" who sought compensation during the state's 1865 presidential Reconstruction convention. However, throughout his narrative, Fleming portrayed loyalists as scalawags or carpetbaggers who betrayed the South for federal political support. Such calls for compensation did not fit neatly into his pro-Confederate narrative. Fleming, *Civil War and Reconstruction in Alabama,* 316–381, 362.

Conclusion

1. Francis Butler Simkins, known for being more balanced than his Dunning School contemporaries, wrote that "a determined minority" of delegates in South Carolina's presidential Reconstruction convention tried to add a clause to compensate former enslavers to the state's constitutional amendment abolishing slavery, but the governor had told them they needed to abolish slavery unequivocally to rejoin the Union. The delegates—and Simkins—dropped the issue there. Simkins and Woody, *South Carolina during Reconstruction,* 39. In his 1935 book, *Black Reconstruction,* W. E. B. Du Bois famously corrected Dunning School histories but still downplayed white Southerners' claims for compensation. Like many other historians of his time, Du Bois concluded that white Southerners were "glad" when emancipation happened because they did not have to "apologize to the world for a system they were powerless to change or reconstruct." He wrote that the "project of compensation for lost capital invested in slaves was permanently dropped" by President Lincoln in 1864. Du Bois, *Black Reconstruction in America,* 150, 165, 213, 326, 607, 671. After dismissing post-1864 compensation schemes Du Bois noted moments when white Southerners sought re-

imbursements for freed slaves after Confederate surrender; see pp. 142, 145, 158, 385, 496, 553, 564.

2. Bright, "Radicalism and Rebellion"; Perman, *Reunion without Compromise*, 86–87, 93–95; Breese, "Politics in the Lower South during Presidential Reconstruction," 139–40, 145; Wolfe, "South Carolina Constitutional Convention of 1865," 26; Foner, *Reconstruction*, 46, 193–95.

3. Hahn, *Political Worlds of Slavery and Freedom*, 51.

4. Araujo, *Reparations for Slavery and the Slave Trade*, 2, 84; Hahn, "Class and State in Postemancipation Societies," 75–98; Foner, *Nothing but Freedom*; Downs, *After Appomattox*, 8–10. For a thorough discussion of historians' treatment of the legality of secession after the Civil War, see Nicoletti, *Secession on Trial*, 2–5.

5. Kurtz, "Emancipation in the Federal City," 264; Commissioners of Claims for Maryland and Delaware, H.R. Exec. Doc. No. 39-22 (1866).

6. Vorenberg, *Final Freedom*, 6; Hamilton, *Limits of Sovereignty*, 9; Perrone, *Nothing More Than Freedom*; Simard, "Citing Slavery"; Graber, *Punish Treason, Reward Loyalty*; Siddali, *From Property to Person*, 8, 81–83; Novak, *The People's Welfare*, 243–44.

7. Janney, *Remembering the Civil War*, 275–76; Kendrick, *Journal of the Joint Committee of Fifteen on Reconstruction*, 350; Flack, *Adoption of the Fourteenth Amendment*, 133–36.

8. Ransom and Sutch, "Capitalists without Capital," 133–34; Axtell, "Towards a New Legal History of Capitalism and Unfree Labor"; Fogle and Engerman, *Time on the Cross*; David et al., *Reckoning with Slavery*; Fogle, *Slavery Debates*; M. M. Smith, *Debating Slavery*, chaps. 1 and 6.

9. Nikole Hannah-Jones, Mary Elliott, Jazmine Hughes, Jake Silverstein, "The 1619 Project," *New York Times Magazine*, August 18, 2019, www.nytimes.com/interactive/2019/08/14/magazine/1619-america-slavery.html. For conversations about quantification in Black digital slavery studies, see J. M. Johnson, "Markup Bodies"; Sharon Leon, "The Peril and Promise of Historians as Data Creators: Perspective, Structure, and the Problem of Representation," November 24, 2019, www.6floors.org/bracket/2019/11/24/the-peril-and-promise-of-historians-as-data-creators-perspective-structure-and-the-problem-of-representation; Gallon, "Making the Case for the Black Digital Humanities"; Brown, "Mapping a Slave Revolt," 134–41. New histories of capitalism include Baptist, *Half Has Never Been Told*; W. Johnson, *River of Dark Dreams*; Beckert and Rockman, *Slavery's Capitalism*.

10. Lincoln, "Second Inaugural Address [March 4, 1865]"; Message to Congress, March 6, 1862, *Collected Works of Abraham Lincoln*, 5:145–46. Historians have also investigated how the slavery debates shaped antebellum regional politics. See Melish, *Disowning Slavery*, chap. 6, 211, 212, 220, 222, 236.

11. Coulter, *Civil War and Readjustment in Kentucky*, 158–59; Marshall, *Creating a Confederate Kentucky*, 2–3, 24. This book focuses on former Confederate states, and the role of the compensation debates in border state politics during Reconstruction deserves more research. Other historians have explored how race relations, Democratic politics, and Civil War memory shaped Reconstruction politics to make the border states "Confederate." Astor, *Rebels on the Border*; Fluker, *Commonwealth of Compromise*; Fields, *Slavery and Freedom on the Middle Ground*, chap. 5. Fields does explore how political debates over compensated emancipation shaped the outcome of emancipation in Maryland during the Civil War. However, more research could be done on Reconstruction.

12. Cong. Globe Appendix, 39th Cong., 1st Sess. 269–72 (1866).

13. Warren, *Legacy of the Civil War*, 59–66.

14. In addition to "The 1619 Project," some economic historians have reframed the debate about slavery's profitability by arguing that previous studies determining that slavery was profitable did not measure the negative externalities that cost enslaved African Americans. Hornbeck and Logan, "One Giant Leap." Nations that abolished slavery in the nineteenth century, like the United States and Britain, celebrated their sacrifice as a moral victory well into the twentieth and twenty-first centuries. For example, in 2018, the British Treasury Department tweeted the "surprising" fact that millions of British citizens "helped end the slave trade through [their] taxes." It continued, "The amount of money borrowed for the Slavery Abolition Act was so large it wasn't paid off until 2015. Which means that living British citizens helped pay to end the slave trade." As British historian David Olusoga pointed out in the *Guardian*, the tweet was erroneous on many levels—the act ended slavery, not the slave trade—not to mention tone-deaf and ill-received. The Treasury Department deleted the tweet after many British citizens pointed out on Twitter that, in many cases, they had been paying taxes to compensate the people who enslaved their ancestors. Almost 200 years later, the British government continued to view the £20 million debt it levied to reimburse former enslavers as an absolution. David Olusoga, "The Treasury's Tweet Shows Slavery Is Still Misunderstood," *Guardian*, February 12, 2018, www.theguardian.com/commentisfree/2018/feb/12/treasury-tweet-slavery-compensate-slave-owners.

15. Tera Hunter, "When Slaveowners Got Reparations," *New York Times*, April 16, 2019, www.nytimes.com/2019/04/16/opinion/when-slaveowners-got-reparations.html.

16. Americans never stopped comparing. In 2021, Larry Elder, a conservative candidate in California's recall election for governor, suggested that Californians should stop talking about reparations for Black Americans because "slavery was legal" and therefore both Black Americans and former enslavers should be compensated. Elder also alluded to the British compensation scheme. Morgan Keith, "California Recall Candidate Larry Elder Says It Could Be Argued That Slave Owners Were Owed Reparations after the Civil War," *Business Insider*, September 4, 2021, www.businessinsider.com/larry-elder-argued-that-slave-owners-were-owed-reparations-2021-9.

17. In this study, I encountered these conversations in primary sources not cited in the preceding chapters, including Brotherhood of Liberty, *Justice and Jurisprudence*; Douglass, "Blessings of Liberty and Education," 623–24. Modern reparations scholars have also likened reparations to an "overdue debt" owed to African Americans. See, for example, Westley, "Many Billions Gone?," 436. Led by W. E. B. Du Bois, who characterized the Civil War as the "general strike of the slaves," historians have explored how enslaved and freed people leveraged their understanding of the slave economy by withholding their labor. Du Bois also explored how Black communities mobilized debt and property collectively after emancipation in *Economic Co-operation among Negro Americans* in 1907. More recently, Justene Hill Edwards has explored how African Americans shaped their own economic enterprises and interacted with markets in slavery and freedom. Other historians, often legal historians, have explored how African Americans offered competing definitions of citizenship before and after the Civil War to secure entitlements like veterans' pensions as well as property and other civil rights. While these histories show how race played a role in securing or denying these individual claims, they do not often extend to collective reparations claims.

Thank you to Kirsten Lee and Justin Leroy for thinking through these topics with me. Du Bois, *Economic Co-operation among Negro Americans*; Du Bois, *Black Reconstruction in America*; Roediger, *Seizing Freedom*; Hahn, *Nation under Our Feet*; Penningroth, *Before the Movement*; Brimmer, *Claiming Union Widowhood*; Kretz, *Administering Freedom*; Penningroth, *Claims of Kinfolk*; Edwards, *People and Their Peace*; McDaniel, *Sweet Taste of Liberty*; J. H. Edwards, *Unfree Markets*; J. H. Edwards, *Savings and Trust*, see 269n20 for additional works on how African Americans invested in their own communities after Reconstruction.

18. Studies of African American Civil War memories are comparatively fewer than those of white Americans, particularly white Southerners. Historians of African American Civil War memory have explored Black Americans' understandings of the Civil War's and slavery's legacies, but we know little about how they discussed the memory of slavery as a financial and legal institution in that context. Some have focused on Frederick Douglass, whose speeches offer revealing connections among the history of the war, slavery, and contemporary politics. At the time of this manuscript's submission, works in progress by Justin Leroy, Hilary Green, Abena Boakyewa-Ansah, Katie Wu, and Ashleigh Lawrence-Sanders promise to shed light on nineteenth-century African Americans' conceptualizations of capitalism and Civil War memories into the twenty-first century. Blight, *Frederick Douglass*; Green, "Persistence of Memory," 131–49; Glymph, "'Liberty Dearly Bought,'" 111–39; J. H. Edwards, *Savings and Trust*, 247–256. Ashleigh Lawrence-Sanders, "Beyond Monuments: African Americans Contesting Civil War Memory," *Black Perspectives* (blog), October 16, 2017, www.aaihs.org/beyond-monuments-african-americans-contesting-civil-war-memory; K. A. Clark, *Defining Moments*; Domby and Cox, "Monuments and Memory," 342–68.

Bibliography

Primary Sources

ARCHIVES AND MANUSCRIPT COLLECTIONS

Georgia
  Georgia Archives, Morrow, GA
    Benjamin Conley Papers, 1839–1875, 1880, and n.d.
    Constitutional Convention—Ordinances & Resolutions, Constitutional Convention of 1865
    Constitutional Convention—Ordinances, Resolutions and Committee Reports, 1867–1868
    Governors' Subject Files, Charles Jenkins
    Henry Dickerson McDaniel Family and Business Papers, 1822–1947
    Legislature Bills and Resolutions, 1865–1866
    Legislature Bills and Resolutions, 1866
  Hargrett Rare Book and Manuscript Library, University of Georgia, Athens, GA
    Benjamin Conley Papers
    Foster Blodgett Papers
    Herschel Vespasian Johnson Papers
    Joseph E. Brown Papers
    Robert Augustus Toombs to John C. Breckinridge
    Walter B. Hill Papers
Louisiana
  The Historic New Orleans Collection, New Orleans, LA
    Williams Research Center
  Louisiana Research Collection, Tulane University Special Collections, New Orleans, LA Louisiana Report of the Committee on Emancipation, 1864, M-451
  Louisiana State University Special Collections, Hill Memorial Library, Baton Rouge, LA
    Benjamin F. Flanders Papers, 1827–1889
    Constitutional Convention Broadside, 1868
    Henry C. Warmouth Papers, 1869–1872
    H. J. Heard Letter, June 11, 1864
    James G. Taliaferro and Family Papers, 1867–1875
    James G. Taliaferro Letters, 1852–1876
    James G. Taliaferro Papers, 1845–1877
    John Pratt, *Address to voters of the Fourth Congressional District, composed of the parishes of Natchitoches, Sabine, Rapides, Calcasieu, St. Landry, Vermilion, Lafayette, Avoyelles, Pointe Coupee, St. Martin, West Baton Rouge, Iberville, Assumption and St. Mary, 1865,* broadside
    Louisiana Constitutional Convention Document

226 Bibliography

  Michael Hahn Pamphlets
  Nathaniel P. Banks Letterpress Copybook
Mississippi
 Mississippi Department of Archives and History, Jackson, MS
  General Records of the State of Mississippi
  Mississippi Governors' Papers
  Papers of the Constitutional Conventions
North Carolina
 North Carolina Collection, Wilson Library, University of North Carolina, Chapel Hill, NC
 Small Manuscript Collections, Rubenstein Library, Duke University, Durham, NC
 State Archives of North Carolina, Raleigh, NC
  Governors' Papers, Holden Correspondence
  Governors' Papers, Worth Correspondence
  North Carolina Department of State Files, Constitutional Conventions,
   1868—Petitions, Committees
  North Carolina General Assembly Session Records
South Carolina
 South Carolina Department of Archives and History, Columbia, SC
  Benjamin Franklin Perry Papers
  Executive Messages, 1865–1871
  Governor Orr, Letters Sent and Received
  Governors Orr and Scott, Executive Messages, 1865–1871
  South Carolina Legislative Papers, Judiciary Committee, Committee Reports
  South Carolina Legislative Papers, Petitions
  South Carolina Legislative Papers, Resolutions of the General Assembly
 South Carolina Historical Society, Charleston, SC
  Whaley, Mitchell & Clancy Records, 1853–1871
 South Caroliniana Library, Columbia, SC
  Francis Lieber Papers
  Benjamin Franklin Perry Papers
Texas
 The Dolph Briscoe Center for American History, The University of Texas at Austin,
  Austin, TX
  Andrew Jackson Hamilton Papers, 1847–1913
  James Webb Throckmorton Papers, 1838–1888
  Lyman J. Bailey Papers, 1905
  Philpott Texana Collection, 1844–1879
 Texas State Library and Archives Commission, Austin, TX
  Andrew Jackson Hamilton Governors' Papers
  Constitutional Conventions Records, 1845, 1860–1861, 1866–1871, 1875, and n.d.
  Executive Records Collection
  John H. Reagan Letters, 1864–1896
Virginia
 Albert and Shirley Smalls Special Collections, University of Virginia, Charlottesville, VA
  Papers of W. E. Bibb and Other Louisa County, Virginia, Families, accession 4171

The Library of Virginia, Richmond, VA
    Executive Papers of Governor Pierpont
    Records and Briefs of the Virginia Supreme Court
    State Government Records Collection
Virginia Museum of History & Culture, Richmond, VA
    United Daughters of the Confederacy, Grand Division of Virginia Records
Washington, DC
    Library of Congress, Washington, DC
        Abraham Lincoln Papers
        Andrew Johnson Papers
        James Madison Papers
        Salmon P. Chase Papers
        Thaddeus Stevens Papers
    National Archives and Records Administration, Washington, DC
        Charles F. Meadows, Jr., Collection, 1864–1865
        RG 15: Records of the Department of Veteran Affairs
        RG 46: Records of the US Senate
        RG 94: Records of the Adjutant General's Office
        RG 128: Records of the Joint Committees of Congress, 1789–1968
        RG 233.16: Records of the Judiciary Committee and Related Committees
        RG 233.2: General Records of the United States House of Representatives
        RG 233.8: Records of the Committee Relating to Claims, 1794–1946
        RG 393.14: Records of Military (Reconstruction) Districts, Department of the Carolinas

ONLINE ARCHIVAL DATABASES

Ancestry.com
    1850 and 1860 US census, slave schedule
    Ex-Slave Pension Correspondence and Case Files, 1892–1922
    U.S., Colored Troops Military Service Records, 1863–1865
Collected Works of Abraham Lincoln, 8 vols., University of Michigan Library Digital
        Collections
David M. Rubenstein Rare Book & Manuscript Library, Digital Collections, Broadsides
    and Ephemera Collection
    United States Ex-Slave Owners Registration Bureau, 1896
    Affidavit for United States Ex-Slave Owners Registration Bureau
Newspapers.com
Nineteenth Century US Newspapers, Gale North America
ProQuest Congressional, Clarivate
Readex, A Division of NewsBank
    African American Newspapers
    America's Historical Newspapers

NEWSPAPERS AND PERIODICALS

Albany Evening Journal (NY)
Alexandria Gazette (VA)
American Citizen (Kansas City, KS)
Atchison Globe (KS)

Atlanta Constitution (GA)
Augusta Chronicle (GA)
Austin Weekly Statesman (TX)
Baldwin Times (Bay Minette, AL)
Bangor Daily Whig and Courier (ME)
Boston Daily Advertiser (MA)
Boston Globe (MA)
Charleston Tri-Weekly Courier (SC)
Choctaw Herald (Butler, AL)
Christian Recorder (Philadelphia, PA)
Cincinnati Daily Gazette (OH)
Cleveland Daily Herald (OH)
Cleveland Gazette (OH)
Colored American (Washington, DC)
Colored Radical (Leavenworth, KS)
Commoner (Washington, DC)
Connecticut Courant (Hartford, CT)
Courier-Journal (Louisville, KY)
Courier-News (Bridgewater, NJ)
Crisis (Columbus, OH)
Daily Citizen (Lowell, MA)
Daily Constitutionalist (Augusta, GA)
Daily Evening Bulletin (San Francisco, CA)
Daily Globe (Washington, DC)
Daily Herald (Atlanta, GA)
Daily Inter Ocean (Chicago, IL)
Daily News and Herald (Savannah, GA)
Daily Picayune (New Orleans, LA)
Daily Times (Cincinnati, OH)
Denver Evening Post (CO)
Douglass' Monthly (Rochester, NY)
Ellis County Star (Hays City, KS)
Emporia Daily Gazette (KS)
Era (New Orleans, LA)
Fayetteville Observer (NC)
Freeman (Indianapolis, IN)
Galveston Daily News (TX)
Galveston Weekly News (TX)
Georgia Weekly Telegraph and Georgia Journal and Messenger (Macon, GA)
Greensboro Patriot (NC)
Greenville Advocate (AL)
Independent Statesman (Concord, NH)
Liberator (Boston, MA)
Linden Reporter (AL)
Loyal Georgian (Augusta, GA)
Memphis Daily Appeal (TN)
Messenger and Intelligencer (Wadesboro, NC)
Milwaukee Daily Sentinel (WI)
Milwaukee Journal (WI)
Mississippian (Jackson, MS)
Morning Republican (Little Rock, AK)
Morning Star (Wilmington, NC)
Nashville Journal (TN)
National Anti-Slavery Standard (New York)
National Reflector (Wichita, KS)
National Tribune (Washington, DC)
Ness County News (Ness City, KS)
New National Era (Washington, DC)
News and Observer (Raleigh, NC)
New York Age (NY)
New York Herald (NY)
New York Times (NY)
New York Times Magazine (NY)
New York Tribune (NY)
North American (Philadelphia, PA)
Oregonian (OR)
Ottawa Daily Republic (KS)
Pine Bluff Daily Graphic (AK)
Providence Press (RI)
Richmond Enquirer (VA)
Richmond Whig (VA)
Ripley Bee (OH)
Roanoke Times (VA)
Rutland Daily Herald (VT)
Sioux City Journal (IA)
St. Alban's Messenger (VT)
St. Louis Globe-Democrat (MO)
Territorial Enterprise (Virginia City, NV)
Times and Democrat (Orangeburg, SC)
Times-Democrat (McCune, KS)
Times-Picayune (New Orleans, LA)
Topeka Tribune (KS)
Tribune (New Orleans, LA)
Tri-Weekly Standard (Raleigh, NC)
Vermont Watchman (Montpelier, VT)
Washington Reporter (PA)
Watchman and Southron (Sumter, SC)
Weekly Georgia Telegraph (Macon, GA)
Weekly Louisianan (New Orleans, LA)
Wisconsin State Register (Portage, WI)

GOVERNMENT DOCUMENTS

Constitution Adopted by the Constitution Convention of the State of Louisiana, March 7, 1868. New Orleans: Republican Office, 1868.

Executive Documents Printed by Order of the House of Representatives during the Second Session of the Fortieth Congress, 1867–'68. 20 vols. Washington, DC: Government Printing Office, 1868.

General Orders from the Adjutant and Inspector General's Office, Confederate States Army, from January 1, 1864, to July 1, 1864. Columbia, SC: Presses of Evans & Cogswell, 1864.

Grider, Henry. *Speech of Hon. Henry Grider, of Kentucky, on Reconstruction; Delivered in the House of Representatives, March 24, 1866.* Washington, DC: Congressional Globe Office, 1866.

Journal of the House of Representatives of the General Assembly of the State of North Carolina, at Its Session of 1868. Raleigh, NC: N. Paige, 1868.

Journal of the House of Representatives of the State of Ohio, for the Regular Session of the Fifty-Eighth General Assembly, Commencing on Monday, January 6, 1868, Being the Ninth Legislature under the New Constitution. Vol. 64. Columbus, OH: L. D. Myers & Bro., 1868.

Journal of the House of Representatives of the United States: Being the First Session of the Thirty-Eighth Congress; Begun and Held at the City of Washington. Washington: Government Printing Office, 1863.

Journal of the House of Representatives of the United States: Being the First Session of the Thirty-Ninth Congress; Begun and Held at the City of Washington. Washington: Government Printing Office, 1866.

Journal of the Missouri State Convention, Held at the City of St. Louis January 6–April 10, 1865. St. Louis: Missouri Democrat, Print, Corner Fourth and Pine Sts., 1865.

Journal of the Senate of South Carolina, 1866. Columbia, SC: F. G. DeFontaine, 1866.

Journal of the Senate of the Commonwealth of Kentucky. Begun and Held in the City of Frankfort, on Monday, the Second Day of December, in the Year of our Lord 1867, and of the Commonwealth the Seventy-Sixth. Frankfort: Kentucky Yeoman Office, John H. Harney, 1867.

Journal of the Senate of the Commonwealth of Virginia. Richmond, VA: J. H. O'Bannon, Superintendent Public Printing, 1895.

Journal of the Senate of the United States of America, Being the First Session of the Thirty-Ninth Congress; Begun and Held at the City of Washington, December 4, 1865. Washington: Government Printing Office, 1865.

Laws of the State of Maryland, Made and Passed at a Session of the General Assembly Began and Held at the City of Annapolis on the Sixth Day of January, 1864, Amended on the Tenth Day of March, 1864. Annapolis, MD: Richard P. Bayly, 1864.

Laws of the State of Mississippi, Passed at a Regular Session of the Mississippi Legislature, Held in Jackson, October, November and December, 1865. Jackson, MS: 1866.

Legislative Document No. 23: Report of the State Agent for Kentucky, in Regard to Credits on Drafts and Certificates for Slaves Muster into the US Service by James P. Flint, Kentucky Documents. Frankfort, KY: State Printing Office, 1866.

Lieber, Francis. *Instructions for the Government of Armies of the United States in the Field, prepared by Francis Lieber, LL.D., Originally Issued as General Orders No. 100, Adjutant General's Office, 1863.* Washington, DC: Government Printing Office, 1898.

Lord, William Blair, and Henry M. Parkhurst. *The Debates of the Constitutional Convention of the State of Maryland.* Vol. 1. Annapolis, MD: Richard P. Bayly, 1864.

Mississippi. *Laws of the State of Mississippi, Passed at a Regular Session of the Mississippi Legislature, Held in Jackson, October, November and December, 1965.* Jackson, MS: Cooper & Kimball, 1866.

Proceedings and Acts of the General Assembly of Maryland, January 2—March 23, 1867. Vol. 133, images 852, 4115–4119, 4559–4562. Archives of Maryland Online. http://aomol.msa .maryland.gov/megafile/msa/speccol/sc2900/sc2908/000001/000133/html/index.html.

Report of the Joint Select Committee to Inquire into the Condition of Affairs in the Late Insurrectionary States. Washington, DC: Government Printing Office, 1872.

Schurz, Carl. *Report on the Condition of the South.* S. Exec. Doc. No. 39-2 (1865).

Sickles, Daniel E. *Major-General D. E. Sickles' Report to the General-in-Chief of the Army, Relating to the Issue Made by the Civil Authorities with the Commanding General of the Second Military District.* Washington, DC, 1867.

Slade, William. *Speech of Mr. Slade, of Vermont, on the Abolition of Slavery and the Slave Trade in the District of Columbia: Delivered in the House of Representatives of the US, December 20, 1837.* Washington, DC, 1837.

Smith Minor. H.R. Report No. 37-58 (1863).

Sumner, Charles. *Ransom of Slaves at the National Capital: Speech of Hon. Charles Sumner, of Massachusetts, on the Bill for the Abolition of Slavery in the District of Colombia, in the Senate of the United States, March 31, 1862.* Washington, DC: Congressional Globe Office, 1862.

The War of the Rebellion: A Compilation of the Official Records of the Union and Confederate Armies. 128 vols. Washington, DC: Government Printing Office, 1880–1901.

RECONSTRUCTION STATE CONSTITUTIONAL CONVENTION JOURNALS
(IN ALPHABETICAL ORDER BY STATE)

Alabama

Journal of the Proceedings of Convention of the State of Alabama, Held in the City of Montgomery, on Tuesday, September 12, 1865. Montgomery, AL: Gibson & Whitfield, 1865.

Official Journal of the Constitutional Convention of the State of Alabama Held in the City of Montgomery, commencing on Tuesday, November 5th, A.D. 1867. Montgomery, AL: Barrett & Brown, 1868.

Arkansas

Debates and Proceedings of the Convention Which Assembled at Little Rock, January 7th, 1868. Little Rock, AK: J.G. Price, 1868.

Journal of the Convention of Delegates of the People of Arkansas. Assembled at the Capitol, January 4, 1864; also Journals of the House of Representatives of the sessions of 1864, 64–65, and 1865. Little Rock, AK: Price & Barton, 1870.

Florida

Journal of Proceedings of the Convention of 1865. Tallahassee, FL: Office of the Floridian, Printed by Dyke & Sparhawk, 1865.

Journal of Proceedings of the Convention of Florida, Begun and Held at the Capital of the State, at Tallahassee, Wednesday, January 20, 1868. Tallahassee, FL: E. M. Cheney, 1868.

Georgia

Journal of the Proceedings of the Convention of the People of Georgia: Held in Milledgeville in October and November, 1865: Together with the Ordinances and Resolutions Adopted. Milledgeville, GA: R.M. Orme & Son, 1865.

Journal of the Proceedings of the Constitutional Convention of the people of Georgia, held in the City of Atlanta in the months of December, 1867, and January, February and March, 1868. And ordinances and resolutions adopted. Augusta, GA: E.H. Pughe, Book and Job Printer, 1868.

Louisiana

Bennett, Albert P., H. A. Gallup, S. W. Burnham, and A. L. Bartlett. *Debates in the Convention for the Revision and Amendment of the Constitution of the State of Louisiana. Assembled at Liberty Hall, New Orleans, April 6, 1864.* New Orleans, LA: W. R. Fish, 1864.

Official Journal of the Proceedings of the Convention for the Revision and Amendment of the Constitution of the State of Louisiana. New Orleans, LA: W.R. Fish, 1864.

Official Journal of the Proceedings of the Convention, for Framing a Constitution for the State of Louisiana. New Orleans, LA: J. B. Roudanez, 1867–1868.

Mississippi

Journal of the Proceedings and Debates in the Constitutional Convention of the State of Mississippi, August, 1865. Jackson, MS: E. M. Yerger, 1865.

Journal of the Proceedings in the Constitutional Convention of the State of Mississippi: 1868. Jackson, MS: E. Stafford, 1871.

North Carolina

Journal of the Convention of the State of North-Carolina, at Its Session of 1865. Raleigh, NC: Cannon & Holden, 1865.

Journal of the Constitutional Convention of the State of North-Carolina, at Its Session 1868. Raleigh, NC: J. W. Holden, 1868.

South Carolina

Journal of the Convention of the people of South Carolina: held in Columbia, S. C., September, 1865: together with the ordinances, reports, resolutions, etc. Columbia, SC: J.A. Selby, Printer to the Convention, 1865.

Proceedings of the Constitutional Convention of South Carolina. Charleston, SC: Denny & Perry, 1868.

Texas

Journal of the Texas State Convention, assembled at Austin, Feb. 7, 1866. Adjourned April 2, 1866. Austin, TX: Southern Intelligencer Office, 1866.

Journal of the Reconstruction Convention: Which Met at Austin, Texas. 2 vols. Austin, TX: Tracey, Siemering, 1870.

Virginia

Journal of the Constitutional Convention, which convened at Alexandria on the 13th day of February 1864. Alexandria, VA: D. Turner, 1864.

Journal of the Constitutional Convention of the State of Virginia, convened in the city of Richmond, December 3, 1867 [. . .]. Richmond, VA: Printed at the office of the *New Nation*, 1867.

The Debates and Proceedings of the Constitutional Convention of the State of Virginia, Assembled at the City of Richmond, Tuesday, December 3, 1867 [...]. Richmond, VA: Printed at the office of the *New Nation*, 1868.

PUBLISHED PRIMARY SOURCES

Avery, Isaac Wheeler. *The History of the State of Georgia from 1850 to 1881*. Brown & Derby, 1881.

Beadle, Delos W. *The American Lawyer and Business-Man's Form-Book: Containing Forms and Instructions for Contracts, Arbitration and Award, [...] and a Map and Seal for Each State in the Union*. New York: Ensign, Bridgman & Fanning, 1854.

Blaine, James G. *Twenty Years of Congress: From Lincoln to Garfield. With a Review of the Events Which Led to the Political Revolution of 1860*. Vol. 2. Norwich, CT: Henry Bill, 1886.

Boutwell, George S. *Speeches and Papers Relating to the Rebellion and the Overthrow of Slavery*. Boston: Little, Brown, 1867.

Brotherhood of Liberty. *Justice and Jurisprudence: An Inquiry concerning the Constitutional Limitations of the Thirteenth, Fourteenth, and Fifteenth Amendments*. Philadelphia: J. B. Lippincott, 1889.

Burritt, Elihu. *A Plan of Brotherly Copartnership of the North and South for the Peaceful Extinction of Slavery*. New York: Dayton and Burdick, 1856.

Campbell, John A. *Reminiscences and Documents Relating to the Civil War during the Year 1865*. Baltimore: John Murphy, 1877.

Child, David Lee. *Rights and Duties of the United States Relative to Slavery under the Laws of War: No Military Power to Return Any Slave. "Contraband of War" Inapplicable between the United States and Their Insurgent Enemies*. Boston: R. F. Wallcut, 1861.

Child, Lydia Maria. *The Right Way, the Safe Way: Proved by Emancipation in the British West Indies, and Elsewhere*. New York, 1860.

Clay, Henry. *Speech of the Hon. Henry Clay, in the Senate of the United States, on the Subject of Abolition Petitions, February 7, 1839*. Boston: James Munroe, 1839.

Coulter, E. Merton. *Civil War and Readjustment in Kentucky*. Gloucester, MA: Peter Smith, 1966.

Curti, Merle. *The Learned Blacksmith: The Letters and Journals of Elihu Burritt*. New York: Wilson-Erikson, 1937.

Cutler, R. King. *Address of Hon. R. King Cutler, United States Senator of Louisiana*. New Orleans, 1865.

Davis, Jefferson. *The Rise and Fall of the Confederate Government*. Vol. 2. New York: D. Appleton, 1881.

De Roulhac Hamilton, Joseph Grégoire. *Reconstruction in North Carolina*. New York: Columbia University Press, 1914.

Dew, Thomas R. "Abolition of Negro Slavery." *American Quarterly Review* 12 (September 1832), 189–265. Reprinted in *The Ideology of Slavery: Proslavery Thought in the Antebellum South, 1830–1860*, edited by Drew Gilpin Faust. Baton Rouge: Louisiana State University Press, 1981.

———. *Review of the Debate in the Virginia Legislature of 1831–1832*. Richmond, VA: T. W. White, 1832.

Douglass, Frederick. "The Blessings of Liberty and Education: An Address Delivered in Manassas, Virginia, on 3 September 1894." In *The Frederick Douglass Papers*, ser. 1, *Speeches, Debates, and Interviews*, vol. 5: *1881–95*, edited by John W. Blassingame and John R. McKivigan. New Haven, CT: Yale University Press, 1992.

Fleming, Walter L. *Civil War and Reconstruction in Alabama*. New York: Columbia University Press, 1905.

———. "Ex-Slave Pension Frauds." *University Bulletin: Louisiana State University* 1, no. 9 (1910): 3–15.

Garland, A. H. *Henry T. Osborn, Plaintiff in Error, vs. Young A. G. Nicholson et al., Defendants*. Washington City: M'Gill & Witherow, 1871.

Garner, James Wilford. *Reconstruction in Mississippi*. New York: Macmillan, 1901.

Hasted, Frederick. "A Copy of a Letter, Written to the President of the United States, on Slave Emancipation." 1859.

Hunter, Robert M. T. "The Peace Commission of 1865." In *Southern Historical Society Papers*. Vol. 3, *January to June, 1877*. Richmond, VA: Rev. J. William Jones.

Jefferson, Thomas. *Notes on the State of Virginia*. New York: Penguin Books, 1999.

Johnson, Andrew. *The Papers of Andrew Johnson*. Edited by LeRoy P. Graf, Ralph W. Haskins, and Paul H. Bergeron. 16 vols. Knoxville: University of Tennessee Press, 1967–2000.

Kendrick, Benjamin B. *Journal of the Joint Committee of Fifteen on Reconstruction, 39th Congress, 1865–1867*. New York, 1914.

Lively, E. H. "Payment for Negroes Suggested." *Confederate Veteran* 18 (March 1910): 120.

Marshall, Thomas. *The Speech of Thomas Marshall (of Fauquier) in the House of Delegates of Virginia, on the Policy of the States in Relation to the Colored Population: Delivered Saturday, January 14, 1832*. 2nd ed. Richmond: Thomas W. White, 1832.

Minutes of the Ninth Annual Meeting and Reunion of the United Confederate Veterans, Held in the City of Charleston, SC. New Orleans: Hopkins' Printing Office, 1900.

Minutes of the Sixth Annual Meeting of the United Daughters of the Confederacy, Held in Richmond, VA, November 8–11, 1899. Nashville, TN: Press of Foster & Webb, 1900.

Minutes of the Tenth Annual Meeting and Reunion of the United Confederate Veterans, Held in the City of Louisville, KY. New Orleans: Hopkins' Printing Office, 1902.

National Union Convention Executive Committee. *The Proceedings of the National Union Convention, Held at Philadelphia, August 14, 1866*. Washington: National Union Executive Committee, 1866.

Niven, John, ed., *The Salmon P. Chase Papers*. Vol. 1, *Journals, 1829–1872*. Kent, OH: Kent State University Press, 1994.

Northup, Solomon. *Twelve Years a Slave: Narrative of Solomon Northup, a Citizen of New York, Kidnapped in Washington City in 1841 and Rescued in 1853, from a Cotton Plantation Near the Red River in Louisiana*. Auburn, AL: Derby and Miller, 1853.

O'Rielly, Henry. *Origins and Objects of the Slaveholders' Conspiracy against Democratic Principles, as well as against the National Union—Illustrated in the Speeches of Andrew Jackson Hamilton, in the Statements of Lorenzo Sherwood, Ex-Member of the Texan Legislature, and in the Publicans of the Democratic League, &c*. New York: Barker & Godwin, 1862.

Owen, Robert Dale. *The Wrong of Slavery, the Right of Emancipation, and the Future of the African Race in the United States*. Philadelphia: J. B. Lippincott, 1864.

Paschal, George W. *Compensation for Emancipated Slaves. Letter of George W. Paschal to Hon. James Harlan on the Issues of the Presidential Contest.* Washington City: M'Gill & Witherow, 1872.

Pendleton, Louis. *Alexander H. Stephens.* Philadelphia: George W. Jacobs, 1907.

Penn, I. Garland. *The Afro-American Press, and Its Editors.* Springfield, MA: Willey, 1891.

Pomeroy, Charles S. *The People's Law Book: An Indispensable Assistant to Business Men: Designed Particularly for the States of Pennsylvania, Ohio, Kentucky, Tennessee, Indiana, Illinois, Missouri, Michigan, Iowa, and Louisiana.* 4th ed. Cincinnati, OH: E. Shepard, 1849.

Proceedings of the Bar and of the Supreme Court, State of MS, on the Occasion of the Death of the Late Hon. George L. Potter. Jackson, MS: Charles Winkley, 1877.

Proceedings of the Twelfth Annual Meeting of the Grand Camp Confederate Veterans, Department of Virginia, Held at Pulaski, Virginia, October 11, 12, 13, 1899. Richmond, VA: J. L. Hill, 1899.

Reagan, John H. *Memoirs, with Special Reference to Secession and the Civil War.* New York: Neale, 1906.

Simkins, Francis Butler, and Robert Hilliard Woody. *South Carolina during Reconstruction.* Chapel Hill: The University of North Carolina Press, 1932.

Stephens, Alexander H. *A Constitutional View of the Late War between the States.* Vol. 2. Philadelphia: National, 1868–70.

Sumner, Charles. *Charles Sumner: His Complete Works.* Edited by George Frisbie Hoar. Vol. 20. Norwood, MA: Norwood Press, 1900.

Taliaferro, James G. *A Protest against the Ordinance of Secession, Passed by the Louisiana Convention, on the 26th January, Presented to the Convention on That Day by James G. Taliaferro, the Delegate from the Parish of Catahoula, Who Asked That It Might Be Entered upon the Journal of the Convention, Which Was Refused.* Catahoula, 1861. www.loc.gov/item/2020770216/.

Thompson, Clara Mildred. *Reconstruction in Georgia: Economic, Social, Political, 1865–1872.* Gloucester, MA: Peter Smith, 1915.

Tucker, St. George. *A Dissertation on Slavery, with a Proposal for the Gradual Abolition of it, in the State of Virginia.* Philadelphia: Mathew Carey, 1796.

Vaughan, William R. *Vaughan's "Freedmen's Pension Bill": Being an Appeal in Behalf of Men Released from Slavery, a Plea for American Freedmen and a Rational Proposition to Grant Pensions to Persons of Color Emancipated from Slavery.* Chicago, 1891.

Warren, Robert Penn. *The Legacy of the Civil War: Meditations on the Centennial.* New York: Random House, 1961.

Whaley, William. *Argument of William Whaley, Esq.: Delivered Before the Supreme Court at Columbia, S.C., on the Negro Bond Question; Against Their Validity: Calhoun v. Calhoun.* Charleston, SC: Courier Stem Book and Job Press, 1869.

Whiting, William. *The War Powers of the President and the Legislative Powers of Congress in Relation to Rebellion, Treason and Slavery.* 3rd ed. Boston: John L. Shorey, 1863.

Williams, George Washington. *A History of the Negro Troops in the War of the Rebellion, 1861–1865.* New York: Harper & Brothers, Franklin Square, 1888.

Wythe [Theodore Dwight Weld]. "The Power of Congress over the District of Columbia." 4th ed. *The Anti-Slavery Examiner* no. 5. New York: American Anti-Slavery Society, 1838.

Secondary Sources

BOOKS

Ackerman, Bruce A. *Private Property and the Constitution.* New Haven, CT: Yale University Press, 1977.
Alexander, Leslie M. *Fear of a Black Republic: Haiti and the Birth of Black Internationalism in the United States.* Urbana: University of Illinois Press, 2022.
Allen, Austin. *Origins of the Dred Scott Case: Jacksonian Jurisprudence and the Supreme Court, 1837–1857.* Athens: University of Georgia Press, 2006.
Ambler, Charles Henry. *Francis H. Pierpont, Union War Governor of Virginia and Father of West Virginia.* Chapel Hill: The University of North Carolina Press, 1937.
Araujo, Ana Lucia. *Reparations for Slavery and the Slave Trade: A Transnational and Comparative History.* London: Bloomsbury, 2017.
Astor, Aaron. *Rebels on the Border: Civil War, Emancipation, and the Reconstruction of Kentucky and Missouri.* Baton Rouge: Louisiana State University Press, 2012.
Ayers, Edward L. *In the Presence of Mine Enemies: The Civil War in the Heart of America, 1859–1863.* New York: W. W. Norton, 2003.
———. *The Promise of the New South: Life after Reconstruction.* New York: Oxford University Press, 2007.
Baptist, Edward E. *The Half Has Never Been Told: Slavery and the Making of American Capitalism.* New York: Basic Books, 2014.
Barreyre, Nicolas. *Gold and Freedom: The Political Economy of Reconstruction.* Translated by Arthur Goldhammer. Charlottesville: University of Virginia Press, 2015.
Beckert, Sven. *Empire of Cotton: A Global History.* New York: Alfred Knopf, 2014.
Beckert, Sven, and Seth Rockman, eds. *Slavery's Capitalism: A New History of American Economic Development.* Philadelphia: University of Pennsylvania Press, 2016.
Berlin, Ira. *Many Thousands Gone: The First Two Centuries of Slavery in North America.* Cambridge, MA: Belknap Press of Harvard University Press, 1998.
Berlin, Ira, Barbara J. Fields, Steven F. Miller, Joseph P. Reidy, and Leslie S. Rowland. *Slaves No More: Three Essays on Emancipation and the Civil War.* New York: Cambridge University Press, 1992.
Berlin, Ira, and Philip D. Morgan. *Cultivation and Culture: Labor and the Shaping of Slave Life in the Americas.* Charlottesville: University Press of Virginia, 1993.
Berry, Daina Ramey. *The Price for Their Pound of Flesh: The Value of the Enslaved, from Womb to Grave, in the Building of a Nation.* Boston: Beacon Press, 2017.
Berry, Mary Frances. *My Face Is Black Is True: Callie House and the Struggle for Ex-Slave Reparations.* New York: Vintage, 2006.
Blair, William A. *With Malice toward Some: Treason and Loyalty in the Civil War Era.* Chapel Hill: The University of North Carolina Press, 2014.
Blanchard, Peter. *Under the Flags of Freedom: Slave Soldiers and the Wars of Independence in Spanish South America.* Pittsburgh, PA: University of Pittsburgh Press, 2008.
Blassingame, John W. *The Slave Community: Plantation Life in the Antebellum South.* New York: Oxford University Press, 1979.
Blight, David. *Frederick Douglass: Prophet of Freedom.* New York: Simon & Schuster, 2018.

———. *Race and Reunion: The Civil War in American Memory*. Cambridge, MA: Belknap Press of Harvard University Press, 2001.
Bradley, Mark L. *Bluecoats and Tarheels: Soldiers and Civilians in Reconstruction North Carolina*. Lexington: University Press of Kentucky, 2009.
Brandwein, Pamela. *Rethinking the Judicial Settlement of Reconstruction*. New York: Cambridge University Press, 2011.
Brimmer, Brandi. *Claiming Union Widowhood: Race, Respectability, and Poverty in the Post-Emancipation South*. Durham, NC: Duke University Press, 2020.
Brophy, Alfred L. *University, Court, and Slave: Pro-Slavery Thought in Southern Colleges and Courts and the Coming of Civil War*. New York: Oxford University Press, 2016.
Byrne, Frank J. *Becoming Bourgeois: Merchant Culture in the South, 1820–1865*. Lexington: University Press of Kentucky, 2006.
Callahan, James Morton. *History of West Virginia, Old and New*. Vol. 2. Chicago: American Historical Society, 1923.
Cantrell, Gregg. *Kenneth and John B. Rayner and the Limits of Southern Dissent*. Urbana: University of Illinois Press, 1993.
Carter, Dan T. *When the War Was Over: The Failure of Self-Reconstruction in the South, 1865–1867*. Baton Rouge: Louisiana State University Press, 1985.
Chemerinsky, Erwin. *Constitutional Law: Principles and Policies*, 4 ed. New York: Aspen, 2011.
Chirelstein, Marvin A. *Concepts and Case Analysis in the Law of Contracts*. 7th ed. St. Paul, MN: Foundation Press, 2013.
Cimprich, John. *Slavery's End in Tennessee, 1861–1865*. Tuscaloosa: University of Alabama Press, 1985.
Clark, Kathleen Ann. *Defining Moments: African American Commemoration and Political Culture in the South, 1863–1913*. Chapel Hill: The University of North Carolina Press, 2005.
Clavin, Matthew D. *Toussaint Louverture and the American Civil War: The Promise and Peril of a Second Haitian Revolution*. Philadelphia: University of Pennsylvania Press, 2009.
Coclanis, Peter A. *The Shadow of a Dream: Economic Life and Death in South Carolina Low Country, 1670–1920*. New York: Oxford University Press, 1989.
Colby, Robert. *An Unholy Traffic: Slave Trading in the Civil War South*. New York: Oxford University Press, 2024.
Cooper, Frederick, Thomas C. Holt, and Rebecca J. Scott. *Beyond Slavery: Explorations of Race, Labor, and Citizenship in Postemancipation Societies*. Chapel Hill: The University of North Carolina Press, 2000.
Cox, Karen L. *Dixie's Daughters: The United Daughters of the Confederacy and the Preservation of Confederate Culture*. 2nd ed. Gainesville: University Press of Florida, 2019.
Crallé, Richard K., ed. *The Works of John C. Calhoun*. Vol. 3, *Speeches of John C. Calhoun, Delivered in the House of Representatives, and in the Senate of the United States* New York: D. Appleton, 1864.
Crofts, Daniel W. *Reluctant Confederates: Upper South Unionists in the Secession Crisis*. Chapel Hill: The University of North Carolina Press, 1989.
Curtis, Michael Kent. *No State Shall Abridge: The Fourteenth Amendment and the Bill of Rights*. Durham, NC: Duke University Press, 1986.

Dailey, Jane. *Before Jim Crow: The Politics of Race in Postemancipation Virginia*. Chapel Hill: The University of North Carolina Press, 2000.
Darity, William A., Jr., and A. Kirsten Mullen. *From Here to Equality: Reparations for Black Americans in the Twenty-First Century*. Chapel Hill: The University of North Carolina Press, 2020.
David, Paul A., Herbert Gutman, Richard Sutch, Peter Temin, and Gavin Wright, eds. *Reckoning with Slavery: A Critical Study in the Quantitative History of American Negro Slavery*. New York: Oxford University Press, 1976.
De la Fuente, Alejandro, and Ariela Gross. *Becoming Free, Becoming Black: Race, Freedom, and Law in Cuba, Virginia, and Louisiana*. New York: Cambridge University Press, 2020.
Dew, Charles B. *Apostles of Disunion: Southern Secession Commissioners and the Causes of the Civil War*. Charlottesville: University of Virginia Press, 2001.
Deyle, Steven. *Carry Me Back: The Domestic Slave Trade in American Life*. New York: Oxford University Press, 2005.
Dilbeck, D. H. *Frederick Douglass: America's Prophet*. Chapel Hill: The University of North Carolina Press, 2018.
Domby, Adam. *The False Cause: Fraud, Fabrication, and White Supremacy in Confederate Memory*. Charlottesville: University of Virginia Press, 2020.
Downs, Gregory P. *After Appomattox: Military Occupation and the Ends of the War*. Cambridge, MA: Harvard University Press, 2015.
———. *Declarations of Dependence: The Long Reconstruction of Popular Politics in the South, 1861–1908*. Chapel Hill: The University of North Carolina Press, 2011.
Draper, Nicholas. *The Price of Emancipation: Slave-Ownership, Compensation and British Society at the End of Slavery*. New York: Cambridge University Press, 2010.
Dubois, Laurent. *Avengers of the New World: The Story of the Haitian Revolution*. Cambridge, MA: Harvard University Press, 2004.
———. *Haiti: The Aftershocks of History*. New York: Metropolitan Books, 2012.
Du Bois, W. E. B. *Black Reconstruction in America, 1860–1880*. New York: Free Press, 1998.
———. *Economic Co-operation among Negro Americans. Report of a Study Made by Atlanta University, under the Patronage of the Carnegie Institution of Washington, DC, Together with the Proceedings of the 12th Conference for the Study of the Negro Problems, Held at Atlanta University, on Tuesday, May the 28th, 1907*. Atlanta, GA: Atlanta University Press, 1907.
Dyer, Justin Buckley. *Natural Law and the Antislavery Constitutional Tradition*. New York: Cambridge University Press, 2012.
Edwards, Justene Hill. *Savings and Trust: The Rise and Betrayal of the Freedmen's Bank*. New York: W. W. Norton, 2024.
———. *Unfree Markets: The Slaves' Economy and the Rise of Capitalism in South Carolina*. New York: Columbia University Press, 2021.
Edwards, Laura F. *Gendered Strife and Confusion: The Political Culture of Reconstruction*. Urbana: University of Illinois Press, 1997.
———. *A Legal History of the Civil War and Reconstruction: A Nation of Rights*. New York: Cambridge University Press, 2015.
———. *The People and Their Peace: Legal Culture and the Transformation of Inequality in the Post-Revolutionary South*. Chapel Hill: The University of North Carolina Press, 2009.

———. *Scarlett Doesn't Live Here Anymore: Southern Women in the Civil War Era*. Urbana: University of Illinois Press, 2004.

Ely, James W., Jr. *The Contract Clause: A Constitutional History*. Lawrence: University Press of Kansas, 2016.

Engerman, Stanley L. *Slavery, Emancipation and Freedom: Comparative Perspectives*. Baton Rouge: Louisiana State University Press, 2007.

Epstein, Richard A. *Takings: Private Property and the Power of Eminent Domain*. Cambridge, MA: Harvard University Press, 1985.

Faust, Drew Gilpin. *The Ideology of Slavery: Proslavery Thought in the Antebellum South, 1830–1860*. Baton Rouge: Louisiana State University Press, 1981.

Fede, Andrew. *People without Rights: An Interpretation of the Fundamentals of the Law of Slavery in the US South*. New York: Routledge, 1992.

Fehrenbacher, Don E. *The Slaveholding Republic: An Account of the United States Government's Relations to Slavery*. New York: Oxford University Press, 2001.

Fields, Barbara J. *Slavery and Freedom on the Middle Ground: Maryland during the Nineteenth Century*. New Haven, CT: Yale University Press, 1985.

Finkelman, Paul, ed. *Defending Slavery: Proslavery Thought in the Old South: A Brief History with Documents*. Boston: Bedford/St. Martin's, 2003.

———. *An Imperfect Union: Slavery, Federalism, and Comity*. Chapel Hill: The University of North Carolina Press, 1981.

———. *Slavery in the Courtroom: An Annotated Bibliography of American Cases*. Washington, DC: Library of Congress, 1985.

Fischel, William A. *Regulatory Takings: Law, Economics, and Politics*. Cambridge, MA: Harvard University Press, 1995.

Fitz, Caitlin. *Our Sister Republics: The United States in an Age of American Revolutions*. New York: W. W. Norton, 2016.

Flack, Horace Edgar. *The Adoption of the Fourteenth Amendment*. Baltimore: Johns Hopkins Press, 1908.

Fluker, Amy Laurel. *Commonwealth of Compromise: Civil War Commemoration in Missouri*. Columbia: University of Missouri, 2020.

Fogel, Robert William. *The Slavery Debates, 1952–1990: A Retrospective*. Baton Rouge: Louisiana State University Press, 2003.

———. *Without Consent or Contract, the Rise and Fall of American Slavery*. New York: W. W. Norton, 1985.

Fogel, Robert William, and Stanley Engerman. *Time on the Cross: The Economics of American Negro Slavery*. New York: W. W. Norton, 1989.

Follett, Richard. *The Sugar Masters: Planters and Slaves in Louisiana's Cane World, 1820–1860*. Baton Rouge: Louisiana State University Press, 2005.

Foner, Eric. *The Fiery Trial: Abraham Lincoln and American Slavery*. New York: W. W. Norton, 2011.

———. *Nothing but Freedom: Emancipation and Its Legacy*. Baton Rouge: Louisiana State University Press, 1983.

———. *Reconstruction: America's Unfinished Revolution, 1863–1877*. New York: HarperCollins, 1988.

Foster, Gaines M. *Ghosts of the Confederacy: Defeat, the Lost Cause, and the Emergence of the New South*. New York: Oxford University Press, 1988.
Franklin, John Hope. *George Washington Williams: A Biography*. Chicago: University of Chicago Press, 1985.
Freehling, William W. *The Road to Disunion*. Vol. 2, *Secessionists Triumphant, 1854–1861*. New York: Oxford University Press, 2007.
Gellman, David. *Emancipating New York: The Politics of Slavery and Freedom, 1777–1827*. Baton Rouge: Louisiana State University Press, 2006.
Genovese, Eugene. *Roll, Jordan, Roll: The World the Slaves Made*. New York: Pantheon Books, 1974.
Ginsberg, Benjamin. *Moses of South Carolina: A Jewish Scalawag during Radical Reconstruction*. Baltimore: Johns Hopkins University Press, 2010.
Glymph, Thavolia. *Out of the House of Bondage: The Transformation of the Plantation Household*. New York: Cambridge University Press, 2008.
Goodell, William. *The American Slave Code in Theory and Practice: Its Distinctive Features shown by Its Statutes, Judicial Decisions, and Illustrative Facts*. New York: American and Foreign Anti-Slavery Society, 1853.
Gordon, Linda. *Pitied but Not Entitled: Single Mothers and the History of Welfare, 1890–1935*. Cambridge, MA: Harvard University Press, 1995.
Graber, Mark. *Punish Treason, Reward Loyalty: The Forgotten Goals of Constitutional Reform after the Civil War*. Lawrence: University Press of Kansas, 2023.
Gross, Ariela J. *Double Character: Slavery and Mastery in the Antebellum Southern Courtroom*. Princeton, NJ: Princeton University Press, 2000.
Gudmestad, Robert H. *A Troublesome Commerce: The Transformation of the Interstate Slave Trade*. Baton Rouge: Louisiana State University Press, 2003.
Hahn, Steven. *A Nation under Our Feet: Black Political Struggles in the Rural South from Slavery to the Great Migration*. Cambridge, MA: Belknap Press of Harvard University Press, 2003.
———. *The Political Worlds of Slavery and Freedom*. Cambridge, MA: Harvard University Press, 2009.
Hahn, Steven, Steven F. Miller, Susan E. O'Donovan, John C. Rodrigue, and Leslie S. Rowland, eds. *Freedom: A Documentary History of Emancipation, 1861–1867*. Series 3, vol. 1, *Land and Labor, 1865*. Chapel Hill: The University of North Carolina Press, 2008.
Hale, Grace Elizabeth. *Making Whiteness: The Culture of Segregation in the South, 1890–1940*. New York: Vintage Books, 1998.
Hamilton, Daniel W. *The Limits of Sovereignty: Property Confiscation in the Union and the Confederacy during the Civil War*. Chicago: University of Chicago Press, 2001.
Hartman, Saidiya V. *Scenes of Subjection: Terror, Slavery, and Self-Making in Nineteenth-Century America*. New York: Oxford University Press, 1997.
Hodges, Graham Russell. *Slavery and Freedom in the Rural North: African Americans in Monmouth County, New Jersey, 1665–1865*. Madison: University of Wisconsin Press, 1997.
Holden, Vanessa. *Surviving Southampton: African American Women and Resistance in Nat Turner's Community*. Champaign: University of Illinois Press, 2021.
Holt, Michael F. *The Rise and Fall of the American Whig Party: Jacksonian Politics and the Onset of the Civil War*. New York: Oxford University Press, 1999.

Holt, Thomas. *Black over White: Negro Political Leadership in South Carolina during Reconstruction*. Urbana: University of Illinois Press, 1979.

———. *The Problem of Freedom: Race, Labor, and Politics in Jamaica and Britain, 1832–1938*. Baltimore: Johns Hopkins University Press, 1992.

Holton, Woody. *Unruly Americans and the Origins of the Constitution*. New York: Hill and Wang, 2007.

Horton, James Oliver, and Lois Horton. *In Hope of Liberty: Culture, Community, and Protest Among Northern Free Blacks, 1700–1860*. New York: Oxford University Press, 1998.

Horwitz, Morton J. *The Transformation of American Law, 1780–1860*. Cambridge, MA: Harvard University Press, 1979.

Huebner, Timothy S. *Liberty and Union: The Civil War Era and American Constitutionalism*. Lawrence: University Press of Kansas, 2016.

Hume, Richard L., and Jerry B. Gough. *Blacks, Carpetbaggers, Scalawags: The Constitutional Conventions of Radical Reconstruction*. Baton Rouge: Louisiana State University Press, 2008.

Hunter, Tera. *Bound in Wedlock: Slave and Free Black Marriage in the Nineteenth Century*. Cambridge, MA: Belknap Press of Harvard University Press, 2017.

———. *To 'Joy My Freedom: Southern Black Women's Lives and Labors after the Civil War*. Cambridge, MA: Harvard University Press, 1997.

Huston, James L. *Calculating the Value of the Union: Slavery, Property Rights, and the Economic Origins of the Civil War*. Chapel Hill: The University of North Carolina Press, 2003.

Hyman, Harold Melvin. *Era of the Oath: Northern Loyalty Tests during the Civil War and Reconstruction*. Philadelphia: University of Pennsylvania Press, 1954.

Hyman, Harold Melvin., and William M. Wiecek. *Equal Justice under the Law: Constitutional Development, 1835–1875*. New York: Harper & Row, 1982.

Inscoe, John C., and Robert C. Kenzer. *Enemies of the Country: New Perspectives on Unionists in the Civil War South*. Athens: University of Georgia Press, 2001.

Irons, Charles. *The Origins of Proslavery Christianity: White and Black Evangelicals in Colonial and Antebellum Virginia*. Chapel Hill: The University of North Carolina Press, 2008.

Jackson, Kelly Carter. *Force and Freedom: Black Abolitionists and the Politics of Violence*. Philadelphia: University of Pennsylvania Press, 2019.

James, Joseph B. *The Framing of the Fourteenth Amendment*. Urbana: University of Illinois Press, 1956.

Janney, Caroline E. *Remembering the Civil War: Reunion and the Limits of Reconciliation*. Chapel Hill: The University of North Carolina Press, 2013.

Jasanoff, Maya. *Liberty's Exiles: American Loyalists in the Revolutionary World*. New York: Knopf, 2011.

Johnson, Michael P., ed. *Abraham Lincoln, Slavery, and the Civil War: Selected Writing and Speeches*. Boston: Bedford/St. Martin's, 2001.

Johnson, Walter, ed. *The Chattel Principle: Internal Slave Trades in the Americas*. New Haven, CT: Yale University Press, 2005.

———. *River of Dark Dreams: Slavery and Empire in the Cotton Kingdom*. Cambridge, MA: Belknap Press of Harvard University Press, 2013.

———. *Soul by Soul: Life inside the Antebellum Slave Market*. Cambridge, MA: Harvard University Press, 1999.

Jones, Martha. *Birthright Citizens: A History of Race and Rights in Antebellum America*. New York: Cambridge University Press, 2018.
Jones-Rogers, Stephanie E. *They Were Her Property: White Women as Slave Owners in the American South*. New Haven, CT: Yale University Press, 2019.
Kennington, Kelly M. *In the Shadow of Dred Scott: St. Louis Freedom Suits and the Legal Culture of Slavery in Antebellum America*. Athens: University of Georgia Press, 2017.
Kilbourne, Richard H. *Debt, Investment, Slaves: Credit Relations in East Feliciana Parish, Louisiana, 1825–1885*. Tuscaloosa: University of Alabama Press, 1995.
Kousser, Morgan J. *The Shaping of Southern Politics: Suffrage Restriction and the Establishment of the One-Party South, 1880–1910*. New Haven, CT: Yale University Press, 1974.
Krauthamer Barbara. *Black Slaves, Indian Masters: Slavery, Emancipation, and Citizenship in the Native American South*. Chapel Hill: The University of North Carolina Press, 2013.
Kretz, Dale. *Administering Freedom: The State of Emancipation after the Freedmen's Bureau*. Chapel Hill: The University of North Carolina Press, 2023.
Kruman, Marc W. *Parties and Politics in North Carolina, 1836–1865*. Baton Rouge: Louisiana State University Press, 1983.
Lawson, Melinda. *Patriot Fires: Forging a New American Nationalism in the Civil War North*. Lawrence: University Press of Kansas, 2002.
Lee, Susanna Michele. *Claiming the Union: Citizenship in the Post-Civil War South*. New York: Cambridge University Press, 2014.
Leemhuis, Roger P. *James L. Orr and the Sectional Conflict*. Washington, DC: University Press of America, 1979.
Leonard, Elizabeth. *Lincoln's Forgotten Ally: Judge Advocate General Joseph Holt of Kentucky*. Chapel Hill: The University of North Carolina Press, 2011.
Les Benedict, Michael. *Preserving the Constitution: Essays on Politics and the Constitution in the Era of Reconstruction*. Fordham, NY: Fordham University Press, 2006.
Levine, Bruce. *Confederate Emancipation: Southern Plans to Free and Arm Slaves during the Civil War*. New York: Oxford University Press, 2006.
Levy, Jonathan. *Freaks of Fortune: The Emerging World of Capitalism and Risk in America*. Cambridge, MA: Harvard University Press, 2012.
Lundberg, James M. *Horace Greeley: Print, Politics, and the Failure of American Nationhood*. Baltimore: John Hopkins University Press, 2019.
Maddex, Jack P., Jr. *The Virginia Conservatives, 1867–1879: A Study in Reconstruction Politics*. Chapel Hill: The University of North Carolina Press, 1970.
Magness, Phillip W., and Sebastian N. Page. *Colonization after Emancipation: Lincoln and the Movement for Black Resettlement*. Columbia: University of Missouri Press, 2011.
Manajpra, Kris. *Black Ghost of Empire: The Long Death of Slavery and the Failure of Emancipation*. New York: Scribner, 2023.
Margolies, Daniel S. *Henry Watterson and the New South: The Politics of Empire, Free Trade, and Globalization*. Lexington: University Press of Kentucky, 2006.
Marshall, Ann E. *Creating a Confederate Kentucky: The Lost Cause and Civil War Memory in a Border State*. Chapel Hill: The University of North Carolina Press, 2010.
Masur, Kate. *An Example for All the Land: Emancipation and the Struggle over Equality in Washington, D.C.* Chapel Hill: The University of North Carolina Press, 2010.

———. *Until Justice Be Done: America's First Civil Rights Movement, from the Revolution to Reconstruction*. New York: W. W. Norton, 2021.
Mathisen, Erik. *The Loyal Republic: Traitors, Slaves, and the Remaking of Citizenship in Civil War America*. Chapel Hill: The University of North Carolina Press, 2018.
McCrary, Peyton. *Abraham Lincoln and Reconstruction: The Louisiana Experiment*. Princeton, NJ: Princeton University Press, 1978.
McCurry, Stephanie. *Confederate Reckoning: Power and Politics in the Civil War South*. Cambridge, MA: Harvard University Press, 2010.
———. *Masters of Small Worlds: Yeoman Households, Gender Relations, and Political Culture of the Antebellum South Carolina Low Country*. New York: Oxford University Press, 1995.
———. *Women's War: Fighting and Surviving the American Civil War*. Cambridge, MA: Harvard University Press, 2019.
McDaniel, W. Caleb. *Sweet Taste of Liberty: A True Story of Slavery and Restitution in America*. New York: Oxford University Press, 2019.
McKitrick, Eric L. *Andrew Johnson and Reconstruction*. Chicago: University of Chicago Press, 1960.
McPherson, James. *The Struggle for Equality: Abolitionists and the Negro in the Civil War and Reconstruction*. Princeton, NJ: Princeton University Press, 1964.
Melish, Joanne Pope. *Disowning Slavery: Gradual Emancipation and "Race" in New England, 1780–1860*. Ithaca, NY: Cornell University Press, 1998.
Merritt, Kerri Leigh. *Masterless Men: Poor Whites and Slavery in the Antebellum South*. New York: Cambridge University Press, 2017.
Miles, Tiya. *All That She Carried: The Journey of Ashley's Sack, a Black Family Keepsake*. New York: Random House, 2021.
———. *Ties That Bind: The Story of an Afro-Cherokee Family in Slavery and Freedom*. 2nd ed. Oakland: University of California Press, 2015.
Milewski, Melissa. *Litigating across the Color Line: Civil Cases Between Black and White Southerners from the End of Slavery to Civil Rights*. New York: Oxford University Press, 2017.
Morris, Thomas D. *Southern Slavery and the Law, 1619–1860*. Chapel Hill: The University of North Carolina Press, 1996.
Murphy, Sharon Ann. *Investing in Life: Insurance in Antebellum America*. Baltimore: Johns Hopkins University Press, 2010.
Myers, Barton A. *Rebels against the Confederacy: North Carolina's Unionists*. New York: Cambridge University Press, 2014.
Nash, Gary, and Jean R. Soderlund. *Freedom by Degrees: Emancipation in Pennsylvania and Its Aftermath*. New York: Oxford University Press, 1991.
Neff, Stephen C. *Justice in Blue and Gray: A Legal History of the Civil War*. Cambridge, MA: Harvard University Press, 2010.
Nelson, Margaret Virginia. *A Study of Judicial Review in Virginia, 1789–1928*. New York: Columbia University Press, 1947.
Nelson, William E. *The Fourteenth Amendment: From Political Principle to Judicial Doctrine*. Cambridge, MA: Harvard University Press, 1998.
Nicoletti, Cynthia. *Secession on Trial: The Treason Prosecution of Jefferson Davis*. New York: Cambridge University Press, 2017.

Novak, William. *The People's Welfare: Law and Regulation in Nineteenth-Century America.* Chapel Hill: The University of North Carolina Press, 1996.
Nunley, Tamika. *At the Threshold of Liberty: Women, Slavery, and Shifting Identities in Washington, D.C.* Chapel Hill: The University of North Carolina Press, 2021.
Oakes, James. *Freedom National: The Destruction of Slavery in the United States, 1861–1865.* New York: W. W. Norton, 2013.
———. *The Ruling Race: A History of American Slaveholders.* New York: W. W. Norton, 1982.
Penningroth, Dylan. *Before the Movement: The Hidden History of Black Civil Rights.* New York: W. W. Norton, 2023.
———. *The Claims of Kinfolk: African American Property and Community in the Nineteenth-Century South.* Chapel Hill: The University of North Carolina Press, 2003.
Perman, Michael. *Reunion without Compromise: The South and Reconstruction, 1865–1868.* New York: Cambridge University Press, 1973.
———. *The Road to Redemption: Southern Politics, 1869–1879.* Chapel Hill: The University of North Carolina Press, 1985.
Perrone, Giuliana. *Nothing More Than Freedom: The Failure of Abolition in American Law.* New York: Cambridge University Press, 2023.
Price, Polly J. *Property Rights: Rights and Liberties under the Law.* Santa Barbara, CA: ABC-CLIO, 2003.
Prince, K. Stephen, ed. *Radical Reconstruction: A Brief History with Documents.* Boston: Bedford/St. Martin's, 2016.
Rable, George C. *The Confederate Republic: A Revolution against Politics.* Chapel Hill: The University of North Carolina Press, 1994.
Ramsdell, Charles W. *Reconstruction in Texas.* New York: Columbia University Press, 1910.
Randall, James G. *Constitutional Problems under Lincoln.* New York: D. Appleton, 1926.
Ranney, Joseph A. *In the Wake of Slavery: Civil War, Civil Rights, and the Reconstruction of Southern Law.* Westport, CT: Praeger, 2006.
Ransom, Roger L., and Richard Sutch. *One Kind of Freedom: The Economic Consequences of Emancipation.* New York: Cambridge University Press, 1977.
Regosin, Elizabeth. *Freedom's Promise: Ex-Slave Families and Citizenship in the Age of Emancipation.* Charlottesville: University Press of Virginia, 2002.
Richardson, Heather Cox. *Greatest Nation of the Earth: Republican Economic Policies during the Civil War.* Cambridge, MA: Harvard University Press, 1997.
Riley, Franklin Lafayette, ed. *Publications of the Mississippi Historical Society.* Vol. 11. Oxford: University of Mississippi, 1910.
Roark, James L. *Masters without Slaves: Southern Planters in the Civil War and Reconstruction.* New York: W. W. Norton, 1977.
Roberts, Alaina E. *I've Been Here All the While: Black Freedom on Native Land.* Philadelphia: University of Pennsylvania Press, 2021.
Robinson, Armstead L. *Bitter Fruits of Bondage: The Demise of Slavery and the Collapse of the Confederacy, 1861–1865.* Charlottesville: University of Virginia Press, 2005.
Roediger, David. *Seizing Freedom: Slave Emancipation and Liberty for All.* Brooklyn, NY: Verso, 2014.
Rose, Willie Lee. *Rehearsal for Reconstruction: The Port Royal Experiment.* New York: Oxford University Press, 1976.

Rosen, Hannah. *Terror in the Heart of Freedom: Citizenship, Sexual Violence, and the Meaning of Race in the Postemancipation South*. Chapel Hill: The University of North Carolina Press, 2009.

Rugemer, Edward. *The Problem of Emancipation: The Caribbean Roots of the American Civil War*. Baton Rouge: Louisiana State University Press, 2008.

Saville, Julie. *The Work of Reconstruction: From Slave to Wage Laborer in South Carolina, 1860–1870*. New York: Cambridge University Press, 1996.

Scalan, Padraic X. *Slave Empire: How Slavery Built Modern Britain*. London: Robinson, 2020.

Schuckers, J. W. *The Life and Public Services of Salmon Portland Chase*. New York: D. Appleton, 1874.

Scott, Rebecca. *Degrees of Freedom: Louisiana and Cuba after Slavery*. Cambridge, MA: Belknap Press of Harvard University Press, 2005.

Scott, Rebecca, and Jean M. Hébrard. *Freedom Papers: An Atlantic Odyssey in the Age of Emancipation*. Cambridge, MA: Harvard University Press, 2012.

Seeley, Samantha. *Race, Removal, and the Right to Remain: Migration and the Making of the United States*. Chapel Hill: The University of North Carolina Press, 2021.

Shugg, Roger W. *Origins of Class Struggle in Louisiana: A Social History of White Farmers and Laborers during Slavery and After, 1840–1875*. Baton Rouge: Louisiana State University Press, 1939.

Siddali, Silvana R. *From Property to Person: Slavery and the Confiscation Acts, 1861–1862*. Baton Rouge: Louisiana State University Press, 2005.

Silber, Nina. *The Romance of Reunion: Northerners and the South, 1865–1900*. Chapel Hill: The University of North Carolina Press, 2000.

Sinha, Manisha. *The Counterrevolution of Slavery: Politics and Ideology in Antebellum South Carolina*. Chapel Hill: The University of North Carolina Press, 2000.

———. *The Slave's Cause: A History of Abolition*. New Haven, CT: Yale University Press, 2016.

Skocpol, Theda. *Protecting Soldiers and Mothers: The Political Origins of Social Policy in the United States*. Cambridge, MA: Harvard University Press, 1992.

Slap, Andrew. *The Doom of Reconstruction: The Liberal Republicans in the Civil War Era*. New York: Fordham University Press, 2006.

Smith, Adam I. P. *The Stormy Present: Conservatism and the Problem of Slavery in Northern Politics, 1846–1865*. Chapel Hill: The University of North Carolina Press, 2017.

Smith, Mark M. *Debating Slavery: Economy and Society in the Antebellum American South* New York: Cambridge University Press, 2012.

Spencer, Charles. *Edisto Island, 1861 to 2006: Ruin, Recovery, and Rebirth*. Charleston, SC: History Press, 2008.

Stampp, Kenneth M. *America in 1857: A Nation on the Brink*. New York: Oxford University Press, 1992.

Stauffer, John. *The Black Hearts of Men: Radical Abolitionists and the Transformation of Race*. Cambridge, MA: Harvard University Press, 2004.

Steinfeld, Robert J., *The Invention of Free Labor: The Employment Relation in English and American Law and Culture, 1350–1870*. Chapel Hill: The University of North Carolina Press, 1991.

Stoebuck, William B., and Dale A. Whitman. *The Law of Property*. 3rd ed. St. Paul, MN: West Academic, 2000.
Storey, Margaret M. *Loyalty and Loss: Alabama's Unionists in the Civil War and Reconstruction*. Baton Rouge: Louisiana State University Press, 2004.
Stroud, George M. *A Sketch of the Laws Relating to Slavery in the Several States of the United States of America*. Philadelphia: Kimber and Sharpless, 1827.
Tadman, Michael. *Speculators and Slaves: Masters, Traders, and Slaves in the Old South*. Madison: University of Wisconsin Press, 1996.
Taylor, Amy Murrell. *Embattled Freedom: Journeys through the Civil War's Slave Refugee Camps*. Chapel Hill: The University of North Carolina Press, 2018.
Taylor, Joe Gray. *Louisiana Reconstructed, 1863–1877*. Baton Rouge: Louisiana State University Press, 1974.
Thomson, David K. *Bonds of War: How Civil War Financial Agents Sold the World on the Union*. Chapel Hill: The University of North Carolina Press, 2022.
Thompson, Elizabeth Lee. *The Reconstruction of Southern Debtors: Bankruptcy after the Civil War*. Athens: University of Georgia Press, 2004.
Tolis, Peter. *Elihu Burritt: Crusader for Brotherhood*. Hamden, CT: Archon Books, 1968.
Tushnet, Mark. *The American Law of Slavery, 1810–1860: Considerations of Humanity and Interest*. Princeton, NJ: Princeton University Press, 1981.
Twitty, Anne. *Before Dred Scott: Slavery and Legal Culture in the American Confluence, 1787–1857*. New York: Cambridge University Press, 2016.
Van Cleve, George William. *A Slaveholder's Union: Slavery, Politics, and the Constitution in the Early American Republic*. Chicago: University of Chicago Press, 2010.
VanderVelde, Lea S. *Redemption Songs: Suing for Freedom before Dred Scott*. Oxford: Oxford University Press, 2014.
Venet, Wendy H. *Neither Ballots nor Bullets: Women Abolitionists and the Civil War*. Charlottesville: University Press of Virginia, 1991.
Vorenberg, Michael. *Final Freedom: The Civil War, the Abolition of Slavery, and the Thirteenth Amendment*. New York: Cambridge University Press, 2001.
Wahl, Jenny Bourne. *The Bondsman's Burden: An Economic Analysis of the Common Law of Southern Slavery*. New York: Cambridge University Press, 1998.
Welch, Kimberly M. *Black Litigants in the Antebellum American South*. Chapel Hill: The University of North Carolina Press, 2018.
Wheeler, Jacob D. *A Practical Treatise on the Law of Slavery: Being a Compilation of All the Decisions Made on That Subject, in the Several Courts of the United States, and State Courts [. . .]*. New York: A. Pollock Jr., 1837.
White, Shane. *Somewhat More Independent: The End of Slavery in New York City, 1770–1810*. Athens: University of Georgia Press, 1991.
Williams, Greg H. *Civil War Suits in the US Court of Claims: Cases Involving Compensation to Northerners and Southerners for Wartime Losses*. Jefferson, NC: McFarland, 2006.
Williams, Kidada E. *They Left Great Marks on Me: African American Testimonies of Racial Violence from Emancipation to World War I*. New York: New York University Press, 2012.
Williams, Robert C. *Horace Greeley: Champion of American Freedom*. New York: New York University Press, 2006.
Winks, Robin. *The Blacks in Canada: A History*. New Haven, CT: Yale University Press, 1971.

Witt, John Fabian. *Lincoln's Code: The Laws of War in American History.* New York: Free Press, 2012.
Wolf, Eva Sheppard. *Race and Liberty in the New Nation: Emancipation in Virginia from the Revolution to Nat Turner's Rebellion.* Baton Rouge: Louisiana State University Press, 2006.
Wood, Kirsten E. *Masterful Women: Slaveholding Widows from the American Revolution through the Civil War.* Chapel Hill: The University of North Carolina Press, 2004.
Woodman, Harold D. *King Cotton and His Retainers: Financing and Marketing the Cotton Crop of the South, 1800–1925.* Columbia: University of South Carolina Press, 1990.
———. *New South, New Law: The Legal Foundations of Credit and Labor Relations in the Postbellum Agricultural South.* Baton Rouge: Louisiana State University Press, 1995.
Wright, Gavin. *Old South, New South: Revolutions in the Southern Economy since the Civil War.* New York: Basic Books, 1986.
———. *Slavery and American Economic Development.* Baton Rouge: Louisiana State University Press, 2006.
Zilversmit, Arthur. *The First Emancipation: The Abolition of Slavery in the North.* Chicago: University of Chicago Press, 1967.

JOURNAL ARTICLES, BOOK CHAPTERS, AND DISSERTATIONS

Abney, M. G. "Reconstruction in Pontotoc County." In *Publications of the Mississippi Historical Society*, vol. 11, edited by Franklin Lafayette Riley. Oxford: University of Mississippi, 1910.
"African Americans and Movements for Reparations: Past, Present, and Future." Special issue, *Journal of African American History* 97, nos. 1–2 (2012).
Alexander, Thomas B. "Persistent Whiggery in the Confederate South, 1860–1877." *Journal of Southern History* 27, no. 3 (1961): 305–29.
Axtell, Max. "Towards a New Legal History of Capitalism and Unfree Labor: Law, Slavery, and Emancipation in the American Marketplace." *Law and Social Inquiry* 40, no. 1 (2015): 270–300.
Aynes, Richard L. "Unintended Consequences of the Fourteenth Amendment and What They Tell Us about Its Interpretation." *Akron Law Review* 39, no. 2 (2006): 289–321.
Bailey, Kenneth R. "Test Oaths, Belligerent Rights, and Confederate Money: Civil War Lawsuits Before the West Virginia Supreme Court of Appeals." *West Virginia History* 7, no. 1 (2013): 1–22.
Bailey-Williams, Sheryl. "An Appraisal of the Estimated Rates of Slave Exploitation." In *The Wealth of Races: The Present Value of Benefits from Past Injustices*, edited by Richard F. America. New York: Greenwood Press, 1990.
Barnhart, Terry A. "Apostles of the Lost Cause." *Georgia Historical Quarterly* 96, no. 4 (2012): 371–412.
Barreyre, Nicolas. "The Politics of Economic Crises: The Panic of 1873, the End of Reconstruction, and the Realignment of American Politics." *Journal of the Gilded Age and Progressive Era* 10, no. 4 (October 2011): 403–23.
Bearss, Sarah B. "Restored and Vindicated: The Virginia Constitutional Convention of 1864." *Virginia Magazine of History and Biography* 122, no. 2 (2014): 156–81.
Benson, Megan. "*Fisher v. Allen*: The Southern Origins of the Married Women's Property Acts." *Journal of Southern Legal History* 6 (1998): 97–122.

Berlin, Ira. "Who Freed the Slaves? Emancipation and Its Meaning." In *Union and Emancipation: Essays on Politics and Race in the Civil War Era*, edited by David W. Blight and Brooks D. Simpson. Kent, OH: Kent State University Press, 1997.

Berlin, Ira, Barbara J. Fields, Steven F. Miller, Joseph P. Reidy, and Leslie S. Rowland. "The Destruction of Slavery, 1861–1865." In *Slaves No More: Three Essays on the Civil War and Emancipation*. New York: Cambridge University Press, 1992.

Bernier, Julia W. "'Never Be Free without Trustin' Some Person': Networking and Buying Freedom in the Nineteenth-Century United States." *Slavery and Abolition* 40, no. 2 (2019): 341–60.

Bierck, Harold A., Jr. "The Struggle for Abolition in Gran Colombia." *Hispanic American Historical Review* 33, no. 3 (1953): 365–86.

Biondi, Martha. "The Rise of the Reparations Movement." *Radical History Review* 87 (Fall 2003): 5–18.

Blair, William. "Friend or Foe: Treason and the Second Confiscation Act." In *Wars within a War: Controversy and Conflict over the American Civil War*, edited by Joan Waugh and Gary Gallagher. Chapel Hill: The University of North Carolina Press, 2009.

Blair, William A., and Karen Fisher Younger. Introduction to *Lincoln's Proclamation: Emancipation Reconsidered*. Edited by William A. Blair and Karen Fisher Younger. Chapel Hill: The University of North Carolina Press, 2009.

Blassingame, John W. "The Recruitment of Colored Troops in Kentucky, Maryland and Missouri, 1863–1865." *Historian* 29, no. 4 (1967): 533–45.

Bowman, Winston. "A Brief History of the Courts of Claims." *Federal Lawyer* 63, no. 10 (2016): 46–51.

Breese, Donald Hubert. "Politics in the Lower South during Presidential Reconstruction, April to November, 1865." PhD diss., University of California, 1964.

Bright, Walter Steven. "Radicalism and Rebellion: Presidential Reconstruction in South Carolina, April 1865 to May 1866." Master's thesis, Clemson University, 2008.

Brophy, James L. "The Intersection of Property and Slavery in Southern Legal Thought: From Missouri Compromise through Civil War." PhD diss., Harvard University, 2001.

Brown, Vincent. "Mapping a Slave Revolt: Visualizing Spatial History through the Archives of Slavery." *Social Text* 33, no. 4 (125) (2015): 134–41.

Calderhead, William. "How Extensive Was the Border State Slave Trade? A New Look." *Civil War History* 18, no. 1 (1972): 42–55.

Carmichael, Peter. "New South Visionaries." In *The Myth of the Lost Cause and Civil War History*, edited by Gary W. Gallagher and Alan T. Nolan. Bloomington: Indiana University Press, 2000.

Charles, Jacob D. "The Debt Limit and the Constitution: How the Fourteenth Amendment Forbids Fiscal Obstructionism." *Duke Law Journal* 62, no. 6 (2013): 1227–66.

Chisolm, Tuneen E. "Sweep around Your Own Front Door: Examining the Argument for Legislative African American Reparations." *University of Pennsylvania Law Review* 147, no. 3 (1999): 677–728.

Chused, Richard H. "Married Women's Property Law: 1800–1850." *Georgetown Law Journal* 71 (1983): 1359–1425.

Clark, John G. "Historians and the Joint Committee on Reconstruction." *The Historian* 23, no. 3 (1961): 348–61.

Cohen-Lack, Nancy. "A Struggle for Sovereignty: National Consolidation, Emancipation, and Free Labor in Texas, 1865." *Journal of Southern History* 58, no. 1 (1992): 57–98.

Davis, Margaret. "Compensated Emancipation in the United States." Master's thesis, University of Nebraska, 1905.

Domby, Adam H., and Karen L. Cox. "Monuments and Memory: Civil War Statuary, Public-Facing Scholarship, and the Future of Memory Studies." *Journal of the Civil War Era* 13, no. 3 (2023): 342–68.

Drake, Winbourne Magruder. "The Mississippi Reconstruction Convention of 1865." *Journal of Mississippi History* 21, no. 4 (1959): 225–56.

Drescher, Seymour. "British Way, French Way: Opinion Building and Revolution in the Second French Slave Emancipation." *American Historical Review* 96 (1991): 709–34.

Eatmon, Myisha. "From the 'Legal Culture of Slavery' to Black Legal Culture: Reimagining the Implications and Meanings of Black Litigiousness in Slavery and Freedom." *Law and Social Inquiry* 48, no. 4 (2023): 1428–47.

Eder, Phanor J. "A Forgotten Section of the Fourteenth Amendment." *Cornell Law Quarterly* 19, no. 1 (1933): 1291–326.

Ely, James W., Jr. "The Contract Clause during the Civil War and Reconstruction." *Journal of Supreme Court History* 41, no. 3 (2016): 257–74.

———. "'That Due Satisfaction May Be Made': The Fifth Amendment and the Origins of the Compensation Principle." *American Journal of Legal History* 36, no. 1 (1992): 1–18.

Engerman, Stanley L. "Emancipation Schemes: Different Ways of Ending Slavery." In *Slave Systems: Ancient and Modern*, edited by Enrico Dal Lago and Constantina Katsari. New York: Cambridge University Press, 2008.

English, William B. "Understanding the Costs of Sovereign Default: American State Debts in the 1840s." *American Economic Review* 86, no. 1 (1996): 259–75.

Fede, Andrew. "Legal Protection for Slave Buyers in the US South: A Caveat concerning Caveat Emptor." *American Journal of Legal History* 31, no. 4 (1987): 322–58.

Finkelman, Paul. "Lincoln, Emancipation, and the Limits of Constitutional Change." *Supreme Court Review* 2008, no. 1 (2008): 362–63.

———. "Lincoln and the Preconditions for Emancipation: The Moral Grandeur of a Bill of Lading." In *Lincoln's Proclamation: Emancipation Reconsidered*, edited by William A. Blair and Karen Fisher Younger. Chapel Hill: The University of North Carolina Press, 2009.

Fladeland, Betty L. "Compensated Emancipation: A Rejected Alternative." *Journal of Southern History* 42, no. 2 (1976): 169–86.

Fogel, Robert William, and Stanley L. Engerman. "Philanthropy at Bargain Prices: Notes on the Economics of Gradual Emancipation." *Journal of Legal Studies* 3, no. 2 (1974): 377–401.

Gallon, Kim. "Making the Case for the Black Digital Humanities." In *Debates in the Digital Humanities*, edited by Matthew K. Gold and Lauren F. Klein. Minneapolis: University of Minnesota Press, 2016.

Genovese, Eugene, and Elizabeth Fox-Genovese. "Slavery, Economic Development, and the Law: The Dilemma of the Southern Political Economists, 1800–1860." *Washington and Lee Law Review* 29 (1984): 1–29.

Glymph, Thavolia. "'Liberty Dearly Bought': The Making of Civil War Memory in Afro-American Communities in the South." In *Time Longer than Rope: A Century of*

African American Activism, 1850–1950, edited by Charles M. Payne and Adam Green. New York: New York University Press, 2003.

Goldin, Claudia. "The Economics of Emancipation." *Journal of Economic History* 33, no. 1 (1973): 66–85.

Goodman, Paul. "The Emergence of Homestead Exemption in the United States: Accommodation and Resistance to the Market Revolution, 1840–1880." *Journal of American History* 80, no. 2 (1993): 470–98.

Green, Hilary N. "The Persistence of Memory: African Americans and Transitional Justice Efforts in Franklin County, Pennsylvania." In *Reconciliation after Civil Wars: Global Perspectives*, edited by Paul Quigley and James Hawdon. New York: Routledge, 2018.

Gronningsater, Sarah L. H. "Born Free in the Master's House: Children and Gradual Emancipation in the Early American North." In *Child Slavery before and after Emancipation: An Argument for Child-Centered Slavery Studies*, edited by Anna Mae Duane. New York: Cambridge University Press, 2017.

Gross, Jennifer Lynn. "'And for the Widow and Orphan': Confederate Widows, Poverty, and Public Assistance." In *Inside the Confederate Nation: Essays in Honor of Emory M. Thomas*, edited by Leslie J. Gordon and John C. Inscoe. Baton Rouge: Louisiana State University Press, 2005.

Hahn, Steven. "Class and State in Postemancipation Societies: Southern Planters in Comparative Perspective." *American Historical Review* 94 (February 1990): 75–98.

Haley, Christopher. "Legacy of Slavery in Maryland: 'Slave Statistics.'" *Journal of Slavery and Data Preservation* 5, no. 2 (2024): 41–45.

Harris, Cheryl I. "Whiteness as Property." *Harvard Law Review* 106, no. 8 (1993): 1707–91.

Harris, William C. "The Hampton Roads Peace Conference: A Final Test of Lincoln's Presidential Leadership." *Journal of the Abraham Lincoln Association* 21, no. 1 (2000): 30–61.

Havrylyshyn, Alexandra T. "Free for a Moment in France: How Enslaved Women and Girls Claimed Liberty in the Courts of New Orleans (1835–1857)." PhD diss., University of California, Berkeley, 2018.

Holt, Thomas C. "'An Empire over the Mind': Emancipation, Race, and Ideology in the British West Indies and the American South." In *Region, Race, and Reconstruction: Essays in Honor of C. Vann Woodward*, edited by J. Morgan Kousser and James M. McPherson. New York: Oxford University Press, 1982.

———. "The Essence of the Contract: The Articulation of Race, Gender and Political Economy in British Emancipation Policy, 1838–1866." In *Beyond Slavery: Explorations of Race, Labor, and Citizenship in Postemancipation Societies*, edited by Frederick Cooper, Thomas C. Holt, and Rebecca J. Scott. Chapel Hill: The University of North Carolina Press, 2000.

Holton, Woody. "Equality as Unintended Consequence: The Contracts Clause and the Married Women's Property Acts." *Journal of Southern History* 81, no. 2 (2015): 313–40.

Jaffe, Caleb A. "Obligations Impaired: Justice Jonathan Jasper Wright and the Failure of Reconstruction in South Carolina." *Michigan Journal of Race and Law* 8 (Spring 2003): 471–501.

James, Joseph B. "Southern Reaction to the Proposal of the Fourteenth Amendment." *Journal of Southern History* 22, no. 4 (1956): 477–97.

Johnson, Jessica Marie. "Markup Bodies: Black [Life] Studies and Slavery [Death] Studies at the Digital Crossroads." *Social Text* 36, no. 4 (2018): 57–79.

Johnson, Walter. "Inconsistency, Contradiction, and Complete Confusion: The Everyday Life of the Law of Slavery." *Law and Social Inquiry* 22 (1997): 405–33.

Kellow, Margaret M. R. "Conflicting Imperatives: Black and White American Abolitionists Debate Slave Redemption." In *Buying Freedom: The Ethics and Economics of Slave Redemption*, edited by Kwame Anthony Appiah and Martin Bunzl. Princeton, NJ: Princeton University Press, 2007.

Kelly, Patrick J. "The Election of 1896 and the Restructuring of Civil War Memory." *Civil War History* 49, no. 3 (2003): 254–80.

Klein, Diane. "Naming and Framing the 'Subject' of Antebellum Slave Contracts: Introducing Julia, 'A Certain Negro Slave,' 'A Man,' Joseph, Eliza, and Albert." *Rutgers Race and Law Review* 9, no. 2 (2008): 243–83.

———. "Paying Eliza: Comity, Contracts, and Critical Race Theory—19th Century Choice of Law Doctrine and the Validation of Antebellum Contracts for the Purchase and Sale of Human Beings." *National Black Law Journal* 20, no. 1 (2006): 1–41.

Kleintop, Amanda Laury. "Life, Liberty, and Property in Slaves: White Mississippians Seek 'Just Compensation' for Their Freed Slaves in 1865." *Slavery and Abolition* 39, no. 2 (2018): 383–404.

Kolchin, Peter. "Some Thoughts on Emancipation in Comparative Perspective: Russia and the US." *Slavery and Abolition* 11, no. 3 (1990): 351–67.

———. "The South and the World." *Journal of Southern History* 75, no. 3 (2009): 565–80.

Kull, Andrew. "The Enforceability after Emancipation of Debts Contracted for the Purchase of Slaves." *Chicago-Kent Law Review* 70 (1994): 493–538.

Kurtz, Michael J. "Emancipation in the Federal City." *Civil War History* 24, no. 3 (1978): 250–67.

Les Benedict, Michael. "Preserving the Constitution: The Radical Basis of Radical Reconstruction." *Journal of American History* 61, no. 1 (1974): 65–90.

Maltz, Earl M. "Moving beyond Race: The Joint Committee on Reconstruction and the Drafting of the Fourteenth Amendment." *Hastings Constitutional Law Quarterly* 42, no. 2 (2015): 287–322.

Martin, Bonnie. "Neighbor-to-Neighbor Capitalism: Local Credit Networks and the Mortgaging of Slaves." In *Slavery's Capitalism: A New History of American Economic Development*, edited by Sven Beckert and Seth Rockman. Philadelphia: University of Pennsylvania Press, 2016.

———. "Slavery's Invisible Engine: Mortgaging Human Property." *Journal of Southern History* 76, no. 4 (2010): 818–66.

Maslowski, Peter. "From Reconciliation to Reconstruction: Lincoln, Johnson, and Tennessee, Part II." *Tennessee Historical Quarterly* 42, no. 4 (1983): 343–361.

Mason, Matthew. "The Battle of the Slaveholding Liberators: Great Britain, the United States, and Slavery in the Early Nineteenth Century." *William and Mary Quarterly* 59, no. 3, Slaveries in the Atlantic World (2002): 665–96.

Masur, Kate. "'A Rare Phenomenon of Philological Vegetation': The Word 'Contraband' and the Meanings of Emancipation in the United States." *Journal of American History* 93, no. 4 (2007): 1050–87.

McClintock, Megan J. "Civil War Pensions and the Reconstruction of Union Families." *Journal of American History* 83, no. 2 (1996): 456–80.
McCommas, Stuart. "Forgotten but Not Lost: The Original Public Meaning of Section 4 of the Fourteenth Amendment." *Virginia Law Review* 99, no. 6 (2013): 1291–326.
McCrary, Peyton, Clark Miller, and Dale Baum. "Class and Party in the Secession Crisis: Voting Behavior in the Deep South, 1856–1861." *Journal of Interdisciplinary History* 8, no. 3 (1987): 429–57.
McCurry, Stephanie. "Plunder of Black Life: The Problem of Connecting the History of Slavery to the Economics of the Present." *TLS*, May 19, 2017, 23–26.
———. "Reconstructing Belonging: The Thirteenth Amendment at Work in the World." In *Intimate States: Gender, Sexuality, and Governance in Modern US History*, edited by Margot Canaday, Nancy F. Cott, and Robert O. Self. Chicago: University of Chicago Press, 2021.
Menard, Russell R. "Financing the Lowcountry Export Boom: Capital and Growth in Early South Carolina." *William and Mary Quarterly* 51, no. 4 (1994): 659–76.
Mering, John Vollmer. "Persistent Whiggery in the Confederate South: A Reconsideration." *South Atlantic Quarterly* 69, no. 1 (1970): 124–43.
Mills, Wynona Gillmore. "James Govan Taliaferro (1798–1896): Louisiana Unionist and Scalawag." Master's thesis, Louisiana State University and Agricultural and Mechanical College, 1968.
Minardi, Margot. "'Centripetal Attraction' in a Centrifugal World: The Pacifist Vision of Elihu Burritt." *Early American Studies* 11, no. 1 (2013): 176–91.
Morris, Thomas D. "The Chattel Mortgages of Slaves." In *Ambivalent Legacy: A Legal History of the South*, edited by David J. Bodenhamer and James W. Ely Jr. Jackson: University Press of Mississippi, 1984.
Neeley, Mark E., Jr. "Colonization and the Myth That Lincoln Prepared the People for Emancipation." In *Lincoln's Proclamation: Emancipation Reconsidered*, edited by William A. Blair and Karen Fisher Younger. Chapel Hill: The University of North Carolina Press, 2009.
Nelson, William E. "The Impact of the Antislavery Movement upon Styles of Judicial Reasoning in Nineteenth Century America." *Harvard Law Review* 7, no. 3 (1974): 513–66.
Nicoletti, Cynthia. "The American Civil War as a Trial by Battle." *Law and History Review* 28, no. 1 (2010): 71–110.
———. "William Henry Trescot, Pardon Broker." *Journal of the Civil War Era* 11, no. 4 (2021): 478–506.
Nolan, Alan T. "The Anatomy of the Myth." In *The Myth of the Lost Cause and Civil War History*, edited by Gary W. Gallagher and Alan T. Nolan. Bloomington: Indiana University Press, 2000.
Olmstead, Alan L., and Paul W. Rhode. "Cotton, Slavery, and the New History of Capitalism." *Explorations in Economic History* 67, no. 1 (2018): 1–17.
Ostdiek, Bennett, and John Fabian Witt. "The Czar and the Slaves: Two Puzzles in the History of International Arbitration." *American Journal of International Law* 113, no. 3 (2019): 535–67.
Ochiai, Akiko. "The Port Royal Experiment Revisited: Northern Visions of Reconstruction and the Land Question." *New England Quarterly* 74, no. 1 (2001): 94–117.
Pincus, Samuel Norman. "The Virginia Supreme Court, Blacks, and the Law, 1870–1902." PhD diss., University of Virginia, 1978.

Penningroth, Dylan C. "Race in Contract Law." *University of Pennsylvania Law Review* 170, no. 5 (2022): 1199–301.

Perrone, Giuliana. "Rehearsals for Reparations." *RSF: The Russell Sage Foundation Journal for the Social Sciences* 10, no. 2 (2024): 132–50.

Ransom, Roger L., and Richard Sutch. "Capitalists without Capital: The Burden of Slavery and the Impact of Emancipation." *Agricultural History* 62, no. 3 (1988): 133–60.

———. "Who Pays for Slavery?" In *The Wealth of Races: The Present Value of Benefits from Past Injustices*, edited by Richard F. America. New York: Greenwood Press, 1990.

Ryder, Karen. "'To Realize Money Facilities': Slave Life Insurance, the Slave Trade, and Credit in the Old South." In *New Directions in Slavery Studies: Commodification, Community, and Comparison*, edited by Jeff Forret and Christine E. Sears. Baton Rouge: Louisiana State University Press, 2015.

Saunt, Claudio. "The Paradox of Freedom: Tribal Sovereignty and Emancipation during the Reconstruction of Indian Territory." *The Journal of Southern History* 70, no. 1 (2004): 63–94.

Shelden, Rachel A., and Erik B. Alexander. "Dismantling the Party System: Party Fluidity and the Mechanisms of Nineteenth-Century US Politics." *Journal of American History* 110, no. 3 (2023): 419–48.

Simard, Justin. "Citing Slavery." *Stanford Law Review* 72, no. 1 (2020): 79–125.

———. "Slavery's Legalism: Lawyers and the Commercial Routine of Slavery." *Law and History Review* 37, no. 2 (2019): 571–603.

Sinha, Manisha. "The Problem of Abolition in the Age of Capitalism." *American Historical Review* 124, no. 1 (2019): 144–63.

Smith, Herbert C., and John T. Willis. "The Maryland Constitution." In *Maryland Politics and Government: Democratic Dominance*. Lincoln: University of Nebraska Press, 2012.

Smith, John David. "The Recruitment of Negro Soldiers in Kentucky, 1863–1865." *Register of the Kentucky Historical Society* 72, no. 4 (1974): 364–90.

Soifer, Aviam. "Status, Contract, and Promises Unkept." *Yale Law Journal* 96, no. 8 (1987): 1916–59.

Stanley, Amy Dru. *From Bondage to Contract: Wage Labor, Marriage, and the Market in the Age of Slave Emancipation*. New York: Cambridge University Press, 1998.

Starnes, Richard D. "Forever Faithful: The Southern Historical Society and Confederate Historical Memory." *Southern Cultures* 2, no. 2 (1996): 177–94.

Stauffer, John. "Frederick Douglass and the Politics of Slave Redemptions." In *Buying Freedom: The Ethics and Economics of Slave Redemption*, edited by Kwame Anthony Appiah and Martin Bunzl. Princeton, NJ: Princeton University Press, 2007.

Stoebuck, William B. "A General Theory of Eminent Domain." *Washington Law Review* 47, no. 4 (1972): 553–608.

———. "Police Power, Takings, and Due Process." *Washington and Lee Law Review* 37, no. 4 (1980): 1057–99.

Stohler, Stephan. "Slavery and Just Compensation in American Constitutionalism." *Law and Social Inquiry* 44, no. 1 (2019): 102–35.

Summers, Mark W. "The Moderates' Last Chance: The Louisiana Election of 1865." *Louisiana History* 24, no. 1 (1983): 49–69.

Treanor, William Michael. "The Original Understanding of the Takings Clause and the Political Process." *Columbia Law Review* 95, no. 4 (1995): 782–887.
Vorenberg, Michael. "Abraham Lincoln and the Politics of Black Colonization." In *For a Vast Future Also: Essays from the Journal of the Abraham Lincoln Association*, edited by Thomas F. Schwarz. New York: Oxford University Press, 1999.
———. "'The Deformed Child': Slavery and the Election of 1864." *Civil War History* 47, no. 3 (2001): 240–57.
———. "Spielberg's Lincoln." *Journal of the Civil War Era* 3, no. 4 (2013): 549–72.
Waldrep, Christopher. "Garrett Davis and the Problem of Democracy and Emancipation." *Register of the Kentucky Historical Society* 11, no. 3/4 (2012): 363–402.
Westley, Robert. "Many Billions Gone: Is It Time to Reconsider the Case for Black Reparations?" *Boston College Third World Law Journal* 19, no. 1 (1998): 429–76.
Wiecek, William M. "The Origin of the United States Court of Claims." *Administrative Law Review* 20, no. 3 (1968): 387–406.
Williams, John C. "Slave Contracts and the Thirteenth Amendment." *Seattle University Law Review* 39 (2016): 1009–29.
Williamson, Samuel H. and Louis P. Cain. "Measuring Slavery in 2020 dollars." *MeasuringWorth*, 2025. www.measuringworth.com/slavery.php.
Wilson, James Grant, and John Fiske, eds. "Roselius, Christian." In *Appletons' Cyclopaedia of American Biography*. New York: D. Appleton, 1898.
Witt, John Fabian. "From Loss of Services to Loss of Support: The Wrongful Death Statutes, the Origins of Modern Tort Law, and the Making of the Nineteenth-Century Family." *Law and Social Inquiry* 25, no. 3 (2000): 717–55.
———. "Toward a New History of American Accident Law: Classical Tort Law and the Cooperative First-Party Insurance Movement." *Harvard Law Review* 114, no. 3 (2001): 690–841.
Wolfe, Harold John. "The South Carolina Constitutional Convention of 1865." Master's thesis, University of North Carolina at Chapel Hill, 1832.

WORKING PAPERS

Ager, Philipp, Leah Platt Boustan, and Katherine Eriksson. "The Intergenerational Effects of a Large Wealth Shock: White Southerners after the Civil War." Working Paper No. 25700. National Bureau of Economic Research, March 2019. https://doi.org/10.3386/w25700.
Bleakley, Hoyt, and Paul Rhode. "The Economic Effects of American Slavery: Tests at the Border." Working Paper No. 32640. National Bureau of Economic Research, June 2024. http://www.nber.org/papers/w32640.
Hornbeck, Richard, and Trevon Logan. "One Giant Leap: Emancipation and Aggregate Economic Gains." Working Paper No. 2023–134. National Bureau of Economic Research, October 2023. https://www.nber.org/papers/w31758.
Miller, Melinda and Rachel Smith Purvis. "'No Rights of Citizenship': The 1863 Emancipation Acts of the Loyal Cherokee Council." Under review with the *Journal of American History*. https://drive.google.com/file/d/1whHc1SP_pF6DG2Dce2k_k2l9Y6vCSwxa/view.
Noll, Franklin. "Repudiation! The Crisis of United States Civil War Debt, 1865–1870." Government Debt Crises: Politics, Economics and History Conference, Graduate Institute of International and Development Studies, Geneva, December 14–15, 2012.

Index

Italic page numbers refer to illustrations.

Abell, Edmund, 56–57, 60
abolitionists, 30–35, 39–40, 91. *See also* compensated emancipation schemes; *names of specific groups and persons*
Adams, John Quincy, 18, 77
Alabama, 35, 71, 220n76
Albany Evening Journal (newspaper), 92
American Anti-Slavery Society, 22, 37
American Colonization Society, 17
American Missionary Association, 121
amnesty oath (Lincoln), 55, 57, 63, 191n40
Antigua, 185n20
An Appeal in Favor of That Class of Americans Called Africans (Child), 21
apprenticeships, 1, 16, 66, 192n47
Ariail, M. R., 59
Arkansas, 38, *71*, 120, 128, 130

Baker, Frank, 36
Banks, Nathaniel P., 53
Banner (newspaper), 153
Barnes, V. M., 78, 79
Bell, James, 73
Berlin, Ira, 2
Bermuda, 185n20
Berry, Harriet, 135
Bibb, William E., 155
Black Codes, 106
Black education programs, 31–32, 66, 192n47
Black military servicemen, 49–50, 67, 74–75, 135, 148, 217n36. *See also* orphan compensation; widow compensation
Black politicians, 119–21, 150–52, 158. *See also names of specific people*
Blaine, James G., 150

bloody shirt campaigning, 97–99, 105, 136, 138, 140, 145–47, 167, 217n43
bond programs, 48, 57, 95–97, 145, 160
Boutwell, George S., 94
Boyce v. Tabb, 112, 131
British colonies, 18, 185n20
Broomall, John, 89–90
Brott, George F., 57–58
Brown, James H., 128–29, 130
Brown, Joseph, 132
Bureau of Refugees, Freedmen, and Abandoned Lands. *See* Freedmen's Bureau
Burgess, Martha, 135
Burritt, Elihu, 30–32, *31*, 33, 151
Butler, Benjamin, 36, 40, 92, 149

Caldwell, Henry Clay, 130
Calhoun, John C., 28–29
Cameron, Simon, 40
Canby, Edward, 119
Cazabat, Anthony, 58–59
Chase, Salmon P., 35, 47, 133–34
Cherokee Nation, 179n11
Chetlain, A. L., 86
Chickasaw Nation, 179n11
Child, David Lee, 40
Child, Lydia Marie, 21–22, 40, 185n27
Choctaw Nation, 179n11
Citizens' Free State Party, 53, 56
Civil Rights Cases (1883), 148
Clay, Henry, 29–30, 79, 130
Cleveland Daily Herald (newspaper), 149
colonization, 17, 33, 190n30
Committee on Emancipation, 55–56
Committee on the Compensation of Loyal Owners for Slaves Emancipated, 59

Commonwealth v. Jennison, 16
compensable taking (term), 15–16. *See also* takings clause
compensated emancipation schemes: abolitionists on, 30–35, 39–40, 91; alternatives to, 65–75; for Cherokee, 179n11; Civil War era and, 36–38; after Confederate surrender, 63–65; and Confederate veterans, 159–63, 195n12; congressional action for, 4–5, 42–44, 61–62, 83–86, 155; constitutional arguments for, 4, 99–103; debates on, 8–9; eminent domain and, 12–13, 23–30, 42–47, 186n44; in Great Britain, 1, 11–12, 18–21, 66, 79; of Johnson, 63–65, 86; in Latin America, 1, 19, 22–23; limits of constitutional change and, 99–103; of Lincoln, 47–52, 67, 159–61, 178n7, 190n30; Lost Cause and, 137–59; loyalty and, 39–40, 45, 50; military service and, 47–52, 67, 135, 148; (im)morality of, 18–23; political compensation for enslavers, 7–8; problem of, 13–18, 177n1; and Southern Unionists, 3–4, 11–13, 38, 52–60, 71, 90, 196n19; in Washington, DC, 29, 40–41, 61, 77, 166, 188n13; for widows and orphans, 75–83. *See also* emancipation, overview; reparations; Fourteenth Amendment: sections overview
Confiscation Acts, 100
congressional action for compensation, 4–5, 42–44, 61–62, 83–86, 155. *See also* names of specific amendments; US Congress
conquered province theory, 69, 89, 129, 197n20
Conservative Party (Virginia), 144
Conservative Unionist Party, 53. *See also* Southern Unionists
constitutional arguments for compensation, 4, 99–103. *See also* compensated emancipation schemes; US Constitution
constitutional conventions, 11, 55–56, 63–64, 75, 82–86, 122–23, 179n9. *See also* names of specific states

Constitutional Union Party, 75–76, 85, 104, 196n19
contraband (concept), 36
Corley, Manuel Simeon, 124
Courier-Journal (newspaper), 160
Cowan, Edgar, 103
Crawford, Thomas G., 81
Creswell, John, 62
Crittenden, John J., 43–44

Davis, Garrett, 10, 42–46, 43, 56, 101, 106, 189n16
Davis, Jefferson, 129, 162
Davis, Reuben, 35
DC Emancipation Act (1862), 40–41, 77, 100
debt relief and repudiation, 110–13; judicial scrutiny of, 127–35; outside courts, 113–27. *See also* economic logics of slavery; labor system logics; national debt; reparations
debts, 7, 20, 95–99
Delaware, 37, 46, 60, 93, 94, 104
Democratic Party, 104, 107, 138, 141, 148–50
Dew, Thomas R., 27–28, 29
Dick, Robert Abraham Lincoln, 157, 159
Dickerson, Isaiah H., 155
Douglass, Frederick, 10, 22, 38–39, 61, 62, 223n18
Downs, Greg, 78, 82
Draper, Nicholas, 19
Dred Scott case, 11, 34, 56
Du Bois, W. E. B., 222n17
Dunmore, Lord, 18
Dunning, William Archibald, 137
Dunning School of Reconstruction History, 137, 138, 163, 165–69, 220n1. *See also* Lost Cause narrative
Durman, Nannie, 111, 113–14
Duval, Thomas, 73

Edwards, Laura, 80
Elder, Larry, 222n16
emancipation, 1–10. *See also* compensated emancipation schemes

Emancipation Proclamation, 49, 119, 154, 169
eminent domain, 4, 12–13, 15, 23–30, 38, 42–47, 186n44
Engerman, Stanley, 21
Enrollment Acts, 52, 67, 72, 93, 95, 100, 103–4, 105, 108, 148, 169
enslaved people: British proclamation on American, 18; children of, 16, 24; as confiscated property, 36; Northup, 24–25; rebellion of, 25–27. *See also* compensated emancipation schemes; emancipation
Equal Protection Clause, 148
extrajudicial debt relief, 113–27. *See also* debt relief and repudiation

Faulkner, Charles, 26
Field, Joseph W., 122
Fifth Amendment, 1–2, 5, 10, 11, 12–13, 28, 30, 156
Finkelman, Paul, 34
First Confiscation Act, 40, 43
Fleming, Walter, 163
Florida, 71, 75, 119, 120
Foner, Eric, 2
Ford, William, 24
Fort Monroe, 36
Fourteenth Amendment: adoption of, 3, 7; judicial scrutiny of, 127–35; language of, 5–6, 100; section 4 adjudication, 127–35; sections overview, 88–89, 202n5
France, 178n2
Frederick Douglass's Paper (Watkins), 32
Freedmen's Bureau, 67, 114, 122
Freedmen's Convention, 153
freedom seekers, 45
Freeman (newspaper), 154
Free State Party, 53, 55, 60
"free womb laws," 16
Frémont, John C., 68–69
Fugitive Slave Clause, 28, 56, 100

Garrison, William Lloyd, 22, 33
Georgia, 65, 71, 75, 78, 85, 125–26, 132, 137
Goodell, William, 22

Gowan, Thomas R., 84–85, 86
Graber, Mark, 6, 202n5
gradual emancipation, 1, 16–27, 166, 167. *See also* compensated emancipation schemes
Gran Colombia, 1, 178n3
Grant, Ulysses S., 141, 215n29
Great Britain, 1, 11–12, 18–21, 66, 79; colonies of, 18, 185n20
Greeley, Horace, 141, 142–43, 143, 145
Grider, Henry, 91, 93, 94
Gronningsater, Sarah L. H., 16
Gross, Ariela, 116

Hahn, Michael, 53, 54
Hahn, Steven, 166
Haiti, 1, 178n2
Haitian Revolution, 1, 23, 166
Hamilton, Andrew Jackson, 73, 74, 86
Hamilton, Joseph Grégoire de Roulhac, 137
Hampton Roads Conference (1865), 67, 159–63
Harlan, James, 147
Harper's Weekly (periodical), 87, 121, 143
Harris, Benjamin G., 148–50
Hart, Levi, 15, 19, 20
Hill, Walter B., 162–63
Hills, Alfred, 56
The History of the Negro Race in America (Williams), 149
A History of the Negro Troops in the War of the Rebellion (Williams), 149
Holbert, Philip, 74–75
Holden, William, 86
Holt, Joseph, 50, 101, 118, 190n33
Hopkins, Samuel, 15
House, Callie D., 155, 163
Hudson, Robert S., 77
Hunter, Robert M. T., 144–46
Hunter, Tera, 170
Huston, James, 179n9

(im)morality, 18–23, 47–49, 57, 120, 123, 169–70

Jamaica, 21
Janney, Caroline, 137–38
Jefferson, Thomas, 17
Johnson, Andrew, 63–65, 70–71, 86, 88–90, 104, 107–9, 118, 194n4
Johnston, Amos R., 82
Joint Committee on Reconstruction, 91, 92, 95, 99

Kansas-Nebraska Act (1854), 30
Kendrick, Benjamin B., 137
Kentucky, 60, 72, 102, 107–8, 116–17, 161
Kilbourne, Richard, 124
Kull, Andrew, 111, 126

labor system logics, 6, 9, 16–17, 19–22, 44–45, 64–66, 100, 155–58, 165, 183n7. *See also* economic logics of slavery
Langley, Landon S., 122
Langston, John Mercer, 158
Latin American independence movements, 1, 19, 22–23
Lawrence, William, 94
Liberal Republicans, 140–42
Lieber Code, 50
Lincoln, Abraham, 10; amnesty oath of, 55, 57, 63, 191n40; on compensation, 37, 46, 67, 159–61, 178n7, 190n30; on confiscated lands, 67; election of, 35; on military emancipation, 47–52; on people as property, 153
Lost Cause narrative, 3, 9, 137–46, 159, 166, 167, 171, 182n21. *See also* Dunning School of Reconstruction History
Louisiana, 11–13, 38, 52–62, 67, 71, 179n9, 212n57
Louisiana Citizens, 118
loyalty and compensation schemes, 39–40, 45, 50

Madison, James, 17–18, 20
Mallory, Shepard, 36
Manning, Joseph C., 152
Marshall, John, 26
Marshall, Thomas, 26

Maryland, 18, 60–61, 93–94, 108, 148, 181n19, 196n13
Maryland Slave Claims Commission (1864), 101, 206n42
Massachusetts, 16–17
McClure, John, 128–29
Memminger, Christopher G., 66
Mendiverri, Antonio, 192n47
Mexico, 149
military emancipation, 47–52, 67, 135, 148, 217n36
Mississippi, 71, 75, 76, 78, 80, 84–85, 194n3
Missouri, 193n64
Missouri Crisis, 17
Mitchell, John, 162
Moore, B. F., Jr., 67
(im)morality, 18–23, 47–49, 57, 120, 123, 169–70
Morning Chronicle (newspaper), 147
mortgage of people as property, 7, 113

National Adjustment Society, 155
National Anti-Slavery Standard (newspaper), 40, 91
National Compensated Emancipation Convention (1857), 31–33, 151
National Compensated Emancipation Society, 30, 33
national debt, 95–99. *See also* debt relief and repudiation; debts
National Debt Office, 20
National Ex-Slave Mutual Relief, Bounty and Pension Association (MRB&PA), 8–9, 155–56, 158–59, 163, 170–71
National Reflector (newspaper), 158
National Union Convention, 105
National Unionist Party, 104
Native Americans, 17, 149, 179n11, 180n11, 218n45
Nat Turner's Rebellion, 25–27
natural law argument, 38–41. *See also* slavery: legal protections of
natural rights discourse, 14
Nebraska Daily Democrat (newspaper), 151

New Era (newspaper), 110
New Jersey, 17
New National Era (newspaper), 110, 135, 141, 143, 145, 151, 171
New Orleans convention (1864), 55–56
New York Tribune (newspaper), 141, 142
Niagara Peace Conference (1864), 142, 215n15
Nicoletti, Cynthia, 84, 110–11, 131
"No Accommodations!" (political cartoon*)*, 87
North Carolina, 68–69, 71, 116
North Carolina Gazette (newspaper), 153
North Carolina Industrial Association (NCIA), 217n44
Northern Democrats, 90
Northup, Solomon, 24–25
Nunley, Tamika Y., 41

Oakes, James, 2
orphan compensation, 75–83, 124–25
Osborn v. Nicholson, 112, 130, 131–32, 134

pacifism, 30
Panic of 1837, 186n44, 187n50
Panic of 1873, 144, 146
Panic of 1893, 154
Paschal, George W., 147, 148
Pease, Elisha, 73
Pennsylvania, 11, 16
pensions, 8–9, 72–73, 151, 155–59, 162, 163, 170–71. *See also* widow's pension
Perrone, Giuliana, 7, 111, 117, 134
plantation reformation, 66–67
Poland, Luke, 99
Populist Party, 152
Potter, George, 76–78, 79
Preliminary Emancipation Proclamation, 48
profitability of slavery logics, 167–70, 181n16, 222n14. *See also* compensated emancipation schemes; debt relief and repudiation; labor system logics
property rights in people, 6–7, 12–13, 18, 42–47, 138–39, 153, 167. *See also* Fifth Amendment

Quakers, 21–22

racial capitalist logics, 167–70, 181n16, 222n14. *See also* compensated emancipation schemes; debt relief and repudiation; labor system logics
Radical Republicans, 5–6, 41, 45, 85, 86, 104. *See also* Republican Party
Randall, Samuel, 99
Rankin, John, 32
Rayner, Kenneth, 68, 71, 75, 196n17
Reagan, John H., 72, 75
Reconstruction, 6, 52, 70–74, 86, 110, 113, 114, 124, 137–38, 149, 155, 165
Reconstruction Act (1867), 118, 119
reparations, 4, 8–9, 10, 22, 155–58, 165, 170–71, 182n20. *See also* compensated emancipation schemes; debt relief and repudiation; National Ex-Slave Mutual Relief, Bounty and Pension Association (MRB&PA)
Republican Party, 34–35, 66, 89, 96, 101, 129, 142, 147, 205n41. *See also* Radical Republicans
"The Restoration of the Union" (C. E. H. Bonwill), 54
Richmond Planet (newspaper), 162
Richmond Whig (newspaper), 115, 141, 152
The Right Way, the Safe Way (Child), 21
Robertson, George, 72, 117
Robertson, John, 186n40
Rollins, James Sidney, 202n7
Rugemer, Edward, 23
Rutland, James M., 124–25

Saint-Domingue, 1, 21
Saulsbury, Willard, 107
Schofield, John M., 51
Schurz, Carl, 93, 98
Second Confiscation Act (1862), 42–46
Seeley, Samantha, 17
Seward, William, 47
Sharkey, William, 113
Sibley, Guy C., 154–55, 157, 158, 171
Sickles, Daniel, 119, 126

Siddali, Silvana, 44, 100
Simkins, Francis Butler, 220n1
Singleton, Benjamin, 155
The 1619 Project, 168, 170, 222n14
Slade, William, 28
Slaughterhouse Cases (1873), 148
Slave Compensation Commission (Great Britain), 20
slave law. *See* slavery: legal protections of
slave rebellion, 25–27
slavery: economic logics of, 167–70, 181n16, 222n14; legal protections of, 6, 12–13, 15, 18, 36, 38–41, 112–13, 127–35, 167, 180n12; as national sin, 18–23, 49, 169–70. *See also* compensated emancipation schemes; debt relief and repudiation; (im)morality; labor system logics
Slavery Abolition Act (Great Britain; 1833), 1, 19–21, 66, 79
Smith, Gerrit, 30, 32–33
South Carolina, 71, 83, 98, 116, 120, 123, 179n9
Southern theory, 70
Southern Unionists, 3–4, 11–13, 37–38, 52–60, 69, 71, 73, 90, 96, 98, 105–6, 126, 128–29, 140–48, 196n19. *See also* Conservative Unionist Party
Stanton, Edwin, 94, 107
state sovereignty, 9, 46, 183n10
state suicide theory, 39, 57, 69–70, 89, 197n20
Steinfeld, Robert J., 100
Stevens, Thaddeus, 88, 126
Stohler, Stephen, 25
suffrage, 106, 119, 166
Sumner, Charles, 35, 39, 126, 133
Swayne, Noah Haynes, 131–33, 134

takings clause, 10, 12–13, 15–16, 28, 36, 37
Taliaferro, James Govan, 69, 179n9, 194n3
Taliaferro, Robert W., 59
Taney, Roger B., 34, 115
Tennessee, 70–71, 71
Ten Percent Plan, 52–53
Texas, 71, 73–75, 199n32
Thirteenth Amendment, 2, 5, 48, 64, 74, 91–95, 100
Thompson, C. Mildred, 137
Thorpe, T. B., 57
Three-Fifths Clause, 56
Tibeats, John M., 24–25
Townsend, James, 36
treason, 44, 51, 92, 97, 103–4, 202n5
Treasury Department. *See* US Treasury
Treasury of Virtue, 170, 171
Treaty of Cherokee Nation and United States (1866), 179n11
Trimble, Lawrence, 102, 169
Trumbull, Lyman, 42, 44, 106
Truth, Sojourner, 155
Tucker, St. George, 16
Turner, James M., 93
Turner, Nat, 25–27

Unconditional Union Party, 60, 104
United Confederate Veterans (UCV), 160–62
United Daughters of the Confederacy (UDC), 160–61
United States Colored Troops, 135. *See also* Black military servicemen
United States Ex-Slave Owners Registration Bureau, 157–58, 159, 163
United States v. Rhodes, 127
US Army, 49, 67, 74–75, 148
US Civil War, 1, 19, 36–38, 139
US Congress, 103–9. *See also* congressional action for compensation
US Constitution: Fifth Amendment, 1–2, 5, 10, 11, 12–13, 28, 30, 36, 37, 156; Thirteenth Amendment, 2, 5, 48, 64, 74, 91–95; Fourteenth Amendment, 3, 5–6; military emancipation and, 47–52. *See also* constitutional arguments for compensation; constitutional reform
US Court of Claims, 72–73, 197n27
US Postal Service, 156, 157
US Slave Claims Commissions, 105, 106, 107
US Treasury, 46, 55, 66, 150, 170, 222n14

Van Cleve, George William, 16
Vaughan, Walter, 8, 151
Virginia, 18, 26–28, 71, 122–23
Vorenberg, Michael, 2, 6, 94
voting rights, 106, 119, 166

Wahl, Jenny, 23
War Department, 39, 50–51, 67, 94, 104, 118, 206n42, 216n33
War of 1812, 18
war powers, 39–41
War Powers (Whiting), 40
Warren, Robert Penn, 170
Washington, DC, 29, 40–41, 61, 77, 166, 188n13
Watkins, William, 32, 33
Watterson, Henry, 160
Wells, James M., 59
West India Committee, 20
Wheeler, Jacob, 24

Wheeling Convention, 128
Whig Party, 68–69, 75–76, 104, 140, 141, 196n19
Whipper, William J., 123
White, Francis, 73
White v. Hart, 112, 131, 132, 134
Whiting, William, 39
widow compensation, 75–83, 124–25
widow's pension, 81, 135, 205n30
Williams, George Washington, 149, 150, 159, 171
Williamson, John H., 152–54, *153*, 171, 218n45
Wilson, Joseph H., 58
Wright, Jonathan J., *121*, 123

Yerger, William, 77, 78, 84, 194n3

Zilversmit, Arthur, 16

www.ingramcontent.com/pod-product-compliance
Lightning Source LLC
Chambersburg PA
CBHW021853230426

43671CB00006B/367